THE RWANDA CRISIS

GÉRARD PRUNIER

The
Rwanda
Crisis

History of a Genocide

Columbia University Press
New York

Columbia University Press
New York

© 1995 by Gérard Prunier
All rights reserved

Printed in Hong Kong

Library of Congress Cataloging-in-Publication Data
Prunier, Gérard.
    The Rwanda crisis : history of a genocide / Gérard Prunier.
      p. cm.
    Includes bibliographical references and index.
    ISBN 0–231–10408–1 (alk. paper)
    1. Rwanda—History—Civil War, 1994. 2. Genocide—Rwanda.
I. Title.
DT450.435.P78 1995   95–18203
967.57104—dc20   CIP

♾

10 9 8 7 6 5 4 3 2

This book is dedicated to two of my Rwandese colleagues, Jean-Népomucène Nkurikiyimfura and Jean Rumiya. The first was a Tutsi, the second a Hutu of mixed parentage. Both were remarkable young historians with a most promising future. Nkurikiyimfura was not politically involved and accepted the Habyarimana regime before it veered off into violence. Rumiya was more involved and even collaborated for a while with some of the intellectuals who were to provide the necessary ideological justifications to the regime as it started to steer a more and more extremist course. But his intellectual clarity and firm moral grounding made him turn against the madness that he felt was coming. Both were killed during the genocide. They are among the people who have maintained the integrity and dignity of our profession at a time when some of their colleagues justified the unjustifiable and collaborated with an evil they were well best placed to denounce.

CONTENTS

Foreword   *page* xi
Map of Rwanda   xiv

Chapters
1. Rwandese Society and the Colonial Impact: The Making
   of a Cultural Mythology (1894–1959)   1

   The physical setting   1
   The Tutsi, the Hutu and the Abazungu   5
   Myths and realities of pre-colonial Rwandese society   9
   —Rwandese society   9
   — The dynamics of Rwandese history   16
   The colonial impact   23
   — The Germans   23
   — The Belgians   26
   — The 'Rwandese ideology'   35

2. The Hutu Republic (1959–1990)   41

   The 1959 muyaga *and its consequences*   41
   The Kayibanda years (1961–1973)   54
   The refugee problem   61
   — The question of numbers   61
   —Life in the diaspora   64
   — The Ugandan factor   67
   The Habyarimana regime   74
   — The good years   74
   — The atmosphere of the regime   80
   — The crisis   84
   — The RPF prepares for war   90

3. Civil War and Foreign Intervention (October 1990–
   July 1991)   93

   The RPF strike and the first days of fighting   93
   Foreign intervention   100
   Settling down into a war culture   108

The reorganisation of the RPF   114
The advent of multiparty politics   121

4. Slouching towards Democracy (July 1991–June 1992)   127
The problems of democratisation   127
War and violence as parts of the political process   135
The new multiparty cabinet and the opening of peace
   negotiations   144
Hardliners, democrats and warriors in the Hutu/Tutsi context   150

5. The Arusha Peace Marathon (June 1992–August 1993)   159
The economic situation   159
Peace and its enemies   160
Negotiations feed the rise of extremism   166
The February war and its aftermath   174
Peace through exhaustion   186

6. Chronicle of a massacre foretold (4 August 1993–
6 April 1994)   192
Waiting for UNAMIR   192
Ndadaye's murder: the shock and its exploitation   198
Hanging on to the cliff's edge   206

7. Genocide and renewed war (6 April–14 June 1994)   213
The enigma of President Habyarimana's death   213
The second week of April 1994   229
The Genocide   237
—Who were the organisers?   239
—Who were the killers?   242
—Who were the victims?   248
—Were there any bystanders?   250
—Patterns of killing   253
— The horrors   255
—Complexities of the situation   257
—Unknown heroes   259
—How long did it last?   261
—How many were killed?   261
— The refugees   265
The war   268
From the outside looking in   273

8. 'Opération Turquoise' and Götterdämmerung in Central
   Africa (14 June–21 August 1994)   281
   Deciding and preparing for the intervention (14–23 June)   281
   From the intervention to the fall of Kigali (23 June–4 July) 291
   *The fall of the northwest and the refugee explosion
   (4–19 July)*   295
   *The new government and the cholera apocalypse
   (19 July–1 August)*   299
   'Turquoise is going away, the problems remain' (1–21 August) 305

9. Aftermath or new beginning? (22 August–31 December
   1994)   312
   The new refugee problem   312
   Reconstruction and internal insecurity   321
   What sort of political structure?   328
   The attitude of the international community   336
   Towards a provisional conclusion   345

Bibliography   356

Glossary   366

Abbreviations   374

Index   379

FOREWORD

'The last battle of the colonised against the coloniser will often be the fight of the colonised against each other.' (Frantz Fanon, *The Wretched of the Earth*)

Any attempt at trying to study the history of a genocide must begin in this author's mind with a basic choice about the moral propriety of his endeavour. In his essay on the Rwandese genocide[1], Rony Brauman, former president of the famous medical emergency organisation Médecins Sans Frontières, rejects the very notion of trying to study the incredibly brutal civil wars now ravaging the African continent from Liberia to Somalia and from the Southern Sudan to Rwanda because 'grading these various sufferings, classifying them according to some form of hierarchy is a pointless exercise verging on the obscene'. As an academic I can understand his position, but cannot agree with it. Humanitarian aid workers can be forgiven for being tired of the emotional and political scavenging carried out on their backs. It is perfectly understandable, in a world where the media shout in the same vulgar way about genocides and sexual scandals, to think that silence is the ultimate form of respect for the victims. But the danger is that this honest search for decency, paradoxically in the same way as the screaming media headlines, will end up obscuring the tragedies, turning them into chaotic convulsions in the primeval mud. The War of the Roses can be written up in dramatic form by Shakespeare; but rumours and ignorance are likely to turn it into a nasty tale full of sound and fury, told by an idiot and signifying nothing.

Respect for the dead does not preclude an effort at understanding why they died. What we have witnessed in Rwanda is a historical product, not a biological fatality or a 'spontaneous'

1. Rony Brauman, *Devant le Mal. Rwanda, un génocide en direct*. Paris: Arléa, 1994.

bestial outburst. Tutsi and Hutu have not been created by God as cats and dogs, predestined from all eternity to disembowel each other because the tall thin men came from Egypt and the short stocky ones were born on the shores of Lake Kivu. This is a long story with complex roots, many contradictions, brutal twists of fate, sudden accelerations and periods of spiritual collapse. The Rwandese genocide is the result of a process which can be analysed, studied and explained. Just as we can analyse, study and explain the genocide of the North American Indians in the nineteenth century or the genocide of the Jews during the Second World War.

And this author thinks that understanding why they died is the best and most fitting memorial we can raise for the victims. Letting their deaths go unrecorded, or distorted by propaganda, or misunderstood through simplified clichés, would in fact bring the last touch to the killers' work in completing the victims' dehumanisation. Man is largely a social construct, and to deny a man the social meaning of his death is to kill him twice, first in the flesh, then in the spirit. The purpose of history cannot be to teach lessons or impose a moral lecture on the reader. But history can have a cleansing effect. Hannah Arendt has taught us that evil was extremely banal. But understanding its nature, stripping it of its emotional shock quality, tracing its ambiguities, looking at a world where the killers can be almost as forlorn as their victims and where the real perpetrators can swiftly turn themselves into the pretence victims of the violence they themselves have organised is an exercise in intellectual hygiene. I hope it can be an antidote to the idea that Africa is a place of darkness, where furious savages clobber each other on the head to assuage their dark ancestral bloodlusts. If this book does nothing other than dispel this feeling (which sneaks even into the recesses of many 'liberal' minds), it would already have fulfilled its main purpose.

For those who are convinced that indeed it is morally proper to attempt to understand even the worst human tragedies, there remains a fascinating tale, an exceptional piece of historical experience. Rwanda, a very small, compact and historically well-defined nation, was built in the late nineteenth and early twentieth century into a complex, unique and quasi-mythological land. With time this cultural mythology *became* reality, i.e. the social and political actors moved by degrees from their real world into the mythological script which had been written for them (in a way, with their complicity). By the 1940s their lives, their actions, probably their feelings were obeying the logic of the script rather than that of their more complex organic past, which by then was receding into historical unreality. In 1959 the red seal of blood put a final label of historical unavoidability on this mythological construction, which from then on became a new *real* historical framework. Can man unwrite what others have written? It is hard to say. But at least one can have the bitter satisfaction of thinking that even the worst of human experiences are not absurd and that they obey a recognisable logic, even if of a rather different kind from Hegel's triumphant march towards the historical incarnation of the spirit.

On a lighter note the author would like to conclude this foreword by saying that he has not been a 'Rwanda specialist' for long. As we shall see, Rwanda and Burundi specialists are a breed apart in the already specialised Africanist world. This author was more conversant with countries to the north, among them Uganda. As a 'Uganda specialist' he got to know several of the men who later created and led the Rwandese Patriotic Front. At the time, when they talked to him of their desire to go 'back' to Rwanda, a country more dreamed about than known, he did not believe that they were capable of doing it. The author was violently proved wrong on 1 October 1990. Since 'experts' hate to be proved wrong, he tried during the next four years to understand, among other things, the present and the past of that tiny land clinging to Uganda's belly. And in the process he succumbed to a fascination which even the horrors of the early summer of 1994 could not destroy. *Amahoro, Rwanda!*

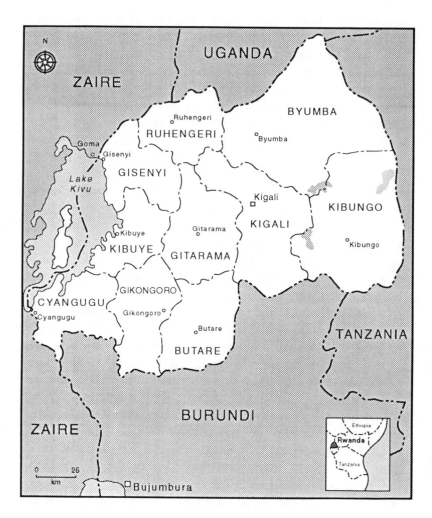

Rwanda

1

RWANDESE SOCIETY AND THE COLONIAL IMPACT: THE MAKING OF A CULTURAL MYTHOLOGY (1894–1959)

The physical setting

Abstract morals notwithstanding, even tragedies do not occur in a vacuum. The country we call Rwanda is not an 'ordinary' African country, supposing that such a thing exists. First of all, it is very small, with an area of only 26,338 km². It is a land neither of teeming jungle nor of arid scrub bush, but rather an area of mild temperate and rather humid climate. The density of human occupation has long ago driven off any remnants of 'African wildlife' and there are no more lions, giraffes or elephants except in the Akagera National Park. The physical terrrain is mostly mountainous. The whole country lies above the 1,000-metre mark, with over half in the 1,500–2,000 m. zone. But neither is it a land of high mountains, except in its northwestern part on the Uganda border where the chain of the Virunga volcanoes culminates in the Kalisimbi at 4,507 m. From west to east we first have the depth of the Rift Valley, mostly filled big lakes (Tanganyika and Kivu) separating Rwanda from Zaïre, then the sharp bluffs of the Zaïre-Nile divide in the 3,000 m. range, then the main Rwandese landscape, the 'land of the 1,000 hills', and finally, further east, the gently sloping lower lands, partly filled with large marshes¹, which extend all the way to the Tanzanian border. Most of the population lives in the medium-altitude area,

---

1. For a more detailed description of the interaction between climate, physical setting and man see François Bart, *Montagnes d'Afrique, terres paysannes. Le cas du Rwanda*, Talence: Presses Universitaires de Bordeaux, 1993. For a quicker but very clear analysis, refer to Jean-Pierre Raison, 'Le Rwanda et le Burundi sous pression' in A. Dubresson *et al.* (eds), *Les Afriques au Sud du Sahara*, Paris: Belin, 1994, pp. 320-9.

a land of breathtaking beautiful vistas dotted with countless hills. The climate is particularly favourable for human occupation with an average annual temperature of 18 °C. and 900 to 1,600 mm. of rainfall per year, according to altitude. There are four seasons in the year, quite different from the European ones since they are divided not according to temperature (which remains quite even throughout the year) but rain levels. In many ways Rwanda (and its twin Burundi) can be called a 'climatic and ecological island'[2]. This peculiar physical environment has had a strong impact on the nature of human settlement. Agriculture has always been very prosperous. Rwandese peasants are in fact large-scale gardeners and, apart from the remaining forested areas (Gishwati in the north and Nyungwe in the south), the whole country looks to some degree like a gigantic garden, meticulously tended, almost manicured resembling more the Indonesian or Filipino paddy fields than the loose extensive agricultural pattern of many African landscapes.

Not only is the land generous but it was also protective. The natural fortress of the highlands acted as a defence against the tse-tse flies and the malarial mosquitoes. It was also a bastion against hostile tribes and, in the nineteenth century, against the coastal Swahili slave raiders. Rwanda always remained free of foreign interference till the coming of the White Man. This prosperity, coupled with freedom from disease and with physical security, was conducive to very high densities of human occupation. The first explorers who reached the Rwandese highlands after crossing the vast malarial and war-torn expanses of the Tanganyika bush felt they were reaching a beehive of human activity and prosperity.

The physical layout of the land, where most of the people live on *musozi* (hills)[3], has determined a very precise and peculiar

2. Jean-Damascène Nduwayezu, *Les fondements physiques, humains et économiques du développement du Rwanda*, Ruhengeri: Editions Universitaires du Rwanda, 1990, p. 44.
3. The popular name given to Rwanda – 'the land of the 1,000 hills' – is fully justified. Seen from the top of a hill in central Rwanda, the landscape is usually made up of other hills of roughly the same altitude, north, east, south and west, as far

form of human occupation. First of all, the Rwandese peasant is
a man of the *rugo*. The word has several meanings. In day-to-day
affairs, it simply means the family enclosure or compound around
which all life revolves. In a polygamous household each wife has
her own *rugo*. But *rugo* is also, at a humbler level than *inzu*
(lineage), the basic unit of social life in Rwandese society. *Rugo*
is the family. Every hill is dotted with dozens of *ingo*. Tutsi and
Hutu, the notorious rival twins of Rwandese society live side by
side, on the same hilly slopes, in neighbouring *ingo* – for better
or for worse, for intermarriage or for massacre. One immediately
realises that such a high density of human occupation, together
with such a capacity for producing all the basic necessities of life
in plenty, led at a very early stage to centralised forms of political
authority and to a high degree of social control.

In fact, it has led to an almost monstrous degree of social
control. Together with the richness of the land, this was also
the first trait which struck the early explorers[4], and it is one
which has endured to this day. As a modern author remarked,
'One can notice a real panic within the power structure as
soon as there is even an inkling of a possible loosening up in
the control of the rural populations.'[5] As we will see, this
was a major factor in the tragedy which unfolded in 1994.
This obsession with control is not due to any special character
trait but simply to the fact that the land is small, the population
density is (and has always been) high and social interactions

as the eye can see. These hills are almost entirely occupied by houses, banana
groves and well tended fields, only broken by the odd clump of trees. The valleys
are marshy and are often the last refuge of wildlife, especially graceful wading
birds such as storks and crested cranes. They are also at times filled by serpentine
lakes coiling around the base of the hills. In the early morning mist, the beauty
of the landscape reminds one of the fragile elegance of a Japanese Zen painting.

4. They were Germans and the two best books on the early contacts (1894–7) with
Rwanda have never been translated. See Graf von Götzen, *Durch Afrika von Ost
nach West*, Berlin: Dietrich Reimer, 1899, and Richard Kandt, *Caput Nili. Eine
empfindsame Reise zu den Quellen des Nils*, Berlin: Dietrich Reimer, 1919 (1st edn
1905), 2 vols. Between 1907 and 1914 Kandt was the first German governor of
Rwanda, affectionately known by the Banyarwanda as *Kaanayoge*.

5. André Guichaoua, *Les paysans et l'investissement en travail au Burundi et au Rwanda*,
Geneva: ILO, 1987. Quoted by Jean-Pierre Raison, op. cit., p. 322.

are constant, intense and value-laden – as is clear from the following table:

	Population	*Gross density*	*Practical density*
1934	1,595,000	61	85
1950	1,954,000	73	102
1970	3,756,000	143	200
1980	5,257,000	200	281
1989	7,128,000	270	380

Source: Jean-Damascène Nduwayezu, op. cit., p. 98. Gross density means population density in relationship to the total surface of the country, i.e. 26,338 km.^{2}, while the practical density reflects the population density related to the arable land surface, i.e. only 18,740 km.^{2}.

Population density can attain incredible heights in certain localities such as in Shyanda *commune* where it had reached 668 people per square km. by 1989. Population projections for the year 2000 topped 10,000,000 people[6], with a 50% increase every ten years leading to over 50,000,000 by 2040 i.e. twenty times the population density of France[7], unless there is some demographic slowing-down in the mean time. Grim as it may seem, the genocidal violence of the spring of 1994 can be partly attributed to that population density. The decision to kill was of course made by politicians, for political reasons. But at least part of the reason why it was carried out so thoroughly by the ordinary rank-and-file peasants in their *ingo* was feeling that there were too many people on too little land, and that with a reduction in their numbers, there would be more for the survivors. The question of knowing who were to be the victims and who the survivors was of course not random, but heavily determined by cultural, historical and political factors. We now turn to that.

6. République Française, Ministère des Relations Extérieures, *Etudes et Documents* no. 55 (July 1983): *Perspectives démographiques à l'an 2000 en Afrique*, vol. 2, pp. 147–57.
7. Jean-Damascène Nduwayezu, op. cit., p. 121.

The Tutsi, the Hutu and the Abazungu[8]

The first explorers who reached Rwanda and Burundi were immediately struck by the fact that the population though linguistically and culturally homogeneous, was divided into three groups, the Hutu, the Tutsi and the Twa. These are the people who have often and inappropriately been called the 'tribes' of Rwanda. They had none of the characteristics of tribes, which are micro-nations. They shared the same Bantu language, lived side by side with each other without any 'Hutuland' or 'Tutsiland' and often intermarried. But they were neither similar nor equal[9]. Each group had an average dominant somatic type, even if not every one of its individual members automatically conformed to it. The Twa, who were very few (1% or less of the population), were pygmoids who either lived as hunter-gatherers in the forested areas or else served the high-ranking personalities and the King in a variety of menial tasks. The Hutu who made up the vast majority of the population, were peasants who cultivated the soil. They had a standard Bantu physical aspect, rather resembling the populations of neighbouring Uganda or Tanganyika. But the Tutsi were something else altogether. Extremely tall and thin, and often displaying sharp, angular facial features, these cattle-herders[10] were obviously of a different racial stock than the local peasants. Given the almost obsessive preoccupation with 'race' in late nineteenth-century anthropological thinking, this peculiarity soon led to much theorising, romanticising and at times plain fantasising. To start with, much was made of the physical features of the three groups in heavy

8. 'Europeans' in Kinyarawanda.
9. Much has been written on these differences – including, as we will see, much that was not very sensible. Before we move on to any more detailed analysis of the Tutsi/Hutu/Twa conundrum, we should point out that the least value-laden 'classical' description of the Rwandese pre-colonial social stratification can be found in Louis de Lacger, *Ruanda*, Kabgayi, 1959, chapters 1, 2 and 3.
10. The term 'cattle-hardens' is more appropriate than the term 'pastoralists' because, due to the limited availability of land in Rwanda, cattle tended to be grazed rather intensively and nomadism was out of the question, except in peripheral areas of the country such as Bugogwe.

pseudo-scientific terms. The small Twa were definitely at the bottom of the pile:

> Member of a worn out and quickly disappearing race ... the Mutwa presents a number of well-defined somatic character- istics: he is small, chunky, muscular, and very hairy; particularly on the chest. With a monkey-like flat face and a huge nose, he is quite similar to the apes whom he chases in the forest.[11]

The description of the Hutu was not much more prepossessing:

> The Bahutu display very typical Bantu features. [...] They are generally short and thick-set with a big head, a jovial expression, a wide nose and enormous lips. They are extroverts who like to laugh and lead a simple life.[12]

But the Tutsi were definitely superior beings:

> The Mututsi of good race has nothing of the negro, apart from his colour. He is usually very tall, 1.80 m. at least, often 1.90 m. or more. He is very thin, a characteristic which tends to be even more noticeable as he gets older. His features are very fine: a high brow, thin nose and fine lips framing beautiful shining teeth. Batutsi women are usually lighter-skinned than their husbands, very slender and pretty in their youth, although they tend to thicken with age. [...] Gifted with a vivacious intelligence, the Tutsi displays a refinement of feelings which is rare among primitive peo- ple. He is a natural-born leader, capable of extreme self-control and of calculated goodwill.[13]

The Europeans were quite smitten with the Tutsi, whom they saw as definitely too fine to be 'negroes'. Since they were not only physically different from the Hutu[14] but also socially supe- rior, the racially-obsessed nineteenth-century Europeans started

---

11. *Rapport Annuel du Territoire de Nyanza* (1925), quoted in Jean Rumiya, *Le Rwanda sous le mandat belge (1916–1931)*, Paris: L'Harmattan, 1992, p. 140.
12. Ministère des Colonies, *Rapport sur l'administration belge du Ruanda-Urundi* (1925), p. 34. Quoted in Jean-Paul Harroy, *Le Rwanda, de la féodalité à la démocratie (1955–1962)*, Brussels: Hayez, 1984, p. 26.
13. Ministère des Colonies, *Rapport*, op. cit., p. 34, quoted in Jean-Paul Harroy, op. cit., p. 28.
14. Although these differences were only statistically relevant. Given the many years

building a variety of hazardous hypotheses on their 'possible', 'probable' or, as they soon became, 'indubitable' origins.

The man who started it all was John Hanning Speke, the famous Nile explorer. In Chapter IX of his *Journal of the Discovery of the Source of the Nile* (London, 1863), entitled 'History of the Wahuma', he presents what he calls his 'theory of conquest of inferior by superior races'. After observing the 'foreign' origin of some ruling groups in several of the interlacustrine kingdoms, he 'deduced' from this 'fact' a 'theory' linking the monarchic institutions he had found in the area with the arrival of a 'conquering superior race', carrier of a 'superior civilisation'. He decided without a shred of evidence, that these 'carriers of a superior civilisation' who were the ancestors of the Tutsi were the Galla of southern Ethiopia[15], an opinion later shared by other nineteenth-century explorers such as Sir Samuel Baker and Gaetano Casati and by twentieth-century missionaries such as Father van den Burgt, Father Gorju and John Roscoe. Father Pagès, on the other hand, thought that they were descendants of the ancient Egyptians, while De Lacger saw them as coming from either Melanesia or Asia Minor. Some of the authors could become rhapsodic about their 'superior race':

> We can see Caucasian skulls and beautiful Greek profiles side by side with Semitic and even Jewish features, elegant golden-red beauties in the heart of Ruanda and Urundi[16].

Or elsewhere:

> The Bahima [a Tutsi clan] differ absolutely by the beauty of their features and their light colour from the Bantu agriculturalists of an

---

of intermarriage since the Tutsi had arrived in Rwanda, many people had the 'wrong' features.

15. They are called today by their real name, 'Oromo'. In Amharic 'Galla' means 'savages', hardly a term to call a 'superior civilisation' coming from the Abyssinian group traditionally linked with the monarchic institution. The Oromo were a nomadic Cushitic group which had persistently fought the Abyssinian kingdom(s) since the sixteenth century before being finally partially culturally assimilated and partially subjugated in the nineteenth century.

16. Father van den Burgt, *Dictionnaire Français-Kirundi*, p. lxxv. Quoted in Emile

inferior type. Tall and well-proportioned, they have long thin noses, a wide brow and fine lips. They say they came from the North. Their intelligent and delicate appearance, their love of money, their capacity to adapt to any situation seem to indicate a semitic-origin[17].

Some of the 'scientific' theories about the 'Hamitic' or 'Semitic' origins of the Tutsi started to get more and more bizarre, although the most respected anthropologists of the time (Ratzel, Paulitschke, Meinhof, Sergi and already Seligman, who was to become the great guru of African racial theories between the two world wars) were competing with each-other to give them not only credence but a wide publicity. The Tutsi (and so-called related groups such as the Maasai) came from a 'primordial red race'. They had 'an absolutely distinct origin from the negroes' which they considered as 'belonging to an absolutely inferior order'. They came from India – or even, as the Dominican Father Etienne Brosse suggested, from the Garden of Eden[18]. Some years later the Belgian administrator Count Renaud de Briey coolly speculated that the Tutsi could very well be the last survivors of the lost continent of Atlantis[19], while as late as 1970 a dignified former French ambassador to the newly independent Rwanda could pass off as serious anthropological literature a long poetical rambling about the Tutsi 'Magi' who had come from Tibet (with a minor branch making it to Iceland), pushing in front of them 'the animal steamroller of their giant herds'[20].

Mworoha, *Peuples et Rois de l'Afrique des Lacs*, Dakar: Les Nouvelles Editions Africaines, 1977, p. 25.

17. Mgr Le Roy in J.B. Piollet, *Les missions catholiques françaises au XIXème siècle*, Paris: Les Missions d'Afrique, 1902, pp. 376–7. Note 'love of money' as proof of Semitic origin!

18. A good study of this astonishing 'scientific' litterature can be found in Jean-Pierre Chrétien, 'Les deux visages de Cham', in P. Guiral and E. Témime (eds), *L'idée de race dans la pensée politique française contemporaine*, Paris. Editions du CNRS, 1977, pp. 171–99.

19. Comte Renaud de Briey, *Le sphinx noir*, Brussels: Albert DeWitt, 1926, p. 62.

20. Paul del Perugia, *Les derniers Rois-Mages*, Paris: Phébus, 1978 (1st edn 1970). The Tibetan origin 'hypothesis' can be found on p. 37. Babylon, Niniveh, ancient Crete and Noah and the Flood are also mentioned on p. 99. On pp. 164–5 the Tutsi king

Despite its semi-delirious aspects, this type of writing is of the utmost importance for several reasons. First, it conditioned deeply and durably the views and attitudes of the Europeans regarding the Rwandese social groups they were dealing with. Secondly, it became a kind of unquestioned 'scientific canon' which actually governed the decisions made by the German and even more so later by the Belgian colonial authorities. Thirdly, it had a massive impact on the natives themselves. The result of this heavy bombardment with highly value-laden stereotypes for some sixty years ended by inflating the Tutsi cultural ego inordinately and crushing Hutu feelings until they coalesced into an aggressively resentful inferiority complex. If we combine these subjective feelings with the objective political and administrative decisions of the colonial authorities favouring one group over the other, we can begin to see how a very dangerous social bomb was almost absent-mindedly manufactured throughout the peaceful years of *abazungu* domination.

Myths and realities of pre-colonial Rwandese society

We should first look at *Rwandese society* as the first Europeans 'saw' it. Von Götzen and all the other whites who followed him were immediately struck by the importance of the kingship institution. The *mwami* (king) lived at the center of a large court and was treated like a divine being. The nature of his power was sacred rather than profane and he *physically* embodied Rwanda[21]. He was surrounded by elaborate rituals carried out by the *abiru* (royal ritualists), and even the vocabulary relating to his daily life was special, with special words to mean 'the King's speech', 'the King's bed' and so on. His authority was

---

is described as having the power to see flying saucers which his poor Hutu subjects are unable to perceive. This does not prevent Mr del Perugia's book from still being frequently included in 'scientific' bibliographies on Rwanda.

21. When von Götzen shook hands with the King, all the courtiers were terrified: not only had the bizarre stranger actually *touched* the *mwami* without his authorisation, but the shaking of his arm might cause an earthquake since he was the personification of the hills of Rwanda.

symbolised by a sacred drum called *Kalinga* on which nobody
ever drummed (there were other ordinary drums for that purpose). Kalinga was decorated with the testicles of slain enemies
and to dare revolt against the King was not only an outrage but
a sacrilege. The King was

> ... the father and the patriarch of his people, given to them by
> *Imana* (God). He is the providence of Rwanda, the Messiah and
> the saviour. When he exercises his authority, he is impeccable,
> infallible. His decisions cannot be questioned. The parents of a
> victim he has injustly struck bring him presents so that he does
> not resent them for having been forced to cause them affliction.
> They still trust him, because his judgements are always just.
> Whatever happens, he remains *Nyagasani*, the only Lord, superb
> and magnificent[22].

But not content with simply trying to understand the nature of
the kingship, several Europeans started to fantasise about it,
along the lines of John Hanning Speke's earlier 'theories'. The
basic reason was it seemed unthinkable at the time that 'totally
savage negroes' could have achieved such a degree of political and
religious sophistication. And since there were other kings in
the other big or small kingdoms of the interlacustrine area
(Buganda, Nkore, Buha, Bushi, Burundi), the fantasies concerned
them all. The explorers, first and foremost Sir Harry Johnston
who was to become the first British administrator of the Uganda
Protectorate, put forward a theory of kingship as having origi-
nated from Ethiopia and having been brought by 'pastoral
invaders' whose memory had been preserved in a set of myths
the Bacwezi[23]. Thus Johnston was the link between the initial

---

22. De Lacger, op. cit., p. 119. For description of the nature of the Rwandese
    monarchy see André Pagès, *Un royaume Hamite au centre de l'Afrique*, Brussels:
    Institut Royal du Congo Belge, 1933, pp. 491 *et seq.*, Jean-Jacques Maquet, *Le
    système des relations sociales dans le Rwanda ancien*, Tervuren: Annales du Musée
    Royal du Congo Belge, 1954, pp.146–7 and 178–80. For a view of the place of
    the Rwandese royal myths and rituals within the interlacustrine cultures, see
    Emile Mworoha, op. cit., pp. 105–11.
23. Sir Harry Johnston, *The Uganda Protectorate*, London: Hutchinson, vol. 2, 1902,
    pp. 486–610.

Speke theory and the late nineteenth-century intellectual fantasies mentioned above. And these theories about 'pastoral invaders' bringing with them the kingship institution were also directly related to the Tutsi/Hutu dichotomy, the invaders having of course been Tutsi who had skilfully subjugated the 'inferior' Hutu peasant masses. This later became an accepted 'scientific' truth during colonial times and was summed up in a matter-of-fact way by Pierre Ryckmans, one of the most important Belgian administrators of the 1920s:

> The Batutsi were meant to reign. Their fine presence is in itself enough to give them a great prestige *vis-à-vis* the inferior races which surround ... It is not surprising that those good Bahutu, less intelligent, more simple, more spontaneous, more trusting, have let themselves be enslaved without ever daring to revolt[24].

But the King was only the apex of a complex pyramid of political, cultural and economic relationships. Typically, as in all traditional societies, including Europe till the eighteenth century, these three different levels of human action were deeply enmeshed and could not be prised apart. Under the King were the chiefs, but of these there were three types[25]: first, the *mutwale wa buttaka* ('chief of the landholdings') who took care of attributing land and of agricultural production (and taxation); then the *mutwale wa ingabo* ('chief of men') who ruled not the land but the bodies and, among other things, was in charge of recruiting fighters for the king's armies; and then the *mutwale wa inka* or *mutwale wa igikingi* ('chief of the pastures') who ruled over the grazing lands. The three functions could be concentrated in a single person for a certain area, but in a difficult or rebellious area, according to the principle of 'divide and rule', the King could separate

24. Pierre Ryckmans, *Dominer pour servir*, Brussels, 1931, p. 26. Quoted in J.P. Chrétien, 'Hutu et Tutsi au Rwanda et au Burundi' in J.L. Amselle and E.M'Bkolo (eds), *Au coeur de l'ethnie*, Paris: La Découverte, 1985, p. 138. For a discussion of the intellectual articulations between the various contemporary theoreticians of East African kinship, see Iris Berger, *Religion and Resistance*, East African Kingdoms in the precolonial period, Butare: Institut National de Recherche Scientifique, 1981, pp. 27–42.

25. Emile Mworoha, op. cit., p. 226.

all three positions and give them to different men. Most of the chiefs were Tutsi, although a number of the *abatwale wa buttaka* were Hutu since agriculture was their domain. And in order to make everything even more complicated (something the King rather relished), the same man could be 'chief of men' and of grazing lands on a certain *musozi* (hill) and have to put up with a rival as *mutwale wa inka* on 'his' hill, while at the same time being also *mutwale wa ingabo* for a couple of different hills where the rest of the power was held by third parties. This was a system aptly described by the first German resident Richard Kandt as that of 'the intertwined fingers'.

These chiefs, like all the administrators of all governments, were there basically to play two roles: controlling and extracting. The controlling varied, as we see later; close to the central core of the kingdom, it was very tight, but it became ever looser as one went towards the periphery. As for the extracting, it took several forms. There were three straightforward duties: maintaining the chiefly enclosures (*kwubaka inkike*), working the land (*gufata igihe*) and minding the cattle (*ubushumba bw'inka*). None of these was purely exploitative, and all entailed some form of 'salary'[26]. Neither these various obligations nor the taxes (paid in kind) rested on each person separately. The chiefs set certain global norms of work/payment for the *umusozi* (hill) and within each *rugo* (household) people made their own arrangements to satisfy the government's demands[27]. The later complaint against the Belgians was that they tightened up the system excessively by obliging each and every able-bodied person to pay/work on the European taxation model instead of retaining the softer form of African collective responsibility. In the late nineteenth century a new form of compulsory work, not previously known by the peasants, called *ubuletwa*, was introduced[28]. This was supposed

26. Non-monetary of course, since money was unknown in precolonial Rwanda.
27. J.J. Maquet, op. cit., p. 29.
28. There is no doubt that this was a late introduction since there is no '*guleta*' verb in Kinyarwanda from which such a substantive could be derived (the *wa* suffix means a passive form). But there is indeed such a verb in Kiswahili where *kuleta* means 'to bring'. So the *abaletwa* are 'those who are brought' and the *ubuletwa* is

to be for works of 'public interest'. It was spread by King Rwabugiri as he extended his dominions in the late nineteenth century, and was seen everywhere it came as a hated symbol of centralist oppression. The Belgian colonisers, who favoured it greatly, abused it. It was much more disliked by the people than the traditional forms of taxation.

But the type of personal dependence which has led to the greatest interest and controversy among Rwandese and foreigners alike has been the *ubuhake*. After the 1959 violence had irremediably split the Banyarwanda into mutually hostile Tutsi and Hutu groups, each camp 'analysed' the *ubuhake* institution in completely divergent ways. For the Tutsi ideologues it was a mild practice amicably linking different lineages into a kind of friendly mutual help contract. For the Hutu ideologues it was an ironclad form of quasi-slavery enabling the Tutsi masters to exploit the poor downtrodden Hutu. Of course the reality was somewhat more complicated[29]. Basically, *ubuhake* was a form of unequal clientship contract entered into by two men, the *shebuja* (patron) and the *mugaragu* (client). In the 'classical' form of *ubuhake* (probably not the original form, as we will see), a Tutsi patron gave a cow to his Hutu client. Since the Hutu were in theory not allowed to have cattle, which were a sign of wealth, power and good breeding, it was not only an 'economic' gift but also a form of upward social mobility. For the cow could reproduce, and the future calves would be shared between *shebuja* and *mugaragu*. This could be the beginning of an upward social climb where, once endowed with cattle, the Hutu lineage[30]

the situation of being brought to the disposal of the Master. And Kiswahili was the new trading language which began to reach Rwanda along with the advance of the coastal Swahili merchants from Zanzibar in the nineteenth century. See Emile Mworoha, op. cit., pp. 232–3, and Catharine Newbury, 'Ubureetwa and Thangata' in Centre de Civilisation Burundaise (ed.), *La civilisation ancienne des peuples des Grands Lacs*, Paris: Karthala, 1981, pp. 138–47.

29. The most astute and objective discussion of *ubuhake* is probably that of Jean-Népomucène Nkurikiyimfura, *Le gros bétail et la société rwandaise. Evolution historique des XIIème-XIVème siècles à 1958*, Paris: L'Harmattan, 1994, pp. 132–40.

30. We must of course remember that in precolonial Rwanda as in most traditional societies, no man was an island and that his family, his lineage and even his whole clan in cases of great success or great infamy would share his destiny.

would become *icyihuture*, de-hutuised, i.e. tutsified[31]. Of course, much depended on the *shebuja*: some were real Scrooges and the poor *mugaragu*, who in the meantime had many social and economic obligations towards his patron, would never get anywhere at all with his deal.

In fact, it seems very likely that originally *ubuhake* was on the whole not between Tutsi and Hutu but between two Tutsi lineages[32], and that it subtly changed form when it became a contract *between* the two groups rather than inside one of them. Thus, for example the 'prohibition' of cattle-owning by the Hutu seems to have been much more loosely enforced before this extension of *ubuhake*. In those times, if and when cows were given to Hutu, it was as a reward for bravery in battle and they remained as purely private property, without any social obligations linked to their ownership. Which brings us to war, a frequent activity in precolonial Rwanda. It was waged for three purposes: defending the kingdom against external enemies, extending the kingdom by conquest, and stealing cattle from neighbouring non-Rwandese tribes. Contrary to what Maquet says[33], the Tutsi were not the only ones to fight. All men were part of the *intore* (fighting regiments). And the scruffy Twa pygmies were greatly appreciated as soldiers. Each regiment had a name, usually a form of boast such as *abashakamba* ('the tough ones'), *imbanzamihigo* ('the ones who are praised first') or

---

31. Similarly a very poor Tutsi who lost all his cattle and had to cultivate the land would in due course become *umuwore* (fallen), i.e. hutuised. Marriage would tend to reinforce either trend, the children of the successful Hutu marrying into a Tutsi lineage and the children of the impoverished Tutsi marrying into a Hutu family.

32. In the peripheral areas of the country where Tutsi/royal control was weaker, there were several forms of Hutu equivalents to *ubuhake*. One, still practised in the early twentieth century in the southwestern province of Kinyaga, was *umuheto* linking whole lineages with each other in mutual cattle exchanges and protection. The other which has survived till modern times in northwestern Rwanda (Gisenyi and Ruhengeri districts) is *ubukonde* which involves the granting of collectively-held clanic tracts of lands to clients for agricultural purposes. See Catharine Newbury, *The cohesion of oppression: clientship and ethnicity in Rwanda (1860–1960)*, New York: Columbia University Press, 1988, chapter 5.

33. J.J. Maquet, op. cit., p. 130.

inzirabwoba ('the fearless ones'). Much of the fighting, especially when it was against rival kingdoms with similarly-minded nobles, took the forms of an almost ritualised ballet, where champions engaged each other in one-to-one combat. This is what De Lacger calls *'the quixotic tendency of Rwandese armies'*. He also notes that the great conqueror Kigeri IV Rwabugiri (1853-95), who meant business when he went into battle, preferred to recruit mostly Hutu armies who were perhaps less elegant but more efficient[34].

If war acted as a kind of 'social coagulant' where Tutsi, Hutu and Twa, although still unequal, were nevertheless first and foremost Banyarwanda facing a common enemy, religion was another social trait which made for the cohesion of society. Rwanda shared with other interlacustrine kingdoms the practice of the *kubandwa* cult. *Kubandwa* is the passive form of the verb *kubanda*, 'to put pressure on', 'to grab'. So the faithful, the *imandwa*, were literally 'the ones who are grabbed'. They were grabbed by *Ryangombe*, the Lord of the Spirits which makes *kubandwa* fall rather neatly into the category of the possession cults[35]. Like many such cults, it had a distinctly popular flavour and seemed to have been of Hutu origin. And although it was socially somewhat frowned upon for a Tutsi to take part in the ceremonies, the adherents were recruited in all three categories of society.

Strangely, even the clans, this basic instrument of social classification in segmentary societies, did not play such a role in Rwanda. If the families *(inzu)* and the lineages *(umuryango)* were either Tutsi or Hutu[36], this was not so with the clan *(ubwoko)* which counted among its members Tutsi, Hutu and even Twa. In fact, the 'clans' could hardly be so called, since there was no

34. De Lacger, op. cit., p. 142.
35. Ibid., chapters 11 and 12.
36. Rwanda is a patrilineal society. So the family went the way of the father and if a Hutu married a Tutsi girl, their children were Hutu. Unless of course the whole family changed its group identity according to the *icyihuture* process outlined above.

memory, even legendary, of an eponymous common ancestor[37]. There are grounds for looking seriously at David Newbury's hypothesis that these clans were in fact a social control device, superseding descent-based 'genuine' clans as the King's rule slowly spread over previously independent areas[38].

From this relatively static picture we have to turn to a different scene.

Dynamics of Rwandese history.   This is a delicate point and we will not try to fudge the dangerous issue of the theories concerning Tutsi origins. Yes, our feeling is that the Tutsi have come from outside the Great Lakes area and that it is possible they were initially of a distinct racial stock. They of course did not come from Tibet or from Ancient Egypt, but their distinct physical features probably point to a Cushitic origin, i.e. somewhere in the Horn, probably southern Ethiopia where the Oromo have long proved to be both mobile and adventurous. The physical evidence seems plain enough when one has lived in the area and the whole accumulated weight of observations since the 1860s cannot be entirely baseless[39]. But the facts we can reasonably accept stop here. Coming from elsewhere does not imply any form of 'superiority'. Anyway, what kind of superiority? The Oromo were simple acephalous pastoral people who developed monarchical institutions only in the nineteenth century, as they became

37. Rwandese clans were superbly studied in Marcel d'Hertefelt, *Les clans du Rwanda ancien. Eléments d'ethnosociologie et d'ethnohistoire*, Tervuren: Musée Royal de l'Afrique Centrale.

38. One good reason for thinking so is the fact that Rwanda is unique in having only eighteen clans while there are 134 in tiny Buhaya and 150 in much less populated Bunyoro. And all the 'exceptions' i.e. the few clans not falling in the group of eighteen, are found in northwest and southwest Rwanda, the two areas where royal conquest took place only in the late nineteenth century and where 'Rwandese order' was still imperfectly enforced at the time of the colonial conquest. See David Newbury, 'The clans of Rwanda: a historical hypothesis', in Centre de Civilisation Burundaise (ed.), *La civilisation ancienne des peuples des Grands Lacs*, Paris: Karthala, 1981, pp. 186–97.

39. Just as the 'different race hypothesis' has caused much crankish writing during the past hundred years, some modern authors have gone to great lengths in the other direction to try to refute this theory and to prove that Tutsi and Hutu belonged

culturally part of the Abyssinian world[40]. The 'superior race' theorists tend to forget that even an author with such a 'classical' view of Rwandese society as De Lacger believed that the monarchic institution in Rwanda was locally-grown from among the Hutu population. Not only were there several other kingdoms in the interlacustrine area, and some such as Buganda which showed no trace of somatically heterogeneous people, but there were also numerous Hutu micro-monarchies. And although many were gobbled up by the royal government, several survived into the twentieth century within Rwanda itself, on the peripheries of the Central state. As De Lacger says ironically of the 'conquest', 'It looks as if the newcomers found nothing better to do than to lie in the bed which had already been made by their predecessors'[41].

----

to the same basic racial stock. For example J.C. Desmarais, 'Le Rwanda des anthropologues, archéologie de l'idée raciale', *Anthropologie et Société*, vol. 2, no. 1 (1978), pp. 71–93, thinks that the Tutsi, as good herdsmen, knew about race selection and systematic breeding and that they applied these bovine techniques to themselves so as to become tall! Another favourite line of argument is that the distinct physical aspect of the Tutsi is due to their consuming exclusively milk products. Thus J.P. Harroy, the last vice governor-general of Ruanda-Urundi, writes (op. cit., p. 29) that 'these giants were created through techniques which have been discarded [why?] during the 1920s.' Yet, crazy as it was, the idea was picked up by the RPF during the war. Keen to play down the Tutsi/Hutu dichotomy, teachers at the RPF Cadre School said that Hutu and Tutsi shared a common racial stock, but that 'Tutsi babies were stretched during infancy' and were given a special high-protein diet, 'like the *Inyambo* cows'. Sober critics pointed out that this 'anti-racist' interpretation ended up being exceedingly racist: for *Inyambo* cows were the best, the royal cattle, the cream of the herd, which meant that the Tutsi had to be the very best human material among the Banyarwanda. The school organisers were annoyed. (Interviews with Christine Ornutoni, Cabinet Director of the Ministry of Social Rehabilitation Kigali, 13 January 1995, and with Journalist Faustins Kagme, Kigali, 17 January 1995. Both were former students of the school.)

40. For an essay on the Oromo social and philosophical vision see Asmarom Legesse, *Gadda: three approaches to the study of African society*, London: Macmillan, 1973. For historical studies of the Oromo or 'Galla' states as they developed after 1800, see Herbert Lewis, *A Galla monarchy: Jimma Abba Jifar (1830–1932)*, Madison: University of Wisconsin Press, 1965, and Mohamed Hassen, *The Oromo of Ethiopia: a history (1570–1860)*, Cambridge University Press, 1990. None of the material even remotely suggests the existence of monarchic institutions at the very early date the proto-Oromo could have come from the Horn.

41. De Lacger, op. cit., p. 88.

But apart from the question of knowing where the Tutsi came from, the main problem in the dynamics of Rwandese history lies with the obstinate expansion of the kingdom under the Banyinginya dynasty. The Rwandese geographical area is a quilt of micro-units, *ibihugu* in Kinyarwanda, which correspond well to the French word *terroirs*. Just as the mountains, coastal plains and islands of ancient Greece created a fragmented environment leading to many micro-states, so did the world of fragmented hills and valleys of Rwanda give birth to hundreds of what De Lacger calls 'toparchies'. It seems that sometime during the eighteenth century one of these 'toparchies', the centrally located Buganza around Lake Muhazi, started to unite under its leadership first the medium-altitude Nduga country and then, as time went on, the eastern lowlands (Ndorwa, Mutara, Gisaka, Bugesera) and later, with much greater difficulty, the western highlands. None of this expansion was planned or systematic, at least in the beginning. And given the fact that after two centuries of 'conquests' the kingdom ruled an area roughly comparable to that of Belgium, the expansion did not take place quickly. One should see it rather as an almost unintended by-product of a society where wars were a normal and accepted part of ordinary life, playing an almost ritualistic role in the relationship of the King with his people.

But, as we see later, this expansion was not always smooth and it carried with it a number of problems[42]. First, the sacred nature of the *mwami*ship meant that, even apart from the obvious problems of material control, the kingdom had to impose a politico-religious vision of quasi-mystical proportions on its conquered subjects. This implied a normalisation of social procedures (*ubuhake*, nominated chiefs) and beyond that a form of symbolic geography reorganising the land according to a strongly enforced world view: *Ryangonbe* lived in the cold Virunga chain to the north, hell was in the Nyiragongo volcano

---

42. For a good detailed view of what was it entailed for the central power to take over a new area, see Jean-Claude Munyakazi, 'Le pouvoir Nyiginya sur le Gisaka, 1850–1916', unpubl. MA thesis, University of Rwanda, Butare.

near Gisenyi, and the river Nyabarongo divided the country into two ritual areas which could not be crossed by certain people, such as a king bearing a certain reign name. Rwanda was at the geographical centre of the world and each of its hills fitted within the King's game plan[43]. The Europeans, when they came, were fascinated by this imperious reordering of the world according to preconceived cultural notions, probably because it was a process with which they were familiar themselves in a different form. But they were slower in seeing the dysfunctions, the various cracks in the system.

And there were several flaws in this otherwise elegantly balanced picture. The main one was that the King's power did not extend evenly over the whole surface of 'Rwanda'. First, there were several Hutu principalities which had survived, especially in the north, northwest and southwest of the country century. They remained defiant till the nineteenth century and in some cases they were incorporated into 'Rwanda' only *after* the arrival of the Europeans and with their help. Thus Kibari was annexed only in 1918, Bushiru 'Tutsified' after 1920 and Bukonya taken over in 1931. And as the King's control extended over the outlying principalities, the nature and style of his authority over the whole land changed gradually towards an ever greater administrative centralisation and more authoritarian forms of political control[44].

This evolution, accompanied and often supported by the European colonisers, represented a considerable departure from the

---

43. See Edouard Gasarabwe, *Le geste Rwanda*, Paris: UGE, 1978, p. 33; also diagram, p. 441.

44. *Historique et chronologie du Rwanda*, Kabgayi, 1956, pp. 128–65. See also the works of Ferdinand Nahimana, 'Les principautés Hutu du Rwanda Septentrional', in Centre de Civilisation Burundaise (ed.), *La civilisation ancienne des peuples des Grands Lacs*, Paris: Karthala, 1981, pp. 115–37, and *Le Rwanda, émergence d'un Etat*, Paris: L'Harmattan, 1993. Ferdinand Nahimana is an excellent historian and a militant Hutu supremacist. He has used his very real academic talent to make many valid points in questioning the nature of kingly power in traditional Rwanda, only to put his intellectual capacities at the service of the most intolerant forms of political activity in the mid-1990s. We will have occasion to find him again under quite a different guise in further chapters dealing with political violence.

situation which had existed in the early nineteenth century and even in many cases up to the 1890s. First of all, central political control became more homogeneous, situations of local particularism, not to say rebellion, even when those were due to Tutsi chiefs, vanished one by one, giving way to the smooth-grained all-encompassing picture of an almost 'modern' state[45]. Secondly, at the central court level the King or some members of his family was able to strengthen and tighten up the functioning of political authority after 'fighting among factions of the dominant Tutsi group which at times had been violent enough to endanger the very survival of this group'[46]. Thirdly, as we have already seen, this double process of local and central strengthening of authority enabled the court to eliminate the last remaining Hutu principalities. And fourthly, to crown this whole process, the relations of personal dependence, which have at times been inaccurately described as 'feudal'[47], changed and indeed *then* became increasingly 'feudalised'.

This period saw the extension of the *igikingi* type of landholding, that is 'granted' land, given by the King or by a Tutsi lineage to *abagaragu* (clients). Theoretically *igikingi* land was for grazing, but in practice the 'legal' determinant (i.e. the fact that it was given and could be held either in freehold[48] or as clanic undivided property in the way of *ubukonde*) became the determining factor when considering this type of land, which in fact was

---

45. There are many scattered references to this process. But the clearest ones can be found in Catharine Newbury, *The cohesion of oppression*, op. cit., pp. 54–7, and in Claudine Vidal, 'Situations ethniques au Rwanda', in J.L. Amselle and E.M'Bokolo (eds), *Au coeur de l'ethnie*, Paris: La Découverte, 1985, pp. 167–84 (see pp. 174–6 on this point).

46. Claudine Vidal, *Sociologie des passions*, Paris: Karthala. 1991, p. 33.

47. This is the word found in J.J. Maquet, De Lacger, Father Pagès and most of the authors presenting what we have called the 'classical' view of Rwandese society, a view which only began to be questioned in the 1960s by Marcel d'Hertefelt. For a discussion of the use of the concept of feudalism in relationship to East African kingdoms, see J.P. Chrétien, 'Vocabulaire et concepts tirés de la féodalité occidentale et administration indirect en Afrique Orientale' in Daniel Nordman and Jean-Pierre Raison (eds), *Sciences de l'Homme et conquête coloniale. Constitution et usage des Sciences Humaines en Afrique*, Paris: Presses de l'Ecole Normale Supérieure, 1980, pp. 47–63.

48. After the Second World War *igikingi* holdings were often transformed into private freehold properties, but this was a completely distinct development to which we return in the next section.

often used agriculturally. The transformation of *ubuhake* into its most unequal form, the introduction of *ubuletwa* forced labour, the extension of *igikingi* land contracts, all went hand in hand, albeit at a slow pace. In the peripheral areas they were resented as hardcore signs of Nduga/Buganza oppression[49]. The kingly title held by the small Hutu princes who were slowly subjugated (*muhinza*) became synonymous with the term 'rebel'[50]. In the areas conquered during the past century but imperfectly controlled (Bugesera, Gisaka, Mubari, Ndorwa, Mutara) the softer forms of *igikingi* land grants and *ubuhake* contracts were tightened up after the 1870s. What is vital for our purpose of understanding the reasons for the tragic split which led to the present Rwandese ultra-violence is the fact that at the time *it was a centre versus periphery affair and not one of Tutsi versus Hutu*. If the King's chiefly agents in this process were mostly (but not all) Tutsi, their 'victims' in the newly 'controlled' situation were both Tutsi and Hutu, and they were defined by their geographical location[51]. And it was worse – in a way – that because the Tutsi and Hutu categories not being the hard unchanging identities which many commentators have purported them to be, many of the newly integrated élites were co-opted by the monarchy in order to turn them into faithful servants of the new order. It is essential to keep this process in mind in order to understand the transformation which took place in Rwanda between 1860 and 1931 and which directly gave birth to its modern society[52] – and its almost intractable problems.

The generalisation of *igikingi* increased the capacity for pressure coming from the political authorities on the inferior and middle

---

49. Catharine Newbury, *The Cohesion of Oppression*, op. cit., p. 82.
50. Ferdinand Nahimana, *Le Rwanda, émergence d'un Etat*, op. cit., p. 211.
51. Jean-Népomucène Nkurikiyimfura, op. cit., pp. 84 and 135.
52. These dates should not be taken as precise expressions of the beginning and end of something which was a very diffuse complex process of political, agrarian, social and economic transformation. But they represent the beginning of the reign of Kigeli IV Rabugiri, the great conqueror, and the end of the reign of his son Yuhi V Musinga. They can be taken as meaning roughly the second half of the nineteenth century and the first third of the twentieth.

social classes. It also contributed to a strengthening of ethnic feelings both at the top and at the bottom of society. Neglecting the poorest strata (mostly Batwa and Bahutu, with a sprinkling of Batutsi), judging that the middle class (made up of Bahutu and Batutsi) was reasonably happy with the situation as it was, the *mwami* (king) and his chiefs thought that several elements, both Bahutu and Batwa could be integrated in the ruling group, that is the Mututsi élite, depending on their capacities, their wealth and their potential for exploiting useful blood connections. *To open up access to the new ibikingi holdings, many people had to be 'tutsified'* something which many authors called 'accession to the nobility', an expression which blurs the distinction between the few high-ranking Batutsi lineages and the ordinary Batutsi ... But this 'enoblement' *prevented the birth of a distinct Bahutu chiefly stratum which could have become a privileged intermediary between the court and the larger population*[53].

This of course, posed the problem of those Hutu (the vast majority) who could not be included in the new royal chiefly élite. The extension and hardening of the new centralised system caused them to slide from a status of inferiority-balanced-by-complementarity into that of a quasi-rural proletariat. By the end of the century the vast majority, if not the totality of the Hutu peasants, were in a position where they had to sell their labour, first as a social obligation, and then as a monetarised commodity in the colonial system[54]. In that way there was a continuity between the late nineteenth century evolution of the Rwandese state and society and the further transformations during the colonial period.[55]

---

53. Jean-Népomucène Nkurikiyimfura, op. cit., pp. 96–7. One should mention here that in spite of what could be perceived as a criticism of the late nineteenth-century development of Tutsi power, Nkurikiyimfura was himself a Tutsi. But he always remained perfectly objective, a model of moderate and intellectually inquisitive scholarship.

54. Claudine Vidal, 'Economie de la société féodale rwandaise', *Cahiers d'Etudes Africaines*, vol. 14, no. 1, pp. 350–84.

55. It is this phenomenon which was later used by the intellectual theoreticians of the 'Hutu revolution' of 1959 to present the social relationships in Rwandese society as eternally and inherently oppressive. The best presentation of this case can be found in Donat Murego, *La révolution rwandaise (1959–1962). Essai d'interprétation*, Louvain:

We now begin to have some elements of an answer to Claudine Vidal's interrogation:

> How can we explain that, within only two generations, a simple form of social antagonism has turned into violent racial hatred, widely shared way beyond its initial nucleus of fanatics?[56]

But to understand better this evolution of Rwandese traditional society at the end of the nineteenth century, we should move on to the effect of colonisation.

The colonial impact

The Germans arrived in Rwanda at a crucial time in the transformation of the country's politics[57]. King Kigeli IV Rwabugiri, who had just died, had been the most active and conscious embodiment of the conquest/centralisation/social standardisation process we have just briefly outlined. As frequently happened in a monarchy where the King was polygamous and where there was no clear system of succession, the old warrior's death was followed by a period of political turbulence. The King had designated one of his sons, Rutalindwa, as the heir to the throne, giving him as Queen Mother not his real mother, who was considered politically too weak, but another of his wives, Kanjogera

---

Institut des Sciences Politiques et Sociales, 1975, which, despite its title, is not a history of the 1959 revolution but a strongly ideological analysis of the traditional Rwandese polity. In a way somewhat similar to its treatment by the colonial anthropologists, the author extracts a still picture from the film of history and presents this moment as an image of eternity. Under the emotional influence of the 1994 genocide, one detects today the opposite tendency, i.e. to present 'traditional' Rwandese society as an example of idyllic mutually beneficial social functionalism.

56. Claudine Vidal, *Sociologie des passions*, op. cit., p. 26.
57. The standard work on the period of the German occupation of Rwanda remains William Roger Louis, *Ruanda-Urundi (1884–1919)*, Oxford: Clarendon Press, 1963. Reinhart Bindseil, *Ruanda und Deutschland seit den Tagen Richard Kandts*, Berlin: Dietrich Reimer, 1987, deals with the early period of the German presence while Gudrun Honke's vivid pictorial essay, *Au plus profond de l'Afrique. Le Rwanda et la colonisation allemande* (1885–1919), Wuppertal: Peter Hammer Verlag, 1990, provides an excellent bibliography on the subject, even containing some items not found in Marcel d'Hertefelt and Danielle de Lame's bibliographical encyclopedia on Rwanda.

of the Ababega clan. This was essential since in the Rwandese monarchy the Queen Mother played a vital political role as manager of the royal household and the focal point of all court intrigues. Rutalindwa's mother was from the Abakono clan, a weak royal uxorial clan[58]. But during the 1885–90 period, Kigeli IV had violently purged his own lineage (the Abahindiro lineage of the Banyinginya royal clan), the reason being that their old habits of haughty independence did not fit well with the new policy of centralisation. As the King's own Abahindiro parentage was marginalised, it was replaced mostly by members of the Ababega clan who had thus acquired inordinate power. Kigeli's choice of a Mubega Queen Mother to 'protect' the heir to the throne was politically sensible but psychologically clumsy. Conscious of the clanic support she could muster, Kanjogera did not take well to seeing the son of a Mukono rival ascend the throne and she was in a perfect position to conspire against her royal charge with the help of her brother Kabera, a powerful chief. Less than a year after the old King's death, Kanjogera and her brother organised a *coup d'état* at Rucunshu in which they killed the King and his main chiefly supporters[59]. They immediately proclaimed as King Yuhi V Musinga, Kanjogera's own son. As Queen Mother, Kanjogera became the most important person in the kingdom and her brother Kabera acted as a kind of regent over the weak and irresolute Musinga. The Banyiginya who had survived Kigeli IV's purges were hunted down pitilessly in order to prevent any attempt at a legitimist revolt[60].

Quite understandably in such a situation, the white newcomers, largely ignorant of the complicated local politics, were

---

58. The *Abami* took their wives from only four of the eighteen clans: the Abakono, the Abaha, the Abagesera and the Ababega (Emile Mworoha, op. cit., p. 225).
59. De Lacger, op. cit., pp. 341–71.
60. There was one anyway, but it did not take place till 1912, a year after the death of the terrible Kabare, and was not led by a real noble but by an adventurer passing himself off as Kigeri's son. See Jean-Pierre Chrétien, 'La révolte de Ndungutse. Forces traditionnelles et pression coloniale au Rwanda allemand', *Revue Française d'Histoire d'Outre-Mer*, vol. 59, no. 4 (1962), pp. 645–80, and Alison des Forges, 'The drum is greater than the shout: the 1912 rebellion in northern Rwanda' in Donald Crummey (ed.), *Banditry, Rebellion and Social Protest in Africa*. London: James Currey, 1986, pp. 311–31.

open to manipulation. And since the Germans maintained only a very light presence in Rwanda (in 1914 there were only ninety-six Europeans in there, including the missionaries) they were ready to overlook the exploitation of their interventions by the central state since they hoped to use it as a tool of colonisation. Thus they had no objections to strengthening it further, i.e. playing exactly the role Kanjogera and Kabera wanted them to play in the period of wobbly authority following the Rucunshu *coup d'état*[61]. Thus from the start the European presence in Rwanda was a determining factor in reinforcing the *mwami*ship, the chiefly hierarchy and the court's increasing hold over the lightly-controlled peripheral areas[62]. And when, due to lack of manpower, the Germans could not directly control a certain area with or on behalf of the royal court, they were not above sub-contracting local control to Tutsi chiefs who, secure in the white man's support, acted as rapacious quasi-warlords[63].

The German presence was structurally essential since it inaugurated a colonial policy of indirect rule, which left considerable leeway to the Rwandese monarchy and acted in direct continuation of the pre-colonial transformation towards more centralisation, annexation of the Hutu principalities and increase in Tutsi chiefly power. But it did not last long (1897–1916) and, given its very light administrative implantation, could not really modify Rwandese society in depth. The Belgian colonial domination, effective on the ground with effect from 1916 military conquest[64] and made official by a League of Nations Mandate in

61. They eventually realised that their actions were playing into the King's hands, and were deepening the Tutsi/Hutu divide, but too late before the war stopped them from making any possible inflexion of policy. See a letter written to his superiors by the temporary Resident Max Wintgens (21 May 1914) quoted in Reinhart Bindseil, *Ruanda und Deutschland seit den Tagen Richard Kandts*, op. cit., pp. 120–2, in which Wintgens warns the Governor in Dar-es-Salaam of 'attracting the hatred of the Wahutu' by giving too much support to the court.
62. Ferdinand Nahimana, *Le Blanc est arrivé, le Roi est parti*, Kigali, 1987, p. 112.
63. Catharine Newbury, *The cohesion of oppression*, op. cit., pp. 118–28.
64. For an idea of the military operations leading to the Belgian occupation of Rwanda in 1916, see Jean Rumiya, op. cit., chapter 1; Ferdinand Nahimana, *Le Blanc est arrivé, le roi est parti*, op. cit., pp. 121–30; and Cdt J. Buhrer, *L'Afrique Orientale Allemande et la guerre de 1914–1918*, Paris: L. Fournis 1922.

1919, was to continue and deepen the German approach to the European presence in Rwanda.

The Belgians. The first years of Belgian administration after the granting of the Mandate were years of 'wait and see'. The 'real' Belgian colonisation policy was progressively implemented between 1926 and 1931 in a series of measures which came to be known as *'les réformes Voisin'* after the then governor, Charles Voisin. These reforms were preceded by a period of soul-searching, essentially in order to decide how to behave towards the court, the whole Tutsi chiefly complex and the system of indirect administration bequeathed by the Germans. There was much uncertainty. Thus Mgr Classe, the bishop who had arrived as a simple priest in the country at the turn of the century and whose advice the Belgians deeply respected, could write in 1927 that although the 'Mututsi youth was an incomparable element of progress' one should not forget that the Rwandese kings of old 'elevated to high dignity Bahutu and even Batwa lineages, giving them rank in the landholding class, them and their descendants'. And then, three years later, fearful that his advice would be too closely followed in the ongoing reform process, he turned about, saying:

> The greatest mistake this government could make would be to supress the Mututsi caste. Such a revolution would lead the country directly to anarchy and to hateful anti-European communism. [. . .] We will have no better, more active and more intelligent chiefs than the Batutsi. They are the ones best suited to understand progress and the ones the population likes best. *The government must work mainly with them*[65].

His second piece of advice was to prove far more popular with the administration than the first and the few fumbling and ineffectual attempts at putting Hutu into chiefly positions came to naught. Even worse, many already existing Hutu chiefs were fired and replaced by Tutsi ones[66]. This eventually led to a

65. Quoted in De Lacger, op. cit., pp. 523–4.
66. See Pierre Tabara, *Afrique. La face cachée*, Paris: La Pensée Universelle, 1992, pp. 84–90. It is noteworthy that the author drawing attention to this policy of the Belgian administration cannot be suspected of being pro-Hutu since he is a Tutsi who fought with the *Inyenzi* rebels against the Hutu republic during the early 1960s.

situation of almost total dominance of the chiefly functions by the Tutsi. By the end of the Belgian presence in Rwanda in 1959, forty-three chiefs out of forty-five were Tutsi as well as 549 sub-chiefs out of 559[67]. One of the central measures taken by Governor Voisin in 1929 was to concentrate chiefly functions into a single hand. As we have seen above, under the traditional Rwandese systems there were three types of chiefs on any given hill, one of whom, the Chief of the Land, was often a Hutu; in 1929 their three positions were fused into one, which was almost always given to a Tutsi. Thus the Hutu peasants, who before had cleverly manipulated one level of chiefly authority against the other, now found themselves tightly controlled by one chief only, whose backing by the white administration was much more efficient than the loose support the traditional chiefs used to receive from the royal court[68]. Also, for the purpose of 'rationalising' taxes and 'public interest work' carried out by the natives, the whole structure of corvée was redesigned by the Europeans. This entailed the introduction or generalisation of *ubuletwa*, the hated forced labour system. And not only was *ubuletwa* generalised where it did not exist before, but its functioning was also radically altered. Where before the royal chief had dealt globally with whole lineages on a hill, the white administration now considered it an *individual* obligation, meaning that a family could no longer delegate a strong young good-for-nothing to sweat for all its members but that every single male (and even at times, when needed, women and children too) had to go and perform the corvée[69].

67. Jean-Pierre Chrétien, 'Hutu et Tutsi au Rwanda et au Burundi', op. cit., p. 145.

68. This fact is noticed by the strongly pro-administration anthropologist J.J. Maquet in *Le système des relations sociales dans le Rwanda ancien*, op. cit., pp. 175–83, and even by the last vice governor-general of Ruanda-Urundi, J.-P. Harroy, op. cit., p. 89. In an added twist of fate, one should keep in mind that the powerful Tutsi chiefs were completely in the hands of the Belgians, who tended to be rough with those they felt had not carried out their tasks correctly. A Tutsi chief would often be whipped with the *chicotte* in front of his Hutu charges. Humiliated, he would then take revenge on them after the departure of the White Man, creating a cascade of increasing resentment. (Interview with a former colonial chief, Kigali, 18 January 1995.)

69. Catharine Newbury, 'Ubureetwa and Thangata' op. cit.

But the 'official' measures were not the only element of transformation of the old Rwandese social system. Sensing the global support of the Belgian administration, the Tutsi felt that they could gradually modify traditional land and contractual rights in their favour. This was helped by Belgian legislation.

> These lands held as undivided usufruct by lineage groups[70] are not considered by the Belgian legislation in Ruanda-Urindi as belonging to the native collectivities. They are not 'occupied' in the legal sense by the natives and are considered as vacant. The state can dispose of such lands after due compensation[71].

Of course, the 'due compensation' was usually rather miserly and slow in coming. Thus the 'state' (i.e. often in practice the Tutsi chiefs who were its embodiment) could gain control of the traditional *ubukonde* Hutu landholdings in the north-west and south-west. This would not be forgotten, and during the 1959 'revolution', Tutsi houses quickly went up in flames in these areas. And beyond explicit legislation, there was the practice, the new atmosphere of individualisation/privatisation, which went along with what one should not shy away from calling the penetration of western capitalism into the traditional collective folds of an ancient society. And of course, as always in such situations, the beneficiaries of the new order were the ones who happened at the time to be closest to the levers of political control – increasingly after 1929, these were the Tutsi[72].

70. The author refers here to *ubukonde*.
71. J. Adriaenssens, *Le droit foncier au Rwanda*, mimeographed course text, Butare: Université Nationale du Rwanda, 1962, p. 42. Quoted in Jean-Népomucène Nkurikiyimfura, op. cit. p. 219.
72. At this point we have to introduce an important caveat. By 'the Tutsi' we mean here those members of the high lineages who were in a position to play ball with the Belgian administration and to benefit from it. They were a minority among their own people, which should never be forgotten if one is not to fall into the 'ethnicist' trap of tribal pseudo-explanations. The missionaries who were probably at the time the Europeans who knew best native Rwandese society, were quite aware of that fact, even if they did not always translate their social awareness into political positions (see for example the revealing quote from the *Archives des Pères Blancs* in Rome by Jean Rumiya, op. cit., p. 198). Rumiya should be trusted on that point since he was a Hutu and since, before eventually breaking with them and being killed by them during the 1994 genocide, he flirted for a while with the Hutu extremists.

Two of the most important institutions in traditional Rwandese society thus slowly moved towards privatisation. The first was the attribution of *ibikingi* grazing lands:

> After 1926–1931, the beneficiaries of *Ibikingi*, in direct or indirect contact with the new legal concepts which had come from the West, moved increasingly towards a private property view of grazing lands. Little by little, every person owning ten cows or more tried to get his own *Ibikingi*. The result was a multiplication of private *Ibikingi*, created with the implicit support of the Belgian administration and through the transformation then taking place in the practice of *ubuhake*[73].

Which means of course that the second aspect of these fundamental changes in socio-economic practice was the transformation of *ubuhake* contracts. In ancient Rwanda *ubuhake* had taken not one but many different forms:
– links of subordination between 'high' and 'low' Tutsi lineages';
– chiefly initiatives to increase control over their 'administrative' subordinates, whether Tutsi or Hutu;
– defensive strategies by either Hutu or Tutsi lineages who owned cattle and felt threatened by an encroaching rich Tutsi lineage and who looked for a powerful *shebuja* to protect them;
– survival strategies by poor families who looked for a patron, Tutsi or even Hutu, in order to improve a particularly sorry economic situation. *Ubuhake* was then close to charity.

In addition to this complexity, not only did *ubuhake* not exist in the remaining independent Hutu principalities which had survived till the arrival of the whites, but it also did not exist in the Tutsi-dominated eastern lowland areas such as Gisaka till they were brought (quite late) under central control. And it was never introduced among the poor Bagogwe Tutsi nomads of the north-west who never quite fitted into the system[74].

73. Jean-Népomucène Nkurikiyimfura, op. cit., p. 228. Here, just as we said in note 72 (but in the opposite ethnic configuration), we should postulate the seriousness of the author's position because he is a Tutsi writing something which is potentially damning for his group. These last two examples from Rwandese authors, both killed in 1994, should act as a reminder (especially to Europeans) against quick intellectual generalisations and hasty politicisation of social analysis.
74. Jean-Népomucène Nkurikiyimfura, op. cit., pp. 83–4.

So we can now see one thing: the *ubuhake* which has been described as 'typical' of Rwandese culture, praised by pro-Tutsi writers as a factor of social cohesion and vilified by Hutu ideologues as a symbol of evil exploitation was in fact largely a synthetic product developed by colonial Tutsi chiefs under the benevolent sponsorship of the Belgian administration. That it came from a set of traditional social practices bearing the same name has the same type of relationship with the original reality as the so-called 'feudal' French society of 1789 with its Capetian origins.

The problem is that the noxious synthetic product spread quickly to areas and to sectors of society where it had not previously been known (at least not in that form) and that it was strongly resented. This was noted both in Kinyaga[75] and in central and southern Rwanda[76] because it was perceived as a 'foreign' imposition, and even in the core Nduga and Bwana-mukari areas because it brought a hardening of the social relationships.

The whole process of Belgian administrative reorganisation was finally and symbolically brought to a close by getting rid of King Yuhi V Musinga in November 1931 and replacing him with one of his sons, a polite young man who was to rule under the name of Mutara III Rudahigwa. The Belgians had never liked Musinga; he had fought alongside the Germans against them, he was haughty and unruly, his mother was a pest, he was openly adulterous, bisexual and incestuous, he never converted to Christianity and he deviously tried to hijack the white man's civilising mission for his political benefit. The Catholic church which hated him was overjoyed at his downfall, especially since 'everything that reeked of paganism, *Ishiriya* charms, all kinds of talismans, fetish iron clubs, *Isubyo* flasks, sacred monkeys, everything disappeared as if in a dream. The whole paraphernalia went to Kamembe [where Musinga was exiled] and never came back.'[77] The new King had been chosen by the Belgians

75. Catharine Newbury, *The cohesion of oppresion*, op. cit., p. 82.
76. Claudine Vidal, 'Le Rwanda des anthropologues ou le fétichisme de la vache', *Cahiers d'Etudes Africaines*, vol. 9, no. 3 (1969). See especially pp. 396–7.
77. De Lacger, op. cit., p. 549.

and his accession to the throne was not accompanied by any of the prescribed rituals. The *abiru* royal ritualists were not even present when Mutara was formally proclaimed King. So for the people he was always to remain, in a way, *Mwami w'abazungu*, 'the King of the Whites'. But for the Belgians he was a pearl of great price. He dressed well in Western clothes (Musinga had always retained his African royal paraphernalia), drove his own car, was monogamous and in due course converted to Christianity. With the zeal of the new convert, he even consecrated his country to Christ the King in October 1946, a measure which put him in the rather bizarre company of General Franco and the quasi-fascist prime minister of Québec, Maurice Duplessis.

The King's conversion was only a recognition of the transformations then taking place in the kingdom. Up to the 1920s Christianity had spread very slowly and most of the converts were poor or marginal people who looked to the church as a sort of white man's *ubuhake* system and aspired to become the *abagaragu* of the missionaries for lack of anything better. What decided the massive wave of conversions which started in 1927 was the impact of the Belgian administrative reforms. The Tutsi realised that the Belgians were going to remodel Rwandese society on the basis of what they perceived as 'real' Rwandese institutions, that Rwanda was quickly becoming 'rwandified' on the white man's terms, and that these developments would not automatically be bad for them if they could only be sure to ride the storm. A necessary prerequisite for membership of the élite of the new Rwanda the Belgians were creating was to become a Christian. Many priests were delighted to see the country's élite suddenly flock to them rather than the social outcasts who used to be their clientele. By 1930, Father Soubielle was writing of what he termed 'a massive enrolment in the Catholic army': 'Our Batutsi have finally made up their minds and, having done so, they have immediately taken the lead in the movement.'[78] Some of the other Fathers were less enthusiastic about the

78. Quoted in De Lacger, op. cit., pp. 519–20.

motivations of their new converts such as the anonymous writer of the Zaza Mission diary who wrote on 19 November 1931: 'Their motives are perhaps not the most disinterested, but with the help of God's Grace, they will be turned into good Christians.'[79]

From that moment on, the Catholic church became a very important element in the Belgian reorganisation of Rwanda[80], which is somewhat paradoxical since Belgian cabinets often contained strongly anti-clerical socialist ministers. But the church had been in Rwanda since the very beginning of the German occupation, and when the Belgians had come they had found the often francophone priests (mostly White Fathers) expert and highly knowledgeable about the country and thus a godsend. While the administrators came and went, the Fathers remained, staying on for their whole lives. They were almost the only whites to speak Kinyarwanda well, and the only ones too who wrote seriously about 'native customs'. Some of them, such as Father Pagès or Father Pauwels, were considered as almost absolute authorities on matters Rwandese, and Mgr Classe, who had arrived in Rwanda as a simple priest in 1907 and become Vicar Apostolic in 1922 (he survived till 1945), was almost a national monument. Before 1927 the church had lacked a firm grounding in Rwandese social reality, but by 1932 it had become its main social institution, presiding over hundreds of thousands of converts, including the King himself.

The church had an impact on many aspects of Rwandese society. First of all, it imparted to the African way of life a strong moralistic streak. Polygamy was evil and adultery was a sin, thrift and hard work were encouraged, and social displays of

---

79. Quoted in Ian Linden, *Church and revolution in Rwanda*, Manchester University Press, 1977, p. 189.
80. For the fundamental role of the Catholic church in Rwanda, in addition to Ian Linden, op. cit., see Julien Kalibwami, *Le catholicisme et la société rwandaise*, Paris: Présence Africaine, 1991, and Allison des Forges, 'Kings without crowns: The White Fathers in Ruanda' in Daniel F. MacCall and Norman Bennett (eds), *Eastern Africa History*, New York: Praeger, 1969, pp. 176–207.

conventional piety were required of all. Rwandese society under the influence of the church became if not truly virtuous, then at least conventionally hypocritical. Later this social hypocrisy was fully carried over from the Belgian colonial microcosm into the new politically independent Rwandese Republic.

The church also had a monopoly on education, something which meant a fairly good quality of teaching but a limited spread of school education, since attendance was paid for and not compulsory. Illiteracy rates remained high, alongside the promotion of good-quality higher education. And since the Tutsi were the *'natural-born chiefs'* they had to be given priority in education so that the church could enhance its control over the future élite of the country. The Astrida (now Butare) College enrolment breakdown by ethnic origin is eloquent:

	Tutsi pupils	*Hutu pupils*
1932	45	9
1945	46	3
1954	63	19 (incl. 13 from Burundi)
1959	279	143

Source: René Lemarchand, *Rwanda and Burundi*, London: Pall Mall/New York: Praeger, 1970, chapter 4.

To obtain any kind of post-secondary education, the Hutu had no choice but to become theology students at the Kabgayi and Nyikibanda seminaries. After graduation they tended to experience difficulties in finding employment corresponding to their level of education, and often became embittered and frustrated, something which was to play an important role in the 1959 social upheaval. But an effect of the christianisation of Rwanda that is less often discussed was the quasi-disappearance of the *kubandwa* possession cult and the changes it brought to spiritual and cultural life in the country. *Kubandwa* had been an element of social cohesion because it was home-grown, trans-ethnic and highly personal. Christianity was also trans-ethnic, although definitely Tutsi-dominated during the colonial years, but it was foreign and rather abstract. As we have seen, the reasons for converting to Christianity were fundamentally social and political. Christian values did not penetrate deeply, even if Christian prejudices and social attitudes were adopted as protective covering. Catholicism, after Mutara III Rudahigwa, became not only linked with the highest echelons of the state but completely enmeshed in Rwandese society from top to bottom. It was a legitimising factor, a banner, a source of profit, a way of becoming educated, a club, a matrimonial agency and even at times a religion. But since it was all things to all men, it could not have any real healing power when faced with the deepening ethnic gap which the Belgian authorities kept absent-mindedly digging.

Kubandwa had been ecstatic and a bit crazy. Christianity was extremely reasonable. It did not transcend social fractures, it reproduced them in many different dimensions and (albeit unwittingly) exaggerated their effects. In Iris Berger's words about *kubandwa*[81], 'In Rwanda, as elsewhere, the themes of symbolic reversal and institutionalised disorder may serve to reinforce rather than to challenge the classificatory categories [of society].'[82] And on the contrary, the moderate institutionalised Christian order, socially hegemonic but almost totally missing the internalised moral underpinning of Christian values, proved to be a terrible element in the violent challenge of these same categories.

---

81. Iris Berger, op. cit., p. 82.
82. Professor Johan Pottier was kind enough to attract our attention to the fact that the *kubandwa* cult had survived in Rwanda right down to the 1980s (see Christopher Taylor, *Milk, Honey and Money: Changing concepts in Rwandan healings*, Washington, DC: Smithsonian Institute Press, 1992, p. 80). But it seems that both *Kubandwa* and the *Nyabingi* cult in the north are personal cults, providing psychological safety-valves for their adepts but with a limited or even non-existent social and political content when compared with Catholicism. In its fight against 'paganism' the Catholic church also destroyed another social practice of great importance, the practice of *kunywana*, the blood-pact ritual which could bind together people of very different social origins. The *Mwami* himself could have Batwa *abanywanyi* (blood brothers).

The Belgian reforms of 1926–31 had created 'modern' Rwanda: centralised, efficient, neo-traditionalist and Catholic – but also brutal. Between 1920 and 1940, the burden of taxation and forced labour borne by the native population increased considerably. Men were almost constantly under mobilisation to build permanent structures, to dig anti-erosion terrraces, to grow compulsory crops (coffee for export, manioc and sweet potatoes for food security), to plant trees or to build and maintain roads. These various activities could swallow up to 50–60% of a man's time. Those who did not comply were abused and brutally beaten[83]. The result was a manpower exodus towards the British colonies, especially Uganda where there was plenty of work[84]. It is worth noting that during the brief period after the First World War when Gisaka (eastern Rwanda) was attached to the British Tanganyika mandate, the people, especially the Hutu, were quite pleased and did not particularly relish the return to Belgian rule two years later[85].

The 'Rwandese ideology'. At this point we should perhaps try to bring together the various strands of the brief but complex narrative in the preceding pages.

First, for the Belgians unlike the Germans[86], Rwanda mattered. It was an important and valued part of their colonial empire.

83. In 1948 the UN Trusteeship Mandate Delegation to Rwanda found that out of 250 peasants they interrogated, 247 had been beaten up, usually many times (R. Lemarchand, op. cit., p. 123). In his memoirs J.-P. Harroy, the last Belgian vice-governor general, complains that the UN was 'short-sighted' when it forbade physical punishments after its visit.

84. See Audrey Richards, *Economic development and tribal change: A study of immigrant labour in Buganda*, Cambridge: Heffer, 1959, and J.P. Chrétien, 'Des sédentaires devenus migrants. Les motifs de départ des Barundi et des Banyarwanda vers l'Uganda (1920–1960)', *Cultures et Développement*, vol. 10, no. 1 (1978), pp. 71–101.

85. De Lacger, op. cit., pp. 479–83.

86. Germany was a great power, with a number of more important colonies. As to how it looked at tiny Rwanda, then part of *Deutsch Ostafrika*, the meagre place it occupies in standard histories of German colonisation is evidence enough, e.g. Horst Gründer, *Geschichte der deutschen Kolonien*, Munich: Ferdinand Schöningh, 1985. But Rwanda and Belgium were the same size, and the Belgians were fascinated with their new toy.

They tried their best to understand it, control it and develop it. But 'understanding', given the accepted 'scientific' vulgate of the time, proved an ambiguous process. On the basis of what was more an ideology than a scientific evaluation, an ancient, rich and complex society was modernised, simplified and ossified.

Administrators, government anthropologists and missionaries, all contributed, at times unwittingly, to an intellectually brilliant ideological reconstruction of Rwanda's past and, from that artificial past, of the present. Unfortunately the 'natives' were keenly aware of this reconstruction and of the advantages – or disadvantages – it offered them according to their ethnic group[87]:

> The newly redefined Rwandese Tutsi aristocracy was particularly sensitive to the 'scientific' guarantees which could be found for its 'nobility'. Even today, among exiled Tutsi, the myth of Egyptian origins still survives in the heads of people who are now its victims after having thought they were its beneficiaries. The crystalization of a genuine 'Rwandese ideology' during the reign of Mutara III Rudahigwa would be worth analyzing in detail . . . 'Traditional Rwanda', as it is now commonly described, [. . .] was basically reconstructed or even constructed at that time[88].

Both the white foreigners and the Tutsi 'aristocracy' worked together to write a beautiful story which, in its hieratic greatness, was closer to H. Rider Haggard's realm of heroic fantasy in *King Solomon's Mines* than to the humbler realities of a small East African kingdom. No one embodied this dream better than the intellectual priest Alexis Kagame (1912–81)[89], 'a member of the native clergy of Rwanda', as he liked to refer

87. Of course this awareness was not noticed at the time. But even if it had been noticed, it would have caused no great concern. Till the mid-1950s, the Europeans still thought they would stay in Africa for another thirty or forty years.
88. J.P. Chrétien, 'Hutu et tutsi au Rwanda et au Burundi', op. cit., p. 146.
89. Claudine Vidal in *Sociologie des passions*, op. cit., pp. 45–61 has written a good essay on his life and work. For a reflexion on the blending of his 'pagan' and Christian themes, see Ian Linden, *Church and revolution in Rwanda*, Manchester University Press, 1977, pp. 200–1. For a critical discussion of his concept of kingship, refer to Ferdinand Nahimana, *Le Rwanda. Emergence d'un Etat*, op. cit., pp. 198–213.

to himself. For many years Kagame was *the* native Rwandese intellectual, before the coming of age of the modern generation of semi-secularly educated academics. Even authors with completely different personal and intellectual perspectives had to agree on the meaning of his intellectual monopoly:

> Alexis Kagame succeeded in captivating very different intellectual milieus, the milieu of the European specialists on Rwanda and the milieu of the Rwandese intellectuals themselves. [. . .] for Kagame there was a constant temptation to go further than simply 'transcribing' precolonial Rwandese society. There was a tendency also to 'europeanise' it. . . . Thus he reconstructed a 'traditional' kingdom and a 'traditional' aristocracy which were mixed figures, borrowing some traits from European historical stereotypes and others from the Rwandese nobility as it had been re-engineered by colonial policies. (Claudine Vidal)

And from the militant Hutu historian Ferdinand Nahimana: 'His work was a projection into the past of the situation he could see in 1943.' Why insist so much on the work of eminent Belgian anthropologists and solemn Rwandese clerics who have been dead for years? Because their influence has remained alive down to this very day and can be traced as the major cause of the violence Rwanda has experienced at recurrent intervals since 1959.

This may seem a rather strong criticism of 'harmless' intellectuals who certainly had no intentions of provoking such a catastrophe[90]. But the cogwheels of what we could call the 'systemic aspect' of the situation had been turning relentlessly:

– First, a mixture of racial prejudice, the *Zeitgeist* and administrative expediency created a 'superior race' vision of the

90. In his opening address at the Budapest University for Central Europe in 1992, the great historian Eric Hobsbawm said that when he was younger he thought that the only scientists who could cause evil were the chemists, physicists and biologists, but that later he came to realise that the apparently innocuous social scientists held even more dangerous powers. He was speaking in the context of Central European and Danubian ethnic nationalisms, but that remark could apply with equal ease to Africa.

Tutsi. Then the vision of the Tutsi was juxtaposed with an equally oversystematised view of the kinship institution. The reality of the central core of the Rwandese kingdom was generalised, codified and legitimised as a 'respect for the national tradition'. By 1931, when King Mutara III Rudahigwa ascended to the throne and Catholicism became the quasi-official religion of the new system, a kind of hologram of Rwanda had been created – bright, shiny, perfect and unreal.

– These visions of the Europeans did not remain intellectual abstractions, but were translated into perfectly real administrative policies. And these in fact dovetailed perfectly with the inner dynamics of the royal system in the late nineteenth century – which was logical since it was their source of inspiration. The Belgian administrative reforms of 1926–31 systematised and rationalised the policies which had been pursued by the Rwandese kings down to Kigeri IV. This did not contradict the fact that the present King and his court had to be politically emasculated because the Belgians had become the real political substitutes of the old *Abami*, whose descendants were kept merely as ceremonial symbols.

– At the same time, 'scientific' anthropologists, doubtless quite honestly and unconsciously, legitimatised the present by projecting it into the past. The system became not only politically dominant but culturally hegemonic, and its distorted version of the past became the generally accepted vision because it 'explained' the present much better than the real complexities of history.

– The Tutsi 'superior race' may have been shorn of all power at the centre, but made up for this by monopolising local administration and contractual means of economic control (*ubuhake*). There again, these forms of authority and exploitation, which were real and had physical substance, were legitimised through a traditionalisation process which purported to show that Tutsi dominance had always existed under such forms. The Tutsi of course did not mind. But the problem was that the racialisation of consciousness affected everybody, and even the 'small Tutsi', who did not benefit from the system in any way, started to believe that they were indeed a superior race and that under the

same rags as their Hutu neighbours wore, a finer heart was beating.
– And of course the Hutu, deprived of all political power and materially exploited by both the whites and the Tutsi, were told by everyone that they were inferiors who deserved their fate and also came to believe it. As a consequence they began to hate *all* Tutsi, even those who were just as poor as they, since *all* Tutsi were members of the 'superior race', something which was to translate itself in the post-Second World War vocabulary as 'feudal exploiters'.

Thus through the actions, both intellectual and material, of the white foreigners, myths had been synthesised into a new reality. And that new reality had become operational, with its heroes, its tillers of the soil and its clowns. Feelings and social actions would henceforth take place in relation to this reconstructed reality because by then it would have become the only one. The time-bomb had been set and it was now only a question of when it would go off.

Those readers who think that the causal chain outlined above is exaggerated should remember one simple but major point: although Rwanda was definitely not a land of peace and bucolic harmony before the arrival of the Europeans, there is no trace in its precolonial history of systematic violence between Tutsi and Hutu as such. There were plenty of wars, both domestic and foreign, 'but they either pitted the Banyarwanda as a group against foreign tribes or kingdoms; or saw chiefly lineages fighting each other to control some seat of local power, with all the *abagaragu* at their *shebuja*'s side, whether Tutsi, Hutu or Twa. These wars, like all wars, caused deaths – probably on the scale of the wars between Picts and Scots or among the Gallic tribes at the time of Julius Caesar. But they were never on the scale we have witnessed since independence and which eventually culminated with the 1994 horror.[91]

---

91. And one cannot apply here the often quoted argument about modern weaponry making Third World conflicts increasingly bloody. The 1994 genocide was largely carried out with weapons comparable to those used in precolonial times.

In the last resort, we can say that Tutsi and Hutu have killed each other more to upbraid a certain vision they have of themselves, of the others and of their place in the world than because of material interests. This is what makes the killing so relentless. Material interests can always be negotiated, ideas cannot and they often tend to be pursued to their logical conclusions, however terrible.

Of course material interests played their role, whether for the Tutsi élite as long as white protection kept them on top or for the Hutu élite when 'revolution' enabled them to grab the benefits of power. But the willingness of the ordinary rank-and-file person to enter the deadly fray cannot be accounted for by material interests. Ideas and myths can kill, and their manipulation by élite leaders for their own material benefit does not change the fact that in order to operate they first have to be implanted in the souls of men.

With the end of the Second World War, new ideas and new myths were going to emerge. But the fact that they grafted themselves so easily on the colonial cultural mythology of Rwanda was proof of how strong, well-implanted and widely believed the latter had become. The new myths did not destroy the old ones, but followed and strengthened them by adding the dynamics of modernity to the now 'traditional' view of Rwandese society.

2

THE HUTU REPUBLIC
(1959–1990)

The 1959 muyaga[1] *and its consequences*

Although they did not decide in the Hutus' favour, church representatives had been alone in expressing, quite early on, some doubts about the place assigned to the Hutu in Belgian colonial society. In a series of private musings analysed by Dr Ian Linden, the future Mgr Classe toyed with the idea of changing the ethnic 'division of labour' he had found in Rwanda, although he finally shrank from it:

> Certain missionaries seem to want to see the Bahutu reigning one day, especially the Christian Bahutu[2] [. . .] Would things be any better? The Batussi are the chiefs . . . the government cannot change in one fell swoop the deep-seated structures of the country. There would be a revolution, something all governments want to avoid at all costs[3].

Mgr Classe had been right for his time, but by 1945, when he died, things were changing. And 'revolution', if properly 'guided', was no longer the bogey it had been in 1912, even in the church's eyes.

The problem was that the changes by then under way were not only due to the new ideas that swept the colonised world

---

1. In Kinyarwanda, *muyaga* means a strong but variable wind, with unpredictable destructive gusts. It is by that name that the Banyarwanda refer to the 1959 disturbances.

2. In 1912 there had been very few conversions, especially of Tutsi, and the missionaries were entitled to think that the aristocracy might continue to refuse Christianity. Hence the idea of promoting those Hutu who had converted.

3. Léon Classe, 'Relations avec les Batussi dans la Mission du Rwanda', undated MS. in Mgr Classe's hand (*ca.* 1912) in which he expressed his private thoughts on the social problems of Rwanda as he saw them. Quoted in Ian Linden, *Church and revolution in Rwanda*, op. cit., p. 97.

41

in the wake of the Second World War, but were also the unavoidable consequences of social and administrative measures taken earlier, at a time when their long term effects certainly had not been foreseen. When the Belgians had taken responsibility away from the families and lineages on the hills and transferred the burden of compulsory labour and taxation onto the shoulders of individuals, they had, without realising it, given a great push to the traditional structures. Individuals were forced to become independent economic agents, which forced them into independent action – and independent thinking. The neo-traditionalist *ubuhake* and the various other measures designed to redesign the 'feudal' social structure also had the same effect of turning collective relations of social subordination into individual relations of economic exploitation. A scholar could remark:

> Thus, as Rwanda entered its fourth decade under European rule, the three major functions performed on the basis of corporate kin groups had either been transformed into responsibilities incumbent upon individual adult men (*ubutaka, urbureetwa*) or abolished entirely (*umuheto*)[4].

Social relationships became grimmer and more full of conflict at a time when, paradoxically, the neo-traditionalist forms of clientship, in spite of retaining their weight in terms of power, had become less and less a way of making money. The War had brought with it a vast expansion of the cash economy in which the Hutu had shared. The old clientship system, which was basically part of the non-monetary economy, was accordingly becoming increasingly obsolete. But in a way that was somewhat typical of all potentially revolutionary situations, the old oppressive forms were perceived (and often wielded by their socially obsolescent 'beneficiaries') more harshly as they lost their real power and as their cultural legitimacy waned.

It is in this progressively hardening social atmosphere that the

---

4. Catharine Newbury, *The cohesion of oppression*, op. cit., p. 112.

church began to favour the growth of a Hutu counter-élite. We have seen above that the possibility of such a choice had been contemplated – and rejected – early on, but several factors led the church to reconsider its social approach between the two world wars. One was that the control of the Rwandese church was slowly slipping from the hands of the whites. By 1951 there were as many black Rwandese priests as white ones. And these native clergy were almost exclusively Tutsi, at a time when the Tutsi élite (of which the clergy formed part) was quickly changing. Being better educated than the Hutu and exercising a quasi-monopoly over the native clerical positions in the colonial administration[5], the Tutsi of exalted lineage had been the first to pick up on the new ideas of racial equality, colonial political devolution and possible self-government. They fully realised that their social position was not impregnable and that they could not wait for too long for the Belgians to transfer power to them if they did not want to see the transfer challenged. They had cleverly taken advantage of the first liberalising measures of the colonial administration in the early 1950s. The decree of 14 July 1952 which had created 'elective councils' at every administrative level (sub-chieftancy, chieftancy, province, state) had not led to elections but to nominations of 'suitable candidates' by the sub-chiefs and the chiefs. So even when Hutu were included in these 'councils', they were the *abagaragu* of the chiefs, and as such perpetually acquiescent to their *shebuja*. Thus, as observers noted, 'This was a process of diffusion of power but principally among the group which already possessed it, that is to say the Tutsi caste'[6]. To be more precise, one should say 'the high-caste Tutsi', because the *'petits Tutsi'*, even if they still believed in their oft proclaimed 'race superiority', did not share in the benefits of this increase in power any more than they had shared earlier in the benefits of the 'traditionally reconstructed' administration of Rwanda.

5. Between them the *abanyinginya* and *ababega* clans controlled almost 60% of all positions (Ian Linden op. cit., p. 227).
6. Jean-Jacques Maquet and Marcel d'Hertefelt, *Les élections en société féodale*, Brussels: ARSOM, 1959, p. 26.

Thus the Europeans in the church were in a position to see their control being challenged, and they realised that this challenge was not isolated but that, on the contrary, it was part of a wider movement of contestation of the colonial order coming from this very Tutsi élite whom the Belgians had been nurturing for the previous thirty years. This occurred at a time when the European component of the church – and its social and political ideas – were also undertaking an important change. The early leaders of the Catholic church in Rwanda such as Mgr Hirth or Mgr Classe had been upper-class men with rather conservative political ideas which were followed by the rest of the white clergy. But in the late 1930s and increasingly after the war, these men were replaced by clerics of humbler social origins, from the lower middle class or even the working class and increasingly Flemish rather than Walloon. They had no sympathy for the aristocratic Tutsi and identified more readily with the downtrodden Hutu.

The combination of changes in white clerical sympathies, struggle for the control of the Rwandese church and increasing challenge of the colonial order by the Tutsi élite, all these combined to bring about a slow but momentous switch in the church's attitudes, from supporting the Tutsi élite to helping the Hutu rise from their subservient position towards a new aspiring middle-class situation. But although nobody was yet aware of it, the hour was very late and there was little time left[7]. Independence was just around the corner and the changes which had been initiated were going to proceed at an accelerated pace under pressure of circumstances, with people's consciousness definitely not keeping up with the speed of social change – a gap which was to have tragic implications.

One of the main organs used in the process of change by the European-led main segment of the church was the periodical

---

7. When in February 1957 A.J.J. van Bilsen had proposed a thirty-year plan for the independance of the Belgian Congo in an article in *La Revue Nouvelle*, he had been criticised as a dangerous anti-colonial agitator. Three and a half years later, the Belgian Congo was independent (J.-P. Harroy, op. cit., p. 258).

Kinyamateka. In the hands of a leading Hutu *évolué*, Grégoire Kayibanda[8], it became the most read organ in Rwanda, with a circulation of about 25,000. At the same time, the creation of the TRAFIPRO (*'Travail, fidélité, progrès'* i.e. work, fidelity, progress) coffee cooperative gave a combination of economic opportunity and leadership training to the growing Hutu counter-élite. Slowly, in various parts of the country, the Hutu, who now felt that they had support from one of the leading institutions of the white man's system, started to organise, creating mutual security societies, cultural associations and, in the north, clan organisations among some of the quasi-Bakiga clans which had submitted most recently to the colonial power. In March 1957 a group of nine Hutu intellectuals, with the aim of influencing the UN trusteeship mission which was about to come to Rwanda, published a text called *Notes on the Social Aspect of the Racial Native Problem in Rwanda*, better known by the name *'Bahutu Manifesto'*[9]. The high-sounding but confused choice of words in the original title reveals the ambiguity of the authors' analytical framework. But the reality they referred to, namely the humiliation and socio-economic inferiority of the Hutu community, could not be doubted:

'The problem is basically that of the political monopoly of one race [sic], the Mututsi. In the present circumstances, this political monopoly is turned into an economic and social monopoly. [. . .] And given the *de facto* selection in school, the political, economic and social monopolies turn into a cultural monopoly which condemns the desperate Bahutu to be for ever subaltern workers, even after an independence that they will have contributed to gain

8. Born in 1924, Kayibanda had been a seminarist at Nyakibanda, the main gateway to social improvement for the nascent Hutu counter-élite. After being a primary school teacher from 1948 till 1952, he became secretary of the *Amitiés Belgo-Congolaises* and chief editor of the Catholic periodical *L'Ami* (1952–6). When the agricultural cooperative TRAFIPRO was created in 1956, he was made its first chairman while at the same time becoming chief editor of *Kinyamateka*. Soon after he became the private secretary to Mgr Perraudin, the Swiss vicar apostolic of Rwanda.

9. The integrality of the text can be found in F. Nkundabagenzi, *Le Rwanda politique (1958–1960)*, Brussels, CRISP, 1961, pp. 20–9.

without even realising what is in store for them. The *ubuhake* has been legislated away[10], but these monopolies have replaced it with an even stronger oppression.

The word 'race' used in this social context was an alarm-bell. It was of course the product of years of European harping on the 'superior race' of 'aristocratic invaders' who had come from anywhere between Tibet and ancient Egypt. But it showed that the ideology had been swallowed whole and that a socio-political problem was now dealt with in 'racial' terms. In a further threat for the future, the *Manifesto* emphatically added:

> In order to monitor this race monopoly we are strongly opposed, at least for the time being, to removing the labels 'Mututsi', 'Muhutu' and 'Mutwa' from identity papers. Their suppression would create a risk of *preventing the statistical law from establishing the reality of facts.*

Here the confusion becomes particularly serious. 'Racial' statistics are set as a guideline, as a monitor of democratisation. We have here the intellectual root of the future 'Quota Democracy' which was to become the law of the land in independent Rwanda.

The reaction of the Tutsi élite to these developments was highly defensive. Starting in 1954, they went on an open counter-offensive, first of all against the liberal Tutsi such as Chief Prosper Bwanakweri and his group of young *Astridiens*. These were young educated Tutsi of the best families who not only sympathised with 'progressive' ideas, but thought that they should be used in the reform of their own society as well as against the colonisers. After the 1953 pseudo-elections Chief Bwanakweri, who was trying to liberalise social relationships in his own chieftancy, was targeted by the King, who asked the Belgians to deport him as a dangerous subversive. He was sent no farther than Kibuye, but his political marginalisation nipped in the bud

---

10. *Ubuhake* had been banned in 1954. But it had had little effect since the *igikingi* land grants remained in Tutsi hands and grazing rights were not given to the Hutu (or the poor Tutsi) unless they remained practically, if not in name, in the old *ubuhake* relationship (see Catharine Newbury, *The cohesion of oppression*, op. cit., p. 146).

any possibility of reform from within the system.

In May 1958, the Court notables (*bagaragu b'ibwami bakuru*) declared that since Kigwa, the ancestor of the Banyinginya dynasty, had reduced the Hutu by force, there could be no fraternity between Tutsi and Hutu[11]. The whole climate became poisoned as political rivalry went into heavily symbolic disputes, not amenable to reason. In October 1958, Joseph Gitera, one of the new Hutu leaders, asked Mgr Perraudin to get rid of *Kalinga*, the sacred royal drum, because, being decorated with the testicles of vanquished Hutu princes, it could not be considered a symbol of national unity. The Tutsi court notables strongly protested.

Political parties were quickly created. In June 1957, Grégoire Kayibanda had been the first to create one, the Mouvement Social Muhutu (Hutu Social Movement) or MSM which had at first only a rather limited appeal. The Association pour la Promotion Sociale de la Masse (Association for the Social Promotion of the Masses) or APROSOMA, created in November 1957 by the Hutu businessman Joseph Gitera, claimed to be a class-based party but attracted almost no one but Hutu. Gitera was a populist, a demagogue, a mystical Christian and a somewhat unbalanced person who practised a particularly rabble-rousing brand of politics. In August 1959 the conservative Tutsi created the Union Nationale Rwandaise (Rwandese National Union) or UNAR, which was strongly monarchist and hostile to the Belgians, and defended the idea of immediate independence. Unexpectedly but logically within the Cold War context of the late 1950s, UNAR began to receive money and diplomatic backing from the Communist countries in the UN Trusteeship Council. The result was immediately to deepen the antagonism between the Tutsi and the Belgian authorities. As the last Belgian vice-governor general was to write in his memoirs:

> From then on, the unspoken agreement which the administration had made in the 1920s with the Tutsi ruling caste in order to further

---

11. For this and for the other political developments which took place in 1957–9, the best source/analysis is René Lemarchand, *Rwanda and Burundi*, London: Pall Mall Press/New York: Praeger, 1970, chapter 5.

economic development ... was allowed to collapse, also tacitly. The Tutsi wanted independence and were trying to get it as quickly as possible by sabotaging Belgian actions, whether technical or political. . . . The administration was forced to toughen its attitude when faced with such obstruction and hostility coming from chiefs and sub-chiefs with whom we had collaborated for so many years[12].

To counter UNAR the Belgians had released Chief Bwanakweri, who created in September 1959 the Rassemblement Démocratique Rwandais (Rwandese Democratic Union) or RADER. This moderate party was hampered by several difficulties. Mainly a Tutsi party, it was frowned upon by the monarchist diehards while the Hutu never quite managed to trust its liberalism. Also, because of its initial Belgian sponsorship, it was constantly accused of being a government plant in the political landscape. Thus Chief Bwanakweri always remained on the fringe of the real action, and liberal Tutsi opinion never had a serious chance of prevailing.

Meanwhile Grégoire Kayibanda had transformed his movement and in October 1959 the MSM had become the Mouvement Démocratique Rwandais/Parti du Mouvement et de l'Emancipation Hutu (Rwandese Democratic Movement/Party of the Movement and of Hutu Emancipation) or MDR-PARMEHUTU. In a development which was to have grave consequences for the future, the two Hutu parties, APROSOMA and PARMEHUTU, had quite distinct regional bases: APROSOMA was mainly based in the Astrida (Butare) area, while PARMEHUTU derived its strength from a mostly Gitarama-Ruhengeri membership.

By late 1959 the situation was so tense that any incident could have caused an explosion. The spark which ignited the powderkeg was very small. As he was walking home on 1 November 1959, the Hutu sub-chief Dominique Mbonyumutwa, a PARMEHUTU activist, was attacked by young members of UNAR and severely beaten. The (false) news of his death spread like wildfire and Hutu activists began gathering their troops to attack Tutsi chiefs and known UNAR members. Confused

12. J.-P. Harroy, op. cit., p. 241.

fighting followed, mostly with traditional weapons such as spears, clubs and *pangas* (machetes). Many Tutsi houses were burnt, without making any distinction between high-lineage Tutsi and ordinary *'petits Tutsi'*. On the 6th, the *mwami* and the UNAR started to retaliate, organising commandos to attack the Hutu, especially the APROSOMA activists who, because of Gitera's fiery rhetoric, were perceived as the most dangerous. There was extreme confusion. Many people thought that the King supported the anti-Tutsi attacks because he embodied justice and the chiefs had been unjust and oppressive. Later, some Hutu actually rallied the King's forces to attack the APROSOMists who were perceived as sacrilegious in their opposition to the throne. From the beginning the Belgian authorities showed extreme partiality for the Hutu, even letting them burn Tutsi houses without intervening[13]. To add to the confusion, Bakiga mountain tribesmen raided Rubengera in the north, purely in order to loot, and killed thirty-eight people in the process. By 14 November, a rough sort of order had been re-established. Around 300 people were dead and 1,231 (919 Tutsi and 312 Hutu) had been arrested by the Belgians.

The key man in this process had been Colonel Guy Logiest. He had arrived in Rwanda on 4 November 1959, having been detached by General Janssens from the Congolese *Force Publique*. He was to stay in the country for three years and play a vital role. From the beginning his approach to the problem was clear:

> Some among my assistants thought that I was wrong in being so partial against the Tutsi and that I was leading Rwanda on a road towards democratisation whose end was distant and uncertain. . . . No, the time was crucial for Rwanda. Its people needed support and protection. My role was essential and it was important that I could play it till the final verdict which would come from the communal elections. Today, twenty-five years later, I ask myself what was it that made me act with such resolution. It was without doubt the will to give the people back their dignity. And it was probably just as much the desire to put down the *morgue* and expose the duplicity of a basically oppressive and unjust aristocracy[14].

13. Pierre Tabara, *Afrique, la face cachée*, op. cit., pp. 179–85.
14. Col. Guy Logiest, *Mission au Rwanda*, Brussels: Didier-Hatier, 1988, p. 135.

So the colonial authorities had finally come around to the idea of social revolution that Mgr Classe thought they would certainly shy away from back in 1912. But this was a very strange 'revolution' indeed. The break between the Belgian authorities and their long-coddled Tutsi élite had come about only because the colonial administrators felt betrayed by their ertswhile protégés. They now considered them as a mixture of backward traditionalists and revolutionary communists, an unlikely combination which was not dissimilar from the way the British then regarded the Mau Mau movement in neighbouring Kenya. What would later be touted as a 'social revolution' resembled more an ethnic transfer of power. To start with, because of the rapid economic changes which had taken place during the last fifteen years, the *average* financial situation of the Tutsi and Hutu groups in 1959 was similar and did not offer the 'aristocratic' picture one could have expected. A survey of incomes undertaken in the mid–1950s (excluding holders of political office) was as shown in the accompanying table.

Group	No. of families	Average family income (BF)
Tutsi	287	4,439
Hutu	914	4,249
Twa	2	1,446

Source: P. Leurquin, *Le niveau de vie des populations du Ruanda-Urundi.* Louvain, 1961, p. 203. Quoted in Ian Linden, op. cit., p. 226.

'Rich' Hutu and poor Tutsi, each one in their group, cancelled each other out on the economic average. In fact, under the banner of 'democratic majority rule' on one side and 'immediate independence' on the other, it was a fight between two competing élites, the newly developed Hutu counter-élite produced by the church and the older neo-traditionalist Tutsi élite which the colonial authorities had promoted since the 1920s. Poor Hutu were used by their new leaders as a battle-axe against a mixed body of Tutsi where, because of the elaborately constructed 'Rwandese ideology' we have sought to outline, the poor stood by the rich on the basis of the myth of 'racial superiority'. In fact poor Tutsi had little choice because the Hutu perception of the same ideology targeted them for elimination along with the chiefs.

Belgium, which was beginning to lose control of itself as well as of the situation, launched the idea of self-government on 11 November in the midst of chaos. Brussels, or at least its local representatives, were moving forward without really knowing where they were going. In January 1960 Colonel Logiest declared: 'Because of the force of circumstances, we have to take sides. We cannot remain neutral and passive.' So forward he went. Sporadic fighting continued and houses were burned down. The Tutsi were getting the worst of it; 7,000 had been regrouped at camps in the Bugesera area and there were 15,000 others displaced between Byumba, Gisenyi and Astrida. The harshest violence was in the north-west, where the Hutu principalities had made their last stand against the Belgian-Tutsi forces in the 1920s and where hatred of the *Banyanduga* ran high. Although it was the area with the smallest Tutsi population, it was where the Tutsi were most relentlessly hunted down. Starting in early 1960, the colonial government began to replace most of the Tutsi chiefs with new Hutu ones. These immediately organised the persecution of the Tutsi on the hills they now controlled, which started a mass exodus of refugees abroad, which eventually took some 130,000 Rwandese Tutsi to the Belgian Congo, Burundi, Tanganyika and Uganda by late 1963[15].

Between 26 June and 30 July 1960, despite the state of insecurity, the colonial authorities organised communal elections. The results were the following:

PARMEHUTU	2,390
Independent candidates	237
APROSOMA	233
RADER	209
UNAR	56
Total	3,125

The turnout at the polls had been roughly 70%, but the electoral process was somewhat confused. In some constituencies the

15. Out of a total population of about 2.7 million at the time.

winning PARMEHUTU camp was split between four or five rival slates. The chiefs became mere figureheads and their offices were suppressed some time later. The new authorities were called *bourgmestres* (burgomaster) on the Belgian model and they ruled 229 *communes*. There were only nineteen Tutsi out of the 229, and 160 were PARMEHUTU. 'The revolution is over,' declared Colonel Logiest in October 1960. This was an appropriate declaration, for inasmuch as the 'revolution' had been a Belgian-sponsored administratively-controlled phenomenon, its end could be administratively proclaimed just as its beginning had been administratively made unavoidable. But reality was still bursting through the administrative seams: on 14 and 15 October, after a quarrel between a local policeman and a Tutsi drifter, thirteen Tutsi were massacred in Kibingo *commune*, triggering a new wave of emigration. The new *bourgmestres* were quickly picking up the old habits of 'feudal' rule and were creating their own Hutu clienteles on the Tutsi model, often in ways as oppressive as those of their predecessors.

The only outside factor which had to be taken into consideration was the United Nations Trusteeship Commission which was displeased with these developments, largely because it was under the influence of the Third World members of the UN who were themselves largely aligned on colonial questions with the Eastern bloc. The communist countries had supported the UNAR party because it seemed to them to be the one most opposed to Belgian, i.e. capitalist western interests[16]. The UN Secretary General Dag Hammarksjöld was also hostile to Belgian rule in the area and agreed with the UN giving its support to the Tutsi party. In December 1960, UN Resolutions nos 1579 and 1580 came as a direct challenge to the policy carried out by the Belgians since November 1959. The world body was asking Brussels to try to organise some form of national reconciliation,

---

16. For the same reason, during the civil disturbances which accompanied the Belgian decolonisation in the Congo, Lumumba and later Gaston Soumialot and his Simbas sympathised with UNAR and offered support to its guerrillas.

something which Colonel Logiest called 'perfectly useless'[17]. At that moment, he was probably right. After the predictable failure of the National Reconciliation Conference at Ostend in Belgium in January 1961, Logiest and Grégoire Kayibanda, to prevent any further tinkering by the UN with the Rwandese situation, arranged a 'legal coup'[18]. On 28 January 1961 they called the 3,125 *bourgmestres* and municipal counsellors to an emergency meeting in Gitarama, Kayibanda's birthplace, where 'the sovereign democratic Republic of Rwanda' was declared by acclamation. During the following months the UN had to reconcile itself to this *de facto* independence of a territory which had theoretically been placed under its mandate. Sporadic violence continued: about 150 Tutsi were killed around Astrida (Butare) in September–October 1961, 3,000 houses were burnt down and 22,000 people were displaced[19]. New waves of emigrants went on foot to the refugee camps in Uganda. On 25 September 1961, legislative elections were held. PARMEHUTU got 78% of the vote and UNAR 17%, which out of a total of forty-four seats gave them thirty-five and seven respectively. The ethnic trap had sprung shut and as a UN report commented grimly,

> The developments of these last eighteen months have brought about the racial dictatorship of one party. . . . An oppressive system has been replaced by another one. . . . It is quite possible that some day we will witness violent reactions on the part of the Tutsi[20].

17. Colonel Logiest, op. cit., p. 185.
18. Ibid., p. 189.
19. Richard Cox in the *Sunday Times*, quoted by René Lemarchand, op. cit., chapter 6. Later, Tutsi émigré circles used these killings (which were bad enough) to claim that 'several hundred thousands of Tutsi were savagely slaughtered' (La Communauté Rwandaise de France, *Mémorandum sur la crise politique actuelle au Rwanda*, Paris, 1990, p. 13). This is a mathematical impossiblity. In 1961 the total population in Rwanda was about 2,800,000, which meant that as 15% of the population, the Tutsi numbered about 420,000. Of these, about 120,000 went into exile. By 1991, if we follow the low Rwandese government estimate 9% for the Tutsi population, there were at least 643,000 out of a total population of 7,148,000 (Ministére du Plan, *Recensement général de la population et de l'habitat au 15 Août 1991*, Kigali, December 1991, p. 86). If 'hundreds of thousands' had died in 1961 (or in the later 1963–4 violence) those 643,000 would have had to appear from nowhere.
20. UN Trusteeship Commission Report (March 1961).

In fact they had already started. Since late 1960, small commandos of exiled Tutsi, called *Inyenzi* (cockroaches) by the Hutu, had begun to attack from Uganda. They were ineffective and behaved more like terrorists than like guerrilla fighters, apparently not caring about the violent reprisals on the Tutsi civilian population which their attacks provoked. But for Colonel Logiest the September 1961 elections had been 'the consecration without appeal of the November 1959 revolution, the total and definitive victory of the Rwandese people'[21]. He was unfortunately not the last foreigner to voice such deadly certainties about the complex realities of the Rwandese situation.

The Kayibanda years (1961–1973)

Rwanda had become formally independent on 1 July 1962, under a republican government. King Mutara III Rudahigwa had died suddenly on 25 July 1959, leaving no children[22]. The *abiru*, the court ritualists, had taken a nostalgic revenge for their marginalisation in 1931 by choosing the 'proper' King according to ancient lore. This was Jean-Baptiste Ndahindurwa, a younger brother of the late Mutara, and he ascended to the throne under the ritual name of Kigeli V. But he was only twenty years old and the unfolding crisis quickly engulfed him. Sent to live in Usumbura (Bujumbura), a prisoner both of the Belgians and of his own entourage, he slipped out of the country and started a life of nomadic exile in East Africa. But he was incapable of providing real leadership and the situation of violent political confrontation with which he was faced was quite beyond his

---

21. Colonel Logiest, op. cit., p. 199.
22. It was he who was sterile because his first wife, whom he divorced precisely on the grounds of sterility, gave birth to several children after remarrying. The King's death occurred in circumstances which added fuel to the political fire of the time: he collapsed suddenly after being given an injection by a Belgian doctor in Usumbura (Bujumbura). Nonetheless foul play seems unlikely, and Laurent Gakuba, a Tutsi doctor and a monarchist, suggests that the King died from anaphylactic shock, i.e. a sudden allergy to penicillin, which Mutara was then using to treat venereal disease (Laurent Gakuba, *Rwanda 1931–1959*, Paris: La Pensée Universelle, 1991, chapter 12).

abilities to control. The Tutsi exiles were organising themselves, albeit confusedly, to attempt a military comeback. One group, under Françqis Rukeba, claimed to be monarchist and at least consulted with Kigeli, but the other *Inyenzi* groups were either left-leaning, such as those who followed the ex-Bwishaza sub-chief Gabriel Sebyeza and of whom some had even gone to China for military training, or they were simply military activists without any particular political leanings. They were constantly divided by personal quarrels, by their politics, by their disagreements on tactical military choices, and by the attitude they felt should be followed *vis-à-vis* the new Hutu government in Rwanda[23].

In May 1962 some exiles agreed to support the new regime while others on the contrary plunged headlong into military confrontation. They fared differently according to their countries of exile. The most favourable country was doubtlessly Burundi where after the death of Prince Louis Rwagasore the new leaders of the UPRONA party sympathised with the Rwandese Tutsi cause. There were about 50,000 refugees in Burundi, which soon became the main base for the launching of surprise attacks against Rwanda. In the Congo the situation was confused by the civil war which lasted till 1964. Because of resentment against the Belgians, the UNAR survivors in Kivu allied themselves with the Mouvement National Congolais (MNC) rebels and they were militarily eliminated when General Mobutu and the Armée Nationale Congolaise reconquered the province. The refugees in Tanganyika were submitted to rigorous control to prevent them from undertaking military operations, but they were also quite generously treated and, as time went on, they tended to integrate with the local population or go to Dar-es-Salaam and start new lives[24]. In Uganda, British and later Ugandan authorities also

23. The best sources for understanding *Inyenzi* politics are René Lemarchand, op. cit., chapter 7 and Pierre Tabara, op. cit., chapters 12–15.
24. For the Rwandese refugees in Tanzania, see Charles Gasarasi, *A tripartite approach to the resettlement and integration of rural refugees in Tanzania*, Uppsala: Nordiska Afrikainstitutet, Research Report no. 71, 1984.

exercised a tight control over *inyenzi* activities. Although the large Ugandan Banyarwanda population showed no interest in their cause[25], they represented a local political problem because they were personally supported by King Mutesa II, which earned them automatic hostility from the Prime Minister Milton Obote[26].

But as time went on the exiles' position became more and more detached from Rwandese reality. In December 1963, feeling this progressive loss of control over their situation, they launched a desperate operation from Burundi and invaded Bugesera. Although they came quite close to Kigali because of the surprise nature of their attack, the whole thing had been poorly planned and they lacked proper military equipment. They were quickly beaten back and the government used the occasion to launch a massive wave of repression in which an estimated 10,000 Tutsi were slaughtered between December 1963 and January 1964. All the surviving Tutsi politicians still living in Rwanda were executed, including Prosper Bwanakweri, a former chief and the founder of RADER[27]. Foreign reactions to these killings, which had no East-West dimension, were muted. The representative of the Swiss government, which was one of the major

25. The Rwandese province of Bufumbira had been attributed to Great Britain's Uganda Protectorate by the Brussels Agreement in May 1910 – see W.R. Louis, *Ruanda-Urundi (1884-1919)*, op. cit., pp. 79–91. In addition, as we noted in the previous chapter, many Banyarwanda migrated to Uganda during the colonial days for economic reasons. As a result, around the time of independance, Banyarwanda were the sixth largest tribe in Uganda, making up about 5.9% of the population (*Uganda Census*, Entebbe: Government Printing House, 1960).

26. A lot has been written on that period of Ugandan politics which ended with the overthrow of the President-King by his Prime Minister in 1966. The best assessments are probably those of I.K.K. Lukwago, *The Politics of National Integration in Uganda*, Nairobi: Coign Publications, 1982, for an anti-Obote (although definitely not monarchist) perspective and T.V. Sathyamurthy, *The Political Development of Uganda (1900-1986)*, Aldershot: Gower, 1986, chapter 8 for a sympathetic view of Obote's positions. Sathaymurthy gives interesting details about politics in Western Uganda in the early 1960s which help to understand better the Banyarwanda situation there at the time.

27. For a grisly account of these massacres see *France Soir* of 4 February 1964. For a vibrantly indignant but more restrained reflection see Sir Bertrand Russell's article in *Le Monde* (6 February 1964).

foreign aid donors, was alone in asking for a commission of inquiry. The result was a report called *Le terrorisme Inyenzi au Rwanda* (*Inyenzi* Terrorism in Rwanda) which whitewashed the government's activity during the crisis. Swiss economic cooperation went on undisturbed. As for *Inyenzi* activities, they dissolved in a sea of accusations and counter-accusations among the various exile politicians. By 1964, exile politics was dead. The only results of *Inyenzi* attacks had been to strengthen the personal power of President Kayibanda, something he did not forget and which he tried to reproduce between late 1972 and early 1973 when he felt that his power was slipping.

Under Kayibanda's presidency the young Hutu republic took on a strange tinge. In many ways the President was in fact the *mwami* of the Hutu. The same style of leadership applied, and his deliberate remoteness, authoritarianism and secretiveness unavoidably recall what the colonial anthropologist Jean-Jacques Maquet wrote of the leadership style of the old kings:

> The role of the ruler was a mixture of protection and paternalistic profit. . . . The subject was expected to fit within this form of leadership. He was supposed to adopt a dependent attitude. Inferiority is the relative situation of a person who has to submit to another in a defined field. But dependence is inferiority extended to all spheres of life. *When the ruler gives an order, he must be obeyed, not because his order falls into the sphere over which he has authority, but simply because he is the ruler*[28].

This unquestioning obedience was to play a tragic and absolutely central role in the unfolding of the 1994 genocide.

But at the time, just as the *Abami* used to manipulate the main Tutsi chiefly lineages in order to balance their power, President Kayibanda played the ex-Nyakibanda seminarians against the Astrida graduates and his Gitarama clansmen against both Butare and Ruhengeri. The northern '*abakonde*' were kept on a leash but they were used by the regime to check the 'Butare mafia'. The southerners were President Kayibanda's main worry because

---

28. J.J. Maquet, *Le système des relations sociales dans le Rwanda ancien*, op. cit., pp. 186–7. Emphasis added.

they had been well organised within APROSOMA, but they were slowly but surely eased out of any political or administrative responsibility between 1964 and 1967.

Like the *mwami*, the President was personally responsible for all appointments and nominations, even at very low levels of the administration, a practice continued by General Habyarimana when he took power. He was supposed to be omnipresent and omniscient, even when, as was his custom, he could not be seen. The old monarchic patterns of governance (a narrow circle of leadership recruitment, regionalism, lineage competition, favoritism, corruption) were quickly fused with the new ones explicitly derived from the 'democratic revolution' (social equality, justice, progress, moralism). But the first set of practices concerned the rulers while the second set of values tended to apply to the ruled.

At a time when the African continent was talking about socialism, revolution and development, Rwanda was strangely silent. Anticolonialism was out of the question, since after their help during the 1959–61 'democratic revolution' the Belgians were seen as heroes[29]. The only values which were repeatedly emphasised were the intrinsic worth of being Hutu, the total congruence between demographic majority and democracy, the need to follow a moral Christian life and the uselessness of politics' which should be replaced by hard work. The style of leadership and the dominant ideology were direct derivations of what in the previous chapter, we have called 'the Rwandese ideology'. They had been coloured with virtuous republicanism for public consumption, but the essential assumptions concerning the roles of rulers and ruled, the very nature of what power meant, were basically the same. It is noteworthy that Abbé Alexis Kagame, the Tutsi monarchist historian, lived quite happily in Hutu-dominated Rwanda till his natural death in 1981. One reason could have been that his work lived on, both

29. See former vice-governor general Jean-Paul Harroy's description of his visit to Kigali for the tenth anniversary of independance and the enthusiasm of the popular welcome he and Colonel Logiest received (J.-P. Harroy, op. cit., p. 399 and p. 511).

at the level of Catholic church social hegemony[30] and at the level of his conception of power. As Claudine Vidal has remarked,

> During the 'fifties and 'sixties Rwandese intellectuals found in Kagame's work a vision of their society rather than of its history. Both camps used his historical themes in ways that suited their struggle for power in ethnic terms, *but both camps were also in agreement with the centralist vision and the élitist project which were at the heart of his work*[31].

President Kayibanda's Rwanda was a land of virtue where prostitutes were punished, attendance at mass was high, and hardworking peasants toiled on the land without asking too many questions. An egalitarian racial ideology buttressed an élitist and secretive authoritarian government in ways which echoed those of Vichy France or Salazar's Portugal. This created an atmosphere much approved of by Christian Democrats, who in Belgium and Germany[32] were the regime's most steadfast supporters. And underdevelopment was no problem since in this atmosphere even poverty, borne with dignity, was only an added virtue. Here again we should quote Christine Vidal who lived in Rwanda at the time:

> Slowly the country turned into an island. The government feared its whole environment: it was horrified by the Congolese rebellions, reserved towards Tanzania, hostile to the Tutsi regime in Burundi and dependant on Ugandan roads for its imports. The inhabitants were inward-looking and bore the country's slow shrinkage in silence. There were several forms of censorship: from a triumphant Catholic church and from the government which was afraid both

---

30. For a first degree vision of the church at that time, see Justin Kalibwami, *Le Catholicisme et la société rwandaise (1900–1962)*, op. cit., pp. 525–45, where the author deals with the reasons for the church's success in Rwandese society and with the post-1962 period.
31. Claudine Vidal, *Sociologie des passions*, op. cit., p. 61. Emphasis added.
32. Germany, as the former coloniser, kept a strong interest in Rwanda, especially in the Catholic *Länder*. Rheinland-Pfalz had its cooperation mission separate from the Federal German embassy, and financed its own projects.

of possible communist-inspired social movements and of the traditional manifestations which could be a reminder of the Tutsi imprint which it considered with something like phobia. To the generalised lack of trust, rumour, secrecy, lack of breathing space: on top of material deprivation — the country was one of the poorest in the world and lacked almost everything — was added something like mental paralysis[33].

In time this stifling atmosphere became too much even for the Rwandese élite. By mid-1972, President Kayibanda, increasingly a recluse in the government palace, knew that his regime was in a state of suspended animation. He tried in a desperate gamble to recreate around himself the atmosphere of unanimity which had accompanied the *Inyenzi* threat, particularly the December 1963 attack. The moment seemed propitious since in May–June of that year Burundi had been ravaged by a massive massacre of Hutu carried out by the Tutsi minority in order to keep its hold on political power[34]. The emotional impact of these events in Rwanda had been considerable and the regime felt this was something it could exploit. Vigilante committees were organised and between October 1972 and February 1973, they scrutinised the schools, the University, the civil service and even private businesses to make sure that the ethnic quota policy was being respected[35]. Those most eager to carry out this 'purification' through the vigilante committees were educated people who could expect to benefit from kicking the Tutsi out of their jobs.

33. Claudine Vidal, 'Situations ethniques au Rwanda' op. cit., p. 171.
34. For an assesment of these tragic events see R. Lemarchand and D. Martin, *Génocide sélectif au Burundi*, London: Minority Rights Group, 1974, and Jean-Pierre Chrétien, *Burundi. L'histoire retrouvée*, Paris: Karthala, 1993, pp. 417–58. For a more general view of the recurrent Burundi massacres, see René Lemarchand, *Burundi: Ethnocide as theory and practice*, Cambridge University Press, 1994.
35. See Jean-Pierre Chrétien, 'Hutu et Tusi au Rwanda et au Burundi', op. cit., pp. 158–9. Since independance Rwanda had steadily followed a policy of ethnic quotas. There were officially 9% Tutsi in Rwanda and so there could be no more than 9% Tutsi students in the schools, 9% Tutsi clerks in the cvil service or even 9% Tutsi in any given sector of employment. In fact, given the long Belgian partiality for the Tutsi in education, they occupied much more than their allotted share of employment and often held good positions. The 1972-3 witch-hunts forced many people out of the civil service where scrutiny was at its highest.

In the hills the peasants showed no interest[36]. Although few people were killed (officially only six, but probably two dozen or more), the economic and psychological effects of this hate campaign were sufficient to trigger another massive wave of Tutsi emigration. But the regime's tactical gamble backfired. The tensions between northern and southern Hutu politicians within the system were such that the vigilante committees soon began to operate according to a different logic. In the hills the peasants started to move, this time to settle personal accounts with figures of authority, quite apart from the ethnic context. These sporadic disturbances encouraged the senior army commander, Major-General Juvénal Habyarimana, to make his move. He was from the north and could count on the support of the long-marginalised '*abakonde*'. When he took power in a bloodless *coup* on 5 July 1973, there was widespread popular relief, even among the Tutsi whose security the new regime immediately guaranteed[37].

The refugee problem

The question of numbers. Violence in Rwanda forced many Tutsi into exile, at first in an almost continuous if irregular stream between 1959 and 1964, and then after a nine-year interval, again but in more limited numbers during 1972–3. There had already been about 120,000 refugees by early 1962 and this figure had

36. Claudine Vidal, *Sociologie des passions*, op. cit., pp. 38–9.
37. The process of President Kayibanda's decline and fall is strangely reminiscent of the reign changes of the old *Abami*. In his introduction to *La Royauté de l'Ancien Rwanda* (Tervuren: MRAC, 1964) Marcel d'Hertefelt quotes the first two verses of part XV of the Royal Ritual: 'When the situation is back to normal and the king is dead . . .' and makes this surprising comment: 'In order to understand the peculiar link postulated here between the king's death and a "normalisation" of the situation, one must realise that in traditional Banyarwanda thinking, the country's prosperity depended on the king's health and strength. Thus, as soon as the king became old, the situation became "abnormal" because the country's well-being was compromised' (p. 4). Like a *Mwami* of old, Kayibanda had 'compromised' the well-being of the country' through his weakness.

grown by late 1964 to 336,000 'official' ones (and some unofficial ones as well).[38] The breakdown was as follows:

Burundi	200,000
Uganda	78,000
Tanzania	36,000
Zaïre	22,000

There are two ways of arriving at a reasonable figure for the 1990s. Either one works from the natural growth of the total Tutsi population, starting from a figure of about 500,000 in 1959, and then deducts from the result the numbers still in Rwanda in 1991, at the time of the census. The result then is a low estimate of about 510,000. Or one applies the average Rwandese population multiplier for the 1960–90 period (2.3) to the 336,000 refugees of the original population, which gives a high estimate of about 775,000[39]. These figures call for some comment, given that much higher ones have been bandied around for propaganda purposes, either to prove that Rwanda could not accommodate all the candidates for repatriation, or on the contrary to stigmatise the evil attitude of the Rwandese government in keeping out 'one-third of its population'[40].

The refugees argue that the 1964 baseline figure of 336,000 is too low because it does not take into account the people who

---

38. UNHCR Banyarwanda Refugee Census (1964) quoted in André Guichaoua, *Le problème des réfugiés Rwandais et des populations Banyarwanda dans la région des Grands Lacs Africains*, Geneva: UNHCR, 1992, p. 26 (henceforth cited as *Le problème des réfugiés Rwandais*).

39. This is done both by André Guichaoua, op. cit., pp. 16–18, and by Catharine Watson, *Exile from Rwanda: background to an invasion*, Washington, DC: US Committee for Refugees, 1991, p. 6. Both their estimates are, in our opinion, somewhat on the low side.

40. Before the war, Rwandese *émigré* circles often talked of 2 million refugees. And a respectable French publication (D. Helbig, 'Le Rwanda entre guerre civile et réformes politiques', *Le Monde Diplomatique*, November 1990) could write of the '500,000 Rwandese refugees in Uganda' (only) soon after the beginning of the conflict. But in a recent Rwandese government document (*Evolution de la population Rwandaise depuis la guerre*. Kigali, 21 November 1994), the global figure, though still high, had been lowered to 900,000.

lived as self-settled refugees outside the camps; they prefer a figure of about 500,000. But this figure is inflated because it includes some of the Banyarwanda living in Zaïre or Uganda *who were previous migrants and not refugees*. But in any case, although we could admit the argument, resulting in a somewhat higher figure than the original UNHCR one (around 400,000), this higher figure cannot be used as a baseline for a very simple reason: just as the numbers of refugees grew by natural demographic increase, they were also whittled away by assimilation. Mixed marriages, blending into the older Banyarwanda settled migrant communities and naturalisations all took their toll. Thus, to arrive at a rough estimate, one can contend that the plus factor (refugees initially not computed) balances the minus factor (refugees – or their children – ceasing to identify themselves as such). As a result, an approximate figure (over which nobody will ever agree because it represents too much of a political and propaganda ammunition store) would seem to be around 600,000–700,000.

Of course it is obvious that there are many more Banyarwanda living outside Rwanda's borders than the number we are mentioning here. But the point is that there are at most 700,000 *refugees*, i.e. people (and their children) who left Rwanda because of political persecution between 1959 and 1973 and who still identified themselves as 'refugees' in 1990. The other Banyarwanda living abroad belong to several different groups:

– those from Zaïre, mostly Kivu province, i.e. at least 450,000 and who may number up to 1.3 million[41] depending on the criteria used. But these are essentially the descendants of migrants who moved to the Belgian Congo from the 1920s till independence (and even after) for economic reasons.

– those from Bufumbira in Uganda, who became 'Ugandans' through the 1910 Anglo-German agreement.

41. A. Gatabazi, 'L'émigration et sa place dans l'équilibre démo-économique et social au Rwanda', *Carrefour d'Afrique*, no. 12 (1973), quoted in André Guichaoua, op. cit., p. 31.

– The Banyarwanda economic migrants to Uganda from the 1920s to the 1950s who live in different parts of the country but mostly in Buganda. Although it is almost impossible to number them[42], a rough estimate would place their descendants at around 700,000 in the present Ugandan population.

But none of these people, whether they speak Kinyarwanda or not, can be taken as 'refugees'. They live with various degrees of integration (or conflict), within the local populations and no longer identify with a country their parents left mostly for economic reasons and of whose language they are often ignorant[43].

Life in the diaspora. The bulk of the refugees had left Rwanda during the early 1960s without knowing that they would remain in exile for nearly thirty years. Many died, and many of their children were in turn born in exile. As time passed, their situations diverged more and more depending on where they were and on how they fared in life. Personal biographies became increasingly diversified to the point where being a Rwandese refugee could mean anything from eking out a precarious living in a refugee settlement in western Uganda to another working as a journalist in Switzerland, by way of peasants in Zaïre, businessmen in Bujumbura and social workers in New York City. As the daughter of a refugee said to a researcher in Uganda, 'We had no land, so we had to use our heads.

---

42. First of all, since 1959, no census in Uganda has been daring (or tactless) enough to include tribal affiliation in its range of questions. Secondly, many immigrants have changed their names and adopted Baganda or Banyankole ones, and their children have often grown up without speaking any Kinyarwanda.

43. Among the three groups mentioned, the Kivu Banyarwanda are probably those whose integration problems are greatest today, given their tense relationship with the local Bahunde population. Thus while RPF guerrillas were made up of refugees who at first came almost entirely from Uganda, other 'Ugandan' Banyarwanda did not join them, while quite a number of young men came from Kivu to fight on their side, even from the traditionally more 'settled' Banyarwanda groups (author's field notes in the RPF guerrilla, June 1992).

Our heads were our only capital.'[44] And they have tended to use that capital well. Even illiterate parents worked desperately to put their children through school and often through university as well, a phenomenon closely resembling the patterns of Eastern European Jews in Western Europe and America at the beginning of the twentieth century and later of Palestinian and Eritrean refugees. Nevertheless, the economic successes of the refugees, though true for many individuals, should not be exaggerated. André Guichaoua sums up the problem well:

> In a way, being mostly excluded from the local labour market, which was monopolised by nationals, pushed the refugees to try new professional paths where the characteristics of their communities (dissemination in various countries, high mobility, strong ties of solidarity) could be helpful. A limited number of individuals acquired a reputation for professional and financial success which was often quite exaggeratedly extended to the whole community in the Great Lakes area. But one should point out that many people remained in precarious social and economic situations: widows and families with a single female parent, lone young adults, people left behind in the camps, and groups in conflict situations with the local populations[45].

Despite their extreme geographical dispersion and their increasing social differentiation, the exiled Tutsi remained in touch with each other. In a way, exile even brought them closer by removing the social barriers which had existed in Rwanda before 1959, especially since in the diaspora the social situation did not always correspond to what they had been before 1959. Thus the daughter of an impoverished *ababega* family might be willing to marry the son of a *'petit Tutsi'* who had gone through school and held a good job, something hardly conceivable in the old Rwanda. As the old UNAR nostalgia receded into the mists of history, younger people created in the 1970s a multitude of social clubs and cultural associations to keep people in contact with

44. Catharine Watson, op. cit., p. 8.
45. André Guichaoua, op. cit., p. 20.

each other. Their diversity and wide geographical spread reflected the diversification of the diaspora. There was the Association des Immigrants Rwandais du Québec, distinct from the Rwandese Canadian Cultural Association in Ontario; in Belgium the *Isangano* ('crossroads') group organised folkloric shows and served as a place for discussion, while the *abadaha* ('Germans') in Germany used their name as a kind of historical in-joke[46]. There were other similar associations in Bujumbura, New York, Los Angeles, Washington DC, Nairobi, Lomé, Dakar and Brazzaville. They put out irregularly published newspapers and magazines with highly polemical and lively cultural and political contents. For a long time, the main title was *Impuruza* (The Mobilizer, the name for a traditional war-drum in ancient Rwanda) which was published in Sacramento, California. There were also *Muhabura* (The Beacon, the name of the highest volcano in the Virunga chain in northern Rwanda), coming out of Bujumbura, *Congo-Nil*, published in Zaïre, *Huguka* (Be alert!) also in Bujumbura, *Ukoloni Mambo Leo* (Emigration News) from Dar-es-Salaam, in Swahili, and a publication which was to play an important role in the 1980s, *The Alliancer* in Kampala.

As the years passed and memories of the real Rwanda began to recede, Rwanda slowly became a mythical country in the refugees' minds. The trend was even clearer for the young who had left as babies or been born in exile. Contrasting an idealised past life with the difficulties they were experiencing, their image of Rwanda became that of a land of milk and honey. Economic problems linked with their eventual return, such as overpopulation, overgrazing or soil erosion, were dismissed as Kigali regime propaganda. The realities of present Rwandese political life, the pervasiveness of the Hutu racial ideology, the problem of the Tutsi image as reconstructed by that same ideology – all these

---

46. In 1940, after Belgium was occupied by the Germans, the supporters of King Musinga (deposed by the Belgians in 1931) hoped for a victory by the Axis Powers. Nervous Belgian administrators then prohibited the use of the words 'Hitler' and 'Germans'. These were quickly replaced by their Kinyarawanda equivalents of '*Hitimmana*' and '*abadaha*', hence the ironically 'subversive' quality of that last name.

obstacles to their dream of an eventual return were blithely ignored. This was particularly true of the Rwandese community in Uganda, where proximity to the real Rwanda did not seem to encourage a clearer grasp of the real situation there.

The Ugandan factor[47]. The Rwandese refugees in Uganda had created the Rwandese Refugee Welfare Foundation (RRWF) in June 1979 to help the victims of political repression after the fall of Idi Amin[48]. In 1980 the RRWF changed its name to Rwandese Alliance for National Unity (RANU). RANU saw itself as more politically militant than the RRWF and openly discussed the question of an eventual return of the exiles to Rwanda. But between 1981 and 1986 the organisation had to migrate to Nairobi and live a somewhat vegetative life there.

This was because in the mean time things had turned sour in Uganda[49]. The 'election' of the former President, Milton Obote, under dubious conditions in December 1980 had driven the political process into a dangerous *cul-de-sac*. Guerrillas sprang up in several parts of the country, including Buganda. One of the three such movements in Buganda was the Popular Resistance Army led by former Provisional Government Defence Minister

---

47. For a more detailed treatment, see Gérard Prunier, 'L'Ouganda et le Front Patriotique Rwandais' in André Guichaoua (ed.), *Enjeux nationaux et dynamiques régionales dans l'Afrique des Grands Lacs*, Lille: Faculté des Sciences Economiques et Sociales de l'Université de Lille I, 1992, pp. 43–9, and Gérard Prunier, 'Elements pour une histoire du Front Patriotique Rwandais', *Politique Africaine*, no. 51. (October 1993), pp. 121–38.
48. Given former President Obote's hostility to the Rwandese exiles, they had welcomed Idi Amin's assumption of power in January 1971. Some even served in his notorious State Research Bureau, although their role has been exaggerated. Nevertheless, in the violent political climate which followed Amin's fall in 1979, they were for a while targeted for repression (see Catharine Watson, op. cit., p. 10).
49. For an assessment of those years, see Holger Bernt Hansen and Michael Twaddle (eds), *Uganda Now*, London: James Currey, 1988, and Gérard Prunier, 'La recherche de la normalisation (1979–1994)', in Gérard Prunier and Bernard Calas (eds), *L'Ouganda contemporain*, Paris: Karthala, 1994. pp. 131–58.

Yoweri Museveni[50]. On 6 February 1981, Museveni and twenty-six companions had started their operations by attacking the Kabamba Military School to get hold of some weapons. Among the twenty-six were two Rwandese refugees who were later to play an important role in the Rwandese exile political movement, Fred Rwigyema and Paul Kagame. Both had been members of the Front for National Salvation (FRONASA), the guerrilla group created by Museveni in 1973 during his exile in Tanzania. FRONASA had been rather ineffective as an anti-Amin organisation but it had played a certain politico-military role in the 1978–9 war, and when Museveni dissolved it after the victory it had remained as a network of friends. Rwigyema had been in Tanzania with Museveni (but not in Mozambique, as Rwandese government propaganda was later to pretend) while Kagame had joined only during the war, when Tanzanian and exile Ugandan troops had pushed into western Uganda where he had lived and gone to school as a youth. Rwigyema and Kagame were among the small nucleus of friends who stayed close to Museveni during his difficult days in the provisional government and stood by him after his party was politically crushed in the December 1980 elections. They shared with him the same left-leaning nationalist views, distrust of the West, hatred of dictatorship and belief in the redemptive powers of 'popular warfare', then the stock-in-trade of young 'progressive' Third World politicians.

As the guerrilla war grew in intensity during 1982, a serious problem began to develop for the Banyarwanda refugees. Yoweri Museveni is a Munyankole from a good Muhima family[51] and since there are not infrequently matrimonial links between Banyankole Bahima and Rwandese Tutsi (this was the case with

---

50. The PRA became the National Resistance Movement (NRM) in June 1981 after joining forces with former President Yusufu Lule's Uganda Freedom Fighters (UFF).

51. The Banyankole are a tribe from western Uganda which is also, in a fashion somewhat similar to the Banyarwanda, divided between two unequal social groups called in this case Bahima (high-caste) and Bairu (low-caste). Although this division is much less sharp and antagonistic than in Rwanda, not having been played on by the British in the same way as the Germans and Belgians used the Tutsi/Hutu

one of his grandmothers who was a Rwandese Tutsi), he was accused by President Obote's propaganda of being Rwandese, i.e. a foreigner meddling in Uganda's internal affairs which were none of his business[52]. This trend was made more dangerous by two factors: Obote's previous hostility to the Rwandese refugees during his first term of office in the 1960s, because as Catholics they had sympathised with the opposition Democratic Party (DP) and not with his Protestant-dominated Uganda People's Congress (UPC), and the fact that in Ankole local politics the UPC was strongly implanted among the Bairu population and had difficulties with the Bahima. Thus some of the men closest to President Obote, including the head of the much feared National Security Agency, Cris Rwakasisi, were Banyankole Bairu who identified with the Hutu and were hostile to what they perceived as a Tutsi/Bahima movement. They ceaselessly intrigued with President Obote to be given a free hand against their 'enemies' and finally got a green light for this in October 1982. Ankole UPC youthwingers (a political name to cover the activities of local thugs), helped by a unit of Colonel Omaria's Special Forces, attacked the refugee communities. Feeling they had government support, they even went after the local Banyarwanda, the Banyankole Bahima and even some Bakiga, the Kigezi hill-dwellers who belong to a completely different tribe. The point was to loot, steal cattle and illegally occupy land. There were some killings (the numbers are not known but they could have been around 100) and many rapes, 45,000 head of cattle were stolen, 35,000 people fled to the old settlements where they quickly found themselves in quasi-detention conditions, and 40,000 people fled towards the border, in an attempt to get

---

dichotomy, it is nevertheless a social division of some significance (on this question see Martin Doornbos, *Not all the King's men: Inequality as a Political Instrument in Ankole, Uganda*, The Hague: Mouton, 1978).

52. In Luwero, the coffee-rich area of Buganda north of the capital and scene of the main military confrontation between the regular army and the NRM guerrillas, the walls of ruined houses were covered by government troops graffiti scribbled with charcoal, many saying 'Museveni, go back to Rwanda'. The theme of Museveni's supposed 'Rwandishness' was constantly harped upon by the government' propaganda (author's field notes, Luwero, 1986).

back into Rwanda. Those who managed to cross were interned in camps on the other side. But those who fared the worst were a group of 8–10,000 who got caught on a narrow strip of land at the border, hemmed in by the Rwandese border guards on one side and the Ugandan thugs on the other. They rotted there for several months, with some Red Cross help, slowly dying of infectious diseases or despair. Under foreign pressure the Ugandan government agreed to a screening exercise in order to determine who was a refugee and who was not. The process dragged on inconclusively for many months while persecution of the refugees continued sporadically[53]. In December 1983 local chiefs and UPC youthwingers evicted 19,000 Banyarwanda, some of them 'old' migrant settlers of the 1930s, from Rakai and Masaka districts. Some fled to Tanzania, others moved to the old camps. Even the Tutsi shepherds who for years had grazed cattle for Langi and Itesot owners in the north, began to be harassed and had to flee southwards.

The 1982 crisis and the sporadic persecutions which were to follow during the next two years marked a turning-point for the Rwandese refugees in Uganda. Many of the young men, like Fred Rwigyema and Paul Kagame, had felt that Rwanda was an old story, their parents' story, and that they were now Ugandans. And then they suddenly discovered that people among whom they had lived for thirty years were treating them as hated and despised foreigners. The shock was tremendous. If the parents could do little but try to weather the storm, their children joined Museveni's guerrillas *en masse*[54]. They took their share of the fighting, first in Luwero and then, as the war developed, in the west. When Museveni's National Resistance Army (NRA) took Kampala by storm on 26 Janurary 1986, about 3,000 of its 14,000 fighters were Banyarwanda[55]. When

---

53. See Catharine Watson, op. cit., pp. 10–11.
54. Their children globally, not only their *male* children. There was a fair percentage of female fighters in the NRA, perhaps 15%, and most of those were Banyarwanda girls. In addition, many Bakiga, who had been caught in the repression, also joined the NRA. (Author's field notes, Kampala, February 1986.)
55. It is useful to keep this figure in mind in order to see in perspective the

the remnants of the now defunct regime regrouped in the Sudan and launched an anti-NRM guerrilla campaign in Northern Uganda, the NRA had to change itself from a guerrilla movement into a regular army. Thus not only were the Banyarwanda in the NRA not demobilised, but others were recruited. Nevertheless, their *relative* place in the new army became smaller, since the size of the forces increased massively from 14,000 in 1986 to an admitted figure of about 80,000 and a real one of probably over 100,000 by 1990. In this massive new army, Banyarwanda soldiers numbered possibly around 8,000 or 8%, down from over 20% in 1986. But the officer corps contained a disproportionately high number of Banyarwanda veterans. They were the boys who had joined NRA in 1982–83, acquired a lot of fighting experience and then been commissioned. After the Alice Lakwena uprising in 1987[56], the situation in the north settled into a nasty low-intensity ethnopolitical confrontation between a southern Bantu-dominated majority government and the desperate Nilotic survivors of several previous regimes and insurgent forces. Banyarwanda officers played a role in that fighting, and as might have been expected in a counterinsurgency situation, their role was sometimes an ugly one. In 1989 two Banyarwanda officers who later fought in the Rwandese war, Majors Chris Bunyenyezi and Stephen Nduguta, were (rightly) accused of having committed human rights abuses during their anti-guerrilla operations in Teso. As a result, President Museveni found the Banyarwanda presence in the army a stumbling-block in his efforts at negotiating some sort of peace with the eastern and northern insurgents. His negotiating partners, particularly those who had served in the Obote regime, remained particularly

Rwandese government's propaganda which later claimed that 'the Tutsi had put Museveni in power so that he could later help them invade Rwanda'.

56. On this astonishing millenaristic movement, see Heike Behrend, 'Is Alice Lakwena a witch?' in Holger Bernt Hansen and Michael Twaddle (eds), *Changing Uganda*, London: James Currey, 1991, pp. 162–77, and Gérard Prunier, 'Le mouvement d'Alice Lakwena. Un prophétisme politique en Ouganda', in Jean-Pierre Chrétien (ed.), *L'invention religieuse en Afrique. Histoire et religion en Afrique Noire*, Paris: Karthala, 1993, pp. 409–29.

hostile to the presence of 'those foreigners' in the NRA. Their hostility was spurred by the fact that Major-General Rwigyema had meanwhile risen to the position of army commander-in-chief and minister of defence.

However, the northerners with whom President Museveni was trying to make peace were not the only ones to resent the Banyarwanda influence in the NRM regime. The Baganda were irritated, not because of their military position but because of their increasing role in the economy. Since Museveni's victory, Banyarwanda exiles had been converging on Uganda from all over the world, often saying openly that 'Now Uganda belongs to us'[57]. The Baganda, who are the traditional business people in Uganda, did not particularly appreciate that attitude. And Museveni could not dispense with Baganda goodwill. Their hostility to Obote and their support for his struggle had been among the main causes – if not the main cause – of his victory. In Uganda it is axiomatic that one cannot govern long in the face of an active Baganda opposition. Thus the Banyarwanda presence in President Museveni's regime began to feel more like a liability than an asset. Imperceptibly things became more difficult for them in government circles. Promises of massive naturalisations which had been made to them in the post-victory euphoria were not kept. Banyarwanda promotions in the army were blocked. In November 1989 Major-General Rwigyema was removed from his position as commander-in-chief and minister of defence. Since, as Museveni's first companion, he had been a symbol of the links between his community and the regime, his firing had great symbolic force. By early 1990, Fred Rwigyema had found new friends.

RANU had had to live in exile between 1981 and 1986. However, its seventh congress could be held again in Kampala in December 1987, and it was during that congress that, under

---

57. Remark made to the author by a young Munyarwanda woman who had just arrived from Brussels where she had eked out a precarious living. Within ten days she had obtained an important and well-paid government job (author's field notes, Kampala, October 1986).

the impulsion of its most resolute militants, RANU changed itself into the Rwandese Patriotic Front (RPF), an offensive political organisation dedicated to the return of exiles to Rwanda, by force if necessary[58]. Since the late 1970s there had always been a small nucleus of exiles who believed that one day they would return to Rwanda with guns. But their efforts had been rather ineffective, to say the least[59]. With the creation of the RPF, they started to get serious.

The 1982–84 Banyarwanda persecutions had come as a shock to a community which felt itself pretty well integrated. But participation in the NRA struggle and wide social acceptance after the victory had seemed like a form of redress. For the young men and women who had believed in the NRA's capacity to provide them with a form of revolutionary integration, Rwigyema's firing and the rumours of a 'Banyarwanda census' seemed like a nightmare revisited. Both in 1969 and in 1983, Obote had also talked of a 'Banyarwanda census'. Keeping all due differences in mind, the position of these young Banyarwanda resembled that of the young German and germanised *Mitteleuropa* Jews who survived the Holocaust, decided they would never again believe in promises of integration, became Zionists and moved to Israel. Museveni's relative cooling off towards them was the last straw, even for those like Rwigyema himself, who had never been much interested in a 'return' to Rwanda.

58. Interview with RPF cadre Tito Rutaremara, Kabale, 11 July 1992. The organisation called itself RPF before it came out, almost as a second thought, with the French version of its name: *Front Patriotique Rwandais* (FPR). This was a direct consequence of the social experience of the 'Ugandan' exiles. But this rather innocent 'English' connotation was to have enormous consequences later *vis-à-vis* the French.

59. Soon after Museveni took power, they had tried to use some Banyarwanda soldiers in the NRA to stage an 'invasion'. The plan was being openly discussed in Kampala bars, and the Ugandan security forces had had no trouble rounding them up and arresting them before they could put any of their plans into action. In a distant echo of the *Inyenzi* of old, their financial backer was an Omani trader who, like most of the Muslim business class in Rwanda, had monarchist sympathies (see *Focus* dated 29 April 1986). The conspirators had been naive enough to come to the French embassy in Kampala and ask a diplomat what would be the French attitude towards them if they took power in Kigali. The French reaction had been one of polite disbelief. (Interview with an embassy staff member, Kampala, April 1986.)

This evolution was happening at a moment when the rest of the diaspora was becoming increasingly militant. A world congress of Rwandese refugees had been held in Washington DC in August 1988 and it had passed very strong resolutions about the 'Right of Return'; these had been transmitted to the Rwandese government which had remained undaunted, as usual in such cases. In February 1988 President Habyarimana had created a joint Rwando-Ugandan commission to look into the problem of Rwandese refugees in Uganda, but it had never done any serious work. For the RPF boys this did not matter: they had set themselves on another course of action: the systematic penetration of key sections of the NRA so that when the time came, they could move a small but well-equipped Banyarwanda-manned segment of the army into Rwanda and make a dash for Kigali.

The Habyarimana regime

The good years. Given the horror in which it ended, there is now a tendency to project back upon the whole of the Habyarimana regime our knowledge of its ultimate evil. This impulse is understandable since the mind tends to look for coherence and meaning in history, even at the price of anachronism. But history is as much the study of discontinuities ('why do things not always stay the same?') as a reflexion on the coherence of things. Tyrants do not always behave in a repellent fashion and, rightly or wrongly, quite a number are popular, at least for a while. Without even having to leave East Africa, this author remembers that the population of Kampala danced and sang in the streets in January 1971 when Idi Amin Dada took power, that before plunging his country back into civil war and religious strife President Jaafar al-Nimeiry of Sudan was extremely popular for years, and that, the final Somali horror notwithstanding, *Jaalle* (comrade) Siad Barre enjoyed the support of his whole nation for the first eight years of his reign. Such examples could be multiplied almost *ad infinitum*.

The case of Habyarimana is somewhat similar. When he took

power in July 1973, the political immobility and the regionalist infighting of the Kayibanda regime had driven the élite into a state of stifled frustration. The artificial and politically-motivated return to the Tutsi persecutions of old had scared both the Tutsi community and reasonable Hutu. The country's dull international isolation had put it in a difficult position diplomatically and even economically. So General Habyarimana's coup had been welcomed with relief among the urbanised population and, in the case of the peasant masses who had little to do with Kigali power games, with indifference.

And the next few years, at least till 1980, posed no particular problem. The country remained small, landlocked and poor as it always had been, but its new leadership appeared pretty mild. Of course, it insisted on the ritualistic reiteration of the ideological slogans of 'rubanda nyamwinshi', equating demographic with democratic rule, and the Tutsi were politically marginalised. Throughout the Habyarimana years there would not be a single Tutsi *bourgmestre* or *préfet*[60], there was only one Tutsi officer in the whole army, there were two Tutsi members of parliament out of seventy and there was only one Tutsi minister out of a cabinet of between twenty-five and thirty members. The quota policy existing under President Kayibanda was retained, although loosely enforced, and proportions of Tutsi in schools or universities were often some way above the required 9%. The same was true in the civil service, although, knowing that they could at any time become victims of officially-sponsored discrimination, the Tutsi preferred whenever possible to work in the private sector. The army was of course the tightest and its members were even prohibited by regulations from marrying Tutsi women. The church, in spite of being Hutu-dominated, remained more open, and a measure of institutional equality existed among the clergy; in the 1980s three of the eight Rwanda bishops were Tutsi. In private employment, higher standards of education and a certain cultural

60. Except towards the very end, the *Préfet* of Butare, who was killed during the Genocide.

savoir faire with foreigners gave the Tutsi a distinct edge over the Hutu[61].

All in all, life was difficult for the Tutsi who were victims of institutional discrimination[62], but in everyday life it was quite tolerable. Compared to the Kayibanda years, things had improved, even to the point where some well-known Tutsi businessmen had made fortunes and were on very good terms with the regime. The unspoken understanding was 'Do not mess around with politics, this is a Hutu preserve'. As long as Tutsi stuck to that principle, they were generally left in peace.

General Habyarimana had brought peace and stability to Rwanda. Like anything else, this had its price. Immediately after seizing power, he outlawed political parties but about a year later, in 1974, he had created his own, the Mouvement Révolutionnaire National pour le Développement (MRND). The President was quite unabashed about his decision: 'I know some people favour multipartyism, but as far as I am concerned, I have had no hesitation in choosing the single party system.'[63] In 1978, article 7 of the Constitution enshrined single-party rule as a basic value of the regime. The MRND was a truly totalitarian party: every single Rwandese citizen had to be a member, including babies and old people. All *bourgmestres* and *préfets* were chosen from among party cadres. The party was everywhere; every hill had its cell, and party faithfuls, hoping for promotion and a professional boost, willingly spied on anybody they were

---

61. Knowing how to deal with foreigners was important given the numerous foreign aid projects with their large expatriate staff. Tutsi men knew how to deal with white employers, and their women knew even better. Inter-racial affairs and even marriages between Rwandese women and expatriate men were frequent, and in over 95% of cases these women were Tutsi, a fact which caused not only jealousy (given the social and financial advantages involved) but also a sort of humiliation: the whites' preference for Tutsi beauty and elegance harked back to the colonial days when they scornfully looked down on the 'ugly primitive' Hutu.
62. Everybody carried an identity card on which a person's ethnic group (*ubwoko*) was mentioned. Those who illegally changed their ethnic classification (*abaguze ubwoko*) were subject to imprisonment or a fine or both.
63. President Habyarimana to the French journalist Philippe Decraene in *Le Monde* (7 October 1982).

told to spy on and on a few others as well. When one looks at Rwanda, one should forget about images of easygoing tropical confusion. All citizens had their place of residence written on their identity cards. Travelling was tolerated, but not changing address without due cause; one had to apply for permission to move. Unless there was good reason, such as going to school or getting a job, the authorisation to change residence would not be granted – unless, of course, one had friends in high places. Administrative control was probably the tightest in the world among non-communist countries. In the early 1980s, this legislation was used to arrest 'loose women' who were living in Kigali without proper authorisation – most of them 'happened' to be the Tutsi girlfriends of Europeans.

If the MRND was the inescapable administrative frame of reference for public life in the country, it was not supposed to be a 'political' party. Indeed, the word 'politics' was almost a dirty word in the virtuous and hard working world of Habyarimanism. Every effort was made to forget – at least officially – that politics existed. When the regime finally decided in November 1981, after eight years in power, to create a 'parliament', it was called the Conseil National du Développement (National Development Council). Rwanda was poor, Rwanda was clean and Rwanda was serious; it had no time to lose in the frivolous business of political discussion. Thus it became what the German pastor Herbert Keiner, long a fan of the regime like many of his brethen, called *'ein Entwicklungsdiktatur'*[64]('a development dictatorship'). Along lines somewhat reminiscent of eighteenth century European theories of 'benevolent despotism', President Habyarimana had decided to take upon his shoulders the heavy burden of the state so that his subjects could devote themselves entirely to the business of agriculture. Given the shortage of arable land and annual population increase of 3.7%, he had a point of sorts. In this system Habyarimana, sole presidential candidate, was triumphantly re-elected in December 1983

64. Pfarrer Herbert Keiner, 'Allmählich schwand die Bewunderung für "Habis" Regime', *Frankfurter Rundschau* (5 November 1992).

and then again in December 1988 with 99.98% of the vote. MRND activists who had hoped for *'Ijana kw'ijana'* (one hundred per cent) were disappointed[65]. The system was authoritarian but somewhat debonair, and it worked at the economic level. In 1962 there had been only two countries in the world with lower *per capita* income than Rwanda. By 1987 there were eighteen and, with a *per capita* income of US$300, Rwanda was roughly comparable with the People's Republic of China (US$310). In fact, if we look at the dynamics of the Rwandese economy, they compared most favourably with the other countries of the region:

PER CAPITA EVOLUTION OF RWANDA COMPARED
WITH NEIGHBOURING COUNTRIES

COUNTRY RANKING AMONG LDCs (FROM BOTTOM UP)

	Rwanda	*Burundi*	*Zaïre*	*Uganda*	*Tanzania*
1976	7	11	16	33	25
1981	16	14	12	13	19
1985	18	11	9	*n.a.*	21
1990	19	11	12	13	2
Variation					
1976–90	+12	—	−4	−20	−23

Source: World Bank Yearly Developments Reports, compiled by Filip Reyntjens in *L'Afrique des Grands Lacs en crise*, Paris: Karthala, 1994, p. 35.

Sectoral evolution was encouraging. Primary activities (i.e. subsistence agriculture), which had accounted for 80% of GNP in 1962, had fallen to 48% by 1986, while secondary activities had gone up from 8% to 21% and services from 12% to 31%. The mortality rate was down, hygiene and medical care indicators were improving, and education, though expensive and difficult to organise given the extremely scattered nature of the dwelling pattern, was improving. The proportion of children at

---

65. This was the official slogan during the 'election campaign'.

school had gone up from 49.5% in 1978 to 61.8% in 1986, despite the tremendous growth-rate of the population[66].

Regionally Rwanda was playing both the francophone 'Central African' card by becoming a key member in the Paris-backed Communauté Economique des Pays des Grands Lacs (CEPGL – Economic Community of the Great Lakes Countries), created in September 1976, and opening up to a more international anglophone world linked with East Africa by taking part in the World Bank-sponsored Kagera River Basin Organisation (KBO) in September 1977. Kigali was hoping to get new transport links, both to Dar-es-Salaam and to Lake Victoria, through its CEPGL membership, while the KBO offered the hope of hydro-electric development for the country.

Of course this modestly bright picture contained some shadows. The much-touted *umuganda* communal development labour, which was supposed to take two days a month out of a peasant's time, often took four or more. And contrary to party cadres' enthusiastic descriptions the work was far from being always voluntary. In some cases it even amounted to forced labour. The fatherly ILO criticism of these practices fell on deaf ears, both in Rwanda and abroad[67]. At a different level the reliance on foreign aid, small at first, had become significant by the late 1970s and enormous by the late 1980s. As one former expatriate joked, Rwanda was not only 'the land of the 1,000 hills', it was also 'the land of the 1,000 foreign aid workers'[68]. According to the OECD, foreign aid, which had represented less than 5% of GNP in 1973, had risen to 11% in 1986 and to 22% by 1991.

---

66. République Rwandaise, *Mémoire présenté à la Deuxième Conférence des Nations Unies sur les Pays les Moins Avancés*, Paris (3–14 September 1990), p. 6. One should keep in mind that in Rwanda in 1991 *57.5% of the population was less than twenty years of age* (Ministère du Plan, *Recensement*, op. cit., December 1991). Part of the violence of the genocide can be traced to the fact that by the late 1980s large numbers of disaffected unemployed youths had drifted to Kigali and to a lesser extent to smaller towns.

67. André Guichaoua, *Travail non rémunéré et développement rural au Rwanda: pratiques et perspectives*, Geneva: ILO, 1990.

68. Alain Hanssen, *Le désenchantement de la coopération. Enquête au pays des mille coopérants*, Paris: L'Harmattan, 1989.

The atmosphere of the regime. It is not possible to assess Rwanda in the way one would assess the Central African Republic or the Gambia. Rwanda was a country with a mystique. Keeping all due precautions in mind, one has to see it in the company of Cuba, Israel, North Korea and the Vatican, that is an ideological state where power is a means towards the implementation of a set of ideas at least as much as a *de facto* administrative structure for governing a given geographical territory.

We saw in the previous chapter how the Belgians, from a mixture of expediency and pseudo-scientific racial fascination, reconstructed a neo-traditionalist Rwanda which by 1945 had become more real than the Rwanda on which Count von Götzen first laid eyes in 1894. The interesting thing is that the Hutu 'democratic revolution' of 1959 had not changed the main traits of that ideological construct, but it had merely inverted its sign. Tutsi were still 'foreign invaders' who had come from afar, but now this meant that they could not really be considered as citizens. Their government had been grandiose and powerful: in the new version of the Rwandese ideology, it had been a cruel and homogeneously oppressive tyranny. The Hutu had been the 'native peasants', enslaved by the aristocratic invaders: they were now the only legitimate inhabitants of the country. Hutu were the silent demographic majority, which meant that a Hutu-controlled government was now not only automatically legitimate but also ontologically democratic.

Just as the first version of the Rwandese ideology had been a perfect construct to legitimise the domination by a few high-lineage Tutsi over everybody else, *petits Tutsi* and Hutu together, the new version was a marvelous tool for the new élite to rule over both the Hutu peasant masses and the disfranchised Tutsi community. The parallels are striking. In the neo-traditionalist 1931–59 version, the *petits Tutsi* felt proud of belonging to the 'ethnic aristocracy', although it brought them very little beyond that sense of superiority. Now it was the Hutu who fell prey to the same error and mostly persuaded themselves that because the government was Hutu, they, the humble peasants from the hills, somehow shared in that power. In both cases the ethnic élites approved and reinforced the delusions of their followers. The Belgians had shared in creating the aristocratic version of the myth and had ended up believing it and admiring their own creation. Now it was the foreign aid workers who collaborated in reinforcing the vision of a 'democratic majority rule' and who ended up admiring their own righteousness in helping such deserving Africans. If there was a link between the two versions of the myth, it was the Catholic church. It had admired the Tutsi and helped them rule, but now admired the Hutu and helped them rule. In both cases, this was perceived (and abundantly explained) as being the work of divine providence and a great step forward in the building of a Christian society in Rwanda[69].

The country lived and breathed in this atmosphere. Everything was carefully controlled, clean and in good order. The peasants were hard-working, clean-living and suitably thankful to their social superiors and to the benevolent white foreigners who helped them. There was almost no crime, the few prostitutes were periodically rounded up for re-education, and the church successfully opposed any attempts at birth control despite the burgeoning of the population. If Belgium remained the main donor of foreign aid, Rwanda also acted as a magnet for Germany, the United States, Canada and Switzerland[70], all of which were well satisfied with the government's attitude towards foreign donors and with the general orderliness of the country. In a way, this was understandable. Parson Keiner made this true observation:

[In the early 1980s] we used to compare the nearly idyllic situation in Rwanda with the post-Idi Amin chaos in Uganda, the Tutsi apartheid in Burundi, the 'real African socialism' of Tanzania and

69. From that point of view, a close reading of the quality Catholic-sponsored review *Dialogue* is interesting. Its Kinyarwanda sister publication *Kinyamateka* evolved in the 1980s towards a more critical stance.
70. Rwanda ranked as first among the recipients of Swiss public foreign aid.

Mobutu's kleptocracy in Zaïre, and we felt the regime had many positive points[71].

But the problem was that this agreeable façade was built on an extremely dangerous ideological foundation. The Hutu-revised version of the Rwandese cultural mythology which had caused the violence of 1959 to 1964 was still alive. And peace could only be kept maintained through sufficient financial lubrication of the élite. Everything rested on a carefully-controlled machinery of hypocrisy, with the church playing the role of Chief Engineer. Violent rumblings could be heard just below the surface if one stopped to listen. Former President Kayibanda had died in detention in 1976, most likely starved to death by his gaolers[72]. Between 1974 and 1977 the security chief, Théoneste Lizinde, and his thugs had killed fifty-six people, mostly former dignitaries of the Kayibanda regime, but also innocuous lawyers or businessmen whom they disliked for one reason or another[73]. The former minister for international cooperation Augustin Muyaneza (he had declared to a French journalist during the last few months of the Kayibanda regime 'Our French partners should realise one thing: our country is completely free from either wastage or corruption.)'[74] was among those who died in detention at an unknown date between 1974 and 1977. There is also uncertainty about the way he died: some sources say that he was buried alive and others that his skull was crushed with a hammer. But such things were usually kept secret and never reached the ears of the foreign aid donors.

The many friends of the regime were later to watch the rising

---

71. Herbert Keiner, op. cit.
72. The author's interview with a former civil servant (Kigali, 4 July 1994). The reason for letting Kayibanda starve rather than killing him seems to have been President Habyarimana's superstitious fear that his blood oath of fidelity to the former head of state would cause him harm if he actually shed the blood of the ex-President.
73. *Chronique d'Amnesty International*, no. 118 (December 1985). These murders only came to light because Lizinde himself had fallen foul of the regime after trying to overthrow President Habyarimana in April 1980. After he had spent some years in gaol, his trial in 1985 suddenly offered a glimpse of the bloody underside of the regime.
74. 'Le Rwanda, pays des vertes collines', *Le Monde* (1 March 1973).

spiral of violence in 1990–4 with stunned disbelief. For them, whatever criticism had been levelled at Kigali had to be maliciously inspired by sympathy for those the MRND called the *féodo-revanchards*, the *Inyenzi* devils lurking in the shadows waiting for an opportunity to pounce on honest little Christian Rwanda. Revelation of the murderous righteousness intrinsic in the Rwandese ideology was a shock which strained their capacity for reflection and self-criticism. Some, like Pastor Keiner whom we have quoted above, found in their independent moral beliefs the strength to reassess their former enthusiasm. Others, motivated by a mixture of genuine if misguided 'democratic' sympathy, refused to accept that hitherto seemingly 'virtuous' associates could be capable of such moral obliquity and an inability to recognise that they could have been wrong, insisted on denying the nature of the reality they were facing[75]. In some extreme cases, as we will see in Chapter 8, this denial has even led virtuous Christian NGOs and otherwise honest individuals, often close to European Christian Democratic circles, almost to overlook the genocide and to try to keep helping the MRND remnants under the guise of 'aid to the refugees'. But even if such developments were a possibility already contained within the Rwandese Ideology Revisited, like a poisonous snake still unborn inside its egg, the Habyarimana regime up till (*circa*) 1988 was in general one of the least bad in Africa if one considers only its actions and not its intellectual underpinnings.

75. Pierre Erny's, *Rwanda 1994*, Paris: L'Harmattan, 1994, is a perfect example of that frame of mind. Professor Erny's book oscillates between a bewildered lament over man's inhumanity to man, pleadings for the Habyarimana regime, and an attempt to cast the RPF in the role of Satan entering the Garden of Eden. Professor Erny also seems to believe that Amnesty International is an organisation run by Freemasons (p. 226), which should invalidate what it says in the eyes of people who 'think religiously'. With an obvious lack of ecumenical political correctness, this author thinks that the difference in attitude between two pro-Habyarimana Christians like Pastor Keiner and Professor Erny could be related to their respective confessions. Protestantism has historically been stronger on independant moral examination and self-criticism than the Roman church, and in this particular case has less of a historical connection with the MRND regime. One should remember that up till December 1989, when Rome ordered him to resign, the Bishop of Kigali, Mgr Vincent Nsengiyumva, had been an active member of the MRND central committee.

The crisis. The only malodorous episode in the fifteen years between 1973 and 1988 had been the conspiracy and *coup* attempt by former security chief Théoneste Lizinde in April 1980. If one were inclined to give somewhat mechanistic Marxist patterns their due, one would have to note that the previously high price of coffee had by then been falling since 1977 – and that they rose again after 1980 before finally collapsing in 1986. Also, world tin prices had collapsed soon after coffee prices (1984–6), leading to the closing down of tin mining in Rwanda. Since it was tin which in 1982–83 had picked up the slack in coffee prices, its share of foreign export earnings rising to 20% (coffee had made up 75% till it progressively fell to around 50%), this second blow struck very hard[76].

And one can say that the political stability of the regime followed almost exactly the curve of those prices. Rwanda is a very poor country built on peasant subsistence agriculture, and little surplus-value can be extracted directly from the peasant mass. For the élite of the regime there were three sources of enrichment: coffee and tea exports, briefly tin exports, and creaming off foreign aid. Since a fair share of the first two had to be allocated to running the government, by 1988 the shrinking of sources of revenue left only the third as a viable alternative. Hence there was an increase in competition for access to that very specialised resource, which could only be appropriated through direct control of government power at high levels. So the various gentlemen's agreements which had existed between the competing political clans since the end of the Kayibanda regime started to melt down as the resources shrank and internal power struggles intensified.

The first sign that things were going wrong was the murder of Colonel Stanislas Mayuya in April 1988. Mayuya had been a close friend of President Habyarimana and there were strong rumours that in due course he might become associated with his power, possibly as vice-president, in a move to groom him for

---

76. République Rwandaise, *Mémoire présenté par le Rwanda à la Deuxième Conférence des Nations Unies sur les Pays les Moins Avancés*, op. cit., p. 3.

the succession. This spelt doom for one of the regime's main political clans, first called in Kigali '*le Clan de Madame*' and later the '*akazu*'[77]. The '*Clan de Madame*', as its name suggests, was made up of members of the President's wife's family and their close associates. The main members of the group were three of her brothers Colonel Pierre-Célestin Rwagafilita, Protais Zigiranyi-razo and Séraphin Rwabukumba, her cousin Elie Sagatwa and close associates Colonel Laurent Serubuga and Noël Mbonabaryi. They were followed by a number of less important but devoted retainers, among whom Colonel Théoneste Bagosora was later to acquire a fundamental role. There were three particular reasons why the '*Clan de Madame*' came to play such an important role in the unfolding of events.

First, in the Rwandese political tradition which the MRND Hutu regime had inherited from both Grégoire Kayibanda and the old Tutsi *Abami*, the ruler needed to have followers who were his ears and eyes, people outside the official power structure who were unequivocally devoted to him and would do anything without asking questions. The *Abami* had found such people among their own Abayinginya clan and within their 'marital' clan, the Ababega. This of course with the accompanying betrayals, conspiracies, reversals of alliance and so on which were the daily lot of this Florentine court. Since, as we have seen, Hutu clans were largely a political construct of the ruling Tutsi political order, they could not easily be used for such a purpose because they elicited only a weak commitment from their members. Thus under the Hutu republic regionalism took the place of clanism. President Kayibanda played various groups off against each other but tended to rely mostly, even to the point of isolation, on people coming from Gitarama. And then, of course, within each 'regional mafia' there would be a tendency to create sub-units according to precise, more narrowly defined geographical origin.

Secondly, as he looked from that angle President Habyarimana

---

77. 'The little house'. In pre-colonial Rwanda this was the name given to the inner circle of the King's court.

had a problem. The 'Second Republic' he created in 1973 had initially been a northern revenge over the PARMEHUTU southerners[78]. But once it became clear that cabinet posts, economic opportunities and foreign scholarships would go first and foremost to northerners, they began competing among themselves to know who would get more. The President and his wife favoured the people of Gisenyi *préfecture* over the Ruhengeri *préfecture* group led by the foreign minister Casimir Bizimungu and public works minister Joseph Nzirorera. So the Ruhengeri boys were forced to take second place to their Gisenyi cousins. But it did not stop there. Favour ranking went by communal affiliation, and there the President was weak. President Habyarimana had been born in Karago *commune*, but he was not 'somebody', i.e. a member of a respectable lineage. In fact, there were persistent rumours that his grandfather had been an immigrant from either the Ugandan province of Kigezi or the Zaïrian province of Kivu. In many ways he was a man alone, self-made. So, although he had become the *mwami* of the Hutu, the top *shebuja* in the land, he did not really have faithful *abagaragu* owing personal loyalty to him.

Thirdly, the case of the President's wife was different. Agathe Kanzinga came from Bushiru and was the daughter of one of those small northern Hutu *Abahinza* lineages who ruled independant principalities till the late nineteenth century and in some cases even into the 1920s. She and her family were proud of their lineage which was large and well-known. So the President relied on his wife's clan and *abagaragu* as his ears and eyes. She became so powerful that she came to be popularly nicknamed 'Kanjogera', in memory of King Musinga's terrible mother, the real power behind his throne. Her husband relied on her and her family for many things, but he also gradually became their

---

78. One could even say that it was more than that. It was a historical revenge by marginalised, fiercely Hutu, anti-royalist Rwanda. It was to that northern revenge that the *engagé* historian Ferdinand Nahimana meant to give intellectual credentials. It is also because the northerners had waited for so long, feeling like second-class citizens, that in 1993–4 the thought of loosing power drove them to the frantic extremity of the genocide.

prisoner and eventually their victim[79]. So in the late 1980s climate, when political competition for the control of a rapidly shrinking economy was becoming fiercer, the succession plans President Habyarimana seemed to entertain concerning Colonel Mayuya were a grave threat to '*le Clan de Madame*', who might lose control at a time when control was more vital than ever because Mayuya was the President's own man (and one of the few![80]). Colonel Serubuga, one of the most powerful *akazu* members, organised Mayuya's murder. The sergeant who actually pulled the trigger was later murdered in jail and the prosecutor in charge of the file was murdered during the inquiry.

The Mayuya affair was the spark which ignited the powder-keg and soon the various clans were at each other's throats. In 1989 the budget was reduced by 40%, a measure which was largely offset by cutting social services[81]. This did not go down well with the peasants who were already overburdened with a variety of taxes (*umusanzu*, water fees, health tax, school fees etc.) and harried by increasing doses of 'voluntary' *umuganda* which looked more and more like forced labour, especially when it had to be performed on lands privately owned by the regime's cronies. The land question was also becoming increasingly thorny. Overpopulation was reaching critical levels and an increasingly marginal food supply made the country heavily dependent on the vagaries of the weather. A mini-drought caused the *ruriganiza* famine which killed about 300 people in 1988–9 and sent thousands of others over the Tanzanian border in search of food. The government tried to impose a press black-out on the question, security chief Augustin Nduwayezu candidly declaring to a Belgian journalist: 'Journalists

---

79. This is a point made by Jean Shyirambere Barahinyura in *Le Général-Major Habyarimana (1973–1988). Quinze ans de tyrannie et de tartufferie au Rwanda*, Frankfurt-am-Main: Izuba Verlag, 1988, p. 143. In spite of the book being a crude political tract, it offers some insights into the intimate workings of the regime.

80. From that point of view an interesting case is that of Colonel Alois Nsekalije, a personal friend of the President, born in his area and a long-time cabinet minister, who was eventually squeezed out of power because he owed nothing to Mme Habyarimana's clan. In the same perspective, the fate of Colonel Elie Sagatwa, a member of her clan who later changed sides, is equally interesting (see chapter 7).

81. André Guichaoua, *Le problème des réfugiés Rwandais*, op. cit., p. 11.

should not write articles which can irritate the highest authorities.'[82] In this climate, stories concerning land-grabbing had an especially exasperating effect on the peasantry:

> The accusation that the highest state authorities had benefited, through the control of an internationally-funded development project, from lands which they used to raise cattle, took on a heavily symbolic value and played a decisive role in the disenchantment with the regime which started to set in at that time[83].

What Professor Guichaoua alludes to here without naming it is the Gebeka project, funded by the World Bank, which caused a big albeit quickly stifled scandal. According to one of its managers[84], the whole thing was a disgrace. Gishwati forest, one of the last primary growth forests in Rwanda, was savagely logged to clear land which was then used to graze exotic cattle imported from Europe in order to start a dairy business. Although both the land and the funds were public, profits accruing from the development were shared between the 'big men' of the regime and crooked World Bank expatriates who had invested in the scheme. The 1959 'democratic revolution' had symbolised Hutu free access to land and to cattle, with its particular significance, and the Gebeka scam was a serious ideological blow to that ideal.

The government was trying to make up through moralistic hypocrisy for what it had lost in terms of blood and financial scandals: *femmes libres* ('loose women') in Kigali were repeatedly rounded up and sent to the Rwamagana 're-education' camp[85],

---

82. The famine in 1988-9 was of course due to the extreme marginality of Rwandese agriculture in a context of deforestation, soil erosion, demographic increase, under-fertilisation and difficult crop selection. But it was also caused by the political vagaries of food marketing and pricing policies. See Johan Pottier, 'Taking stock: Food marketing in Rwanda (1982-1989)', *African Affairs*, no. 92 (1993), pp. 5-30.

83. André Guichaoua, *Le problème des refugiés Rwandais*, op. cit., p. 12.

84. Personal communication to the author, Paris, 2 August 1994. After he had denounced some of the corrupt practices in the Gebeka scheme, our informer had to protect himself from assassination attempts by having some members of his family who served in the army act as his permanent bodyguards.

85. See *Le Monde* (20 July 1983 and 29 April 1984). These arrests were occasions

radical Catholic pro-life commandos raided pharmacies to destroy condoms with the approval of the Ministry of the Interior, young urban unemployed, arbitrarily called *abanyali* ('bandits'), were grabbed in the streets, had their heads shaved and were packed off to 're-education' centres, and some shantytowns were partly torn down under the pretext that they harboured 'criminals'. These had little lasting effect and certainly did not stop the political tensions from rising. In August 1989, member of Parliament, Félecula Nyiramutarambirwa, was deliberately run over by a lorry after criticising the government for corruption in road-building contracts. She also came from Butare and was thought to encourage political opposition there. In November the same year, Father Silvio Sindambiwe, a vocal and outspoken journalist who had written too freely about certain dubious government practices, was also killed in a stage-managed 'traffic accident'. Other journalists who tried to write about these events were arrested[86]. In April 1990 President Habyarimana came to Paris and later in June attended the Franco-African summit at La Baule[87]. President Mitterrand, who was then on a 'liberal' political course concerning African affairs and who seemed to want to link economic aid with political democratisation[88], advised Habyarimana to introduce a multi party system in

---

of personal revenge against women who had also aroused jealousy. In 1984 the US ambassador had to threaten that he would leave the country in order to get his secretary out of detention.

86. Amnesty International, *Republic of Rwanda: a spate of detentions and trials in 1990 to suppress Fundamental Rights*, London: A.I. (October 1990).

87. Over the last fifteen years, France had slowly replaced Belgium as the tutelary power in Rwanda because it offered financial and especially military guarantees which Belgium could not provide. In 1975 Paris had signed with Kigali a military cooperation and training agreement (but not a defence agreement, something which put the October 1990 French intervention on an illegal footing) and had regularly increased its economic aid. France kept over 400 *coopérants* in the country and its development aid was second only to that of Belgium with US $37.2 m. in 1990 (OECD sources quoted in Economist Intelligence Unit, *Rwanda: Country Profile*, London: EIU, 1993, p. 18).

88. Scared by the effects of his La Baule speech supporting democratisation, President Mitterrand radically changed his tack within the next eighteen months. For an analysis of the contradictions of French policy in Africa, see Antoine Glaser and Stephen Smith, *l'Afrique sans Africains*, Paris: Stock, 1994.

Rwanda. The advice was quickly followed and Habyarimana, who had always stringently enforced the MRND political monopoly, suddenly declared that he supported a multiparty system (July 1990). But his personal conviction on the matter seems to have been rather shallow. In any case, this did not prevent thirty-three intellectuals from signing a manifesto which demanded immediate democratisation (August 1990). There were rumblings in the hills and the Butare students who had rioted in June for non-political reasons and seen one of their number shot dead, quickly found that their movement was picked up and amplified[89]. By the early fall of 1990 the Rwandese political scene was one of deep and pervasive crisis.

The RPF prepares for war.   This crisis acted as a multidimensional spur on the RPF invasion preparations in Uganda. First, two influential men came out of Rwanda during the summer of 1990 to meet the RPF leaders and discuss with them the state of affairs in the country. The wealthy Tutsi businessman Valens Kajeguhakwa and former civil servant Pasteur Bizimungu, a Hutu, told the same story: the Rwandese political system was on the verge of collapse and any strong push from outside would complete the process. This of course was music to the ears of the young Tutsi exiles who had positioned themselves within the NRA and were now preparing to attack Rwanda[90].

Secondly, some elements of the government in Kigali who were well aware of the Tutsi invasion plans thought seriously of ways to deflect them. The *Commission Spéciale sur les problèmes des émigrés Rwandais*, which had been created in February 1989, had been allowed to lie dormant, but by May

---

89. The Ruhengeri campus went on a solidarity strike and there were numerous manifestations of sympathy.
90. This impression was reinforced by the general tone of the foreign press in dealing with Rwanda: see for example 'Rwanda. fin de règne', *Africa Confidential*, vol. 30, no. 21 (20 October 1989); Marie-France Cros, 'Une ambiance de fin de règne', *La Libre Belgique* (31 October 1989); and François Misser, 'Rwanda: Death and Intrigue', *The New African* (February 1990).

1990 it had been reactivated and fused with the older *Comité Ministériel Conjoint Rwando-Ougandais sur le Problème des Réfugiés*. Its third session in July 1990 led to the drafting of a document which made arrangements for Rwandese government delegates to visit Uganda and select lists of candidates for a repatriation exercise due to be carried out in November. This new development augured ill for the RPF militants who were now in danger of losing their support among the refugees if the latter felt that their return to Rwanda could be achieved without fighting. Accordingly they accelerated their preparations to beat the November deadline. Without knowing it, they benefited from the discreet complicity of those extremists in the MRND regime who wanted a war in order to get rid of the opposition once and for all.

The third development which spurred the RPF to faster action was the political movement inside Rwanda. The intellectual circles responsible for the August manifesto were busy preparing to launch opposition political parties. Given his speech in July and the French pressure in the background, President Habyarimana could not long delay the acceptance of a multiparty system – which would deprive the RPF of one of its best public relations points, i.e. that it was fighting a totalitarian single-party dictatorship.

The time was ripe. Since early 1988, militants of the Front had infiltrated key areas of the NRA, which would enable them to act decisively at the crucial moment. The fact that Commandant Musitu who headed the NRA Training Service was a Munyarwanda had been quite helpful. Commandant Samuel Kanyemera (alias Kaka), who had been made head of the military police was Rwandese, as were 80% of the computer service employees, the head of the medical service Dr Peter Banyingana, and the acting head of military security Paul Kagame, one of the Front leaders. But the biggest boost for recruiting ordinary soldiers had been the rallying of Major-General Fred Rwigyema after he had been fired from his position as commander-in-chief. Rwigyema was a warm and congenial personality, unlike many of the Front leaders who were cold political types; he was popular with the rank-and-file with whom he had shared all the sufferings and hardships of war for nine years. He was a soldiers' soldier and the moment he went over to the Front, every Munyarwanda NCO or enlisted man in the NRA was ready to follow him[91].

By July 1990, the decision to attack Rwanda had been firmly made, and Fred Rwigyema set out on a fund-raising mission among Tutsi *émigré* communities in Europe and North America[92]. Paul Kagame had been sidetracked by being sent to the United States for further training in June, and he had accepted in order not to attract attention[93]. The final touch of the conspiracy was almost comical: to explain his having ordered troop movements when no longer commander-in-chief, Major-General Rwigyema explained that the President had put him in charge of organising the military parade to celebrate the Ugandan Independence Day (9 October); Rwigyema was so well known and on such good terms with everybody that nobody bothered to check with State House whether this was true or not.

91. Contrary to later Rwandese government propaganda, there were very few non-Banyarwanda NRA soldiers in the RPF. The only non-Munyarwanda this author ever met inside Rwanda during the war was a Musoga soldier, ADC to a Munyarwanda officer, who replied to a question about his presence: 'I have followed him everywhere since 1982. How could I not follow him here?'
92. Catharine Watson, op. cit., pp. 13–14.
93. This episode is at the root of another old rumour, namely that 'the RPF has been trained by the Americans'. Major Kagame stayed in the United States for a total of three and a half months and he was already an experienced soldier when he went to Fort Leavenworth. There were about nine or ten Banyarwanda NRA officers who at some time went to the United States, together with a much larger number of their fellow-officers from various Ugandan tribal origins, within the framework of a US military training program. When the 1 October 1990 invasion got under way, it took the CIA and the State Department several days to realise that one of the Front leaders was actually present on US territory. They then had to phone Fort Leavenworth to request his file (author's interview with a former US State Department official, Washington DC, 9 September 1994).

3

CIVIL WAR AND
FOREIGN INTERVENTION
(October 1990–July 1991)

The RPF strike and the first days of fighting

At 2.30 on the afternoon of Monday, 1 October a group of about fifty armed men came out of the bush near the Rwandese border post of Kagitumba and opened fire on the guards, killing one and setting the others to flight. Within minutes, hundreds more men clad in Ugandan army fatigues had joined the attackers and were crossing into Rwanda. The civil war had begun. The Rwandese Patriotic Army forces[1] now on the move numbered around 2,500, out of about 4,000 Banyarwanda still in the NRA[2]. They were led by Major-General Fred Rwigyema, Lt.-Colonel Adam Wasswa, five majors (Peter Banyingana, Christopher Bunyenyezi, Samuel Kanyemera, Paul Kagame[3] and Stephen Nduguta) and about 150 other officers of various ranks and NCOs. This gives some idea of the then declining importance of Banyarwanda in the NRA, especially in its officer corps, since it had at the time around fifty lieutenant-colonels and 250 majors. The invading forces had taken with them a fair amount of equipment including heavy machine-guns, mortars, BM-21 multiple rocket-launchers, recoilless rifles and Russian ZUG light automatic cannons. Some of President Museveni's own bodyguard even stole the presidential staff radio communication vehicles, a feat they later recalled with a mixture of

---

1. This was the 'official' name the invaders had adopted for the armed branch of the RPF. In practice it was little used and everybody kept referring to both the political and military wings of the movement as 'RPF', a practice we will also follow.
2. Estimate given by RPF founding member Tito Rutaremara (interview with the author, Kabale, 11 July 1992).
3. Major Kagame was not part of the invading force, being in the United States at the time.

childish glee and embarrassment. But they had not managed to steal either heavy artillery or armoured vehicles, and because they expected a short war they carried limited supplies of fuel and ammunition. Facing them were the Forces Armeés Rwandaises (FAR) a small but fairly well-equipped regular army of 5,200 men supplied by the French with Panhard armoured cars, heavy artillery and some Gazelle helicopters. During the first few days of the fighting, they benefited from a surprise effect, advancing some 60 km. down to Gabiro. But they were by now cut off from Uganda, the Kampala government having quickly thrown up roadblocks on the roads in the west of the country to prevent them from being further reinforced by deserting NRA soldiers. A few stragglers were caught that way. They also had to deal with a fairly large number (about 3,000) of Tutsi civilian refugees who had enthusiastically and irresponsibly rushed to the border when they learned of the attack. Getting them to return to Uganda was not easy.

It was not long before things started to go wrong for the attackers. The first setback was of major importance: Major-General Rwigyema, the charismatic RPF leader, was killed on the second day of the attack. His death, which was long kept secret, has been the subject of much controversy. According to certain sources, he was killed by his second-in-command, Major Banyingana, after a quarrel over military tactics. Banyingana and his friend Major Bunyenyezi were supposed to have favoured a lightning conventional strike towards Kigali, while Rwigyema would have preferred a more cautious approach involving the organisation of guerrilla areas to achieve a progressive political and military erosion of the Habyarimana regime. According to this version, Banyingana and Bunyenyezi were later tried and shot by an RPF military court on Major Kagame's orders[4], but there are many contradictions in this account which was disseminated at the time by the Kigali regime and discreetly supported by the French. One of these concerned the psycho-

---

4. Interview with a diplomat at the French embassy in Kampala (28 January 1991).

logical aspects. Rwigyema was a legend among the Ugandan Banyarwanda, and his long and distinguished military career, his personal charisma, his success in having achieved the highest rank in the NRA and his cheerful comradely attitude with the frontline soldiers had made him extremely popular. It is doubtful whether anybody would have dared to murder him and even more doubtful that his killers would have survived more than a few minutes after shooting him. The second discrepancy in the murder version is that the 'killers' of 'Commandant Fred', as his men affectionately called him, were alive and free several days after his alleged assassination. A Ugandan journalist, Teddy Ssezi-Cheeye, interviewed Major Peter Banyingana inside Rwanda on 5 October 1990 and saw him very much in charge and respected by his subordinates[5]. And finally there is a third factor making the murder theory unlikely. In contrast to some other African guerrilla movements such as the Eritrean EPLF or the Sudanese SPLA, there were no later rumours of bloody feuds among the top leadership. If 'Commandant Fred' had been murdered by some of his own subordinates, further factional infighting would almost certainly have broken out, and it is doubtful that the dead men's friends would have failed to at least spread the story.

The reality seems in fact to have been much more prosaic – that Rwigyema was killed by one of the bizarre yet frequent hazards of war. It seems that he was standing on a small hill watching retreating Rwandese government forces through his binoculars when a fleeing soldier turned around and killed him with a single shot. He actually was the only RPF casualty on that day. This panicked the Front leadership, who feared that the reality would never be believed and in addition that news of Rwigyema's death would damage the morale of their troops.

5. See Teddy Ssezi-Cheeye, 'Encounter with Rwanda rebels in the bush', *The Weekly Topic*, no. 41 (19 October 1990). It is doubtful that Ssezi-Cheeye could have been acting in support of the pro-RPF forces in Uganda because he could not, by any stretch of the imagination, be described as pro-Museveni. He was then writing for an independent paper linked with the left oppostion to the NRM and he later created a scandal-sheet called *Uganda Confidential*, obsessively devoted to denouncing the real or imaginary financial misdemeanours of the Ugandan regime.

They decided to cover up his death and when they later had to admit to it, they attributed it to his having stepped on a mine. This was such a remote possibility that it contributed to creating suspicion[6].

Whatever the truth, Rwigyema's death was a big blow to the RPF and their offensive wavered. The Forces Armées Rwandaises rapidly recovered from their initial shock, especially since the French government had quickly come to their rescue. On 7 October the Rwandese regular forces made a counter-offensive and retook Gabiro on the 9th – they lost it again but retook it on the 23rd. Caught in a conventional warfare situation without the necessary equipment, RPF forces started to fall back. The retreat soon turned into a rout, and there were many desertions. Contacted by telephone in the United States, Major Kagame hastened back, only to witness increasing confusion. It was in the midst of these difficulties that Peter Banyingana and Chris Bunyenyezi were apparently killed when they and their troops walked into a government ambush (23 October). By the end of the month there was no more 'battle front', the last RPF stragglers having either crossed back into Uganda or else taken refuge in the Akagera national park. They had suffered heavy losses during the fighting, due to battlefield casualties and even more to desertions. In the national park some of their men starved to death and on 30 October the Kigali authorities could announce with every semblance of truth that 'the war had ended'. When on the next day RPF troops briefly occupied the Gatuna border post, it looked more like a desperate act of defiance than a calculated military move. But for Major Paul Kagame, who had now taken over the RPF military leadership, this was what, as a good ex-Maoist, he called 'the beginning of a protracted popular war', a long-term struggle which was to last the next four years and see the death of President Habyarimana, the collapse of his regime, and the accession of the RPF to power after an extraordinary succession of events including the second largest genocide since the Second World

---

6. At that early stage of the war, the government forces had had no time to lay mines.

War and the exodus abroad of most of the country's surviving civilian population.

Seen in retrospect, the whole madcap adventure of the early invasion begs one basic question: how much did President Yoweri Museveni know and what was his real attitude to the whole thing? The answer is complex[7] but it seems that the two extreme positions, namely the official Ugandan line ('our good faith was surprised by cunning conspirators') and the Kigali propaganda line ('this is a planned invasion supported by the Ugandan government with the aim of establishing a Tutsi empire in the Great Lakes area[8]) are both untenable. President Museveni and his security advisers knew, if not the precise date of the invasion, at least its general outline: first, because a conspiracy of this magnitude cannot be completely hidden; secondly, because the men who led it were among the President's closest friends; and thirdly because the political activities of Rwandese exiles in Uganda (and elsewhere in the world) were public knowledge[9]. But these arguments are in themselves a mitigating circumstance. Rumours of an invasion of Rwanda had become routine by the late 1980s and were no longer taken seriously by most people (except probably by the Rwandese security, as we shall see). The accepted wisdom on the subject was that this was a sort of ultimate option, both a threat and a bargaining element in the negotiations then taking place between the Kigali authorities, the Red Cross, the UNHCR and the Ugandan

7. For a more detailed treatment of this point see Gérard Prunier, 'L'Ouganda et le Front Patriotique Rwandais' in André Guichaoua (ed.), *Enjeux nationaux et dynamiques régionales dans l'Afrique des Grands Lacs*, Université de Lille: Faculté des Sciences Economiques et Sociales, 1992, pp. 43–9.
8. This view is presented in République Rwandaise, Ministère des Affaires Etrangèes et de la Coopération Internationale, *Livre Blanc sur l'agression dont le Rwanda a été victime à partir du 1er octobre 1990*, Kigali, January 1991.
9. President Museveni was in the United States attending a UNICEF conference on 1 October 1990. Just before leaving he had still begged Rwigyema and some of his friends to wait and negotiate with President Habyarimana, not out of sympathy for the Kigali regime (in fact be strongly disliked Habyarimana) but because he feared the international consequences of the invasion for Uganda. (Author's interview with a Ugandan civil servant, Kampala, July 1992.)

government[10]. But even if President Museveni did not believe an attack to be imminent, why did he tolerate the creation of a clandestine Rwandese network within his armed forces? There are various reasons. One, which is rarely mentioned, is that he had no way of stopping it without a major politico-military showdown. The place of the Banyarwanda in the NRA, the social, political and matrimonial alliances they had developed in western Uganda and even in Kampala, their presence at every level of both the civilian and military administrations – all this made them into a formidable potential foe in case a course of open repression against them was to be chosen. In the late 1980s northern and eastern Uganda were in a state of nearly constant insurrection, with the government waging war simultaneously against UPDM guerrillas and the remnants of Alice Lakwena's mystical bands (both of which drew their forces mainly from the Acholi clans), against the Iteso-based Uganda People's Army and against roving bands of Karamajong cattle thieves armed with RPG-7 rocket-launchers and heavy machine-guns. In neighbouring Kenya President Daniel Arap Moi, who disliked and feared the new 'revolutionary' Ugandan regime, gave whatever help he could to any and all of these rebels. In view of such a situation, it was unlikely that President Museveni would deliberately create another adversary, especially one that could seriously destabilise the western district of Ankole where the Banyarwanda exiles were based and which was one of his government's main area of support.

Yet another reason for his tolerating the RPF organising within the NRA was that he knew perfectly well that President Habyarimana also knew of it, and that he believed the invasion threat would merely soften the Rwandese President's position on the refugee question in future negotiations. Though understandable, this was a miscalculation. President Habyarimana had no intention of accepting the refugees back, except on his own personal terms. But, as a French publication later remarked,

---

10. The author shared this misconception and as a result was completely taken aback by the invasion on 1 October 1990.

President Habyarimana had to know about the coming invasion
. . . and he took advantage of it in order to try to liquidate his
internal opposition. In this tiny and almost perfectly controlled
country, where practically everyone was under the direct scrutiny
of the administration and the cadres of the single party, it seems
unbelievable that the Security Services could have ignored the rebels
oncoming attack[11].

The game was not *two-sided* as the later tragic events in
Rwanda have tended to make onlookers believe, but in fact *three-sided*, between the Habyarimana regime jockeying for survival,
the internal opposition struggling to achieve recognition, and the
Tutsi exiles trying to make some sort of a comeback. In trying
to use the external threat to quell the internal one, Habyarimana
held a major trump-card – the French fear of an 'Anglo-Saxon'
erosion of their position on the African continent – and it was
this which probably made him decide to embark on the risky
course of not trying to deflect the invasion through serious
negotiation[12]. We have already seen that the 'danger' of a
negotiated refugee repatriation programme was one of the factors
that pushed the RPF into acting quickly. As so often in the
Rwandese tragedy, extremisms tended to feed on each other, and
the honest accommodation of conflicting interests was never the
order of the day. Part of the problem was that France, as a sort
of protectorate power on the Rwandese political scene, also did
not act as a moderator. Habyarimana calculated that Paris would
back him in any event, and he was right.

11. *Afrique Défense* (January 1991. p. 23). This monthly publication, now defunct,
    was not an ordinary magazine. It was very close to the French Ministry of Defence
    and its 'articles' were in fact almost *verbatim* renderings of French military attachés'
    reports. Thus its 'positions' can reasonably be taken as reflecting those of the
    French military at the time in a given country.
12. Whether this was a real possibility will remain unknown. But the Habyarimana
    regime definitely chose not to try. During the summer of 1990 the Kigali
    government envoys who were supposed to have gone to Uganda to select
    'a representative group of refugees' to launch the repatriation process were told
    'not to hurry' (Interview with a diplomat from the Rwandese embassy in
    Kampala, 10 June 1993).

Foreign intervention

The timing of the invasion had been strange, since none of the international players concerned was at home. Both Museveni and Habyarimana were in New York, to attend a UNICEF conference on children's problems in the Third World, and François Mitterrand was on a state visit to the sultanate of Oman. While the French President's visit was probably an independant factor, it is quite likely that the RPF decided to take advantage of the Ugandan and Rwandese Presidents being absent to give him greater freedom of action. And for both of them this trip abroad provided, in turn, a convenient excuse and a way of affecting shocked innocence. In a half-admission of foreknowledge a top member of the Ugandan presidential delegation in New York later admitted to the author[13]:

'We were woken up by a call in the middle of the night telling us that the boys had gone over the border. The President was quite disturbed. We knew they were up to something but we did not think they would act so soon. With our presence in an international forum, it was quite embarrassing.'

As for President Mitterrand, he was told of the invasion while flying back to Paris from Oman. It seems that he made his decision almost immediately. After a short consultation with the Defence Minister Louis Joxe and Foreign Minister Roland Dumas he ordered the despatch of troops to bolster the Rwandese government army[14]. But the Rwandese head of state was sufficiently worried about the French attitude to call the Africa Unit at the Elysée palace from New York on 2 October. In a brief conversation lasting no more than ten minutes, Jean-Christophe Mitterrand, the President's own son who ran the Africa Office at the Elysée, gave a bland and reassuring answer to President Habyarimana[15], adding with a wink: 'We are

---

13. Interview in Kampala (unrecorded date in 1992).
14. Author's interview with a French Foreign Ministry official, Paris, October 1993.
15. The conversation took place in the author's presence. The Africa Unit (*Cellule*

going to send him a few boys, old man Habyarimana. We are
going to bail him out. In any case, the whole thing will be over
in two or three months'.

The next day Casimir Bizimungu, the Rwandese Minister for
Foreign Affairs, arrived in Paris where he was received by Jacques
Pelletier, Minister for Cooperation[16]. To avoid hard feelings
from Rwanda's one-time colonial masters, contact had already
been made with Brussels. Promises of military intervention were
immediately confirmed, although the military training and
technical cooperation agreement, dating back to 1975, was not
a defence treaty. On Thursday 4 October, a company (150 men)
of the 2éme Régiment Etranger Parachutiste stationed in the
Central African Republic flew down from Bangui to Kigali,
immediately taking up positions around the airport. The
Belgians soon followed, sending down 400 paratroopers from
Brussels. Seeing a chance to get himself back into the good graces
of his French and Belgian allies who had tended to cold-shoulder
him more and more in the recent past, President Mobutu Sese
Seko of Zaïre also sent several hundred troops belonging to his
crack military unit, the Division Spéciale Présidentielle (DSP).
In total contrast to the European troops, they immediately went
into action against the RPF.

However, for the Rwandese regime this was not quite
enough, and the non-combat status of the French and Belgian
troops left something to be desired. So in order to dramatise

---

Africaine) is part of the French presidential office which benefits from a high
degree of independence where decision-making in Africa is concerned. It is under
the direct control of the President himself. Its existence, an oddity in administrative terms, is a reflection of the very peculiar status Africa enjoys in the French
political landscape.

16. The Ministry of Cooperation has often been called the 'Ministry of Africa'.
It is mainly concerned with the *'pays du champs'* ('countries of the field'), i.e.
ex-French Africa. A few other countries – mostly French-speaking – have been
included in the 'field', and Rwanda was one of them. Although theoretically
concerned with *all* foreign countries, the French Foreign Ministry (often called
the Quai d'Orsay) tacitly acknowledges that the *Cellule Africaine* and the Ministry
of Cooperation are the real players in the African field.

the perceived gravity of the situation, it staged a fake attack on Kigali by 'enemy troops' during the night of 4/5 October. Beginning at 1 a.m., shooting started in the capital, lasting with varying intensity till around 7 a.m. Thousands of shots had been fired, but miraculously there was not a single casualty and there was very little damage to buildings. The international press was deceived[17] and the French ambassador Georges Martre duly reported 'heavy fighting in the capital', thereby achieving the desired effect in Paris. Within the next few days, French troop numbers had been increased to 600 although the government had started a campaign of massive arrests in Kigali (and to a lesser extent in the provincial capitals) and news of civilian massacres in the countryside had started to filter out[18].

At this point a question springs to mind: what could have caused Paris to send troops to a distant African country in order to protect a faltering dictatorship from an attack launched by its own refugee population trying to return home by force? This unanswered question was to become more and more disconcerting as the fighting developed, eventually reaching a hauntingly sinister quality when France's erstwhile allies cracked up and went genocidally mad. But there is no easy answer to this point. As a somewhat puzzled American journalist pointed out[19], within the mutually-accepted Franco-African political culture, 'it is not when the French government intervenes that he has some explaining to do, it is when it *doesn't.*' Alone among the former colonial powers that once ruled Africa, France has kept the will and the political breathing space, both at home and on the African continent, to use military power whenever it feels the need to add muscle to its policies. And up till the time of the Rwandese genocide there had been no post-modern

---

17. See for example *Le Monde* dated 6 October 1990. More seasoned observers soon saw through the deception which had also been staged in order to justify the massive wave of arrests then taking place (see Filip Reyntjens, *L'Afrique des Grands Lacs en crise*, Paris: Karthala, p. 94).

18. The first stories about the massacres which had then just started in the Mutara region came out in the Belgian daily *Le Soir* on 5 October 1990.

19. John Darnton, 'France in Africa: why few raise a fuss', *International Herald Tribune* (27 June 1994).

moralistic qualms about using humanitarian excuses for such interventions; good old-fashioned arguments about 'national interests' were usually enough. In fact the need for Paris to dig up 'humanitarian' justifications for its armed return to Rwanda in June 1994 can be seen as a weakening of French will and a sure sign that Paris felt ill at ease about the whole thing. France had needed no such rationale for sending its troops to Kigali – its 'special relationship' with Africa was enough.

Since the global re-legimisation process engendered by General de Gaulle in his 'self-determination' referendum in its black African colonies, France has seen itself as a large hen followed by a docile brood of little black chicks. Its former African colonies are not 'foreign' countries just like any other, but 'part of the family', hence the special unit in the President's office. Hence also the ministry to dole out the special funds for the somewhat irresponsible children who need to be helped. This is what French political circles call *'le pré carré'* (our own backyard). Of course, the whole exercise is not completely disinterested. There are some material rewards, not so much in the 'exploitation of the black continent', as surviving Third World Marxists are fond of saying, but rather in using Africa as a money-laundering machine. Overpriced government contracts are given to good trusted friends and dull public money becomes vibrantly alive in private hands. French political parties are partly financed through such operations, political friends are 'rewarded' and loyal Africans get their share. Those who lose elections are excluded from the benefits of this modest cornucopia. But the casual observer imagining that money is the cement of the whole relationship would have the wrong impression. The cement is language and culture. Paris' African backyard remains its backyard because all the chicks cackle in French. There is a high degree of symbiosis between French and francophone African political élites. It is a mixture of many things: old memories[20], shared material interests, delusions of

---

20. Between 1945 and 1960 many of the future politicians of 'independant' French Africa were elected to the French Parliament. Some even became cabinet ministers, and all played their role in the fast moving politics of the Fourth Republic. Apart

grandeur, gossip, sexual peccadilloes – in short a common culture for which there is no equivalent among ex-colonial powers with the possible and partial exception of Portugal.

Of course, the arch-enemy of this cosy relationship, the hissing snake in the Garden of Eden is the 'Anglo-Saxon', the modern reincarnation of *'les Anglais'*. Everybody in France knows that *'les Anglais'* are among the worst enemies the French ever had: they burnt Jeanne d'Arc alive, they stole Canada and India from us in 1763, they exiled Napoleon to a ridiculous little rock in the South Atlantic, and they sank our battlefleet at Mers-el-Kebir in 1940. And to top it all, their women are ugly and their food is terrible, traits which show a basic lack of civilisation. From all eternity they have tried to spoil things for the French, and unfortunately they have usually succeeded. Nowadays they are greatly weakened and do not represent the threat they once did, but they have spawned an evil brood scattered over the four continents, the 'Anglo-Saxons'.

The notion of 'Anglo-Saxon' is hazy yet it also has a deadly clarity. Anybody who speaks English can be 'Anglo-Saxon', and indeed northern Europeans such as the Scandinavians and the Dutch are honorary 'Anglo-Saxons' because they tend to speak English so well[21]. Of course 'Anglo-Saxons' are usually white, but not always. President Yoweri Museveni, as we shall see, was definitely an incarnation of the 'Anglo-Saxon' menace in its truest form: because an 'Anglo-Saxon' is an English-speaker who threatens the French. In the South Pacific, for example, New Zealanders who protest against French nuclear tests are clearly

---

from the surviving Djiboutian autocrat Hassan Gouled Aptidon, this generation of African politicians is now passing away. But it has left behind a certain climate and a nostalgia. Today the Africa unit in the President's office still routinely takes care of African presidential families' medical emergencies, First Ladies' shopping sprees and of freeing a kleptomaniac presidential relative caught shoplifting by the Paris police.

21. The author of this book, being French, is also obviously a traitor because he writes in English. He was told so in no uncertain terms by an interestingly wide cross-section of academics, army officers and politicians. Only journalists seemed immune, probably because they had fallen under the spell of the modern worldwide Anglo-Saxon culture.

'Anglo-Saxon' and ecologists' boats have to be blown up in order to quell the imperialistic threat they represent. In Canada 'Anglo-Saxons' sit in the seats of power in Ottawa, hatching their plots – with some luck *'le Québec Libre'* will soon escape their clutches[22]. In New York devilish Anglo-Saxon cultural activists plan hamburger invasions against French *cuisine* and the mixing of old Edith Piaf songs into rap versions. The Anglo-Saxons want our death – that is, our *cultural* death. They threaten our language and our way of life, and they plan our ultimate anglo-saxonisation. Look at our own children: they all wear base-ball caps with the visor turned backwards, they ride skateboards and they drink Coca-cola. This sounds absurd, but in fact it is both so deadly serious and so crazy at the same time that only humour can bridge the existential gap. The whole syndrome, which for the sake of convenience we could call the 'Fashoda syndrome'[23], is still very much a part of French political thinking today. And it is the main reason – and practically the only one – why Paris intervened so quickly and so deeply in the growing Rwandese crisis.

According to the Fashoda syndrome, the whole world is a cultural, political and economic battlefield between France and the 'Anglo-Saxons'. There is no possible peace, any lull in the confrontation is only tactical; nothing less than the total victory of one of the contending parties will bring an end to the conflict. In fact, the French already know they are doomed, but they will fight on for *'la beauté du geste'*. The French Academy and other

---

22. Unfortunately, the long association of the Quebeckers with the 'Anglo-Saxons' has left them somewhat tainted and unsound politically. Private French remarks about (French) Canadian UN General Roméo Dallaire in Rwanda were often sarcastically aggressive about his 'double dealing' as if, being francophone, he had a 'special duty' towards France.

23. Fashoda is a small southern Sudanese village where, in 1898, the eastbound French forces of Captain Marchand met the southwards-moving British army of Lord Kitchener. The Cape-to-Cairo and Dakar-to-Djibouti dreams were in collision. The result was nearly a European war. For more details see Darrel Bates, *Encounter on the Nile: the Fashoda incident of 1898*, Oxford University Press, 1984. For a nationalistic French view, published in Vichy France soon after the Mers-el-Kebir tragedy, see Général Baratier, *Fachoda. Souvenir de la Mission Marchand*, Paris: Grasset, 1941.

language-purifying devices are important tools in the struggle[24], and of course the African family of nations is a vital ally. At the UN francophone African countries tend to vote along the lines of French suggestions and they share our dislike of the 'Anglo-Saxons' in their black local versions[25]. So they have to be kept happy, first by giving them large amounts of financial help and also by securing the power of their autocrats. This simple policy has been scrupulously followed by every French President from General de Gaulle onwards, and it has worked – in its own way – according to its aims.

From that point of view, the invasion of Rwanda on 1 October 1990 by a group of rebels coming from Uganda was a typical test-case – an obvious 'Anglo-Saxon' plot to destabilise one of 'ours', and one we needed to stop right away if we did not want to see a dangerous spread of the disease. The reaction had to be quick and unambiguous. The message to the rest of francophone Africa was clear: never mind about 'democracy' or 'human rights', these had to be included for public consumption in the President's speech at the La Baule Franco-African summit of 1990, but you do not really have to take them seriously, we will support you whatever happens. The message was well-received and several francophone African heads of state privately congratulated the French government for the speed of its

24. France is probably the only country in the world (together with some Arabic countries who share in their own way the Gallic obsession with linguistic purity) which can boast a cabinet minister for language. The present (1994) holder of that office, Jacques Toubon, tried to have a law passed by Parliament outlawing the use of a number of foreign terms in certain contexts, cutting off public funding from scientific conferences where French would not be the dominant language, and restraining the use of English in movie titles. To his great chagrin, the Constitutional Council ruled the proposed law illegal as contradicting the Declaration of Human Rights which serves as a preamble to the 1958 Constitution.

25. Togolese scapegoating of Ghana to explain away its internal problems and Anglo-baiting in Cameroonian politics are two cases in point. A telling example of the convergence of France's obsession with its own language and of the 'African Connection' is the case of Léopold Sedar Senghor, ex-President of Senegal and today a member of the prestigious French Academy, who is always referred to as an '*Agrégé de Grammaire*'. The fact that a black man can so love the French language as to become '*Agrégé de Grammaire*' fills the French soul with a sweetness making up for years of 'Anglo-Saxon' petty insults.

reaction in Rwanda[26]. So all was well in the family, the cherished 'credibility' of French African involvement was buttressed and a routine consensus developed between the Socialist government and the Gaullist opposition around the intervention issue.

This is how Paris found itself backing an ailing dictatorship in a tiny distant country producing only bananas and a declining coffee crop without even asking for political reform as a price for its support. This blind commitment was to have catastrophic consequences because, as the situation radicalised, the Rwandese leadership kept believing that *no matter what it did*, French support would always be forthcoming. And it had no valid reasons for believing otherwise.

Although prey to its own contradictions, Belgium felt no such automatic need to give blind support to the Habyarimana regime. Sending troops to Rwanda had been its instinctive response to the possible security threats which could have developed for the large Belgian expatriate community there (about 1,700 people), but after a few days, doubts began to appear. The Belgian community was not threatened at all but distinct political problems started to develop: a massive wave of arrests, news of civilian massacres, the unquestioning nature of French support for the Kigali regime regardless of its behaviour, President Habyarimana's refusal to address seriously the root-causes of the emergency[27] – all these factors combined to make politicians in Brussels question the intervention. But then the debate quickly changed its shape in order to fit into the traditional battle-lines of Belgian domestic politics. Habyarimana's regime had for many years been the darling of the international Christian Democratic Movement, which had sprung to its

26. Interview with a staff member of the Presidential Africa Unit, Paris, 10 October 1990.
27. President Habyarimana had declared (*Le Soir*, 30 October 1990) that he would 'agree to talk with the forces backing the rebels once they will have left Rwandese territory'. This meant, first, that he would not talk with the rebels themselves; secondly, that the rebellion was largely manufactured from outside (i.e. by Uganda) and that the rebels had no right to stand on Rwandese soil. This seemed like a poor start for a negotiated settlement.

support after 1 October. In Belgium Christian Democratic support (and to a degree Flemish support) meant an almost automatic francophone Liberal anti-clerical reaction[28]. After Prime Minister Willy Martens and Foreign Minister Mark Eyskens had gone to East Africa on 18 October to meet Presidents Habyarimana, Museveni and Arap Moi in an attempt at regional mediation, they came home to face a medium-size political storm. The ensuing debate soon convinced them that the domestic political price to be paid was much too high if one took into account the extremely uncertain peace prospects of the intervention. As a result, on 27 October Brussels announced its intention to withdraw from Rwanda as of 1 November. The declaration was accompanied by an urgent appeal to France, the Netherlands and Germany to help organise and transport an inter-African peace-keeping force for Rwanda, the first of many such ineffectual plans designed to enable western powers to dodge any responsibility behind conveniently neutral excuses.

Settling down into a war culture

Given the tense political situation which had prevailed in Rwanda before the October invasion, war could be used by the government to take advantage of the 'Tutsi feudalist threat' and recreate around itself the atmosphere of unanimity it used to enjoy before the onset of the democratisation movement. Using the fake attack on Kigali as a pretext, it launched a massive wave of arrests[29]. It soon became obvious that these arrests did not target supporters of the RPF (there were very few and even these few were not all known to the police) but indiscriminately swept

28. On this aspect of the problem, see Filip Reyntjens, *L'Afrique des Grands Lacs en crise*, op. cit., pp. 101–3.
29. On 9 October the Ministry of Justice admitted the arrest of about 3,000 people. The real numbers were soon to swell to nearly 10,000, some of them being held till April 1991. There were very few charges and almost no trials (see Fédération Internationale des Droits de l'Homme (henceforth FIDH) *et al., Rwanda. violations massives et systématiques des Droits de l'Homme depuis le 1er Octobre 1990*, Paris, 1993, p. 14).

up educated Tutsi, opposition-minded Hutu, anyone who was in the bad books of the power élite (and even of their friends or business connections: arrests were often seen as a way of cancelling outstanding debts) and foreign African residents, mainly Zaireans and Ugandans, who as small businessmen were generally good for a financial squeeze[30]. Conditions of detention were terrible, people being herded like cattle into buildings unsuitable for holding such large numbers and at times not given food or water for several days. Beatings, thefts and rapes were commonplace; some of the prisoners were beaten to death simply because they happened to do something to displease a drunken guard[31]. Many people had believed the fake fighting on the night of 4–5 October to be genuine and they expected RPF fighters to attack Kigali at any time. Everyone was on edge and the soldiers threatened to shoot all the detainees if the RPF entered the capital. In the north the army was fighting around Gabiro but the Zaïrean 'allies' had caused such havoc by looting and raping Rwandese civilians as if *they* were the enemy, that Habyarimana had to ask President Mobutu to withdraw them. MRND activists saw spies everywhere and the Justice Minister Theodore Mujyanama had declared 'There is cast-iron proof of guilt against all those who have been arrested ... and to be released does not mean that one is innocent.'

The public prosecutor, Alphonse-Marie Nkubito, was considered too liberal, and replaced by a hardliner. On the national radio the Minister of Defence asked the population to 'track down and arrest the infiltrators'. This licence to kill had immediate effects in the Mutara region where some of the defeated RPF had actually taken refuge. Between 11 and 13 October an estimated 348 Tutsi civilians were massacred and

30. See Véronique Kiesel, 'Une épuration qui ne vise pas que les Tutsi' (*Le Soir*, 9 October 1990) and Filip Reyntjens, *L'Afrique des Grands Lacs en crise*, op. cit., pp. 95–6.
31. Interview with L.M., a Tutsi university professor who was detained for about one month starting on 6 October (Paris, 12 July 1994).

more than 500 houses burned in the Kibilira *commune*[32]. None of the victims was a RPF fighter or a civilian supporter, of whom there seemed to be none. In almost every case, the killings were organised and led by the local authorities, a pattern that was to become only too famliar. When questioned about these events at a press conference, President Habyarimana answered: 'Civilians? Why should we kill civilians if they are not involved in the fighting? There is no revolt. Everybody is obeying.' Retrospectively, the last (true) sentence strikes a particular chill.

The French military mission deployed in Rwanda (code name '*Noroit*', French for 'north wind') did not seem unduly disturbed by the civilian human rights situation. On Friday 6 October the French Prime Minister, Michel Rocard, had declared on the French TV channel TF 1 that: 'We have sent troops to protect French citizens and nothing more. This is a high security mission and a republican duty.' This may have been a brave statement but it was an inaccurate one since France had evacuated all its expatriates within a few days[33] while the soldiers stayed on. They were not directly involved in combat duties[34], but they performed a variety of tasks which not only freed Rwandese troops for frontline duty but also bolstered their morale and increased the efficiency of the FAR as a fighting machine. They took care of the airport guard and logistics (large amounts of

32. See FIDH, *Rwanda*, op. cit., pp. 18–22, and Association Rwandaise pour la Défense des Droits de la Personne et des Libertés Publiques (henceforth ADL), *Rapport sur les Droits de l'Homme au Rwanda*, Kigali, 1992, pp. 101–16. The French press had carried the story as early as 16 October (Jean Hélène in *Le Monde*: 'Les réfugiés dénoncent les massacres perpétrés par l'armée').

33. All those who so desired were allowed to go back to Rwanda by early November 1990. But, although the fighting was limited to the extreme north of Rwanda where there were no French expatriates, the pretext of 'protecting French citizens' was the one used up till the very end, when French troops finally withdrew in December 1993.

34. At least not officially. In June 1992, while on a research trip to the RPF-held area around Byumba, the author was caught in a Rwandese government artillery bombardment. From inside the shelter, the RPF fighters could tune in on the FAR frequency and it was possible to follow quite clearly on the radio the orders given by the officer commanding the government battery. They were given in French, with an accent that could not conceivably have been that of a native African.

weapons and equipment were being flown in), looked after the government's helicopters and when necessary flew them, organised artillery positioning and ammunition supply, and ensured radio communications. In addition, they undertook rather more sinister duties such as supervising Rwandese military security operations (including the interrogation of detained suspects) and even manning roadblocks[35]. For the men of *'Noroit'*, the point of their presence in Rwanda was clear: short of direct infantry combat, they had to help the Forces Armées Rwandaises in every possible way in winning the war they were fighting against the invading RPF.

Their perception of the war situation was simple. French forces had been sent in to help an allied country against a foreign invading force. All this refugee business was merely a cover-up. It was *'les Angliches'*[36] who were behind it all and even *'les Ricains'*[37] through their buddy Museveni. In fact, it was all good fun, a way of fighting it out with the 'Anglo-Saxon' enemy by proxy, without the need for a major war. A sort of real life war-game, and a good chance to practise a bit of operational training. And by God, we were going to win, because our boys were the best and these FAR chaps were well trained and well equipped and had good morale! They also had a good cause. The French army, though conservative, had definitely rallied to the Republic since its last political flirtation with right-wing authoritarianism during the Algerian war (1954–62). The officer corps was by now fully persuaded, probably for the first time in its history, that democratic ideals were the only acceptable form of legitimacy for a political regime. This feeling coexisted with a strong streak of almost archaic

---

35. Their instructions appeared to have been rather crude since most of the time they simply asked bluntly: 'Are you Hutu or Tutsi?', causing a certain amount of irritation among the civilian population (interview with RPF civilian cadre Roger Rutikanga, Kabale, 6 July 1994). As for the interrogations of POWs by French officers, they are mentioned in the mission account of Maître Eric Gillet, a human rights lawyer from the Brussels bar association who went to Rwanda between 12 and 20 August 1991 to inquire (see *Africa Confidential*, 22 October 1991).
36. A somewhat outmoded French slang word for 'the Brits'.
37. Same for 'the Yanks'.

republicanism dating back to the wars of the French Revolution
and the Empire, and with a decided taste for law and order.
Republicanism and democracy, yes, but *'pas le bordel'* ('not a
bloody mess'). These simple ideological features made up the
somewhat uncomplicated political creed of the French Army.
They fitted perfectly with what it perceived as the reality of
Rwandese politics and as the causes of the war. For the men
of *'Noroit'*, the Habyarimana version of the situation, which their
Rwandese counterparts never tired of repeating, made perfect
sense. There had been a 'social revolution' in 1959 (a little like
the French one in 1789, and therefore an event with a strong
legitimacy content), in which the 'aristocrats' had been chased
from power. Many of them had fled abroad and were now
'émigrés', like ours during the French Revolution – and they
were trying to stage a come-back to take up the reins of power
once more. Like ours too, they had the support of foreign
powers hostile to the new popular regime. So in Rwanda the
French army was in the position of those revolutionary soldiers
of 1792 who fought Prussians and 'émigrés' alike. A bit outdated
perhaps, but after all this was Africa, where history runs behind
schedule. As for a proof that the Habyarimana regime was
democratic, they were perfectly satisfied with the argument that
since the Hutu represented 85% of the population (and since
in Africa everything is tribal), a Hutu regime was *ipso facto*
democratic[38]. Civilian Hutu opponents were merely ambitious
men who wanted to *'foutre le bordel'* ('raise hell'), using 'democracy' as a pretext for replacing the existing government and
pocketing the money. Since, as we shall see, this crude view of
the opposition contained an element of truth and strongly
encouraged by the MRND cadres and FAR officers with whom
the French were in constant contact, it became an accepted creed.

38. This somewhat simplistic view of 'democracy' by ethnic consensus in the context
of African politics was rather widely shared, especially by the expatriate community in Rwanda which appreciated the regime's good law and order record,
its quite efficient handling of the communication infrastructure and its deference
to the whites. That it would also be democratic was to have your soul and your
money on the same side (see 'Manifeste des 101 expatriés pour soutenir le régime',
Le Soir, 22 October 1990).

Their African comrade-in-arms of the Forces Armées Rwandaises (FAR) were quickly ceasing to be the small, rather professional and disciplined army they had been at the time of the RPF attack. The Tutsi invasion had rekindled strong irrational, partly self-induced fears in the Hutu MRND élite. As we shall see, many opposition Hutu were far from feeling reassured, and felt caught between the devil and the deep blue sea. These fears translated themselves into a frantic recruitment drive for the army. The FAR, which had numbered 5,200 on 1 October 1990, had grown to 15,000 by mid-1991, 30,000 by the end of that year, and 50,000 by the time the Arusha peace negotiations began in mid-1992. Of course, this tenfold growth in the space of two years did pose a few problems. One that was easily resolved was weapons: France supplied all that was needed, either directly or, as we see later, by arranging foreign contracts, mainly with Egypt and South Africa. The second problem was manpower itself. If some idealists enlisted to 'fight the feudalists', most of those who joined did so in order to have an opportunity to eat, drink[39] and loot since pay was minimal and irregular. The volunteers were mostly landless peasants, urban unemployed and even some foreign drifters[40]. They had little or no education, which complicated the process of military training. Nevertheless, for most of the war the FAR maintained fairly high professional standards for an African army. The officers were usually capable and the discipline remained reasonably good. Although rough and at times rowdy, the Rwandese army was several notches above that of Uganda during the time of Idi Amin or the motley crew of bandits that calls itself the Zaïrean army. This discipline eventually weakened in mid-1992 when the first cease-fire and contradictory rumours of forced demobilisation led to rioting and indiscipline among the troops. But they fought courageously, though at times ineptly, and kept their cohesion even in defeat. This reasonable degree of

39. Each soldier was entitled to two bottles of beer a day, a luxury by Rwandese standards.
40. In June 1992, near Byumba, the author met a Kenyan FAR prisoner of war.

efficiency has an interesting political corollary: contrary to some African armies which loot and kill civilians as they please, one can say that when the FAR went on the rampage against the populace, with extremely few exceptions, it was acting on orders from above.

The final problem posed by the growth of the army was financial. Its budget grew out of all proportion between 1990 and 1992 and, even if the French did their best to plug the gap, there remained a growing deficit. The international community was not unsympathetic, and even the International Monetary Fund, where the hated 'Anglo-Saxons' hold sway, decided to approve a credit of SDR 30.66 million (about US $41m) for Rwanda[41]. But money was desperately short and in spite of the Rwandese government introducing a new 'solidarity tax' of 8% on all salaries in May 1991, by the middle of the year the budgetary deficit was estimated at around 23 billion Rwandese francs (US $188m).

The reorganisation of the RPF

By early November 1990 the RPF had looked almost finished. Shaken by the deaths of Fred Rwigyema, Peter Banyingana, Chris Bunyenyezi and several hundred soldiers and NCOs, the guerrilla movement was reeling. Some of the men hid in the Akagera national park where a few starved to death[42], while a group led by Captain Kayitare and Major Nduguta reached as far south as the Rusumo-Kayonza road, but then found itself completely cut off and without communications with the main body of the RPF further north. Confusion was at its height. Paul Kagame, who had hastened back from the United States,

---

41. *Africa Economic Digest* (6 May 1991).
42. To give a measure of the extremes soon reached by propaganda, they were accused by government supporters to do so in order to create ecological havoc and to ruin the tourist industry. See Jean Rumiya, 'La guerre d'Octobre, une agression préméditée pour la reconquête du pouvoir' in François-Xavier Bangamwabo *et al.* (eds), *Les relations interethniques au Rwanda à la lumière de l'agression d'Octobre 1990*, Ruhengeri: Editions Universitaires du Rwanda, 1991, pp. 209–22.

decided on a desperate measure: to regroup what was left of his forces in a totally inaccessible area out of reach of the Rwandese army, lie low, bide his time and then, if he managed to survive, strike a spectacular blow. He asked President Museveni to let them cross back into Uganda and was granted permission, provided the RPF troops crossed at night, on foot, and would have gone back into Rwanda by the morning. The survivors completed the exhausting march during the night and then started to climb up into the high cold country of the Virunga volcanoes[43]. They stayed there for about two months without operating. The surroundings were very harsh and at a height of some 5,000 metres, with only light clothing, several soldiers froze to death. But Major Kagame[44] managed to use the respite they had bought so dearly to reorganise.

The first task he addressed was to strengthen the leadership. Colonel Alexis Kanyarengwe, Habyarimana's old accomplice and later rival who had been living in exile[45], had joined the Front and been appointed chairman. Having a Hutu as nominal head of the RPF was of course good politics but it also raised a number of questions on the nature of the Tutsi/Hutu relationship within (and without) the organisation. We will come back to those later.

Apart from Colonel Kanyarengwe and a couple of others, the leadership of the RPF was solidly Tutsi and exiles from Uganda played a major role in it. The vice-chairman Patrick Mazimpaka, a bright young geologist who had come back from Canada where he was studying in order to join the Front, had grown up in Uganda. So had Colonel Frank Mugambage, who over time developed into the Front's second-ranking military man after Kagame. Théogène Rudasingwa, the Front's secretary-general, was also of 'Ugandan' origin, as was Aloysia Inyumba, the tireless financial commissioner who, from her Kampala base, operated a worldwide fund-raising network. Wilson Rutaysire, the commissioner for information; Ann Gahengayire,

---

43. Catharine Watson, 'War and Waiting', *Africa Report*, Nov./Dec. 1992.
44. He later gave himself the rank of major-general, more in keeping with his leadership of the whole organisation.
45. He had been involved in the Lizinde coup attempt of April 1980.

the commissioner for social affairs; Christine Omutoni, the commissioner for refugees; and even Frank Tega, the commissioner
for youth and sports, had also all been raised in Uganda. This
inevitably posed certain problems because the Front was quickly
diversifying its sources of recruitment and the 100% 'Ugandan'
fighting core was rapidly becoming much more geographically
diversified. Volunteers were joining from all over the Tutsi
Banyarwanda diaspora, at first in a trickle and later in ever larger
numbers. The first to come in late 1990 were members of the
large exile community in Burundi. Then other volunteers arrived
from Zaïre, Tanzania and even such exotically distant places as
Brazzaville, Brussels and New York City. The Front acted as
a magnet for the exile youth, none of whom knew Rwanda but
who had all grown up hearing about it as a land of plenty which
their parents dreamed about and where they would one day
return. But just as with the young European Zionist Jews in
1945, there was a basic ambiguity in not being able or willing
to face the fact that others living on the same land felt they had
an exclusive right to it and would try to keep the newcomers
out.

But in spite of this diversification of recruitment, few of the
main Front leaders came from outside Uganda. Among those one
can mention Denis Polisi, the Second Vice-Chairman, who had
fled to Burundi during the 1973 pogroms; Gaspard Nyirinkindi,
also from Burundi; Jacques Bihozagara, who had abandoned his
job in Bujumbura to become the Front's representative in
Europe, based in Brussels; Dr Emile Rwamasirabo, commissioner for Health, who had fled to Belgium in 1973 but who,
disenchanted with life in Europe, had later gone to Uganda to
practise medicine at Mulago hospital; or Tito Rutaremara who
joined the Front as a sort of resident philosopher after spending more than ten years as a Parisian Left Bank intellectual.
Although well respected, these men could not really represent
a counterweight to the original Uganda core group[46].

46. It is up to this point (and to this point only) that the French reasoning about
    'Anglo-Saxon' influence held a certain amount of validity. If the majority of the

The *émigré* component of the early RPF recruitment gave it a very high average standard of education: almost all its soldiers had gone to primary school, around half had attended secondary school and nearly 20% had reached university, making it probably the best educated guerrilla force the world had ever seen[47]. These high standards declined later in the war when very young boys, at times almost children, joined from inside Rwanda itself. These recruits came to the RPF more or less in self-defence because the insecurity and persecution of the Tutsi minority were increasing as the conflict dragged on. By early 1991 the RPF had grown to over 5,000 men, by the end of 1992 it numbered nearly 12,000, and when the country exploded in flames in April 1994 it had probably had more than 25,000. But by then the recruitment patterns had changed radically.

RPF finances, as well as its fighters, came from the Tutsi diaspora scattered abroad. In a pattern similar to that which made Jewish communities all over the world give financial support to Zionism and motivated the regular contributions of Eritreans in exile to their National Liberation Fronts, Tutsi Banyarwanda from Kampala to Brussels and from Paris to Kinshasa gave what they could for 'the cause'. The main contributions came from exile communities in Canada and the United States because they were the richest, but many small contributions were also gathered from among the larger and poorer communities in Africa. An additional source of funding came from a few Rwandese businessmen who had had political problems with the regime and hoped to recoup their losses. This was the case for example with the Tutsi Valens Kajeguhakwa,

---

RPF frontline fighters were definitely not English-speakers after 1992, the Front's top leadership remained 'Ugandan'. These divisions are of course only mildly relevant since the actors did not see the problems according to such categories.

47. See Catharine Watson, 'War and Waiting', op. cit. This author met inside Rwanda in June 1992 several young fighters who matter-of-factly asked him about the health of some of his university colleagues with whose writings they seemed perfectly familiar. This high level of education is one of the reasons for the RPF's efficiency as a fighting force, the other being the long military experience gained on Ugandan battlefields by the ex-NRA officers in its top leadership.

former manager of the Rwandese national petroleum company and of the Hutu Silas Majyambere, former president of the Kigali chamber of commerce; in helping the Front, they were motivated by very down-to-earth economic considerations. But even when these different sources of financing were added together, the Front was not rich. Its representatives abroad tended to lead Spartan lives and the leadership was very money-conscious. Contrary to what had happened in several African guerrilla organisations where leaders routinely used the movement's money for their private ends, there were never any rumours of financial misappropriation in the RPF.

The last problem faced by the Front was weapons and ammunition. RPF soldiers had carried with them a fair-sized quantity of armament taken from the NRA, but growing numbers had to be equipped and they were also short of ammunition. A simple calculation shows that the number of shells they fired at the government troops between the invasion and mid-1992 was vastly greater than what that they could possibly have brought down with them from Uganda[48]. So, where did the difference come from? Obviously, although an increasing proportion of its military supplies was bought on the international arms market as the war went on[49], the RPF continued for a long time to rely on its Ugandan connection. The exact nature of the supply process is not clear but it seems to have been somewhat decentralised. Notwithstanding his friendship with Paul Kagame and of his sympathy for the RPF cause, President Museveni was too keenly aware of the displeasure of OECD countries and the downright hostility of France not to be prudent, especially at a time when more than 60% of Uganda's foreign currency resources came from international aid. So rather than give large amounts of direct help to his RPF friends, in the way that the Ethiopians had helped the Sudanese SPLA

48. *Source*: French Ministry of Defence, April 1992.
49. The early 1990s were the years during which the collapse of the former Soviet Union sharply drove down international weapon and ammunition prices as large quantities of these commodities were put on the market by dollar-starved inheritor regimes.

between 1983 and 1991, Museveni seems to have decided not to promise anything but rather to look the other way when Major-General Kagame and his colleagues used their old NRA contacts to obtain help from their former comrade-in-arms. An NRA officer in Mbarara almost admitted as much to the author[50]:

'I have fought side by side with these chaps not only against Obote but later in the North. One of them saved my life when we were fighting against Alice [Lakwena]. Would you expect me to refuse them now when they come to me because they haven't any more ammunition?'

So NRA target practice consumed disproportionately high quantities of ammunition, supplies vanished from military stores and later, when the World Bank was pressing for drastic reductions in NRA troop numbers, the surplus weapons left idle by demobilisation found their way south[51].

Major-General Kagame had two things in mind when he took his men into the cold volcanic highlands of the Virunga chain: to buy time and regroup after the October disasters, and to be ready to swoop down on Ruhengeri. The latter had several attractions for the RPF. Given its geographical location, it was the only *préfecture* seat which they could think of storming without being spotted long enough in advance for the FAR to move troops forward to anticipate their attack. It was also a key center of the 'blessed region', the heartland of the regime. Striking it would create a climate of insecurity in the country, giving a feeling that the guerrilla was capable of reaching even the most strongly protected targets. Furthermore it contained the largest prison in Rwanda, with more than 1,000 inmates, many of them political prisoners. Among those was Théoneste Lizinde, detained since 1980, one of the men who knew most of President

---

50. Interview with the author, 12 June 1992.
51. Actually, this quite important source of equipment was what enabled the RPF to rearm during the uneasy period between the signing of the Arusha peace agreement on 4 August 1993 and the country's explosion on 6 April 1994. So the World Bank contributed unwittingly to the RPF victory in the Rwandese civil war.

Habyarimana's old secrets, especially about the circumstances under which former President Grégoire Kayibanda and his ministers had died. Lizinde was detained under conditions of maximum security, and his gaolers had instructions to kill him if he tried to escape.

Kagame attacked Ruhengeri on 23 January 1991, causing immediate panic. When the prison authorities called Kigali to report the assault, they were ordered to kill all the inmates immediately. The prisoners had already been told by their guards that this was the fate which awaited them and they had no doubt that the threat would be carried out[52]. But an officer, Colonel Charles Uwihoreye, refused to obey the execution order and saved the prisoners, who were freed when the RPF stormed the prison[53]. Among these was Colonel Lizinde, who was immediately recruited by the Front in spite of his dubious past. The guerrillas held the town for a day and then withdrew before reinforcements could be brought in. Apart from the freeing of the prisoners, the RPF had managed to recover a fairly large amount of military equipment and, more importantly, to cause a psychological and political shock throughout Rwanda. The message was clear: even if it could not win and occupy ground in a conventional military fashion, the Front still had a military capacity that had to be taken seriously, and any political reform undertaken in the future would have to take its existence into account.

52. Interview with L.M. (Paris, 12 July 1994). L.M., who had already been arrested in October 1990 in the first wave of detention following the RPF attack, then freed and later re-arrested without ever being charged. It seems his main offence was being a Tutsi university professor. He was freed from gaol by the RPF but refused to join the guerrillas. He was left free by the government and later came to France for further studies. His whole family – wife, children, parents and collaterals, some twenty people in all – were slaughtered in April 1994, with the single exception of his fifteen-month-old baby daughter who was grabbed by a neighbour and carried all the way to Burundi.

53. Colonel Uwihoreye was later arrested and jailed for a year after a parody of judicial process. He took refuge abroad after being temporarily released and publicly denounced the reasons for his arrest (*The New African*, November 1992; *Africa Confidential* [French version], 11 November 1992).

The advent of multiparty politics

The RPF invasion had acted as a violent outside catalyst on an internal political situation which had been on the verge of transformation. If President Habyarimana had hoped to intimidate the democratic opposition through the wave of arrests in October, he had miscalculated. The effects of these harsh measures were rather to reinforce resolution on both sides. The opposition felt that it had to push for quick political changes in order to prevent the possiblity of such arbitrariness becoming 'normal' in the war situation; for its part, the MRND hardcore grumbled at the President's 'softness' and started to denounce the Hutu democrats as *ibyitso* ('accomplices'), meaning pro-RPF fifth-columnists. This was far from being the truth, as we shall see, but the accusation stuck – with terrible consequences.

In any case, moving from thirty years of single-party dictatorship to multiparty democratic politics at the same time as fighting a civil war was bound to be a rough exercise. The first 'independent party' to appear was created in exile by Silas Majyambere, the former president of the Kigali chamber of commerce and crony of Habyarimana who had flirted for a while with the RPF. On 9 November 1990, barely more than a month after the invasion, he created in Brussels the Union du Peuple Rwandais (UPR). But rather than offering a political programme, his opening document[54] was a broadside, first going back over the various political assassinations of recent years, then moving on to cases of government corruption, press intimidation and arbitrary arrests. While most of the facts he denounced were true, the general tone of the document (the author presented himself as 'one of the most popular economic operators in Rwanda and in the whole world') and the life-history of its author called for a minimum of caution[55].

54. 'Déclaration de M. Silas Majyambere, industriel, à l'attention de tout le peuple Rwandais brisé par le pouvoir dictatorial du Président Habyarimana Juvénal et sa clique' (no place, no date – Brussels, November 1990).
55. Within a year, Majyambere had lost all his urge for political reform (some say after obtaining some personal reassurance from Kigali) and moved to Kampala

Probably thinking that with such adversaries he could always work out some kind of a deal, President Habyarimana had made on 11 November 1990 a very liberal speech in which everybody could find something to be pleased with[56]. For the Hutu opposition a multiparty system would soon be allowed and there would be a constitutional referendum in June 1991, and for the Tutsi who could be attracted by RPF propaganda there was a promise that the mention of ethnicity (*ubwoko*) would be removed from all future identity cards and other official papers[57]. For the foreigners the President praised the Structural Adjustment Plan (SAP) and said it was an excellent thing for the Rwandese economy. On 28 December the National Synthesis Commission published the first draft of a proposed National Charter which was supposed to open up the rules of Rwandese political life[58].

During the winter of 1990-1, with a feeling that change was in the air, opponents held a series of clandestine meetings. But Article 7 of the 1978 Constitution, which gave legal sanction to the one-party state, was still officially in operation and aspiring democrats were careful, especially remembering the selective killings of 1988-9. Finally, in March 1991 a group of 237 opponents decided to come out in the open and publish an 'Appeal for the recreation of the Mouvement Démocratique Républicain (MDR)'[59]. Although not very innovative the choice was quite interesting in terms of Rwandese history. The old Parmehutu had been closely associated with the anti-Tutsi pogroms of

---

where he got into trouble with the law for selling lorries he did not own. He then announced that he was going to open a supermarket, but only took the money of his Belgian business partner and vanished.

56. See the Kigali weekly *La Relève* (16 November 1990).

57. Two weeks later, on the morning of 25 November the Minister of the Interior himself went on the air on Radio Rwanda to set matters straight: the mentioning of *ubwoko* in official documents was to be kept and nothing would be changed. And that was that. This ethnic mention was to cost thousands of lives during the terrible days of April-May 1994.

58. *La Relève* (28 December 1990). The draft Charter was never actually voted but a process of constitutional reform based on the use of art. 91 of the 1978 Constitution was eventually to lead to an abrogation of monopartism six months later.

59. Published in *Le Démocrate* (March 1991).

1959–61, and the name MDR (Mouvement Démocratique Rwandais at the time) had only been added later to project a more sedate image. MDR-Parmehutu had been outlawed in 1973 after the Habyarimana coup. It had been a party with a strong bipolar geographical base in the Gitarama region, Kayibanda's home area, and around Ruhengeri in the north. As time passed, the old party became quite idealised for a number of people, especially in the old MDR-Parmehutu bastions. This is apparent in the March 1991 'MDR appeal' which describes its predecessor in glamorous terms:

> MDR-Parmehutu was the party of the ordinary man and it never betrayed its democratic and republican principles: respect of multipartism, freedom of adherence to the party, free elections at all levels and clear separation of powers.

This is in fact a fairy-tale view of a party which, without having gone through the constitutional step of declaring itself legally a single party, had nevertheless eliminated all its competitors, rigged its own internal candidacy processes, and acted with almost as much intolerance as Habyarimana's MRND. But the key to its retrospective glamorisation was regional feeling, a very strong factor in Rwanda. In the final stages of the regional struggles caused by the shrinking of the country's wealth since the mid-1980s, the northerners had started to fight among themselves, the Gisenyi mafia against the Ruhengeri group. And the Gisenyi/Bushiru boys, supported by Mme Habyarimana, had usually won. The hard-core *akazu* (as opposed to the outer circles of the privileged group) came from there. So the MDR represented not only a vehicle for abstract 'democratic' demands, but was also a reconstruction of the old Kayibanda regional alliance against the Gisenyi *akazu*. In the new published party lists, 30% of the MDR supporters came from Gitarama and 17% from Ruhengeri[60], thus recreating the regional axis which had been the driving force of the 1959 anti-Tutsi revolution and which could now be used instead against the regime's northwestern

---

60. Filip Reyntjens, *L'Afrique des Grands Lacs en crise*, op. cit., p. 106.

Hutu hard core. But in order to reap the advantages of the old mental associations while at the same time avoiding their more unsavoury aspects, the Parmehutu name with its violent-connotations had to be dropped and MDR, with its milder associations, put forward. It is interesting to note that when, about a year later, an ethnically more radically-oriented group took shape within the reborn MDR, it chose to use the name Parmehutu to indicate its different character without formally splitting the party.

But this recycling of the old MDR-Parmehutu was not attractive to the whole opposition, especially the more liberally-inclined inhabitants of Butare *préfecture*. Butare, under its colonial name Astrida, had been the administrative capital of Rwanda during the Belgian times. It was where the first university had been built, and the town boasted a certain intellectual sophistication which led it to consider Kigali people as *parvenus* and the northern university campus of Ruhengeri created by the Habyarimana regime as a fake. It had very mixed memories of the old Kayibanda regime and was traditionally a milder area in terms of ethnic relations. Tutsi were numerous in the *préfecture*, and this had never posed any particular problem. The virulent anti-Tutsi image of the MDR was not considered attractive, and Butare became the centre of a second opposition party which quickly organised itself in April-May, named Parti Social Démocrate (PSD). If the MDR had a broad populist approach, the new PSD tried to position itself on the centre-left and to attact a clientele of teachers, civil servants and professionals.

A third opposition party emerged in the spring of 1991 as the Parti Libéral (PL). This was a very urban party which tended to attract businessmen and was generally considered centre-right in European political terms. With no particular geographical base, it was disseminated all over the country and soon counted in its ranks a large number of well-to-do Tutsi. Since its attitude on the ethnic question was obviously liberal, it also tended to attract people whose ethnic status was ambiguous, such as the 'Hutsi' (children of mixed parentage[61]) or people married to

---

61. Rwanda being a patrilineal society, children of mixed parentage belong to their
    father's group. But this tended to be less true in urban situations among educated

members of the other ethnic group. As Landwald Ndasingwa, one of the PL leaders, was fond of saying, 'I am a Tutsi, my wife is a white Canadian, several members of my family are married to Hutu, in fact we are all tired of this ethnic business.' Attractive as this open-mindedness was, it was of course more typical of the urban cultural background of the PL cadres than of feelings among the population at large, or even of the opposition in general. As we see in more detail in the next chapter, opposition parties were far from being automatically liberal on the ethnic issue, and positions *vis-à-vis* the RPF were something else again.

A fourth party appeared early in 1991, the Parti Démocrate-Chrétien (PDC), a genuine Christian Democratic group which had great difficulty coming into being because the Catholic church had always solidly supported President Habyarimana and because the MRND had always been warmly welcomed in the Christian Democratic international circles. The church's game in Rwanda had always been clear: total support for the regime in exchange for a rather open-minded ethnic policy and a free hand in social, educational and even financial matters. And even if the church had lately distanced its politics from those of the ruling party, this was not the case with the Christian Democratic International which still invited the MRND minister of commerce François Nzabahimana as Rwanda's official representative at its November 1991 conference in Brussels[62]. In such circumstances it was difficult for an opposition Christian Democratic party to make political room for itself, but the PDC gamely tried to do so.

---

people, where 'half castes' were usually aware of their mixed parentage and felt more reluctant to adopt strong 'Tutsi' or 'Hutu' positions.

62. *Africa Confidential*, (22 November 1991). Christian Democrats and the Catholic Church had a definite pro-Hutu slant, whoever these Hutu could be, probably because of the 'sociological majority' line of reasoning. The clandestine extremist PALIPEHUTU movement was also present at the Brussels conference, and two weeks later it carried out several terrorist attacks in Burundi. On the other hand the Belgian missionary priest Jeff Vleugels, who headed the province of Rwanda for the White Fathers, described RPF soldiers in the following terms: 'Thirteen- or fourteen-year-old children, drugged and given weapons by their leaders who coldbloodedly send them to certain death' (Provincial Letter, dated 29 March 1991).

On 28 April 1991 the MRND held an extraordinary congress and changed its statutes to adapt to the coming of multipartism. On 10 June a new constitution was proclaimed, allowing the existence of several political parties and a week later the law governing the way they would function was voted in. By early July all the existing *de facto* opposition parties were in the process of officially registering. On 5 July, in keeping with the time the MRND added another 'D' to its name to become the Mouvement Révolutionnaire National pour le Développement *et la Démocratie*. It seemed that Rwanda had made its choice and was heading down the democratic road. A wave of optimism swept the country. It was somewhat premature.

4

SLOUCHING TOWARDS DEMOCRACY[1]
(July 1991–June 1992)

The problems of democratisation

One of the first things the young democratic parties came to realise after the proclamation of the new constitution was that President Habyarimana's view of their existence was largely decorative. Nothing much had changed from his point of view since the famous 5 July 1990 speech where he had announced the advent of multipartism. His concept of democracy seemed to be having a number of fashionably 'democratic' political parties around while the old MRND(D) would carry on very much as before, the whole point of the exercise being to please the French. In order to achieve his purpose, he tried a number of delaying tactics. The first was to favour the birth of a great number of small ineffectual 'opposition parties': the Parti socialiste Rwandais (PSR), the Rassemblement Travailliste pour la Démocratie (RTD), the Parti Révolutionnaire du Rwanda (PARERWA) and many others of various hues and colours. There was even an ecologist party, the PECO, a Muslim party, the Parti Démocratique Islamique (PDI)[2] and a bizarrely-named Mouvement des Femmes et du Bas-Peuple (MFBP or 'Movement of the Women and of the Lower Classes'). In all there were ten of them and they played no active part in actual political life up till the day in March 1993[3] when the President decided to start using them to block the peace negotiation process.

1. This title is derived from a paper by Irving Gershenberg on the 1966 'revolution' in Uganda: 'Slouching towards socialism: Obote's Uganda', *African Studies Review*, vol. 15, no. 1 (April 1972), pp. 79–95.
2. There is a small and complex Muslim community in Rwanda, both native and foreign, which is well described in José Hamim Kagabo, *L'Islam et les 'Swahili' au Rwanda*, Paris: Editions de l'Ecole des Hautes Etudes en Sciences Sociales, 1988.
3. See Chapter 5.

But in March 1992 an eleventh offspring of democracy was born, this one with a fire and brimstone capacity for future trouble. It was the Coalition pour la Défense de la République (CDR), a radical Hutu racist party working on the right of the MRND and goading it and the regime for their supposed 'softness' towards the RPF and its democratic *ibyitso* ('accomplices').

The CDR was the brainchild of a rather unusual character on the Rwandese political scene – Jean Shyirambere Barahinyura, a well-educated man who had studied first in the Soviet Union and then in West Germany. In 1988 he had published a violently muckracking pamphlet against Habyarimana[4], which seemed to have been largely motivated by the fact that his wife Immaculée Mukamugema had been imprisoned for six years after allegedly being involved in the Lizinde/Kanyarengwe coup plot of 1980. Despite its intemperate tone, the book had caused quite a stir in the parochial world of pre-1990 Rwandese politics and its author had definitely been put on the country's political agenda. In late 1990, he had briefly joined the RPF which, being short of known Hutu members, was apt to accept them without much concern for their quality. He then quit after accusing the RPF

4. Jean Shyirambere Barahinyura, *Le Général-Major Habyarimana. Quinze ans de tyrannie et de tartufferie au Rwanda*, Frankfurt-am-Main: Izuba Verlag, 1988. The story of how this book came to be published is in itself interesting. After being alternatively threatened and offered money by the Rwandese embassy in Bonn not to publish his broadside, Barahinyura had been contacted by a Frenchman introducing himself as Pierre Gilleron and pretending to work for the *Cellule Africaine* in the President's office in Paris. A man of this name had indeed worked earlier at the Elysée palace in the special anti-terrorist unit under the command of Major Christian Prouteau. Major Prouteau in turn worked in close contact with Captain Paul Barril, head of the Groupement d'Intervention de la Gendarmerie Nationale (GIGN), the crack anti-terrorist unit of the Gendarmerie. Captain Barril had to resign his position in 1983 and leave the army after being convicted of tampering with evidence during a political court case involving alleged IRA terrorists. Gilleron had left the Elysée in 1986. But by then ex-Captain Barril had become a soldier of fortune and started a private 'special services' company together with none other than his friend Pierre Gilleron. We see in Chapter 7 how Barril ended up in the service of the Habyarimana family. But the Gilleron phone-call to Jean Barahinyura means that he at least – and very likely his friend Barril – were already acting on behalf of the Habyarimana regime as early as January 1990 when Gilleron was trying to prevent distribution of the book in France (see *Africa Confidential*, 9 March 1990, for part of this story).

of being a Tutsi supremacist organisation and of not giving enough power to its Hutu members.

After making up with the Habyarimana regime in unknown circumstances, he wound up in Kigali where, with a number of associates, he created the CDR[5]. The organisation's leaders – with such people as Jean-Bosco Barayagwiza or its secretary general Martin Bucyana, were on the lunatic fringes of radical Hutu extremism, but they were far from being without talent or intelligence. It was from their political circle that the journalists of Radio Télévision Libre des Mille Collines (RTLMC), the famous 'independent', radio station which was to play such a firebrand role during the time of the genocide, were later recruited. The Kinyarwanda paper *Kangura* ('Wake him up!'), run by Hassan Ngeze a close associate of the CDR, was sleazy but politically quite efficient. And its French-language publication, *Le Courrier du Peuple*, was a hard-hitting scandal sheet which dealt low but well-aimed blows at liberal opposition figures. Unfortunately, dealing such blows was easy, since the main opposition figures were far from being a blameless lot, an almost unavoidable situation in the wake of a dictatorship as Eastern Europeans came to realise at about the same period. The MDR leadership was largely composed of ex-establishment figures who had had personal fights with President Habyarimana and/or the *akazu* and who could be criticised for their freshly-acquired democratic 'convictions' and the rattling financial skeletons in their cupboards. Both the former Minister of the Interior Thomas Habanabakize and the former Speaker of the National Assembly Thadde Bagaragaza, who were now MDR luminaries, had long been part of the ruling MRND circles. As for the party president, Faustin Twagiramungu, he had been the long-time (1977–89) general manager of the Société des Transports Internationaux Rwandais (STIR), a parastatal company

5. In 1992 he published a second book, *Rwanda. Trente-deux aus aprés la révolution sociale le 1959*, Frankfurt-am-Main: Izuba Verlag, in which he violently attacked the RPF as 'terrorists and murderers'. The book cover sported the colours of the CDR flag.

with a monopoly on all of Rwanda's international freight movements. As such, it issued licences for foreign transport companies (usually Kenyan running from Mombasa) which were allowed to take freight into Rwanda, and it charged a 5% levy on the freight invoices. Twagiramungu had been accused of pocketing bribes to give cheaper permits and even briefly arrested, an episode which he attributed to political persecution rather than to financial misbehaviour[6].

The PSD leadership was generally less open to criticism even if the secretary general, Félicien Gatabazi, had been arrested for using his position as manager of the emergency aid programme for the refugees deported from Uganda in 1982 to enrich himself. But his associates such as Théoneste Gafaranga, Félicien Ngango or the former Minister of Agriculture Frédéric Nzamburambaho were reputed to be men of integrity.

In moral terms, the worst liability for the opposition was probably the presence of Justin Mugenzi at the helm of the Parti Libéral. He was a convicted murderer who was condemned to life imprisonment in March 1976 for killing his wife and who was free only because he had been pardoned by President Habyarimana in December 1981. On top of this unsavoury past, he was notoriously corrupt. He had used political connections in order to borrow money from parastatal bodies without repaying it. In the spring of 1993, under threat of having to repay since his being in opposition now made his government debts collectable, he tried to use the fact that there was now a coalition cabinet in order to secure the position of minister of commerce because this could give him an opportunity to clear the books of what he owed (12 m. Rw. francs to the Kigali municipal authorities and 319 m. Rw. francs to the Banque Rwandaise de Développement)[7]. He eventually succeeded, but only after a change in his political position which will be seen in the next chapter.

---

6. This is not entirely false, since the same offence would have been overlooked for a protected *akazu* member.
7. *Le Courrier du Peuple*, 6–13 May 1993. In 1993 there were officially 144 Rwandese francs to the US dollar and 182 on the parallel market.

This embarassing list might give the wrong impression about the democratic opposition. There were many men of integrity in its ranks (with a definite plus for the PSD) and even more among the ordinary militants. In fact, the difficulty of democratisation in Rwanda came largely from the conjunction of two forces: the obdurate resistance of the power structure to any type of genuine democratisation and the selfish greed of a large part of the opposition leadership. Caught in the middle were the honest reformers and the mass of the electorate who did not always get the leadership they deserved. For democratisation was giving many people high hopes and having a dynamic effect on civil society. Strong and well organised human rights organisations were being developed[8] and their militants were taking personal risks in gathering what were soon to become very precise and damning reports on the situation in the country. A vibrant press had been born almost overnight, with all the titles openly defending (at times in terrible bad faith) the colours of their political favourites: *Kamarampaka* (the name given to the referendum on 25 September 1961 which prepared the way for independence) was the MRND(D) organ, with its more militant sister publication *Interahamwe* ('those who work together') a name which had not yet acquired its later murderous connotation; *La Nation* and *Isibo* ('Forward'), run by the very capable Sixbert Musamgamfura, were the French and Kinyarwanda titles defending the MDR-Twagiramungu tendency; *Le Soleil* was the PSD paper; *Kangura* preached the CDR

8. The oldest one was the Association Rwandaise pour la Défense des Droits de l'Homme (ARDHO), supported by the ex-public prosecutor Alphonse-Marie Nkubito and close to the PSD. The Association Rwandaise pour la Défense des Droits de la Personne et des Libertés Publiques (ADL), led by Emmanuel Ntezimana and Monique Mujawamaliya, had been created late in 1991 and was close to the MDR, while the Ligue Chrétienne de Défense des Droits de l'Homme (LICHREDOR), led by Innocent Mazimpaka, was close to the Catholic church. All had a predominantly Hutu membership. The Association des Volontaires du Progrés (AVP), presided over by Charles Shamukiga, was predominantly Tutsi and close to the PL while Kanyarwanda, also mostly Tutsi, was sympathetic to the RPF. With the friendly persuasion of the Belgian Flemish NGO coordination group NCOS, they had created a coordination committee called Comité de Liaison des Associations de Défense des Droits de l'Homme au Rwanda (CLADHO).

racist creed; *Rwanda Rushya* ('New Rwanda'), published by André Kameya, was openly sympathetic to the RPF guerrillas, *Le Libéral* stood for the party of the same name; and, born somewhat after the others, *Paix et Démocratie* and later *Umurangi* fought for different anti-Twagiramungu lines within MDR.

Even the Catholic church, for so long a silent ally of the regime[9], was now moving towards more audacious positions. The ground had been prepared by the action of two successive liberal papal nuncios, first Morandini (1985–90) and then Giuseppe Bertello after 1990, who had both played important roles in making the Vatican aware of the church's political problem in Rwanda, also in marginalising Mgr Vincent Nsengiyumva and promoting his namesake Mgr Thaddée Nsengiyumva. In a daring and innovative document[10], the primate of Rwanda first offered a strong self-criticism of the church itself, for its cosy association with the regime. He then went on to denounce a political situation where 'assassination is now commonplace', where the government refused to play the democratic game fairly, where opposition parties were mostly opportunistic, where nobody seemed serious about reaching a negotiated peace with the guerrillas and finally where there was no serious debate on the real social sins of the country which were buried under political verbiage, namely of discrimination

9. This is in fact a rather severe judgement that needs to be nuanced. Such Catholic periodicals as *Kinyamateka* or *Dialogue* had represented before 1990 the only intellectual and political breathing space the regime had tolerated. But this élite toleration could be bought only by the church-supported subservience of the peasant masses to the MRND.

10. Mgr Thaddée Nsengiyumva (primate of Rwanda), *Convertissons-nous pour vivre ensemble dans la paix*, Kabgayi, 40 pp. (mimeo), December 1991. The title chosen for this publication seemed paradoxically provocative (Let us convert [to Christianity] in order to live peacefully with each other). In fact it was a lucid and almost desperate assessment of the religious situation of Rwanda from a moral point of view. After a century of Christian proselytisation, the country was catholicised but not christianised. Ritual was generally followed but the spirit was missing. This became tragically evident for the church only after April–May 1994 when its people slaughtered their brethren wholesale *inside* the churches on orders from civil authorities, which obviously conveyed a kind of 'moral override' to the population.

in education and neglect of the living conditions of the peasantry. With this radical document the socially conservative Catholic church of Rwanda publicly parted company with Caesar.

In this context every single new step on the road to democracy was going to have to be fought for against a stubbornly conservative power structure bent on keeping its money and privileges, and by 'democrats' who were not always of the purest type, but who had the support of a large segment of the population for whom democracy meant peace, an end to political corruption, financial accountability by the government and freedom of expression.

The first fight took place around the question of the formation of a new cabinet. The new political parties had created an interparty Comité de Concertation de l'Opposition which was agitating for a number of precise demands:

– A de-institutionalisation of MRND(D) not only in words but in practice, something which implied among other things that President Habyarimana would resign from his position as president of the former single party. It also implied equality of treatment for all political forces [11].
– The disbanding of Parliament and the convening of a national conference.
– An opening up of the audiovisual media. In a country like Rwanda where more than 60% of the population could not read or write, the existence of a free press only had meaning for the literate sector of the population, who were already politically aware anyway. The audiovisual scene was a tremendously important battlefield and here the government still reigned supreme: its version of events was the one carried out to the hilly countryside by radio. The licence given to 'free' extremist radio RTLMC (and to nobody else who might have supported a more moderate line) only made things worse.

11. As an example, the military curfew resulting from the war was not applied to all in the same way. MRND(D) cadres had special passes which enabled them to move anywhere around the country by day or night, while the militants of opposition parties would be harassed at roadblocks or even detained by the police when they travelled on party business.

Only a new – neutral – cabinet could start on such a programme. Instead, on 13 October 1991, President Habyarimana asked Justice Minister Sylvestre Nsanzimana to form a new cabinet. Nsanzimana was a moderate who had been a cabinet minister under President Kayibanda and had later chosen to leave Rwanda to pursue a diplomatic career which had brought him the position of assistant secretary general of the Organisation of African Unity (OAU). After returning home, he replaced the hardline Théodore Mujyanama as minister of justice in February 1991 and was instrumental in discreetly releasing the victims of the October 1990 mass arrests who were still in detention. Given the circumstances, he was probably doing his best, but his liberal attitude over the detainees had alienated the MRND(D) hardliners and his being called to form a new MRND(D) cabinet immediately alienated the whole opposition. Shorn of any independent influence, he became no more than the President's tool. The cabinet formation process soon sank into a procedural quagmire, the opposition asking for fundamental reforms as a prerequisite to any participation in government, and the President trying to dodge any basic change and just to co-opt the opposition into a docile business-as-usual 'new' cabinet.

On 17 November 1991, the main opposition parties (MDR, PSD, PL) signed a common memorandum to the President detailing the obstacles the government was putting in the way of further democratisation (harassment of their militants, use of the government radio and TV for MRND propaganda, use of government vehicles, buildings and other equipment to help MRND(D) candidates for party propaganda, and so on). They also complained that in spite of the multiparty legislation, local authorities – all solidly MRND(D) – kept behaving as if the government's party was still the only one allowed and accused them of being unable to distinguish between their duties as civil servants and their role as MRND(D) activists. For the first time there were mentions of 'MRND(D) armed bands' who had attacked MDR sympathisers after a party meeting, leaving ten wounded, one of whom had had a hand cut off by a machete blow. The memorandum concluded by calling for a national conference which would carry on with a real process of democratisation. To press home their point, on the same day the *Comité de Concertation de l'Opposition* got more than 10,000 militants and sympathisers of their parties to demonstrate in Kigali against the lingering MRND(D) political hegemony and in favour of the national conference. A week later, the MRND(D) hit back by having 20,000 demonstrators march through the streets of the capital chanting slogans against the convening of a national conference. The swearing-in of the Nsanzimana cabinet (30 December 1991) only made matters worse, since it included no opposition ministers apart from a single PDC member in a secondary post. On 8 January 1992, 50,000 demonstrators filled the streets of Kigali to protest against the new cabinet while thousands of others marched in Butare and Gitarama. A new demonstration planned for 15 January was forbidden, and illegal demonstrators were attacked by the police and arrested. The democratisation process, though formally legalised, appeared in practice to be blocked.

War and violence as parts of the political process

One should keep in mind that this whole process of political struggle was taking place not in ordinary circumstances but while the country was engaged in a limited-scale civil war. A Zaïrean-sponsored cease-fire agreement signed in N'Sele (near Kinshasa) on 29 March 1991 had had no effect whatever on the actual military operations. After their daring raid on Ruhengeri, the RPF fighters had withdrawn again and settled down to a typical guerrilla hit-and-run pattern of operations in the northern *préfecture* of Byumba. Low-intensity operations dragged on, without either side gaining any definite advantage. The Forces Armées Rwandaises, especially with continued French support, kept the upper hand, but they could not prevent constant RPF attacks and even the closing down of the road to Uganda, Gatuna remaining under guerrilla control[12]. Contrary to the

---

12. This placed a particular strain on Rwanda's landlocked economy since all transport to and from Mombasa now had to use a longer, harder and more expensive route through Tanzania.

expectations of the RPF, local Hutu peasants showed no enthusiasm for being 'liberated' by them – they had run away from
the area of guerrilla operations. There were about 100,000
displaced persons in camps directly to the south. Later, in early
1992, when the RPF pushed its advantage still further in the
area around Byumba, even more peasants ran away from them,
the number of the displaced reaching to around 300,000.

But politically civil violence was even more distracting than
the war. In January 1991 a new wave of massacres had started
in Bugogwe. This area of north-western Rwanda had already
seen several acts of collective violence in October 1990, at
the time of the Mutara massacres. And on 27 January 1991,
apparently in retaliation for the taking of Ruhengeri by the RPF,
the killings started again, following a very similar pattern[13].
The Bourgmestre[14] of Kinigi commune, Thaddée Gasana, led
his charges in a massacre of several members of the Bagogwe
community[15], claiming between thirty and sixty victims. In the
following days the massacres spread sporadically to Ruhengeri
itself and to Gaseke and Giciye communes. This area is in the
heart of Bushiru, the 'blessed country' which was the government's stronghold, and information about the violence filtered
out only very slowly and inaccurately to the rest of the country.
Then the massacres spread west towards Kanama, Rwerere and
Gisenyi itself during early February and lasted till mid-March.
Although the systematic killings stopped at that time, sporadic
harassments and murders of Bagogwe and other Tutsi kept
taking place till around June 1991, when the authorities allowed
the potential victims to leave the area if they so wished. Most

13. FIDH, *Rwanda*, op. cit., pp. 27–41, and ADL, *Rapport*, op. cit., pp. 117–34.
14. The name had been kept from the old Belgian administrative system. A
    bourgmestre was the (appointed, not elected) official in charge of a commune,
    a sub-unit in a Préfecture. He was directly answerable to the central government.
    There were 145 communes in the whole country.
15. The Bagogwe were a Tutsi group which had kept the pastoral way of life of
    their ancestors till quite recently. They were very poor, even poorer than the
    average Rwandese rural dwellers, and they had slowly moved to the towns and
    villages to eke out a living doing odd jobs as land pressure and administrative
    abuses caused a shrinking of their traditonal pastures.

of them then went down to Kigali where they felt more secure. The total number of victims is not known, but it seems to have been between a low estimate of 300 and a maximum of about 1,000. The bodies were summarily buried in several unmarked graves.

As the pace of the political struggle quickened, another round of massacres took place in the Bugesera region in early March 1992[16]. This time the ground had been psychologically prepared through the purported 'discovery' of a Parti Libéral leaflet calling on the Tutsi to rise up and massacre their Hutu neighbours. This leaflet had supposedly been found in Nairobi by a human rights group, and the five radio broadcasts where it was repeatedly mentioned were in the form of a warning by the government to the Hutu population. The massacres which started on 4 March could then be presented as 'self-defence'[17]. They lasted till 9 March and led to the death of an estimated 300 people (government sources admitted to 182). The police and part of the judiciary tried to react and 466 people were arrested in connection with the massacres, but pressures from up above caused them to be discreetly released without charges ever being pressed. When the guilty parties in the false leaflet story were found to be civil servants, all the Prime Minister Sylvestre Nsanzimana did was to give them an administrative reprimand[18].

Since these massacres had already occured and since they were to happen again, and as they present on a small scale all the characteristics of the April-May 1994 genocide, it is not without interest to pause for a while and try to understand how they worked. A common feature of all the massacres is that they were preceded by political meetings during which a 'sensibilisation' process was carried out. These seemed to have been designed to

16. FIDH, *Rwanda*, op. cit., pp. 42–7, and ADL, *Rapport*, op. cit., pp. 193–234.
17. See *La Libre Belgique* dated 9 March 1992. The allegation that the Parti Libéral had made this seditious call was due to the fact that it had many Tutsi in its ranks. The deception was rumoured to be the brainchild of Ferdinand Nahimana, the university professor turned Hutu radical activist.
18. *Jeune Afrique* (19–25 March 1992) and *Africa Events* (May 1992). This was the last straw in discrediting the Prime Minister.

put the local peasants 'in the mood', to drum into them that the people they were soon to kill were *ibyitso*, i.e. actual or potential collaborators of the RPF arch-enemy. These meetings were always presided over and attended by the local authorities with whom the local peasants were familiar; but they also usually featured the presence of an 'important person' who would come from Kigali to lend the event an aura of added respectability and official sanction. After the 'sensibilisation' process had been carried out, the order would come sooner or later, either directly from the Ministry of the Interior in Kigali or from the *préfet*. People would then be called for a special *umuganda* (collective work session). The vocabulary of the ordinary agricultural *umuganda* would be used and the *bourgmestre* would usually talk about 'bush clearing'. It is interesting that even as the killings were about to happen euphemisms and metaphors had to be used, as if the naked truth was too much to stomach. It is possible that the fragile and shameful complicity between officials and peasants would not have withstood too blunt an exposure of the bloody reality that was to follow. In any case, the peasants were prepared for the punitive expedition which could turn out to be more or less violent according to the situation. In some cases, when the *bourgmestre* refused to carry out his distasteful task, he could stop the massacre[19]. But mostly the *bourgmestres* and their charges carried out orders unquestioningly. Of course, some of the *bourgmestres* such as Fidèle Rwambuka in Kanzenze and Rémy Gatete in Kibungo became famous for their enthusiasm for the killing business. They enjoyed what they did and derived abundant material benefits from it. But they seemed to have been the exception rather than the rule – like their exact opposites, the courageous defenders of civil peace. Most *bourgmestres* involved seem to have carried out their orders without either enthusiasm or

---

19. See FIDH, *Rwanda*, op. cit., p. 39, where the commission quotes the case of the *bourgmestre* of the *commune* of Kayoye who, rather than carry out a killing expedition, called the *gendarmes* (rural police) to quieten down the crowd. They did so and nobody was killed.

reluctance like any other job the government required of them. And the same seems to have been true of the ordinary peasants. There are of course other descriptions of these killings. The government, which always tried to minimise the massacres, attributed them to the 'righteous anger of the people' who spontaneously launched themselves at the Tutsi. The implication here seems to be that these Tutsi richly deserved what they got since they all sympathised with the RPF. However, this version of 'spontaneous popular violence' does not seem to be corroborated by the many eyewitnesses[20].

The other version, usually offered by believers in a deep-seated Hutu-Tutsi brotherhood among Banyarwanda which only the evil Habyarimana regime had been able to destroy[21] describes these massacres as being carried out purely by 'militiamen'. This seems to be an oversimplification, although it came closer to the truth as time went on, as massacres became better coordinated and militias more organised. But the Mutara massacres of October 1990, the sporadic killings of the Bagogwe between the beginning of 1991 and early 1993, and the Murambi killings of November 1991 were all carried out by ordinary peasants organised on the spot by their local authorities. And even later, when militiamen did play a greater role (mostly after the Bugesera massacres of March 1992), local peasants were still involved every time, up to and including their participation in the massive genocidal killings of April-May 1994.

How is this to be explained? This is a hard and subjective

---

20. On 10 March 1992, during the Bugesera massacres, the Italian lay sister Antonia Locatelli was killed for trying desperately to denounce this government rationalisation. During the two days before her death, she called Radio France Internationale in Paris several times to protest against the government version of the killings, saying that as someone who had lived in the area for twenty-two years, she was perfectly well able to see that the murders had not been committed by a spontaneously angry crowd. She added that several of the killers were people she had never seen before, who had been brought from outside in government-registered vehicles. (Interview with a Radio France Internationale employee, Paris, 12 March 1992.)

21. This for example is the official RPF version, although in private RPF cadres tend to be more realistic.

question to answer. For some European commentators[22], the question is simple: African 'tribes' are possessed by 'ancestral hatreds' and periodically slaughter each other because it is in their nature to do so. But this does not explain why 'tribes' suddenly start to kill each other, or why they stop doing so. Enlightened people tend to frown on such archaic explanations. Liberal intellectuals (that is the majority of academic Africanists) prefer to attribute these outbursts of violence to either political or economic causes (or both) and to consider that the 'tribal' guise is just a useful cover-up for dark forces one no longer quite dares to call 'imperialist'.

In fact tribal violence in Africa is infinitely complex and no two cases are similar. This does not mean that there are no general causes, but it would probably be more productive intellectually to turn around the methodological approach and ask oneself why violence (which in any case has a certain logic given the economic, social, cultural and political contradictions on the continent) usually takes a tribal rather than, say, a 'clean' political form[23]. The answer is that if tribes did not exist, they would have to be invented. In a world where illiteracy is still the rule, where most of the population has horizons which are limited to their parochial world, where ideologies are bizarre foreign gadgets reserved for intellectuals, solidarity is best understood in terms of close community. In

---

22. For example Jacques de Barrin in a front-page article on civil strife in East Africa in *Le Monde* (3 January 1986).
23. The European perception of violence is in itself very culturally determined. Political violence, especially if it has a clear-cut ideological context (the maximum having probably been achieved during the Spanish civil war) is felt as being more legitimate, more acceptable, than less 'noble' violence, e.g. the tribal outcry. From this point of view, the civil war in ex-Yugoslavia, with its strong ethnic base, has been a sobering and humbling experience for European consciousness. The same is true where the methods of killing are concerned. During the April–May 1994 Rwandese genocide, journalists always insisted that the victims were killed with machetes, as if the use of a cold steel rather than a bullet made the killing worse. Nobody ever thought of blaming the Roman army or European medieval knights for their use of the sword, any more than journalists were able to realise that using machetes reflected a certain level of economic functioning rather than cultural barbarity.

turn, these positive (or negative) group feelings are manipulated
by the élite in their struggles for controlling scarce and even
shrinking financial, cultural and political resources. Rwanda
offers a perfect example of this process. The ruling fraction of
the country's élite manipulated the existing 'ethnic' raw material
into an attempt at political survival. Killings were merely one
of the means used in a broad spectrum of political tools which
included war, bribery, foreign diplomacy, constitutional manipulations and propaganda, though not necessarily in that order.

The nagging question which remains is: 'How do the ordinary
peasants let themselves be manipulated into such situations?' And
this is where there is no single answer. Since this could be called
a political (and nearly military) mobilisation process, we have to
see that, despite broadly comparable situations, mobilisation
patterns are quite different according to time and place and that
each depends on the culture, history, geography and traditions
of the country. In other words, although somewhere way back
up the line of causality they have similar general causes, the
massacres in Liberia, the Sudanese civil war, the Somali anarchy
and the Rwandese genocide are all individual cases which need
to be studied in detail if they are to be understood and which
cannot be explained away by wide generalisations.

In the Rwandese case, as we saw in the first chapter, there
are several reasons why political slaughter could be organised
along fairly systematic lines[24]. We could perhaps at this point
go back and list them in a formalised way:

– Rwandese political tradition, going back to the Banyiginya
kingdom through the German and Belgian colonial periods, is
one of systematic, centralised and unconditional obedience to
authority. President Habyarimana was, from that point of view,
the direct inheritor of the *abami* of old.

---

24. Something which for example it would have been almost impossible to do in
Somalia. Bloody as it was, the Somali conflict remained a war, where civilians
died as secondary casualties. Somali culture is not nicer than Rwandese culture,
it is simply too individualistic to enable such systematic slaughter to be organised
among civilians. One more note of caution for commentators who glibly talk
about 'Africa' as if it were a coherent whole.

– Most people were illiterate. Given their authoritarian tradition, they tended to believe what the authorities told them. And what they were told was quite fantastic. The RPF Tutsi fighters were pictured as creatures from another world, with tails, horns, hooves, pointed ears and red eyes that shone in the dark. Anybody who could be their accomplice (*ibyitso*) was bound also to be a very evil creature[25].

– There was a 'rural' banalisation of crime. Killings were *umuganda*, collective work, chopping up men was 'bush clearing' and slaughtering women and children was 'pulling out the roots of the bad weeds'. The vocabulary of 'peasant-centred agricultural development' came into play, with a horrible double meaning. But, somewhere deep down, it brought about another sphere of justification: all these people who were about to be killed had land and at times cows. And somebody had to get these lands and those cows after their owners were dead. In a poor and increasingly overpopulated country this was not a negligible incentive[26].

So one could (in a somewhat simplified fashion) sum up the psychological causal chain of massacre participation in this way: our wise political authorities gave us orders (to be obeyed) so that we would eradicate those (dangerously evil) people like weeds and we will be rewarded for this hard but necessary work by getting some of the material benefits we dearly need.

Of course, this presupposes one absolutely basic thing: the total dehumanisation of the Evil Other and the absolute legitimisation of Authority. Both had been achieved by what we have called 'the democratic majority ideology' in Chapter 1.

25. From that point of view, it is interesting to notice the double semantic reference, to the European Christian pictorial imagery of the devil and his cohorts on the one hand and to African witchcraft on the other. This is where Mgr Nsengiyumva's intuition about 'the need to convert to Christianity' comes in: Christian imagery is present in simplified pictures of Good and Evil, but there is no widespread spiritual understanding of these categories.

26. David Waller, *Rwanda: Which way now?*, London: Oxfam, 1993, gives a simple down-to-earth picture of the psycho-economic pressure of land hunger on ordinary peasants, all the more chilling for having been written a few months before the genocide.

And Europeans who are horrified when contemplating this prospect should ask themselves what were the psycho-political mechanisms which enabled German Nazis during the Second World War to cleanly remove from 'civilised' society five and a half million Jews, around one million Gypsies and another million or so homosexuals, mentally retarded people, racial half-castes, underground resistance fighters and assorted social deviants without much protest from the local populace, and at times with their active support[27].

In any case, violence was used by the power structure in Rwanda to try to stop any form of genuine democratisation, and it was not used only in the form of massacres. Massacres were good for some purposes but not for others: they served to reinforce group solidarity through shared guilt, they projected an image of spontaneous popular hatred for the RPF and its *ibyitso* and they could also have been a tactic in the process of trying to soften up the RPF itself[28]. But there were also other forms of violence for other purposes. Early March 1992, saw the start of terrorist attacks. Twice grenades were thrown blindly into the crowds at the Kigali bus park, killing five the first time and killing one and wounding thirty-four the second time. On 2 May a bomb exploded in a taxi, killing four people. The origin of these attacks has been discussed and

---

27. In a parallel with the Rwandese genocide, it is notable that in most of Europe (including *Western* Europe), the folk representation of Jews before the Second World War was still almost medieval. An old Jewish gentleman told the author that once, while travelling through central France in the 1930s as a salesman, he was asked by a villager, in rather embarrassed tones, to remove his shoes to verify that he had feet and not cloven hooves. After he had done so, the farmer triumphantly turned to his wife and said: 'You see! I told you so! Our priest is just talking rubbish!' Similarly, the author has collected several accounts by RPF fighters of their having had to show Hutu peasants that they had no tail or cloven hooves.

28. This had been a common practice during the *Inyenzi* attacks of the 1960s. A number of Tutsi – preferably socially prominent ones – would be arrested and then killed one by one. Through friends and family abroad, the message of distress would soon be carried to the *Inyenzi* leadership and fighting would die down. (Interview with Radio Rwanda journalist Jean-Marie Vianney Higiro, Kigali, 15 June 1993.)

some sources have tried to attribute them to the RPF[29], citing as 'proof' the type of Russian and Chinese equipment found on the spot. This proves RPF involvement, so it was said, because the Forces Armées Rwandaises use French equipment. This makes no sense, first because the FAR were also buying from Egypt, where replicas of Russian and Chinese equipment are produced, and secondly because the FAR had also captured RPF equipment at the front and could have used it for whatever purposes they wanted; and thirdly because by early 1993, French explosives had begun to be used in these attacks[30]. In any case, the political logic was clear: unclaimed terrorist attacks could be chalked up to the RPF, bringing several benefits to the government: the RPF was once more portrayed as particularly brutal and evil; the civilian Hutu opposition which refused to believe in the RPF origin of these attacks would now be tarred with the same brush; and the whole democratisation process could be treated as a slide towards anarchy which should be stopped by every means possible. On the other hand, what benefits the RPF could have derived from such attacks is difficult to figure out.

The new multiparty cabinet and the opening of peace negotiations

Opposition politicians felt largely powerless to repay the government's use of violence in kind. As the PSD President Félicien Gatabazi had declared, 'Each time there are some difficulties (in the democratic process) there is is a flare-up of tribal violence instigated by the regime, and threats of civil war are used to justify the *status quo*.'[31]

29. See the French *gendarmerie* report quoted by Stephen Smith in *Libération* (29 July 1994). Later, the preferred *modus operandi* of the killers became to lay mines on the roads. Somehow, this was mainly in the restive south and never in the pro-government north, although this was close to the operational zone of the RPF.
30. The Kirambo killings, near Cyangugu were the first instance. In that case, the terrorist attacks were coupled with a wave of selective rapes targetting Tutsi women (interview with the chief editor of *Isibo*, Sixbert Musamgamfura, Kigali, 13 June 1993).
31. Interview in *Le Monde*, 14 March 1992.

The Bugesera massacres and the recent terrorist attacks were answers to the new popular mobilisation capacity the opposition had shown in January 1992 when more than 50,000 people took to the streets in protest against Nsanzimana's solidly MRND(D) cabinet. But violence was not enough in itself to stem the tide unless it could have been used on a much larger scale, a temptation some segments of the *akazu* were beginning to feel in the face of mounting popular pressure. Tension was such that on 14 March President Habyarimana had to accept the signature of an historic compromise agreement with the united opposition: a genuine coalition cabinet would be installed to replace that of Nsanzimana, with the premiership going to the largest opposition party (MDR), there were to be peace negotiations with the RPF, and the principle of a national conference was agreed upon.

On 7 April, under the aegis of Premier Dismas Nsengiyaremye (MDR), a new cabinet was sworn in, where for the first time the MRND(D) had to share power. This was not exactly a surrender. The former single party had nine cabinet portfolios out of twenty and including those for Defence (James Gasana), the Civil Service (Prosper Mugiraneza), the Interior (Faustin Munyazesa) and Transport (André Ntagerura). But the opposition had obtained some of the other key ministries: Boniface Ngulinzira (MDR) had become Minister for Foreign Affairs, Mme Agathe Uwilingiyimana (MDR) held the vital Education portfolio, Marc Rugenera (PSD) was Finance Minister, Stanislas Mbonampeka, a (very wet) PL member, was Minister of Justice, and Agnes Ntamabyaliro, the PL secretary-general, was Minister of Commerce. Altogether the MDR held four portfolios (including the premiership), the PL and the PSD three each, and the PDC one.

The new cabinet courageously went on the offensive to try to redress some of the regime's most obvious injustices. The new Minister for Education, Agathe Uwilingiyimana, abolished the so-called 'policy of equilibrium' which enabled the government to choose the ethnic (i.e. Tutsi or Hutu) origin of students and even in practice, within the Hutu community, the regional origin of candidates. She replaced it with simple and fair entrance examinations[32]. The notorious Service Central de Renseignements (SCR), the all-powerful secret service, was cut up and its attributions divided between four different ministries. The worst *préfets* were fired and replaced by opposition members. The proportion of *préfets* coming from the 'blessed country' of the north-west was reduced in order to ensure a better regional balance. The judiciary was encouraged to become more independent and it actually dared to declare some past presidential decrees unconstitutional. Ferdinand Nahimana, the extremist director of ORINFOR[33], was fired, and in order to comply with the June 1991 constitution, President Habyarimana resigned from his position as head of the armed forces.

But these changes were fragile, and the political climate remained tense. In April and May, directly in the wake of the swearing-in of the new cabinet, there were several terrorist attacks all over the country, unclaimed as usual, in which twenty-two people were killed and over 100 wounded. At every step MRND(D) civil servants kept countermanding the orders of their opposition ministers. The SCR reformed itself clandestinely in cooperation with what was soon going to be known as the 'Zero Network' of death squads (see Chapter 5). And Ferdinand Nahimana simply went back to his university position, waiting for an opportunity that was soon to come. Times were hard for the democrats, especially as some of them were playing strange games.

Early in the year, as the transition towards an opening up

32. Contrary to some stories written after her assassination in April 1994, Mme Uwilingiyimana was a Hutu. The only Tutsi minister in the cabinet was the minister of labour and social affairs, Landwald Ndasingwa (PL). For a defence of the nitpicking excesses to which the 'policy of equilibrium' could lead, see Eustache Munyantwali, 'La politique d'équilibre dans l'enseignement' and Laurien Uwizeyimana, 'La politique d'équilibre ethnique et régional dans l'emploi' in François-Xavier Bangamwabo *et al.*, *Les relations interethniques*, op. cit., respectively pp. 300–7 and 308–22.

33. Office Rwandais d'Information, a parastatal body in charge of press and radio control. The new minister for information, Pascal Ndengejeho, was a PSD member with little sympathy for Nahimana's brand of CDR politics.

of the MRND(D) monopoly of power seemed unavoidable, a new tendency had appeared. Launched by the ex-MRND(D) Minister of Commerce François Nzabahimana, Nkiko Nsengimana and Emmanuel Gapyisi, the *Initiative Paix et Démocratie* presented itself as a 'middle of the road' independent force, equidistant from the regime and the opposition. Its sponsors attempted a write-in campaign to support their initiative, their target being to gather 100,000 signatures, and in this they failed. But they remained a new trend in the political landscape, one apparently not without friends in government circles since ORINFOR echoed widely what they did while it usually kept a complete blackout on opposition initiatives. Gapyisi especially soon became a charismatic figure in the somewhat lacklustre Rwandese political landscape. Dynamic, intelligent and well-educated, he had spent the last few years abroad working as an engineer and thus escaped being tarred with the same brush as most of the political class. He had joined the MDR but was felt to be a new figure in politics, anyway. His rhetoric was simple: the Habyarimana regime was worn out, but the 'principles' of the 'social revolution' of 1959 were still valid. Overhauling the regime and opening up democratically did not need to be in opposition to the 'sociological majority' ideology everyone had been taught to respect for the past thirty years. The implication was that, as the regime was always hinting, the rest of the regular democratic opposition was in fact a fifth column of the RPF. The message was sweet for a certain segment of the power structure which wanted to keep the reality of political control but realised that at least cosmetic changes were needed, since President Habyarimana was indeed worn out.

With all these changes on the way for the regime they had saved in its hour of need, what was the attitude of the French eighteen months after their initial intervention 'to protect the security of French nationals'? One can say without exaggeration that it remained one of total, uncritical and unconditional support for President Habyarimana and his close circle. In March 1992, after the Bugesera massacres had become public knowledge, the French ambassador Georges Martre refused to join a delegation of the OECD countries' diplomatic representatives in Kigali which went to see President Habyarimana to express their concern at this new wave of violence[34]. The delegation was led by the US and Canadian ambassadors, a sure sign of 'Anglo-Saxon' plotting. On the military side, weapons and ammunition kept flowing in on direct orders from the highest circles at the Elysée. Nevertheless, the vast size of the deliveries caused some problems for General Huchon who ran the *Mission Militaire* at the Ministère de la Coopération for Rwanda in Paris, and he had at times to struggle at meetings of the Interministerial Committee for War Material Exports meetings to get approval for the impressive volume of lethal equipment which high government officials wanted to send to Kigali[35]. In fact, these administrative difficulties became so pressing that other solutions were found. In March 1992 the French government underwrote the financial risk of weapon deliveries to Rwanda from Egypt through its nationalised bank Crédit Lyonnais. The total amount involved was US $6 million[36]. Later in the year, French agents acted as

34. The common joke in Kigali diplomatic circles at the time was that Ambassador Martre was not the French ambassador to Rwanda but rather the Rwandese ambassador to France. President Habyarimana appreciated him so much that when he was about to leave, he wrote personally to President Mitterrand asking that he might stay in Kigali. In a letter the opposition leaked to the foreign press, President Mitterrand answered that he would keep Mr Martre in his post for a further six months, but that the retirement rules of the French civil service did not allow him to stay any longer.

35. Confidential interview with a French Foreign Ministry representative, Paris, 30 March 1992.

36. The deal was reported on 25 May 1992 by the Paris-based confidential letter *La Lettre du Continent*. But it was not widely noticed until its publication in the Human Rights Watch Report, *Arming Rwanda: The arms Trade and Human Rights Abuses in the Rwandan War*, New York, January 1994, which printed the Egyptian contract as an annex. Out of prudence or a need to protect their sources, the Human Rights people had blanked out the mention of the bank involved in the transaction. However, in its piece on the subject, *La Lettre du Continent* had been able to give not only the bank's name but the precise account number used for the operation. After the legislative election of March 1993, the new conservative majority in the French Parliament started to investigate the operations of Crédit Lyonnais and found it to have been almost slavish in its devotion to the Socialist government's orders and to have undertaken a number of operations which were politically motivated and without justifiable business reasons. Accounts were in the red for over US $9bn. Its general manager, Jean Yves Haberer, was dismissed (see Martine Gilson and Claude Soula, 'Crédit Lyonnais. une facture de 50 milliards, *Le Nouvel Observateur*, 29 September–5 October 1994).

intermediaries to facilitate the signing of a supply contract with South Africa for US $5.9 million[37]. French involvement in the situation was not only at the level of arms delivery, but went right down to the level of operations on the ground. The French army was in fact in complete control of counterinsurgency operations and Lieut.-Colonel Chollet of the French military mission had been caught in the public spotlight when the press got hold of a leaked Rwandese government letter giving him overall command of operations[38]. He just laid low for a while, and then passed on his operational command of the FAR to his right-hand man, Lieut.-Colonel Maurin[39]. In view of all this the visit of the French Cooperation Minister Marcel Debarge to Kigali in mid-May 1992 appeared more like a check on how operations were progressing than an attempt at mediation[40].

And indeed, despite their extra-legal violence, things were not going so well for the regime hardliners. In application of the 14 March agreement, which had opened the way for a coalition government, negotiations were also supposed to start with the RPF. On 24 May Foreign Minister Boniface Ngulinzira met the RPF vice-chairman Patrick Mazimpaka in Kampala for a first

37. This was in direct violation of UN Resolution no.558 of 13 December 1984 prohibiting arms imports from South Africa, then subjected to international sanctions because of its apartheid policies. The amounts in question may seem small, but to have a point of comparison, one should note that between 1981 and 1988 Rwanda had only bought a total of US $5 million of military equipment (Human Rights Watch, *Arming Rwanda* op. cit., p. 22).
38. See *La Libre Belgique* (21 February 1992).
39. Stephen Smith, 'Dans le plus grand secret. La France fait la guerre au Rwanda', *Libération*, 11 June 1992.
40. Certain sources describe the French government using its position as the main source of military supplies and/or financier to Rwanda to apply pressure in favour of democratisation (interview wtih James Gasana, former MRND Minister of Defence, Geneva, 13 June 1994). But these pressures were always light and threats of military sanctions were never carried out. In any case it would have been difficult for the French political authorities to apply such pressure since the French military establishment felt itself in duty bound to support the regime in its fight against the RPF (several interviews between the author and French army officers in Paris between 1992 and 1994). Bruno Delhaye, head of the French Presidential Africa Unit since June 1992, even told the author (13 October 1992) that an army general involved in the '*Noroit*' expeditionary force had declared to him that he would regard any abandonment of the Habyarimana regime as 'an act of high treason'.

contact and announced that direct negotiations would begin in Paris in June. This immediately caused several violent reactions. On 30 May, both the opposition and the MRND(D) youth wing went on the streets, either to support the announced peace process or to denounce it as a betrayal, and seven people were killed in the ensuing clashes. The next day, the army mutinied in Gisenyi and Ruhengeri, areas where the soldiers knew they would have the support of both the civilian population and the local authorities. They had been stirred up by rumours that peace would bring large-scale demobilisation and that demobilised men would be set to work on swamp reclamation. They also complained that in spite of the special 'Solidarity Tax' having brought the government some 300 million Rw. francs, they still got their pay very irregularly. They asked for cash and, when they were refused, went on a rampage, killing twenty-seven people and wounding almost 100. It took several days and additional contingents of Forces Armées Rwandaises to restore order.

Meanwhile, the opposition had made a radical choice. Braving the risk of being branded as traitors, its members had decided to meet directly the RPF and on 6 June a common MDR, PSD and PL delegation arrived in Brussels for talks. The next day, realising that for the first time it had found, if not political allies at least partners who were willing to renounce the use of violence in their dealings with them, the RPF leadership announced that the armed struggle was over and that from now on the struggle would be political. On 6 June, an agreement was reached in Paris on 'the technical modalities of the peace process' and soon after the actual peace talks started at Arusha, in Tanzania. On 14 July, a cease-fire was signed and peace seemed to be just round the corner.

Hardliners, democrats and warriors in the Hutu/Tutsi context

As they prepared to talk peace, we should pause for a moment and try to understand the rules of the complicated three-cornered game played between the old Habyarimana regime, the democratic opposition and the guerrillas, as seen in the context of the infernal Tutsi/Hutu dichotomy. First of all, there is the global paradox that almost all the clichés on the question are both true and also wrong. For example, although the whole ideological construction of the Rwandese regime was based on demonisation of the Tutsi as beyond-the-pale quasi-foreigners, in fact, after 1973, President Habyarimana was a protector of the Tutsi and no harm befell them in the twenty years of his reign. Since they were politically castrated by their 'untouchability', they could be allowed to do business and to flourish. In fact, it was better for the President to have a prosperous Tutsi business class than having independently powerful Hutu businessmen who would have autonomous political ambitions of their own and eventually pursue them.

Another paradox was that although the democratic opposition and the RPF guerrillas were both fighting the same enemy, namely a twenty-year-old dictatorship which was desperately trying to block any form of political or social change, they were far from being allies, at least for the first two years of the war. This is why for example the MDR in one of its early programmatic documents could still describe the RPF as 'the *Inyenzi*, the armed branch of the unreconstructed feudalists who have not accepted the people's will as expressed in the 1959 revolution and especially through the Kamarampaka referendum of 25 September 1961'[41]. In the same way, despite its 'progressive' ideology, the RPF counted among its members (and even more among its outside sympathisers) a considerable number of Tutsi supremacists for whom the Hutu were a despicable and backward mass of peasants.

To some extent, the Tutsi/Hutu question was a kind of voluntary blind spot for the RPF. The main leaders of the movement, not only the best-known ones such as Major-General

---

41. *Analyse de la situation actuelle du Rwanda et perspectives d'avenir. Esquisse d'un projet de société pour le Rwanda de demain*, Kigali, January 1992. The part on the RPF is on page 29. The Kamarampaka referendum mentioned here was the tool used by Parmehutu to pressure the Belgians into accelerating independence. It was an operation that gave 'democratic' legitimacy to the *de facto* political exclusion of the Tutsi.

Rwigyema or Paul Kagame, but also the less well-known core
leaders such as Patrick Mazimpaka, Théogène Rudasingwa
or Frank Mugambage – were all pure products of a 'Ugandan'
political world. Their politically formative years had been spent
in Uganda where the NRA struggle between 1981 and 1986 had
deeply affected their political vision, and all of them had imbibed
a sort of mildly populistic post-Maoist political philosophy
adapted to the context of Uganda's politico-tribal wars. The
lesson they had derived from these violent and confused years
was ambiguous. On the one hand, tribalism was theoretically
considered an absolute evil and 'progressives' were supposed to
fight it relentlessly; seeing over and over again how absolutely
destructive African tribal conflicts could be had strengthened
their determination to avoid them. But they had realised at the
time that without a solidly trustworthy tribal core and attendant
network the new 'revolutionary' power which came to replace
the 'primitive tribalists' of old would in practice be blind and
dangerously exposed.

Their political ideal was Yoweri Museveni, who had finally
brought peace to his troubled land. And Museveni's brand of
'broad-based government' was an ingeneous elaboration on
the theme of tribal politics. It was open to all and any tribal
force which cared to join, but there was a subtle gradation
between 'being in government' (with all the attendant perks and
privileges) and 'being in power' (often without so many perks
and privileges, but with a real decision-making capacity). In the
first group, there could be just about anybody. In the second
group there were two types of people: the tribal inner core and
a limited number of friends from other tribal origins but whom
the President knew had been able psychologically to go beyond
their tribal origin. On the basis of this selection of the leadership
which was at once security-conscious and popular, President
Museveni had been able to combine a nationalist approach
rejecting 'gross tribalism' with the security of a tribally-safe
political inner-core.

The RPF approach was broadly similar: keep essential
decision-making within a familiar inner core of Uganda Tutsi

refugees, add a select number of 'outsiders' including a few trusted Hutu, and then try to build a broader, apparently 'multi-ethnic' official leadership for public consumption. Thus anti-tribalism was delegated to a tribal élite, much in the same way that the task of creating the communist classless society had been delegated to 'the vanguard of the proletariat'. Whether or not it would turn out that this anti-tribalist tribal élite would follow its ideals rather than its sociological bent remained an open question. It would be a hard course to keep to because of its loneliness. On the one hand, in the eyes of the Hutu opposition, the RPF was a Tutsi outfit and therefore to be treated with a good deal of prudence, if not outright mistrust. People like Pasteur Bizimungu and Seth Sendashonga, the main Hutu cadres of the RPF, were well respected but considered as having gone a bit off the deep end. Few Hutu, whether educated or not, were willing to imitate them and join the Front[42].

And on the other hand, the conservative right-wing (and at times monarchist) elements which had figured so prominently in pre-war *émigré* circles[43] and which had had to yield precedence to the Uganda-based 'progressives' within the RPF, were just biding their time. And they, especially those based in Burundi had no patience for the 'social equality' theories of the 'Ugandans'.

42. Nevertheless, there were a few Hutu fighters. They were usually descendants of Hutu agricultural migrants who had moved to Uganda in the 1920s and '30s to escape the harshness of Belgian colonialism and take advantage of the economic opportunities Uganda then offered. During the 1982–4 anti-Banyarwanda repression, they had been targeted by the Obote government in the same way as the Western Tutsi Banyarwanda refugees. As a result some had joined the NRA and they had later followed their Tutsi Banyarwanda comrade-in-arms into the RPF.

43. From this point of view it is interesting to consult Franois-Xavier Bangamwabo and Emmanuel Rukiramakuba, 'Le vocabulaire et le discours des Inkotanyi et de leurs alliés' in Franois-Xavier Bangamwabo *et al.*, *Les relations interethniques . . .*, op. cit., pp. 223–68. In spite of their heavy anti-RPF slant, their linguistic and textual analysis is good and shows quite convincingly how backward-looking and unaware of contemporary Rwandese reality émigré literature was. But that is where the demonstration reaches its limits. It is almost entirely based on emigration publications such as *Impuruza, Huguka, Le Patriote* and *Isangano*. And by 1 October 1990 the dynamics of RPF action had made most of them obsolete. This does not mean of course that nostalgic Tutsi supremacists could not come back later to the forefront of Rwandese politics.

From the regime's point of view, the fact that a group of Tutsi could organise and later sustain military operations against the government of the Republic of Rwanda, the very government of the 'democratic majority', seemed to stupefy and silence the establishment Hutu moderates (they existed) and exasperate the most violent and extremist elements. In retrospect this seems 'logical', but only because the extremists did 'win' the day, even if their 'victory' ended up in disaster. The Habyarimana regime contained various trends and none but the most extreme of the Abashiru *akazu* finally remained in control, it is partly because the existence of the Tutsi RPF acted as a repulsion magnet: moderate Hutu who thoroughly disliked the regime and its dictatorial bent were always semi-paralysed by the fear of 'giving aid and assistance to the enemy' when they went too far in their opposition. Similarily, as we will see in the next chapter, it was always possible to play on the chord 'Neither Habyarimana nor the RPF', which Emmanuel Gapyisi had already begun to strike, and that playing on such a chord inevitably led to an ethnic position as extremist (if not more so) than that of the regime. 'Opposition' could then even be made to stand on its head, and the reason for criticising President Habyarimana could be presented as his being 'too soft' on the RPF and the Tutsi. One could truthfully say that by late 1993 the ultra-racist CDR had become an opposition party and that in turn some segments of the opposition had become more racist than the MRND of old[44].

44. This is the line chosen by the French when they try to defend their support for the Habyarimana regime, and was implied by the French ambassador Jean-Philippe Marlaud, successor to George Martre, when he declared in 1993, 'We are in a country at war and despite the war it has been able to pursue democratisation. It is not perfect, but the trend is towards democratisation' (quoted in Human Rights Watch, *Arming Rwanda*, op. cit., p. 36). The best presentation of the official French position on Rwanda at that time can be found in Philippe Decraene, 'Impasse militaire, diplomatique et politique au Rwanda', *Marchés Tropicaux* (9 April 1993), where President Habyarimana is described as 'a moderate democrat . . . whose image has been tarnished by the clumsiness and excesses of some Hutu extremists'. The fact that Mme Decraene had been for many years President Mitterrand's personal secretary and her husband one of his informal advisers on African matters lends a special quality to this statement.

The RPF benefited greatly in political terms from this drift towards extremism. For obvious reasons it had very much needed to demonise its enemy. The equation present in every 'Ugandan' RPF fighter's mind was MRND = UPC, Habyarimana = Obote and RPF = NRA[45] – or in other words, 'The victory will be ours'. Elements of reality which did not fit into this mechanistic transfer of the Ugandan past on to the Rwandese future were simply denied, and among them was the difference in popularity between the guerrillas and of the regime. For example the fact that the RPF was a largely Tutsi organisation and that Tutsi made up less than 15% of the Rwandese population, while the NRA, with the backing of most of the Bantu tribes of southern and western Uganda, had been able by 1985 to rely on the support of almost half the country's population; and the fact that Obote was a brutal and (in the end) drunken tyrant whose support, even among his Nilotic fellow-tribesmen, had been steadily declining while President Habyarimana would probably have won an honest democratic election without too much trouble as late as early 1991 – such reflexions were discounted as 'pro-government propaganda'[46].

It is astonishing that, as it persevered in this unrealistic appreciation of its political situation, the RPF by its very existence turned many of these misconceptions into realities. The hitherto roughly authoritarian Habyarimana regime did become a full-fledged tyranny, the RPF did become the only hope for a transition to democracy, and the ethnic radicalisation of the government did eventually drive liberal Hutu into the arms of the RPF. But none of this happened as stages in a planned progress. On the contrary. It was only when all other hopes were exhausted and frustrated, when extremists were completely in the ascendant on the government side, and a near apocalypse had occurred, that the war aims of the RPF finally became attainable, but in a completely different context from anything the Front had ever anticipated.

45. And later in the war, Kagame = Museveni.
46. The author's personal discussions with RPF cadres in Europe, Kenya, Uganda and Rwanda between 1990 and 1994.

This is why in a way the RPF programmatic stance never had much importance. Its eight-point programme, which Filip Reyntjens rightly describes as 'Not very original and having already been widely debated in Rwanda before the war, even within the ruling MRND',[47] was quite sufficient for the role it had to play. It served merely to occupy the ground and to pre-empt any openly monarchist or racially supremacist line from surfacing within the Front. It had to keep the organisation's purity of purpose crystal clear and steer the political quarrel on a moral course. At that level it was unbeatable. The Habyarimana regime rose to the bait with no glimmer of awareness and no understanding of the workings of world public opinion. The RPF's eight-point programme was hardly ever an issue since foreign public opinion (insofar as it knew or cared about Rwanda) rapidly took it for granted that the Tutsi guerrilla movement, representing poor downtrodden victims, refugees from their own country where a dictatorial regime denied them their birthright, could not but be fighting for democracy and social equality. This winning of the high moral ground had shifted the burden of proof from the guerrillas to the government, the Habyarimana regime having clearly lost any respect it ever had for the most basic human rights. Few paused to ask themselves whether human rights and politics were the same thing, whether victims were always innocent and the evil quality of the enemy was guaranteed.

During the brief occupation of Ruhengeri town by the RPF in January 1991, an old Tutsi man had remarked to one of the young guerrilla fighters who had come to 'liberate' him: 'You want power? You will get it. But here we will all die. Is it worth it to you?' The question was worth asking, but it is improbable that in late 1990 when Paul Kagame was working day and night to turn the RPF from an alienated band of exiles into an efficient fighting machine, he ever stopped to ask himself what was really going to happen. And in a way it is quite normal. Action carries with it its own logic, and in such

47. Filip Reyntjens, *L'Afrique des Grands Lacs en crise*, op. cit., p. 93.

situations men who stop to think far too long are likely to end up dead. But given the peculiar nature of the Hutu/Tutsi historical conundrum, historical myths, Belgian colonisers and all, any military action in this context had the inescapable quality of a bull let loose in the proverbial china shop. There is no reason to doubt the genuineness of the political ideals motivating the Front's leaders when they launched their action. But their 'Ugandan' political rationality and their rock-hard conviction of being right both morally and politically seem to have caused them to underestimate the depth of the irrational myths, fears and hatreds they were about to confront – including probably those lurking on their own side.

Everybody was wading in mythology[48]. For the Hutu supremacists of the Habyarimana regime, the RPF was the serpent entering the Garden of Eden where industrious, God-fearing, law-abiding members of the 'sociological majority' were peacefully attending to their bucolic tasks. As for the battle-hardened yet naive veterans of Uganda's revolutionary wars, they saw themselves as the legions of justice who had come, after years in which 'their' country had been hijacked by evil usurpers, to

---

48. Even the *wazungu* (whites). Rwanda and Burundi, these diabolical East African twins with their Tutsi and Hutu populations deadlocked in an apparently intractable love/hate relationship, are dangerous mythology-spawning enchanted castles. The disease is so strong that most genuine foreign specialists of these countries have either been contaminated or at least accuse each other of having been contaminated by Hutu-demonising or Tutsi-hating. See for example the polemical exchange between René Lemarchand, 'L'Ecole historique franco-burundaise. une école pas comme les autres', *Canadian Journal of African Studies* vol. 24, no. 2 (1990), pp. 235–48, and Jean-Pierre Chrétien, 'Burundi, le métier d'historien – querelle d'école?', *Canadian Journal of African Studies*, vol. 25, no. 3 (1991), pp. 450–67. Although the present author is not a true Rwanda specialist (and as such claims a limited immunity), he has probably by now also been contaminated, or in any case will be accused of having been as soon as this book appears. The evils of colonialism versus the dark recesses of the African soul, economic versus political determinants, killer victims versus victim killers, contradictory interpretations of ancient oral traditions – the stuff of conflicting visions abounds. And somewhere in the dark recesses of *our* own culture, the obsessive duality of the Hutu/Tutsi dichotomy probably has to do with Manichean fascination with good and evil – with our compulsive need to take sides which Zoroastrian deviants infiltrated centuries ago into medieval Christianity.

claim their birthright with the help of all good and decent citizens who were bound to agree with them and rush to their support. If they did not, it was because the government had brainwashed them.

As we have tried to show, the truth was somewhat more complicated. But it did not matter, myths are much stronger than the reality they purport to represent. And those twin conflictual myths, together, had just started to screw on the fuse of one of the biggest human bombs since the Nazi Holocaust.

5

THE ARUSHA PEACE MARATHON
(July 1992–August 1993)

The economic situation[1]

By mid-1992 war had taken its toll of an economy which had already been in a state of crisis when it had started. Exports had remained steady at 8.9 billion Rw. francs (compared to 9.2 in 1990) but imports had increased drastically from 23 to 38 billion Rw. francs. The resulting balance of payments deficit had been financed by spending a large chunk of the country's foreign currency reserves, which by early 1993 were down to US $56.7 m. from US $110.1 m in 1991. The foreign debt, which had already been sharply on the increase before the war, rising from US $452.2 m. in 1986 to $736.2 m. in 1990, was touching the $1 billion mark by 1993. Global public debt increased even quicker, going from 6,678 m. Rw. francs in 1990 to 13,702 m. in 1992, i.e. a 105% increase due almost entirely to military purchases. During the same period the Ministry of Defence budget had increased from 3,155 m. to 8,885 m. Rw. francs, a rise of 181%[2].

The result of this massive inflationary spending had been a quick depreciation of the Rw. franc, a currency which in the previous years had been quite steady.

AVERAGE EXCHANGE RATE *(Rw. francs per US $)*

1987	1990	1991	1992	1993
79.7	82.6	125.1	133.3	144.0

---

1. Unless otherwise mentioned, the statistics that follow are from IMF and OECD sources as quoted in Economist Intelligence Unit, *Rwanda: Country profile*, London: EIU, 1993.
2. Filip Reyntjens, *L'Afrique des Grands Lacs en crise*, Paris: Karthala, 1994, p. 117.

159

The last figure was theoretical since by 1993 everybody exchanged money on the black market, where the rate had risen to 182 Rw. francs to the dollar.

At the same time, while the war economy was rapidly devouring the country's resources, the government carried out unperturbed the Structural Adjustment Programme (SAP) it had agreed upon with the World Bank in 1990 and which had resulted, as a first measure, in a 40% devaluation of the national currency just before the outbreak of hostilities. A second devaluation (by 14.9%) was carried out in June 1992 to adjust for the pressure of inflation since the start of the war. The one element of the SAP which could not be carried out under the present circumstances were the planned reductions in public service employment. The army alone dwarfed all other civil service sectors and it continued to grow relentlessly. But in early 1993, in order to respect its other obligations, the government undertook a number of important privatisations, notably that of Electrogaz, the largest of its parastatals with 3,400 employees, which was US$58 m. in the red. The new management did exactly what Pasteur Bizimungu, who had briefly been its general manager in 1990, had been prevented from doing by President Habyarimana: he raised electricity rates, fired 2,000 workers from the politically-padded payrolls and cut off power from those who did not pay, including government departments. A 'national assets company' was created to manage the non-privatised parastatals, with the understanding that they would be disposed of later.

It was horse medicine and it could possibly have worked if it had been used ten years before. But between the coffee price decline and the war economy crisis, the SAP merely contributed to weakening further an already exhausted economy.

Peace and its enemies

The announcement of the cease-fire signed in Arusha brought great satisfaction to the ordinary population but caused consternation among the supporters of the extremist Hutu state.

Within days, the MRND(D) ministers were boycotting cabinet meetings and demonstrations hostile to Prime Minister Dismas Nsengiyaremye had erupted in the strongly conservative *préfectures* of Gisenyi and Ruhengeri[3]. On 17 August President Habyarimana, who sensed the displeasure of his supporters, gave a long speech on the radio, trying to explain and justify the need for peace. Speaking directly to his worried followers, the President declared:

'Our negotiating team in Arusha has been fully briefed . . . so that the positions they adopt are no longer improvised . . . This is why I think that the Rwandese people can rest assured that all the precautions have been taken to ensure that individual actions do not lead our country into an adventure it would not like.'[4]

The words used were coded. The 'improvised positions' alluded to by Habyarimana were those taken by Prime Minister Nsengiyaremye and Foreign Affairs Minister Ngulinzira, both members of the opposition and considered as 'suspect' by MRND(D) hardliners in their attitude towards the RPF. The hardliners had a nagging doubt that President Habyarimana was 'selling out' and that he would be prepared to accept a compromise on essentials in order to reach an understanding with 'the enemy' and safeguard his own position. The essentials of course were the 'sociological majority' principle of the 1959 revolution, ensuring systematic dominance for the Hutu in all spheres of life and, possibly even more strongly, the monopolistic grip which faithful party figures had been allowed to keep on the economy for the last twenty years. Jeopardising those were the 'adventures our country would not like'. The problem for the regime hardliners was how to avoid these dangers if peace and political pluralism were to become the order of the day. In the end, the answer had to be quite radical: regardless of international

---

3. BBC Summary of World Broadcast (henceforth SWB), Radio Kigali, 4 and 5 August 1992.
4. SWB, Radio Kigali, 17 August 1992.

opinion[5], if the new developments really threatened the *status quo*, they should be fought and destroyed.

On 18 August, Radio Muhabura, the RPF radio station, answered the President's long speech of the day before, saying that he did not wholeheartedly support the peace process and was actually undermining the cabinet's action in Arusha. This was an understatement. That very same day an agreement was reached between a government delegation and the RPF on the creation of a 'pluralistic transitional government' i.e. one in which the guerrillas would have a place. Four days later, 'ethnic' massacres started in the Kibuye area[6]. Once more, violence took a very organised aspect and arrested killers were mostly members of the MRND(D) or their affiliates. Félicien Gatabazi, the PSD leader, denounced the killings and was in turn denounced by the CDR as an *ibyitso*.

The Arusha 'peace' negotiations continued, but in a climate of increasing tension. Part of the problem came from the fact that the Presidential faction (and 'even more' the CDR activists who were now increasingly critical of the President) felt that

5. International concern about the Rwanda question by mid-1992 should not be exaggerated. France discreetly and firmly supported the Habyarimana regime and most other OECD countries displayed little interest in the problem. The United States had just declared: 'Our relations with Rwanda are excellent . . . and there is no evidence of any systematic human rights abuses by the military or any other element of the government.' (US Department of Defense and Department of State, *Congressional Presentation for Security Assistance Programs, Fiscal Year 1993*, Washington DC, 1992, p. 291, quoted in Human Rights Watch, *Arming Rwanda*, op. cit., p. 21). Apart from Belgium – which, knowing the country and the regime well, was growing increasingly nervous – only the German government had distanced itself from Kigali. Following the all too enthusiastic embrace it gave to the Habyarimana regime in the 1970s and '80s, even the CDU had by then grown very reserved. When Ferdinand Nahimana, after being fired from his Orinfor job, was given the position of cultural attaché at the Rwandese embassy in Bonn, the German government refused his accreditation as a diplomatic representative.
6. These have been documented in detail in ADL, Rapport, op. cit. pp. 235–64. This report was written quite early in the events (26 August) and could account for only about twelve victims. The final tally went up to about eighty-five dead and 200 wounded. About 500 houses were burned and more than 5,000 people were displaced.

they were not represented in Arusha. They felt that the Nsengiyaremye cabinet was playing its own game. Specifically they also considered, first, that they were not being consulted, and that the 'governmental' delegation in Arusha was acting as if it were purely an opposition delegation even if it now shared power in the cabinet. Secondly, that it was discussing the future allocation of government portfolios directly with the RPF without referring back to Kigali; and thirdly, that the principle of a chosen rather than an elected transitional assembly had been accepted, which was an intolerable surrender to RPF positions[7].

In Arusha Foreign Minister Ngulinzira and Defence Minister Gasana were negotiating with the RPF delegation (Pasteur Bizimungu, Théogène Rudasingwa and Patrick Mazimpaka) together with Ambassador Pierre-Claver Kanyarushoki (based in Kampala), who was the Habyarimana hardliner-in-residence. Since he did not seem able to impose his line, Colonel Théoneste Bagosora, who was later to coordinate the genocide, made frequent trips to Arusha to keep an eye on what was going on. He almost never spoke, but he remembered everything, and shortly before signing the final Peace Agreement in August 1993 James Gasana had to flee to Switzerland in fear for his life. Foreign Minister Ngulinzira was not so prudent, and was among the first to be killed in April 1994. Ambassador Kanyarushoki was of course left in peace.

On 18 October the CDR extremists took to the streets to demonstrate against the way the peace process was being negotiated. It is not without interest that thay chanted such slogans as 'Thank you President Mitterrand!', 'Thank you French People!', 'Free Radio Rwanda!', 'We want the Prime Minister and his government out!', and 'We want a broad-based cabinet!'. The hostility towards Prime Minister Nsengiyaremye

---

7. SWB, Radio Kigali, 20 October 1992. The RPF favoured a nominated rather than an elected Transitional Assembly because it felt that the MRND(D) still retained enough influence to win a large share of the vote, by legal or illegal means, and that the rest of the seats would be largely swept by the civilian Hutu opposition parties, leaving the RPF with a miserably small share of the seats.

was logical, but the allusion to a 'broad-based' cabinet was something new. It alluded to the latest anti-democratic manoeuvre which President Habyarimana had then been preparing[8], namely an attempt to circumvent the serious MDR, PSD and PL opposition by using some of the small inconsequential parties. Those which had agreed to enter into his plan were the PSR, the PECO, the PDI and the Union Démocratique du Peuple Rwandais (UDPR), four of the miniature political parties created the year before which, together with the MRND(D), now asked to be consulted on *all* decisions, *all* to have representatives in Arusha and *all* to have cabinet posts in the future transitional cabinet. To complete the sabotage, skirmishes were organised the next few days on the RPF lines around Byumba and negotiations ground to a halt.

As for the 'Free Radio Rwanda' slogan, it arose from the fact that the Radio Rwanda reporters, feeling that change was in the air, were beginning to show a sense of independence and to report what was actually going on, even if the news they carried was not particularly favourable to the regime. It was at this time that the CDR extremists began to think about the need to have their own radio station. More intriguing was the gratitude expressed to the French people and to President Mitterrand himself. However, the reason was simple. France had discreetly been backing the CDR in various ways. Even as the negotiations in Arusha were beginning, reinforcements of about 150 men had been brought up before the cease-fire. This was seen by the French military mission in Rwanda as contingency planning 'just in case something happened'. It is not clear whether some of the other decisions taken then were always made in full agreement with explicitly-stated policies from the ministry in Paris[9], but they were taken none the less. The

8. He made it public four days later on 22 October 1992.
9. A French army colonel bragged in the author's presence how, by playing on the dates and rotation patterns of the various units, it was possible to keep up to 1,100 men in Rwanda while admitting only 600 to the press (Paris, 11 April 1993). This was a period when, after some initial emotion from East Africa specialists (see Jean-Pierre Chrétien, 'Le régime de Kigali et l'intervention française

French instructors were very lax over the screening of the candidates they accepted for military training, especially at the Bigogwe commando camp. An excuse might be that at the time the FAR were progressively losing their discipline and that the French military mission both had to face a flow of ill-chosen recruits and at the same time wished to improve the quality of their training. However, the result was that, possibly without realising it, the French trained the MRND(D) and CDR militiamen, the notorious *Interahamwe* and *Impuzamugambi* who were later to organise and lead the April-May 1994 genocide[10].

Some other friendly gestures could not have been the result of absent-mindedness, such as when President Mitterrand's office 'thanked' Jean-Bosco Barayagwiza, the extremist CDR leader, for his letter and sign-in campaign in support of French intervention[11]. In any case, for the Rwandese extremist press, things were clear and Paris was seen as a staunch ally in the fight against the 'Tutsi feudalists'. In the famous number of *Kangura* in which the CDR journalist Hassan Ngeze had published his 'Ten commandments of the Hutu', the very official-looking picture of President Mitterrand on the back of the magazine had

au Rwanda – sortir du silence', *Bulletin du CRIDEV* no. 105 (Feb.-March 1992), awareness of the ambiguities of French intervention in Rwanda was beginning to spread to the general press. See for two examples Stephen Smith, 'La guerre secrète de l'Elysée en Afrique de l'Est', *Libération* (11 June 1992) and Jean-François Dupaquier, 'La France au chevet d'un fascisme africain', *L'Evènement du Jeudi* (25 June 1992).

10. This is an accusation the French have always denied, more with moral indignation than with concrete proof (see Coopération Minister Michel Roussin's interview on Radio France Internationale, 30 May 1994). But there are testimonies to the contrary from some of the trainees themselves (see Frédéric Filloux, 'Rwanda. Un ancien des escadrons de la mort accuse', *Libération*, 21 June 1994). But in Rwanda the accusation stuck, and President Mitterrand was nicknamed '*Mitterahamwe*'.

11. Letter from the President's office, dated 1 September 1992 and signed by Bruno Delaye, head of the *Cellule Africaine*. The letter was adressed to Jean-Bosco Barayagwiza in his capacity as director of political affairs in the Rwandese Ministry of Foreign Affairs, and a few days later in a private conversation M. Delaye pretended that the President's good faith had been surprised. If this is the case and Barayagwiza's true political personality was not known at the Elysée, one wonders what kind of political reports were coming from the French embassy in Kigali.

carried the following caption in Kinyarwanda: 'It is during the hard times that one comes to know one's true friends.'[12]

Negotiations feed the rise of extremism

In fact, although they pretended always to act in support of President Habyarimana and against his enemies, the CDRs and the hardline fraction of the MRND(D) were increasingly taking an attitude of almost open defiance of their official leader. This reflected growing tensions within the *akazu* itself, where Mme Habyarimana and her brothers, always a law unto themselves, were becoming ever more suspicious of what they saw as the President's new 'middle of the road' line. The President knew it and he also knew that the danger of a military coup coming from that direction would increase as the prospect of a genuine peace with the RPF came nearer.

In Arusha between September 1992 and January 1993 the discussions had dealt initially with the power-sharing arrangements. Surprisingly, this had gone down quite smoothly; the RPF resigned itself to keeping a politically-diminished Habyrimana as President; much haggling took place over how long the transition period would last (it was finally set at eighteen months), and the cabinet itself was the product of many complex bargainings. But the discussions around the creation of a new army, which started in February 1993, proved much more difficult. The original government offer was to include 20% RPF soldiers into the future new national army, but everyone knew the RPF would not accept such a low figure and that the FAR leadership was very nervous about having

12. *Kangura*, no. 6 (December 1990). These 'Ten Commandments' made up a racist anti-Tutsi decalogue which said among other things (commandment no. 8) that the Hutu 'should stop taking any pity on the Tutsi' and that (commandment no. 10) 'the 1959 Social Revolution, the 1961 Referendum and the Hutu ideology have to be taught to every Hutu at all levels and widely disseminated'. For a discussion of the *Kangura* phenomenon, see Jean-Pierre Chrétien, 'Presse libre et propagande raciste au Rwanda', *Politique Africaine*. no. 42 (June 1991) pp. 109–20.

more[13]. As soon as the Nsengiyaremye cabinet was sworn-in, the President asked the new Prime Minister and his Minister of Defence, MRND(D) moderate James Gasana, to prepare a plan for reorganising the Armed Forces top leadership, with the aim of eliminating the most resolute extremists. This reorganisation had been made effective on 6 June 1992. Colonels Laurent Serubuga, Bonaventure Buregeya, Pierre-Célestin Rwagafilita and Pontien Hakizimana had been administratively retired. A relative moderate, Colonel Deogratias Nsabimana, had been made new army commander-in-chief and another moderate, Colonel Marcel Gatsinzi, had received the command of the military school. But Colonel Ndindiliyimana, who had been given the command of the *Gendarmerie* (the paramilitary rural police), certainly could not be called a moderate and Defence Minister Gasana had not managed to get rid of one of the worst extremists, Colonel Théoneste Bagosora[14]. Bagosora was linked with the '*Clan de Madame*' and was close to Mme Habyarimana's three brothers who had been among the most powerful men in the country[15]. But he had also always played his own game and seen himself as presidential material. He had intrigued tirelessly but unsuccessfully to become commander-in-chief of the FAR, bombarding the ministry with memos. He knew about the drug business developed by the FAR officer corps in the previous few years and was even rumoured to be one of its beneficiaries. Now that other members of the hardline *akazu* in the army had been eliminated, he became more useful than ever for their group and Gasana was forced to postpone his retirement by one year and

---

13. Commandment no. 7 of Ngeze's racist decalogue was adamant that 'the Armed Forces have to be solidly Hutu'. The majority of the FAR officer corps heartily agreed.

14. In a way, President Habyarimana had been using his Minister of Defence as a security fuse and when faced with the anger of the extremists he pretended that Gasana had acted on his own, to please the new opposition in the cabinet. Under constant threat from the military extremists, Defence Minister Gasana finally had to flee Rwanda before the August 1993 Arusha Peace Agreement later to see Colonel Bagosora became the chief organiser of the massacres. (Interview with former Minister of Defence James Gasana, Geneva, 13 June 1994.)

15. See Chapter 2.

to accept him as Director of Services in the Ministry of Defence, a position from which he could keep his network informed about everything that went on inside the army.

And some of the things that were going on inside the army had begun to filter out, causing a certain amount of scandal. On 2 October 1992, Professor Filip Reyntjens organised a press conference at the Belgian Senate in Brussels with the help of Senator Willy Kuypers[16], during which he revealed the existence of a civilian-military organisation nicknamed 'Zero Network' which constituted a death squad on the Latin American model. This death squad, according to several testimonies, had taken part in the Bugesera massacres of March 1992 and planned various political killings. It was made up of a mixture of off-duty soldiers and MRND(D) militiamen who were given weapons by the army. The list of the death squad's leaders given by Professor Reyntjens read like an *akazu* 'who's who': Mme Habyarimana's three brothers; Alphonse Ntirivamunda, son-in-law of President Habyarimana and Director of Public Works[17]; Colonel Elie Sagatwa, the President's personal secretary who was married to one of his sisters; the head of G 2 military intelligence; the commander of the presidential Guard (GP); several top civil servants and of course Colonel Théoneste Bagosora, cabinet director of the Defence Ministry. There was no official Rwandese government denial of the Reyntjens/Kuypers revelations, but a few days later[18] the RPF radio referred to 'the persistant rumours which are now circulating concerning a new plan to massacre Rwandese civilians in an indiscriminate way. . . . If such a thing should occur, our armed forces could not remain inactive.'

It now seems likely that the genocide plan was first put

16. See his short mimeographed note, 'Données sur les Escadrons de la Mort', Brussels, 9 October 1992. For other material on the death squads see François Misser, 'Inquiry into death squads', *The New African* (January 1993), and FIDH, *Rwanda*, op. cit., pp. 78–84.

17. Public Works pick-up trucks had been used to transport some of the militiamen to the killing spots of Bugesera in March.

18. SWB, Radio Muhabura, 25 October 1992.

together in outline at that time. Certainly nothing had yet reached an organised stage, and such plans were probably limited to the most hot-headed CDR and *Interahamwe* extremists. But it is probably during those late months of 1992 that the general notion of 'solving' the power-sharing question by a large-scale slaughter of most Tutsi and of all the known Hutu opposition supporters, began to look to the hardline *akazu* circles like both an attractive and a feasible proposition. The *Amasasu* ('bullets') secret society had been created in the army sometime in early 1992, and consisted of extremist officers who felt that the fight against the RPF was not being carried out with the necessary energy. It was its members who had begun to hand out weapons to the militias organised by both the CDR and the extremists within the MRND(D). They were also probably the link between the respective recruitment programmes of the FAR and the militia which the French military mission did not seem too concerned to sort out. And they worked hand-in-hand with the 'Zero Network' boys.

By late 1992, the protoganists in the future genocide had all found their places as shadowy counterparts of the official institutions. The FAR had its secret society, the extremist parties their militia, the secret service its killer squads. But all were still doing little more than flex their muscles, killing on a small scale and hoping that their sporadic murders and massacres would somehow lead to a change of policy inflexion and that the opposition parties would be terrorised into submission, President Habyarimana dynamised into an all-out political confrontation and the army pushed to total war with the RPF. In other words, they were apprentice extremist totalitarians within a semi-totalitarian regime. Habyarimana had been a semi-totalitarian in the sense that he had created a seamless social and political system in which civil rights were narrowly controlled. But it was a society with its own (restricted) freedoms. What the new brand of extremists now emerging from the ranks of the old order wanted was absolute power through absolute terror. When facing the members of their society who wanted to liberalise and broaden the limited openings it had offered, they reacted by attempting not only to tighten up but to destroy the adversary completely. The only way they could hope to succeed in the radical political-realignment-through-mass-murder of which they were now beginning to dream was by gaining the total support of the Hutu peasant masses. And that could be achieved only by making the peasants feel that they had no choice but to kill to protect themselves from an evil that was both facelessly abstract and embodied in the most ordinary person living next door. To succeed in carrying out a plan of mass slaughter they had to achieve two things: one was to drape themselves with the mantle of legitimate power in order to benefit from the instinctive Rwandese cultural bent towards obeying authority, and the second was to instil a powerful, all-encompassing fear of the dreadful change evil stangers were about to inflict on us into the minds of a credulous and naive peasantry already shaken by two years of conflict and political confusion.

In the short term, the extremists' main preoccupation was how to stop the growing dynamics of peace both in the country and at Arusha. The MRND(D) kept protesting against the lack of consultation concerning the negotiations[19] while the CDR, in a more aggressive style, was demonstrating in the streets and fighting it out with MDR and PSD militants[20]. For his part, President Habyarimana kept insisting that the big oppositon parties now represented in the cabinet should accept to meet with the small opposition parties and take them seriously. He also suggested holding elections, a proposal the opposition parties declined for obvious reasons. Irritated by these failures, he then disavowed the government delegation in Arusha, accusing it of 'going beyond its mandate'[21] and on 15 November, while giving a speech in his Ruhengeri home base, he went as far as to call the July cease-fire agreement 'a piece of trash . . . which the government is not obliged to respect'[22]. In Arusha, Boniface

19. SWB, Radio Rwanda, 28 October 1992.
20. Ibid., 30 October 1992.
21. Ibid., 3 and 6 November 1992.
22. This speech, which was given in Kinyarwanda, was not retransmitted by the National Radio, and President Habyarimana later denied having spoken these words about the Arusha agreement. But the speech had been taped by several people and was commented on all over the country.

Ngulinzira, the Foreign Affairs minister and head of the government delegation, declared in frustration: 'The MRND keeps talking in contradictory ways. On the one hand, it pretends to support the peace negotiations and on the other hand it keeps sabotaging them. This party has to choose: either it supports the negotiations or else it fights them.'[23] The deadlock was complete and President Habyarimana stuck to his guns, declaring in Bujumbura where he had flown to meet President Museveni in a vain attempt at mediation:'There are sixteen political parties in opposition, only five of which are in government. [...] The others should be there too.'[24]

There were frequent demonstrations throughout December 1992 and January 1993, either in support of the Arusha negotiations or to condemn it. They all ended up in street fights between the opposition and the CDR/*Interahamwe*. As usual in such situations, the hardliners tried to end the deadlock by pushing the situation to extremes of ethnic violence. On 22 November 1992, Léon Mugesera, Vice-President of the Gisenyi MRND(D) Section and influential within the party, addressed the party militants of the Kabaya *sous-préfecture* as follows:

'The opposition parties have plotted with the enemy to make the Byumba *préfecture* fall to the *Inyenzi*[25]. [...] They have plotted to undermine our armed forces. [...] The law is quite clear on this point: 'Any person who is guilty of acts aiming at sapping the morale of the armed forces will be condemned to death.' What are we waiting for? [...] And what about those accomplices

23. SWB, Radio Rwanda, 16 November 1992.
24. Ibid., 22 December 1992. President Habyarimana's arithmetic seemed to have been somewhat off the mark. There were 'only' fifteen opposition parties – unless one also counted the MRND(D) – and there were four and not five represented in the government. But the President could be forgiven for not remembering too well, since most of the Rwandese population did not even know about the existence of the small opposition parties. The President had created on 11 November the Alliance pour le Renforcement de la Démocratie (Alliance to Strengthen Democracy or ARD) which regrouped the MRND(D), the CDR, the PDR, PARERWA and PECO. It was little more than a paper structure.
25. 'Cockroaches', the name given to Tutsi guerrillas during the conflicts of the 1960s.

(*ibyitso*) here who are sending their children to the RPF? Why
are we waiting to get rid of these families? [...] We have to take
responsibility into our own hands and wipe out these hoodlums.
[...] The fatal mistake we made in 1959 was to let them [the Tutsi]
get out. [...] They belong in Ethiopia and we are going to find
them a shortcut to get there by throwing them into the Nyabarongo river [which flows northwards]. I must insist on this point.
We have to act. Wipe them all out!'[26]

A few days later Mugesera was repeating the same speech in the
Kibilira commune, where massacres had already taken place in
October 1990[27]. Stanislas Mbonampeka, the opposition (PL)
Minister of Justice, charged Mugesera with inciting racial hatred
and issued a warrant for his arrest. Mugesera took refuge in a
military camp and the police were too frightened by his army
protection to go after him. Out of frustration, Mbonampeka
resigned and President Habyarimana, quite content to have a
headless Ministry of Justice at this juncture, postponed finding
a successor till June 1993.

The area where Mugesera had so energetically preached for
radical action soon answered his call and violence began. Even
some of the MRND(D) faithful balked at the prospect of what
they now saw rising on the political horizon. In a letter
addressed to Mugesera whom he knew well, the university
professor Jean Rumiya, a former member of the MRND(D)
central committee accused him of 'openly calling for murder . . .
in order to launch an operation of ethnic and political purification'. He added: 'Like many other Rwandese, I had hoped that
the time when ritual murders were committed for political
purposes was over.'[28] He was unfortunately wrong as the
movement was just gathering momentum.

26. FIDH, *Rwanda*, op. cit., pp. 24–5.
27. See Chapter 3.
28. Filip Reytjens, *L'Afrique des Grands Lacs en crise*, op. cit., p. 120. Jean Rumiya
    is the author of the book on the Belgian colonial mandate in Rwanda which we
    mentioned in Chapter 1. As an MRND(D) militant, he had collaborated in the
    already quoted propaganda work edited by François-Xavier Bangamwabo, *Les rela-
    tions interethniques. . . .*

Sporadic violence occurred during late December 1992 and early January 1993, killing a dozen people and forcing hundreds to flee. But when an international commission arrived in Rwanda on 7 January to monitor human rights abuses, the violence receded. The *bourgmestres* in the *communes* declared openly that the violence would be restrained for the duration of the visit, but that it would flare up again as soon as the commission left.[29] On 9 January, the negotiators at Arusha signed an agreement on power-sharing, whereby the future Broadened Base Transitional Government (BBTG) would have five MRND(D) cabinet posts; the RPF would also get five, the MDR four, the PSD and the PL three each and the PDC one. In the transitional assembly which was to function until enough peace and calm had been restored to enable elections to be held, the main parties MRND(D), RPF, MDR, PSD and PL would each have eleven members of parliament and the PDC four, while the 'eleven pygmies' minor opposition parties would each get one seat out of a total of seventy. This was a more or less equitable way out of a terribly thorny situation but it was not acceptable to the MRND(D) or CDR extremists who knew that they would be slowly ground down by such a set-up till they reached their real place in the political sociology of the country. On 19 January the MRND(D) and the CDR organised violent demonstrations against the proposed settlement and on 21 January MRND(D) national secretary Mathieu Ngirumpatse declared that, signature or no signature, his party had rejected the agreement. The same day, the International Commission on Human Rights mission left the country and, as the *bourgmestres* had foretold, violence immediately engulfed the whole north-west.

29. The Commission was composed of the Fédération Internationale des Droits de l'Homme (Paris), Africa Watch (London), the Union Interafricaine des Droits de l'Homme (Ouagadougou) and the Centre International des Droits de la Personne et du Développement Démocratique (Montreal). This visit led to writing the report we have quoted several time as FIDH, *Rwanda*.True to their work, the *bourgmestres* restarted the killings on 21 January, the very day the Commission left the country. (Author's interview with a commission member, London, 14 December 1994.)

Groups of extremist militiamen, acting either on their own or more often with the support of the local people and the collaboration of FAR elements, went on a murder rampage, torturing prisoners and burning houses. The violence lasted for about six days, till 26 January, and an estimated 300 people were killed. The effect on the whole area was traumatic[30]. The contacts in Arusha were suspended and on 8 February RPF forces decided to break the cease-fire and attack around Byumba.

The February war and its aftermath

The RPF offensive was immediately successful, causing the Forces Armées Rwandaises to withdraw in disarray. The main reason for their failure to resist was the lowering of morale and military discipline in its recruits since the May 1992 mutinies. The formerly disciplined army was living in ever worse material conditions as the government's financial situation deteriorated, and in completely contradictory ways it felt not only that it was both the mainstay of the regime but also that the cease-fire and coming peace had made it useless and redundant. During the last few months it had more and more often indulged in drunkenness and abuses of civilians, quite independently from the ethnic violence to which some of its militant members were increasingly prone. A popular and moderate Catholic publication had recently written about them in harsh terms:

> Soldiers are the biggest cause of insecurity. When they have had too much to drink, they will do anything: shoot at people, ransack houses, rape girls and women. . . . We have to discipline our soldiers if the public is to retain confidence in its armed forces. The civilian population have supported the war effort with all available means, and now the soldiers are turning against their benefactors. The civilians have had enough and will defend themselves with their traditional weapons. In several places bad soldiers have been found dead[31].

---

30. Africa Watch, *Beyond the Rhetoric: Continuing Human Rights Abuses in Rwanda*, London. June 1993, pp. 4–5.
31. *Kinyamateka*, no. 1383, December 1992, pp. 10–11 (quoted in FIDH; *Rwanda*, op. cit., p. 59)

Such an awful relationship between regular army and population would, in most other countries, have paved the way for a successful popular guerrilla campaign. But the ethnic contradiction was such that the Hutu peasants fled massively before the arrival of their Tutsi 'liberators'. The 300,000 displaced persons who had already moved during the 1990–2 fighting ran away from their camps and started moving south in company with new refugees. By late February there were an estimated 600,000 people on the move[32] and by early March about 860,000[33]. Nothing seemed capable of stemming the RPF advance and there were distinct fears that it might take the capital by storm.

For the first time, the RPF was clearly guilty of a number of atrocities. In Ruhengeri town, which they took on 8 February, their forces shot eight civil servants and nine of their relations, some of them children. While at least one of the dead, *bourgmestre* Thaddée Gasana of Kinigi *commune*, had been guilty of ordering some of the Bagogwe killings a few days before, the cases of the others were much less clear-cut, and in any case wives and children had never been involved. It seems that the victims were shot simply in reprisal for the recent massacres. Other executions were reported elsewhere, although they were not as clearly documented as the ones in Ruhengeri[34]. Whether these killings were carried out deliberately or whether they resulted from the anger felt by some of the fighters after the recent massacres is not clear. But they contributed to blackening the

---

32. *Le Monde*, 24 February 1993.
33. *Libération*, 8 March 1993. The author visited the RPF-held areas about three months after the 'February War' and found them eerily empty of life. RPF soldiers had not looted anything and houses could be seen with chairs still set around a table and mouldy food on the plates where people had fled so hurriedly as not to eat their last meal. The RPF admitted that only 1,800 Hutu peasants were left in an area which had had a population of about 800,000 before the war. The killings in and around Ruhengeri (see note below) which were not immediately known were not the motive for this exodus. It came from the deep fear which Hutu peasants felt (and were encouraged to feel) for the RPF 'feudalist devils'.
34. Africa Watch, *Beyond the Rhetoric*, op. cit., pp. 23–5, and interview with Radio Rwanda opposition journalist Jean-Marie Vianney Higiro, Kigali, 14 June 1993. The figures for the February RPF killings vary between 50 and 200 according to sources.

RPF image among the liberal Hutu opposition in Kigali, a process that was to have serious political consequences. The French reaction to the RPF attack was quite sharp: in Paris it was regarded as unprovoked aggression. Ambassador Georges Martre had told a French member of the International Human Rights Commission on his recent visit to Rwanda that the massacres in the north-west were 'just rumours'[35]. The Direction Générale des Services Extérieurs (DGSE), the French secret service, accused Uganda of helping the RPF offensive, and for good measure accused the guerrillas of burning villages, adding that 'mass graves had been found in their area'[36]. How government troops could have found mass graves in the growing area of enemy territory while they themselves were retreating was not explained. The DGSE was active in passing on disinformation, which resurfaced in various forms in several French newspapers[37]. The general trend of this disinformation was to present the renewed fighting as something completely new (the public were not supposed to remember the vague happenings of a few years ago in that distant country) and as a straight foreign invasion, the RPF being presented merely as Ugandans under a different guise. A few days later, a 'RPF massacre' was providentially 'discovered'[38]. The disinformation played its role in preparing the ground for increased French involvement in the war. Three hundred new troops were rushed to Rwanda and a massive quantity of ammunition was sent for the FAR artillery.

35. Stephen Smith, 'Massacres au Rwanda', *Libération*, 9 February 1993.
36. Dispatch of Agence France Presse (AFP), 16 February 1993.
37. See for example, 'L'Ouganda envahit le Rwanda. Mitterrand nous cache une guerre africaine', *Le Canard Enchainé*, 17 February 1993, and 'Selon les Services de Renseignement français, les rebelles bénéficieraient du soutien de l'Armée Ougandaise', *Le Monde*, 17 February 1993.
38. *Le Monde*, 21 February 1993. This 'massacre' was supposed to have occurred at the Rebero refugee camp. When some priests (usually rather hostile to the RPF because of their long association with the regime) went to check, they found no trace of any massacre, but the population had decamped. When they had heard on the radio that they had been 'massacred', they chose to hide for fear that the army would actually kill them in order to corroborate the announcement.

The French line of argument in defending renewed intervention in Rwanda was to insist that

. . . France has supported the Arusha negotiations which have led to an agreement between the government and the opposition to create a transition cabinet. . . . In any case, the World Bank and the other donors keep their representatives in Kigali only because of our military presence which – need I remind you – is there only to protect our citizens[39].

The fact that the renewed fighting had been caused by the regime systematically sabotaging the agreement France had 'supported' was obviously not to be discussed. France – and this was an article of faith only questioned by ill-intentioned persons – 'supported democratisation everywhere in Africa'. As for the January massacres, 'they were committed by fanatical elements and would have been even worse if it had not been for the French-trained *Gendarmerie* who saved people everywhere and did not hesitate to fire on the murderous crowds'[40].

But regardless of the ambiguities, (to put it mildly) of the French intervention, it had one beneficial effect: to safeguard Kigali itself which, despite its denials, the RPF might have been tempted to take by storm. And a storming of Kigali could only have led to a major bloodbath and removed any chance of a negotiated political solution. Where the French intervention fell tragically short of its target was when, once Kigali had been turned into a safe refuge, Paris instead of following military with political action turned its back on the whole dismal non-process, leaving the Arusha and post-Arusha witches' brew to simmer nastily until it blew up in everybody's faces.

RPF troops had arrived about 30 km. north of Kigali when on 20 February Colonel Kanyarengwe proclaimed a unilateral cease-fire from Byumba. There were several strong reasons for the guerrillas to stop at the last moment before attacking

---

39. Marcel Debarge, Minister of Cooperation, in an interview in *Le Monde*, on 17 February 1993.
40. Bruno Delaye, head of the Elyseé *Cellule Africaine*. Conversation with the author on his return from Kigali 15 February 1993.

the capital. On the one hand France was most likely to help President Habyarimana defend Kigali, possibly involving French troops in the fighting, and a direct military confrontation with the French army was obviously hazardous for the RPF. Then its agents were also beginning to bring back from the capital information on the very negative psychological and political effect of the offensive on the Hutu population. Everybody, including the most resolute opponents, was prepared to fight. President Habyarimana could count on massive popular support, and the offensive risked undoing years of political work[41]. So, while the guns almost fell silent[42], politics and diplomacy came back to the fore. But the renewed fighting had considerable impact.

On 28 February, Marcel Debarge, the French Minister for Cooperation arrived in Kigali and quickly asked the opposition parties to 'make a common front' with President Habyarimana against the RPF. Even if the desire on the part of Paris to exploit the closing of Hutu ranks against the Tutsi RPF was understandable, the public nature of the French minister's declaration was shocking. In such a tense ethnic climate, with massacres having taken place in recent weeks, this call for a 'common front' which could only be based on race was nearly a call to racial war. It seemed that some of the French authorities involved in the Rwandese crisis were in danger of globalising the conflict in ever cruder and more paranoid terms. In another DGSE-inspired article one could read: 'In Rwanda, humanitarian organisations are almost all under Anglo-Saxon control and as a result pro-Uganda.'[43] The equation thus suggested was 'Uganda equals Anglo-Saxons equals RPF'. M. Debarge's call for a 'common front' went one step further in adding equals Tutsi'. This of course implied another equation: 'Rwanda equals France equals "common front" equals Hutu.' But there

41. Interview with journalist Sixbert Musamgamfura, Kigali, 13 June 1993.
42. Sporadic fighting lasted another two weeks, till on 5–7 March the meeting of the RPF and the Rwandese government in Dar-es-Salaam.
43. Frédéric Pons, 'Tango à Kigali', *Valeurs Actuelles*, 1 March 1993.

should have been no problem about a 'common front' because in the same article, President Habyarimana was described as 'a moderate'.

For the Hutu opposition parties in government the whole thing was a disaster. They sent a delegation to Bujumbura to meet the RPF on neutral ground and try to mend fences. The meeting lasted a whole week (25 February to 2 March) and resulted in a common communiqué calling for: a durable cease-fire; the withdrawal of 'foreign troops' (i.e. the French); a renewal of the peace negotiations in Arusha; the return of inter-nally displaced persons to their homes; and legal action against the persons responsible for massacres.

But President Habyarimana was busy organising his 'common front'. On the day the Bujumbura meeting ended, he had called a 'national conference' in Kigali, grouping around the MRND(D) and the CDR not only seven of the ten minor opposition parties[44], but representatives of the four opposition parties in government (MDR, PSD, PL and PDC) as well. With an almost perfectly symmetrical anti-Bujumbura agenda, the resolutions of this meeting

– condemned the 'RPF-*Inkotanyi*' for 'trying to take power by force of arms';
– thanked the armed forces for their 'bravery' and assured them of full support;
– welcomed the French military presence;
– condemned Uganda for its support of the RPF; and
– asked for 'coordination' between the Council of Ministers, the President and the Prime Minister.

So there was the paradoxical situation of one set of delegates from four political parties condemning in Kigali what another set of delegates of the same four political parties had supported in Bujumbura on the same day. This paradox reflected a fierce

44. PDI, PECO, RTD, Parti Démocrate, PADER, MFBP plus a hitherto unknown member in that folkloric band, the PPJR-Ramarwanda. The conference document claimed that the meeting had been called at the initiative of the Rwandese bishops' conference and of the Protestant Council of Rwanda.

political struggle within the opposition as a result of the 'February war'.

The RPF attack on 8 February had caused a real trauma for a broad section of the now-legal and mostly Hutu opposition. Faustin Twagiramungu, president of the largest opposition party and as such its informal leader, and even Prime Minister Dismas Nsengiyaremye, had represented the RPF as a moderate political force, which only wished to regain full political and social rights for the exiled Tutsi refugee community. Since the regime had always presented the guerrillas as bloodthirsty feudalists bent on seizing power by force, the Hutu opposition had progressively accepted the milder MDR view of the RPF and shrugged off its virulent conqueror image as a propaganda fabrication. Now, suddenly, it seemed as if the Habyarimana regime had a point after all, and a major and dangerous point at that. The exact circumstances of the RPF attack were not clear. The official line of the guerrillas was that they had attacked to stop the massacres in the north-west. But these had stopped almost two weeks before the offensive. So there could be only two reasons for the RPF to break the cease-fire. If one wanted to believe the Front's good faith, it could be explained by its exasperation in the face of constant and repeated sabotage of the Arusha negotiations by the regime, but if one did not hold such a positive view, one could think that the extent of the exasperation had resulted in an attempt to seize power. This doubt about the RPF's motives had a tremendous effect on the Hutu opposition. On one side, even the most resolute and honest opponents of the regime began to fear that they had been naive and that, through their actions, they were running the risk of exchanging a Hutu military dictatorship for a Tutsi one. And on the other, both the genuine, basically unreconciled Tutsi-haters and the ambitious politicians who thought that there was new political mileage to be made out of deliberate Tutsi-baiting moved to create a 'new opposition' which would be both anti-Habyarimana and anti-Tutsi. The formula had already been tried by Emmanuel Gapyisi almost a year before, without success because the time was not ripe. It was going to happen again, this time with much more far-reaching effects.

Already on 1 March Donat Murego, the MDR executive secretary and a personal enemy of the MDR president Faustin Twagiramungu, had issued a strange communiqué in which he expressed strong support for the French military presence in Rwanda, adding that this presence 'could in no way have the effect of supporting directly or indirectly the dying dictatorship of *retired*[45] Major-General Habyarimana Juvénal which the MDR will keep fighting with all its strength'. This from the same man who, two days later, represented the MDR at the meeting supporting President Habyarimana's initiative. This is what can be called tactical manoeuvring, and it was erupting in all the opposition parties. The representative of the PL at the Habyarimana-sponsored conference had been the veteran politician Stanislas Mbonampeka, a rival of the party president Justin Mugenzi, while the PDC representative was Gaspard Ruhumuliza, a challenger of the party's founder Jean-Népomucène Nayinzira. The PSD representative, Paul Secyugu, was a lacklustre party member – the best that the Habyarimana team had been able to attract. Contrary to the other parties, the PSD remained united and coherent under its Nzamurambaho-Gatabazi-Gafaranga leadership. But within the PL, the PDC and particularly the MDR it was a free-for-all. Within twenty-four hours of the Habyarimana-sponsored meeting splitting the opposition, the 'official' leadership of the four parties[46] issued a communiqué disavowing their representatives who had 'neither the mandate nor the power to start such negotiations'. In fact, the whole opposition, with the partial exception of the PSD, was now split down the middle between those who thought accommodation with the RPF should be pursued in order to fight the regime and those who saw the RPF as the enemy even if the regime also had to be fought (albeit with temporary tactical alliances).

This provided a perfect opportunity for two political groups.

---

45. Emphasis in the original.
46. That is Faustin Twagiramungu for the MDR, Frédéric Nzamurambaho for the SPD, Justin Mugenzi for the PL and Jean-Népomucène Nayinzira for the PDC: it was soon to be known as the 'cartel of the presidents' since all were presidents of their respective parties.

The first of these was made up of what could be called the 'CDR constellation' in the sense that the CDR was its above-ground official incarnation but that a whole world of dark underground forces ('Zero Network', the *Interahamwe* militia wing of the MRND(D), army extremists) followed in its wake. These people, though closely linked to the *akazu* presidential circles or even members of them, had now lost faith in the die-hard resolution of the President. For them Habyarimana should have reacted much more strongly to the RPF attack on 8 February. They started compiling lists of those who, as 'traitors to the country', deserved to die. And the notion that the President himself should perhaps figure on those lists probably began to be considered. On 9 March , the CDR issued a very violent communiqué condemning the recently signed Dar-es-Salaam ceasefire:

> Mr Habyarimana Juvénal, President of the Republic, has approved the contents of an agreement obviously detrimental to the interests of the Rwandese people. This shows clearly that Mr Habyarimana Juvénal, President of the Republic, does not care any more about the interests of the Nation and is now defending other interests. [The Dar-es-Salaam cease-fire agreement] constitutes an act of high treason. [...] The CDR solemnly calls on its adherents, on other authentic democratic forces and on the FAR to refuse categorically the capitulation accepted by Prime Minister Dismas Nsengiyaremye and President Habyarimana Juvénal.

On 27 March the CDR announced its resignation from the ARD, the paper-alliance of anti-opposition parties, and by this action positioned itself as an opposition party, but as a 'new opposition', more radically opposed to the former 'opposition' now in government than to the President himself.

The second group to benefit from the opposition split consisted of Emmanuel Gapyisi and his friends. During March Gapyisi had worked frantically to revive his Peace and Democracy 'club' of the year before, and he had started to recruit from inside every party, with the aim of creating a large anti-Habyarimana anti-RPF movement. The ground was well prepared. He engineered the organisation of a PARMEHUTU current within the MDR with the help of his associates Donat Murego and Frodwald Karamira. Mbonampeka brought him part of the PL and Ruhumuliza a little piece of the PDC. The ten small opposition parties were interested but they waited to see who would win. The idea was not to create a new party but to give the impression of a broad multi-party movement which would preach 'common sense' by giving a new 'intrinsically democratic' voice to the *rubanda nyamwinshi* – the 'majority people', i.e. the Hutu. This was the practical application of the 'common front' which Minister Debarge had been calling for, even if President Habyarimana looked like being at the losing end of the combination. The new movement immediately proved enormously popular with a public opinion which was both tired of the Habyarimana regime and wary of the RPF and its opposition 'allies'[47]. In an apparently paradoxical but in fact totally logical move President Habyarimana, as an old political fox, felt the new wind blowing, and quickly moved closer to the 'old' opposition. His calculation was that since the 'new opposition' was the most dangerous because it was increasingly popular, the 'old opposition' in its present weakened state represented less of a threat.

Violence, or rather its mediatisation, had now become an important element in the propaganda war. The report compiled by the International Human Rights Commission, which had come to Rwanda in January was published on 9 March and immediately caused a political mini-scandal in France[48]. President Habyarimana answered with a seven-page public letter which denied most of the accusations, especially the existence of the death squads[49]. In late March, the discovery of the Ngarama mass-grave containing 134 bodies was the pretext for a war

---

47. See Emmanuel Gapyisi, 'La fin d'un régime et la fin d'une guerre', *Paix et Démocratie*, April 1993, pp. 11–13.
48. See Laurent Bijard, 'Les charniers du Réseau Zéro', *Le Nouvel Observateur*, 11 March 1993.
49. Interestingly Premier Dismas Nsengiyaremye, who knew better, co-signed the letter. This was one of the signs of the rapprochement between the Presidency and the 'old opposition'.

of communiqués and counter-communiqués between the RPF and the government, the bodies being described as those of RPF victims while the guerrillas countered by saying that this was an old government mass-grave which had been only temporarily in its area[50]. In the main towns and especially in Kigali, violence had become a daily occurrence. The army was slipping more and more weapons to the *Interahamwe* and *Impuzamugambi*, who were using them with abandon to kill Tutsi, and 'old opposition' sympathisers or simply to settle private quarrels[51]. The economy was in a shambles and communications were getting ever harder with the RPF mining some of the access roads through Tanzania. The refugee situation caused huge problems. In order to feed the displaced people from the north, the World Food Programme of the United Nations had put together a massive airlift. They were trucking a vast quantity of food from Mombasa and then, with hired Russian Ilyushin 76 cargo planes, flying it from Entebbe to Kigali. There was a constant stream of planes, carrying up to several hundred tons of grain a day. In accordance with the Dar-es-Salaam ceasefire agreement, the RPF was trying to get the refugees to move back north to their own *rugos* but the FAR were intercepting the refugee groups who were walking out of their camps towards the guerrilla-held zone. This was the beginning of a process which culminated in the summer of 1994, when half the country's population were on the roads, having become political shuttlecocks between the collapsing government, the RPF and the French Turquoise Force.

50. *Le Monde*, 30 March 1993. By then, the RPF in compliance with the Dar-es-Salaam ceasefire agreement, had withdrawn to its pre-8 February positions. So Ngarama had been in government hands *before* the offensive, in RPF hands between 10 February and 20 March 1993, and then again under government control.

51. French arms deliveries during the February emergency had been so plentiful that grenades, resold on the side by the Army, were openly on sale on public markets. The author saw some, sold side by side with avocados and mangoes, at a market near Kigali in June 1993, but was stopped from photographing them by a policeman who told him that 'it was not nice to take such pictures'. See Stephen Smith, 'Dans Kigali, chronique de la terreur quotidienne', *Libération*, 22 March 1993.

Emmanuel Gapyisi was driving home on 18 May 1993 when he was shot by five bullets accurately pumped into his chest as he opened his gate. The murder immediately caused havoc on the political scene. An unsigned leaflet appeared the next day, accusing the MDR of his assassination but giving no details. By the 20th another leaflet was out, this time accusing both Twagiramungu and the RPF. On the 21st there was a third leaflet, still unsigned, which accused Charles Shamukiga, the Tutsi businessman and civil rights activist. All these seem to have been clumsy fabrications designed to get the public off the track and present the murder as part of an MDR internal struggle, but hardly anyone believed them. Although Gapyisi represented a danger for Faustin Twagiramungu, the MDR president had neither the personality nor the necessary social contacts to hire efficient professional killers easily and discreetly. It was obvious that the contract on Gapyisi's head came either from CDR circles or from among the President's friends. But the only motivation for a CDR murder would have come from competition, both Gapyisi's *Forum* and the CDR being seen as bidding for the same electorate. Yet this was not really true: Gapyisi's appeal was different from that of the CDR: he made extremism seem normal and even respectable, something which was not the case of the *Coalition*. The CDR needed Gapyisi, even if they were in a relationship of competitive collaboration with him, because his personal respectability and his friendly and matter-of-fact approach, attracted to the extremist cause people who would otherwise have shied away from the vociferous CDR brand of politics. Because of Gapyisi, CDR ideas, once derided as crackpot extremism, had acquired an aura of acceptability. If there was a political family Gapyisi was really harming, it was the mainstream MRND (D), the respectable Hutu supremacists, the official practitioners of internationally-approved racism. If a peace agreement would be reached in Arusha, Gapyisi's position would have been extremely comfortable: 'I did not sign it, I don't even approve of it, but I am realistic and reasonable: I will give it a chance. But not blindly: I will give it a chance as a true guardian of the interests of the *rubanda nyamwinshi*, of my Hutu fellow-countrymen.' Meanwhile Prime Minister Nsengiyaremye and President Habyarimana, exhausted by their mutual fight, would both have been discredited. This scenario was so likely that politicians had recently been flocking to the Gapyisi camp. His death had changed everything. A new situation had been created in the 'old' versus 'new' opposition contest, and in the relationship of both with the desperately struggling President Habyarimana.

Now, paradoxically, there was only one way for the President to steal the thunder the dead Gapyisi had been playing with, and that was to sign the peace agreement – and play with the 'real' or 'old' opposition. During the past few months, President Habyarimana had increasingly been caught in the crossfire between those who traditionally reproached him for his authoritarianism and a new 'moderate' group which attacked him for his softness. The second group was the more dangerous even if it had now been decapitated. Alliance with the 'old' opposition, on the other hand, would enable the President to buy time, something he desperately needed. He would just have to play shy, and make it clear that the agreement had been signed in the face of his extreme reluctance. And then time had to be allowed to play its role: by making use of the contradictions that would unavoidably develop between the disunited gaggle of his enemies, he probably would have recuperated many of his 'opponents' within a few months. Violence could still be used, but also accommodation – always say yes in principle but always procrastinate in practice. President Mobutu had been playing that game for years in Zaïre and he was still in power after having been written off as finished at least a dozen times. The CDR were too rough. They were just crude bullies who could be useful in a rough spot but who did not understand the finesse of politics. Now the way towards peace – of a sort – had been opened up.

Peace through exhaustion

By early June the government delegation had agreed to a protocol on the repatriation of the refugees, something which had once been a major political issue but had now completely paled in the political agenda. But the final signing was blocked by a much more important point from the President's point of view: the make-up of the new post-war Forces Armées Rwandaises. The 20% share offered to the RPF had been abandoned after the February fighting, and the proportion now agreed upon was 40–60, in favour of the government forces. The stumbling block was the composition of the officer corps. The RPF wanted a 50–50 distribution of posts while President Habyarimana wanted dominance for the old army. He had in mind a precise organigram for the Army and did not want to give way over some key positions. The talks dragged on, to the exasperation of Prime Minister Nsengiyaremye who was scapegoated by both sides[52]. He was also worried by the increasingly threatening utterances of the extremists and did not know exactly what game the President was playing, and in an open letter accused him of encouraging them:

> Terrorist groups are now preparing attacks on various politicians and disturbances in the whole country in order to try to restart the war. In other words, you seem to want to find a trick that would enable you to avoid signing the peace agreement and that would force the present cabinet to resign so that you could put together another pro-war cabinet and start the conflict again. This so as to keep all the power and prerogatives you now have as President of the Republic. (6 July 1993).

Prime Minister's Nsengiyaremye's scenario was quite close to the reality that was shaping up, but there was one shade of uncertainty – namely that the extremists were not so certain that President Habyarimana was their champion. Among these were some of the dismissed military men such as Colonel Rwagafilita or Colonel Serubuga who by now were strongly opposed to the President. The key factor was Mme Habyarimana who up till then had always supported or manipulated her husband. But her

---

52. On 14 June 1993 the Arusha delegation announced that the agreement would be signed on the 19th in presence of the President. The author was then in Kigali and the signs of popular satisfaction were unmistakable. However, the deadline passed, nothing happened, and the popular mood turned to despondency.

trusted brothers now favoured a change of tack and a more radical orientation. In other words the tempting but hazardous notion of a 'big clean-up' was gaining ground though it remained to be seen whether the President would agree and be prepared to lead it.

The 'new opposition' had restructured itself through the creation of an informal club-like structure called (in English) 'Hutu Power'. The supporters of this tendency, which the Rwandese public called in French '*les power*', were roughly the members of the old Gapyisi network: the Donat Murego-Frodwald Karamira Parmehutu fraction of MDR, a few lost PSDs, Ruhumuliza and his friends in the PDC. The big change was in the Parti Libéral. A few days before Gapyisi's assassination, Stanislas Mbonampeka was the target of a grenade attack, and not being particularly heroic by nature, he decided to take a back seat in the tumultuous politics of the day. His place was filled by hitherto die-hard opponent Justin Mugenzi, someone who occupied a special position. He had received large sums of money from the presidential circles[53] and was soon to be given the commerce portfolio he had long desired in the new cabinet then being formed. So although he became the leader of his party's 'Power' fraction, he was clearly no longer in opposition, but acted as a kind of Habyarimana spokesman to the 'Power' group, half in and half out. But in any case he had broken with the 'old opposition', and the frankly anti-Habyarimana fraction of the party remained under the control of Landwald Ndasingwa. Since all the Tutsi members stayed on that side, the split took on an added ethnic tinge[54].

The 'half in, half out' position of Mugenzi was also the editorial line of the new Radio Télévision Libre des Mille Collines (RTLMC), brainchild of the CDR intellectuals, which began broadcasting in July. For the last year, since the new

---

53. *Kanguka*, no. 78, 1 July 1993, and interview with former PL member, Paris, 29 June 1994.
54. As a result, to escape being targeted, many Tutsi left the PL to join the PSD which was holding up better in the 'Power' storm.

coalition cabinet had started negotiations with the RPF in Arusha, the CDR extremists had felt ill-at-ease with the gradual slide of Radio Rwanda into liberalism. They felt that the national radio journalists were opportunists who were betraying 'the Cause' and toadying to the opposition. So RTLMC, which had been licenced to broadcast as an 'independent' station, was in fact loyalist. However while fiercely loyal to the Hutu cause, it was only conditionally loyal to President Habyarimana. In its own way it was effective. It knew how to use street slang, obscene jokes and good music to push its racist message. During the genocide, it became what one listener at the time called 'a vampire radio' openly calling for more blood and massacres. Yet people went on listening to it with a kind of stupefied fascination, incredulous at the relaxed joking way in which it defied the most deeply cherished human values. The fascination extended to the RPF fighters in the battle who preferred listening to it than to Radio Muhabura ('Radio Beacon'), their own 'politically correct' and rather preachy station[55].

On 17 July 1993, the mainstream MDR politician and ex-Minister of Education Agathe Uwilingiyimana became the Prime Minister of a new cabinet which had a mandate from the President to sign the peace agreement[56]. Mme Uwilingiyimana was the choice of Faustin Twagiramungu, who did not want to exhaust himself in the final episodes of the negotiations, preferring to keep somewhat aloof. But his choice had been made in close consultation with the President himself. This caused a furore among the anti-Twagiramungu forces within the MDR, who decided to try by every means possible to stop him from becoming Premier in the future Broad Based Transitional Government (BBTG) to be formed after the signature of the

55. Interview with journalist Faustin Kagame, Geneva, 28 July 1994. Kagame is a Tutsi whose life was saved by the RPF in early April 1994 and thus cannot be suspected of hidden sympathies for the RTLMC. But despite (or because of) its message of hate, this radio station represented one of the most interesting political and media phenomena of the whole tragedy.
56. The sharing-out of the portfolios between the parties was exactly the same as the one in the outgoing Nsengiyaremye cabinet: MRND(D) 9, MDR 4 (including the premier), PSD 3, PL 3 and PDC 1.

peace agreement, for which the Murego-Karamira group put forward Jean Kambanda as the MDR candidate. In spite of having three-quarters of the MDR political bureau and most of the regional party delegates against him, Twagiramungu coolly designated himself as the future BBTG Premier on 20 July. The party called a congress to stop him and confirm the candidature of Kambanda, but to no avail[57]. In a desperate move the anti-Twagiramungu group sequestrated Mme Uwilingiyimana on 23 July and forced her to write a letter of resignation, which was immediately made public. But she went on the air the next day, told the country what had happened, and declared that she had no intention of resigning. She retained her Premiership, but on the same day the Murego-Karamira-inspired MDR congress meeting deposed Twagiramungu from his position as president of the party. He refused to recognise this decision and the split became official, with the former party president retaining control of only a minority of the old MDR.

By then everybody was exhausted. The political rigmarole had reached a point of almost total absurdity. Hutu supremacists were sniping at President Habyarimana, who was consorting with liberals who wanted to see him fall; in Arusha the appetite of the RPF seemed to grow by the day; extremists were arming almost openly; politicians who were verbal enemies shared the same party label and sat side by side in the same cabinet; and the public was growing cynically bored with the antics of 'democracy'. The only thing that seemed equally distributed between all the political actors was corruption money, and an independent press organ could write: 'Political parties have now become money-making concerns.'[58]

---

57. The Kigali *préfet* refused a permit to hold the congress and MRND(D) militants scuffled with the congress delegates. This was an apparent paradox since Twagiramungu was radically opposed to President Habyarimana, while the Murego-Karamira MDR faction was aligned on his positions. But, as we have seen, Habyarimana had by then embarked on a certain course of *realpolitik* and, temporarily at least, was playing a reverse game.

58. *Le Flambeau* no. 13, 20 September 1993, quoted in Filip Reyntjens, *L'Afrique des Grands Lacs en crise*, op. cit., p. 125. On the same page Reyntjens quotes several other Rwandese newspaper articles with the same disenchanted tone, all published between August and November 1993.

On 4 August 1993, the peace agreement was signed in Arusha at a solemn ceremony attended by President Juvénal Habyarimana of Rwanda, President Ali Hassan Mwinyi of Tanzania, President Yoweri Museveni of Uganda, President Melchior Ndadaye of Burundi and Prime Minister Faustin Birindwa from Zaïre. The French were only represented by a member of the Dar-es-Salaam embassy staff. The agreement carried precise provisions for the future Broad Based Transitional Government (BBTG), National Transition Assembly (NTA), united armed forces and many other things. But despite all these detailed provisions, all the participants in the ceremony were aware of the extreme fragility of the document they were signing and celebrating. One episode was closing and another was about to start.

6

CHRONICLE OF A MASSACRE FORETOLD
(4 August 1993–6 April 1994)

Waiting for UNAMIR

The Arusha peace agreement was made up of many different parts tacked on as the last twelve months of negotiations progressed:

– the initial cease-fire agreement signed on 12 July 1992;
– the power-sharing agreements defining the modalities of the Broad Based Transitional Government (BBTG) signed on 30 October 1992 and 9 January 1993;
– the protocol on the repatriation of refugees signed on 9 June 1993; and
– the armed forces integration agreement signed on 3 August 1993.

The whole complex structure would be unworkable in practice without goodwill, an element in short supply.

The BBTG cabinet was made up of a rigorously defined coalition of parties (the four big opposition parties, the MRND(D) and the RPF), which would not only hold predetermined numbers of portfolios; each portfolio was also precisely attributed – the Premiership to the MDR, the Ministry of the Interior to the RPF, the Ministry of Defence to the MRND(D) and so on. There were twenty-one ministers in all, including the Premier, and decisions required a two-thirds vote. This meant that for any decision to become effective it had to have the support of the RPF (five ministers), the MRND(D) (also five) and the MDR (four) for a total of fourteen votes. This sounded like a recipe for the constant blocking of any decision more contentious than the purchase of paper-clips.

And paralysis of the BBTG meant paralysis of the whole state

because theoretically it held almost absolute power. It was supposed to make the laws and carry them out since the presidential
function had been shorn of almost all its power[1] and a two-
thirds majority was needed for a vote of no-confidence in the
cabinet, and with the National Transition Assembly (NTA)
being made up of the same parties as the BBTG (plus representatives of the minor opposition parties) it was highly unlikely
that the NTA would censure the BBTG. Being the product of
so many tensions, the agreements were pervaded by an almost
obsessive concern to avoid dominance by any force of any other.
The result was that the whole carefully-balanced construction
ended up being based on almost strict consensus between
mutually hostile elements. Nobody seemed to have had any idea
of how it would work in practice.

The military integration agreement signed on 3 August had
been the last element of the compromise and the most difficult
to achieve. It provided for a 60–40 share-out of troops in favour
of the FAR, and 50–50 in of the officer corps, with the
principle that no two hierarchically consecutive positions (i.e.
commander and second-in-command) in a given unit be held
by the same side. If the commander was going to be RPF, his
second-in-command ought to be FAR and vice versa. Beyond
the 'Angolan'-type tensions inherent in such a set-up, another
problem was the demobilisation issue: the new army was
supposed to be only 20,000 strong, but because there might be
40,000 troops in the FAR and 15,000 in the RPF (both low
estimates), Filip Reyntjens calculates that the financial incentives
for demobilisation (set at between 100,000 Rw. francs for
soldiers and NCOs and 500,000 for high-ranking officers) would
have cost at least US $200 million[2], an amount nobody knew
where to find.

---

1. As defined by the Arusha series of Agreements, presidential power was reduced
   to no more than representing the Republic: the President had to promulgate laws
   without any power to modify or even veto them. Not only did he have no power
   to nominate civil servants, but he could not even offer names for nominations.
   His 'messages to the nation' had to be approved by the BBTG.
2. Filip Reytjens, *L'Afrique des Grands Lacs en crise*, op. cit., p. 255.

On top of these complexities, implementation depended on a tricky external condition: the setting-up of an international military monitoring force. On this point the RPF had been adamant: it wanted the French troops to leave and be replaced by a UN force. Up till then, the history of international involvement in the Rwandese crisis had been quite limited. A Groupe des Observateurs Militaires Neutres (Neutral Military Observer Group or GOMN) had been set up by the OAU after the February war to monitor the application of the Dar-es-Salaam cease-fire agreement. It consisted of about sixty African military observers, and had worked well technically but been unable to contribute any political input to the situation. Then on 23 June 1993, to facilitate the negotiations in Arusha and quieten the government's fears of the RPF being rearmed from Uganda, the United Nations created by its Resolution no. 846 the United Nations Uganda-Rwanda Observation Mission (UNUROM)[3]. But after the signing of the Arusha agreement, the signatories turned to the UN to obtain the deployment of a neutral military monitoring force to ensure a fair application of the Agreement. On 25 September 1993 the UN Secretary-General agreed on the principle and by Resolution no 872 on 5 October created the United Nations Assistance Mission to Rwanda (UNAMIR). Then began the usual round of diplomatic consultations to find out which countries would be willing to send troops to give UNAMIR its muscle. France of course was excluded, given the RPF's hostility[4].

President Habyarimana had consented to sign the Arusha peace agreement not as a genuine gesture marking the turning-over of a new political leaf and the beginning of democratisation in Rwanda, but as a tactical move calculated to buy time, shore up

3. UNUROM was very slow in getting organised and was only deployed after the signing of the Arusha agreement. Because of a very formal approach to border control work, its efficiency was extremely low, as the author was able to verify on the ground at both Gatuna and Kagitumba in 1994.
4. As part of the Arusha agreement, the RPF was supposed to send a 600-man battalion to Kigali, as a kind of 'security' for its politicians. On 29 September the RPF declared that it would refuse to send this battalion to the capital for as long as French troops were there (SWB, Radio Rwanda, 30 September 1993).

the contradictions of the various segments of the opposition and look good in the eyes of the foreign donors.

In an attempt to gauge the regional situation after the Arusha ceremony he first went to Uganda to check Museveni's frame of mind (31 August 1993). The visit was a disaster. The Ugandan President was adamant over the need to comply with the Arusha documents. He had invited several of the RPF leaders (Paul Kagame, Colonel Kanyarengwe, Tito Rutaremara, Pasteur Bizimungu) in the expectation that Habyarimana would want to chat with them in an informal atmosphere, but the Rwandese President coldly turned his back on Museveni's guests, nearly creating a diplomatic incident[5]. A few days later (4 September), he went to Burundi to meet President Melchior Ndadaye, who had been elected only a few months before, and ask him to prevent the recruitment of RPF troops among the Rwandese Tutsi refugees in northern Burundi. But President Ndadaye was wary in case his controversial guest should make ripples in the fragile post-election peace Burundi was enjoying if he were invited for a state visit in the capital, and therefore instead of going to Bujumbura, the Rwandese President flew by helicopter directly to Ngozi in the north. The meeting was inconclusive. Habyarimana had expected to be able to appeal to a common 'Hutu solidarity' in the face of 'Tutsi arrogance' but he found a cautious and moderate politician who, in spite of having decided to prevent refugees in Burundi from becoming embroiled in the Rwandese crisis, was far from willing to give his Kigali counterpart a blank political cheque.

The domestic situation had turned sour. Political change was in the air and many people were hurrying to settle various accounts before the new political order took shape. Large amounts of money were flowing out of the country because the MRND(D) stalwarts feared that their usual foreign exchange

---

5. SWB, Radio Muhabura, 2 September 1993, and interview with RPF President-designate Pasteur Bizimungu, Mulindi, 4 July 1994. The RPF group which went to Uganda to meet President Habyarimana insisted that it had been invited by him through President Museveni and that his attitude was a last-minute change of mind.

channels might be tampered with by the future BBTG. They were also afraid of losing control of the insititutional levers of the economy and the President's men were busy making their own preparations before the BBTG took over by privatising many parastatal or semi-parastatal outfits in the hands of their friends at bargain prices[6]. There were also measures for changing the designations of the various levels of local administrative authorities[7] and new civil service affectations in the ministries which were supposed to go to the RPF. Refugee movements, which according to the Arusha peace agreement were supposed to be free, continued to be hampered by the FAR when the refugees were trying to move northwards back to RPF-controlled areas[8].

Some accounts were settled in more brutal fashion. In several parts of the country, some of the men of blood who had organised and carried out massacres since 1990 were killed, either by friends and relations of their victims seeking vengeance or even by some of their powerful political bosses who were afraid that they might talk too much. There were several murders in the south, probably *Abanyanduga* revenge killings, and among the victims was Fidèle Rwambuka, the notorious Kanzenze *bourgmestre*, assassinated on 21 August. In the north-west, a series of murders which took place during mid-November were attributed to the RPF. They could have been revenge killings

---

6. This was presented as being in compliance with the World Bank recommendations within the framework of the SAP.
7. In agreement with the Arusha decisions, *all* the local authorities, whether at *préfecture, sous-préfecture* or *commune* level had to be changed. It is interesting to note that part of the MRND(D) fear of being wiped out of the political map might have been exaggerated. In September, in the demilitarised zone which was controlled neither by the FAR nor by the RPF, a partial election for *bourgmestres* took place in several *communes sous-préfectures* of Kinihira (Byumba) and Kirambo (Ruhengeri). All the seats went to the MRND(D). Of course this area had always been a stronghold of the Habyarimana regime, but it showed that in free and fair elections the MRND(D) might lose nation-wide but would still make a strong showing in some regions.
8. In a letter dated 2 October 1993 Colonel Kanyarengwe, the RPF chairman, protested against 'these manoeuvres which go against both the spirit and the letter of the Arusha agreement'. He received support from the President of the supreme court, Joseph Kavaruganda, an act which marked him out to be eliminated when the genocide got under way.

for the Bagogwe massacres, or cases of lukewarm *Interahamwe* being eliminated by their more radical brethen.

In the face of this deterioration of the political climate, the 'opposition' parties acted in ever more confused and conflicting ways. The CDR had been calling openly for an alliance with the MDR-Power and the splits inside both that party and the PL were now such that the initial cabinet list informally agreed upon in Arusha was the object of raging controversies[9]. The problem came from the consensus system also agreed upon during the negotiations. Cabinets posts had been shared *along party lines*, but if several opposed groups claiming ownership of the same party tag now brandished different lists of cabinet candidates, to which list should the portfolios go? There was of course no answer and these divisions played right into the hands of the President and the extremists, even if both seemed to be less and less on the same political track[10]. It was in this tense atmosphere that the news of President Melchior Ndadaye's assassination broke.

9. This informal list communicated to the author by former Defence Minister James Gasana in Geneva in June 1994 seems to have been as follows. The RPF were to have five ministries, including the newly-created position of Vice-Prime Minister, and they were to go to Jacques Bihozagara, Pasteur Bizimungu, Seth Sendashonga, Mme Immaculée Kayumba and Dr Colonel Joseph Karamira. André Ntagerura, Prosper Mugiraneza, Ferdinand Nahimana, Mme Pauline Nyiramashuhuko and Augustin Bizimana were the nominations for the MRND(D). All were hardliners. Frédéric Nzamurambaho, Félicien Gatabazi and Marc Ruganera were to stand for the PSD. There was no disagreement over those names since the PSD had remained in a coherent position *vis-à-vis* the old régime. Jean-Népomucène Nayinzira, the PDC candidate, had his name challenged by the PDC-Power which wanted instead Gaspard Ruhumuliza. Faustin Twagiramungu was the MDR 'choice' for Premier and he was supposed to be in the company of Dismas Nsengiyaremye, Mme Agathe Uwilingiyimana and Boniface Ngulinzira. Nseng'yaremye's attitude was ambiguous but he was getting closer and closer to the 'Power' group. The others were fiercely opposed to it. And for the PL Justin Mugenzi and Mme Agnès Ntamabyaliro were strong 'Power' members while Landwald Ndasingwa, initially slated to accompany them in government, had split from the party with all the 'old oppositon' sympathisers, most of them Tutsi.

10. The situation was well summed up by Marie-France Cros in an article prophetically entitled 'Il est minuit, Messieurs' ('It is midnight, gentlemen') in *La Libre Belgique*, 4 October 1993.

Ndadaye's murder: the shock and its exploitation

To understand the impact of President Ndadaye's assassination on the political situation in Rwanda, we have to remember that Rwanda and Burundi have been, since independance, the two opposite ends of a political seesaw. Their parallel – and at times common – past histories, their comparable social structures, their constant and almost obsessive mutual scrutiny, fated them to be natural mirrors of each other's hopes, woes and transformations. It was largely the fear aroused in the Tutsi community of Burundi by the Rwanda massacres of 1959–63 which led to the construction of a Tutsi dominated political system in Bujumbura. It was the renewed fear caused by Rwanda-inspired Hutu restlessness in the late 1960s which drove Tutsi extremists to start the 1972 mass killings of Hutu intellectuals in order to deprive any future Hutu movement of its potential élite. In turn, it was the 1972 Burundi horror which led President Grégoire Kayibanda to think in 1973 that a demagogic persecution of the Tutsi community in Rwanda would help him prop up his faltering dictatorship. This paved the way for the Habyarimana coup instead. Then in 1988, it was the Rwandese support for the radical Burundese Hutu movement Palipehutu leading to the Ntega/Marangara uprising and repression which convinced President Pierre Buyoya that he should try to overhaul the Burundi system of ethnic dictatorship. And it was the courageous democratisation process in Burundi between 1988 and 1993 which largely contributed to making the Habyarimana dictatorship in Rwanda seem more and more anachronistic and its position more and more untenable[11].

11. For a more detailed view of this process, see (among others) Jean-Pierre Chrétien, 'Hutu et Tutsi au Rwanda et au Burundi', pp. 129–65, in Jean-Louis Amselle and Elikia M'Bokolo (eds), *Au coeur de l'ethnie*, op. cit., for the fundamentals of the relationship see René Lemarchand, *Rwanda and Burundi*, op. cit., for the violence of the early years of independence see Jean-Pierre Chrétien, 'Pluralisme politique et équilibre ethnique au Rwanda et au Burundi', pp. 51–8, in André Guichaoua (ed.), *Enjeux nationaux et dynamiques régionales dans l'Afrique des Grands Lacs*, op. cit., for the early 1990s and Filip Reyntjens, *L'Afrique des Grands Lacs en crise*, op. cit., for the recent past.

Melchior Ndadaye, a Hutu engineer, was elected President of Burundi by 64.8% of the electorate on 1 June 1993 in a free and fair election. Less than a month later on 29 June his Frodebu party won sixty-five parliamentary seats out of eighty-one with 71.4% of the vote. His Tutsi opponent, the former President Pierre Buyoya, loyally accepted the election result and the hand-over of power took place smoothly. After this, in spite of great difficulties caused both by impatient Hutu radicals and frustrated Tutsi extremists, the President managed to steer a moderate course and minimise the tensions inherent in such a situation. Then, on 21 October 1993, he was kidnapped by extremist Tutsi army officers, taken to a military camp and murdered. He had been the first Hutu President in Burundi's history and the rage and frustration of his Hutu fellowcountrymen were boundless. But instead of trying to quieten down these feelings, several ministers and many local civil servants encouraged the Hutu population to take revenge directly on the local Tutsi peasants. The situation was complicated by the fact that the cabinet, several of whose members had been killed by the unsuccessful putschists, took refuge first at the French embassy and later at a lakeside resort camp and remained there confused and apathetic, neglecting to undertake the (admittedly dangerous) task of calming down the popular anger. After a few days, the Tutsi-controlled army moved in to restore order in a very heavy handed way.

The combination of anti-Tutsi pogroms and anti-Hutu army killings seems to have caused about 50,000 deaths, roughly 60% Tutsi and 40% Hutu. An estimated 150,000 Tutsi fled to army-controlled towns where they could feel safe and became internally displaced, while some 300,000 Hutu fled across the borders to neighbouring countries, mostly Rwanda[12].

The impact of these events on Rwanda was considerable. They were of course interpreted in different ways by the different political actors. For the radical Hutu groups, whether CDR or 'Power', what had happened was a clear example of Tutsi

12. Commission Internationale d'Enquête sur les Violations des Droits de l'Homme au Burundi depuis le 21 Octobre 1993, *Rapport final*, Brussels, July 1994.

perfidy and strengthened them in their decision to resist the Arusha peace agreement at all costs, including for the most extremist the cost of a preventive genocide. We saw in Chapter 5 that the notion of a 'big clean-up', a 'final solution to the ethnic problem', had begun to circulate in extremist circles in late 1992. But it was the murder of President Ndadaye which convinced the CDR and their allies that the time had come for action. They knew that the shock felt in Rwanda after Ndadaye's death would enable them to rally many simple or hesitant people. They presented the situation in terms of almost biblical urgency. To the fear of losing one's privileges (rational level) they added the fear of losing one's life (visceral level) and the fear of losing control of one's world (mythical level). Their radio station, RTLMC, poured out a torrent of propaganda, mixing constant harping on the old themes of 'majority democracy', fears of 'Tutsi feudalist enslavement' and ambiguous 'calls to action'. A monstrous answer to a monstruously misrepresented problem was beginning to be turned into a deliberate, organised, cold-blooded political programme. This paranoid vision had existed for years, but till then as a minority syndrome, limited to the CDR, the 'Zero Network' and *Amasasu* activists and assorted militiamen. With President Ndadaye's murder the hysterical choice of kill-first-not-to-be-killed could be developed into a general feeling shared by large segments of the population. This was a godsend for the 'Power' fractions of the 'opposition' parties which could both pretend to have been 'moderates' hitherto and to have turned to 'rightful extremism' only as a response to an intolerable threat. The psychological impact of the Hutu President's murder and of the arrival in Rwanda of hundreds of thousands of Hutu refugees spreading tales of terror and massacre at the hands of the Tutsi army of Burundi[13] had enormous negative consequences on the already overcast Rwandese political weather. Riding that wave of popular shock and fear, the 'Power' groups moved closer to the CDR and to the hardline

---

13. They of course omitted to relate their own massacres of Tutsi peasants before the army intervention.

fraction of MRND(D), to the point where together they formed a new pole in Rwandese political life[14]. The CDR had broken out of its isolation and the most extremist racist notions about a 'final solution', though still not entertained by the majority of the population, were now becoming almost familiar and spreading out to the rural areas. It was certainly at that time that the extremist network gained sufficient popular acceptance to be able to start giving orders to the local MRND(D) administration, speaking with the voice of authority as if it were the government itself.

If the shock of President Ndadaye's assassination helped the Hutu supremacists of various hues to solidify behind them a block of increasingly armed hatred, for the 'old opposition' it acted as a double warning: first, by identifying themselves with the Frodebu moderates, they realised that institutional change was fragile and that at any time violence could overturn what a moderate process, either electoral or negotiated, had achieved. Then seeing themselves as a (mostly) Hutu political group forced to collaborate with an armed Tutsi group brought back the uneasiness they had felt at the time of the February RPF offensive. What were really the aims of those *Inkotanyi*? Would they remain content with what they had achieved at Arusha or would they want a monopoly of power, in which case the Hutu opposition would have been a quickly-discarded Trojan horse? The Burundese tragedy made the old opposition parties fully aware of their powerlessness: unlike the RPF and the Hutu supremacists, they had no guns. The death of mild, moderate President Ndadaye was a chilling reminder of how defenceless one could be without a gun when the extremists decided that the time was ripe for action.

The attitude of the RPF was ambiguous. It issued a conventional communiqué condemning both the killing of President

---

14. On 23 October 1993 during a public meeting organised to 'support the Burundese people', Frodwald Karamira, one of the leaders of the MDR-Power, declared that 'Hutu should unite against the danger represented by anti-democratic Tutsi'. This was exactly the usual CDR line.

Ndadaye and the ensuing violence, but its reaction was extremely formal: coming from a self-defined 'democratic' organisation, it conveyed no sense of genuine indignation at the murder of a popularly elected head of state. Worse still, some sectors of the Front openly rejoiced at the death of the Hutu President. In Kampala several of the failed Burundese putschists were, if not officially granted political asylum, at least welcomed and allowed to stay and to live in style[15]. The RPF used its connections there to help them. This attitude was ambivalent, to say the least, and was clearly perceived as such by the Hutu democratic opposition in Kigali. Thus, it did not help to assuage their fears.

The last group of people on which the death of President Ndadaye had an effect consisted of President Habyarimana and his old guard. The President's first conclusion was not very different from that of the democratic opposition: institutional arrangements were very weak indeed in the face of violence. But in his position the causality looked different: both President Buyoya and President Ndadaye had been idealists. Power was power, and entrusting it to pieces of paper was not safe. This reinforced the President's resolution to resist the Arusha peace agreement. Who could guarantee what would happen to him if he once agreed to a virtual abdication of power to his enemies? He might be put on trial to answer for the 1990–3 massacres or even be asked questions about the pre-1990 political murders. He might be queried about his use of public money. And he would have no weapons to defend himself. On the other hand,

15. They were Major Bernard Busakoza, Lieut.-Colonel Sylvestre Ngaba, Lieut.-Colonel Paul Kamana, five other officers and two NCOs. Lieut.-Colonel Kamana is thought to be the person who actually killed President Ndadaye. They stayed in Kampala as well-received guests of RPF circles between late October 1993 and early February 1994 when, because their presence had begun to cause political problems for President Museveni, they were politely told to take a hoiyday. After some time in Zaïre, they discreetly came back to Uganda where they were finally arrested in late November 1994. At the time of writing they are still waiting to be extradited because the present uncertainty of Burundese politics makes their return to Bujumbura an embarrassing problem both for the government and for the opposition. (Interview with Ugandan journalists, Kampala, 7 July 1994. *Le Monde*, 25 November 1994. Interview with Filip Reyntjens, Ashburnham Place, England, 14 December 1994.)

the Hutu supremacists who had been his supporters now considered him increasingly a has-been, incapable of really defending the interests of the *rubanda nyamwinshi* in general and their own in particular. He, as President, could still conceivably make a deal with his enemies, weak as that would be. The whole of the *akazu* and even more the flocks of provincial small-time beneficiaries of the regime could not. There were too many of them, they had gone too far, and they could not turn back. They now figured they had no choice but to go on to more radical solutions. Just as President Ndadaye had probably been discreetly abandoned by his own party extremists who found him too moderate, quite apart from his openly murderous Tutsi enemies, President Habyarimana also knew that the CDR and 'Power' people might decide at any time to ditch him in favour of a more radical solution since they had the necessary contacts within the army. His margin for manoeuvre was extremely limited and danger threatened him on all sides. Buying time, without knowing exactly for what purpose, became a kind of survival reflex.

The popular demonstrations caused by the shock felt at President Ndadaye's murder were immediately exploited by the MRND(D) hardliners, the CDR and the 'Power' extremists. RPF sympathisers were murdered, sporadic killings of Tutsi took place in various *préfectures*, and some *Interahamwe* who were no longer considered trustworthy were liquidated[16]. Old private accounts were settled in blood[17]. It was in this atmosphere that the Arusha agreement provisions began slowly to be implemented.

The first UNAMIR troops had started to arrive in Kigali in

16. There were twenty such murders in Butare *préfecture* and thirteen in Kigali *préfecture* during November 1993 alone. Near Butare town a mine blew up eleven people. Nobody claimed to have carried out the attack (*Le Monde*, 5 December 1993).
17. It was at this time (November) that the journalist Calixte Kulisa, who had worked on the movie *Gorillas in the mist*, was killed. He had been a witness in the Dian Fossey murder case in which Protais Zigiranyirazo, Mme Habyarimana's brother, was a strong suspect (see Nicholas Gordon, *Murders in the mist: Who killed Dian Fossey?*, London: Hodder and Stoughton, 1994).

November[18], and so had the 600-strong RPF battalion. The French troops, whose withdrawal had been decided by Paris in late October[19], were being flown out of the country. On 28 December three of the future RPF ministers, Jacques Bihozagara, Paul Kagame and Pasteur Bizimungu, also arrived in the capital. Apparently there was no longer any reason to postpone the transfer of power. But the MDR-Power and the PL-Power were still adamantly opposed to accepting their 'old opposition' ex-party comrades into the cabinet. And nobody could prove conclusively who was the owner of each particular party label and therefore who had the right to choose the party candidates for government. This led Prime Minister-designate Faustin Twagiramungu, at the height of frustration to declare: 'I am waiting for the President of the Republic to stop interfering in MDR and PL business so that we can go ahead and implement the institutions agreed upon at Arusha.'[20] The United Nations special representative, Jacques-Roger Booh-Booh from Cameroon, seemed somewhat lost in the midst of all this confusion. Trying not to take sides, at one moment he strongly criticised the President for what he perceived (rightly) as his systematic procrastination[21] and later infuriated the RPF and the democratic opposition by supporting the CDR's demand to be included in the future government. Generally, the United Nations gave the impression of trying to consider the situation as a 'technical problem' that could somehow be magically solved by further injections of men and matériel. While it had no notion of which policy it should choose, the UN decided in any case on 6 January to send another 1,000 Blue Helmets to reinforce UNAMIR.

The fact that weapons had been distributed to the extremist militia was now public knowledge. The RPF frequently denounced 'purchases of weapons abroad in order to start a

18. The three countries contributing the largest contingents were Bangladesh, Ghana and Belgium.
19. See *Le Monde*, 13 October 1993.
20. SWB, Radio Rwanda, 17 January 1994.
21. Ibid., 3 January 1994.

war'[22] and the UN tried to organise a last-chance meeting between the MRND(D) and the RPF. But such meetings were by now almost useless. The MRND(D) cadres who were still willing to take part in them were either middle-of-the roaders, who no longer had any control over what went on, or extremists who just wanted to buy time. Major-General Kagame had left Kigali in frustration and was now back in Mulindi. On 30 January Pasteur Bizimungu warned President Habyarimana that if no progress was made towards implementing the Arusha agreement, the RPF might unilaterally break the cease-fire. And indeed Kagame was busy rearming with Ugandan help, getting light weapons for the new soldiers he was busy recruiting both from the Tutsi refugee diaspora and among some Ruhengeri Hutu, who were coming in because of Colonel Kanyarengwe who was a local boy[23]. But Bizimungu's threat was in fact empty and President Habyarimana knew it, because with the presence of UNAMIR the Front could not afford to put itself into the position of being the aggressor.

The transfer of power had been scheduled for 10 February and once again been postponed. On the 17th the UN Security Council, which was beginning to lose patience, issued a communiqué saying that its action in Rwanda could be carried on only if the contending parties reached a minimum agreement on the implementation schedule of the Arusha agreement. But on the same day, in Kigali, UNAMIR was putting out a much more terse communiqué calling on all the parties to refrain from their military training programmes and from the 'massive arms distributions' that were being carried out[24]. The Belgian Foreign Minister Willy Claes then flew to Kigali and told President Habyarimana that the community of donors was also beginning

22. SWB, Radio Muhabura, 29 January 1994.
23. In fact, Colonel Kanyarengwe had been recruiting young men from his area ever since the March 1993 cease-fire, both to strengthen the RPF and to develop his own political base within the organisation. Kanyarengwe had no real military power because, although he was chairman of the Front, he did not belong to the RPA, its armed branch, which was headed by Major-General Kagame. (Interview with Faustin Twagiramungu, Kigali, 14 June 1993.)
24. *Le Monde*, 19 February 1994.

to lose patience. The next day he met the UN's special envoy, Booh-Booh, who told him that UNAMIR, under its present mandate, was quite incapable of stopping the distribution of arms to civilians that was now being done openly[25]. While they were talking, demonstrations were rocking the streets of the capital, leaving five killed and more than a dozen wounded. The UN hoped that the inauguration of the BBTG, scheduled for 22 February, would give a new margin for manoeuvre to the concertation process which now seemed completely stuck. On the next day (21 February) the Twagiramungu fraction of MDR tried to hold a public meeting in support of the BBTG inauguration, but it was attacked by the rival 'MDR-Power' fraction. The city was wracked by violence which caused eight deaths and left many wounded. And in the evening, when he was driving home at around 11 p.m., the PSD executive secretary Félicien Gatabazi was shot dead by an unidentified armed commando, exactly in the same way as Emmanuel Gapyisi had been killed less than a year before.

Hanging on to the cliff's edge

The surgical precision of Gatabazi's murder was equivalent to a signature. The extremists had once again succeeded in putting off the transfer of power to the BBTG, but this time they almost triggered the long-awaited general explosion. Gatabazi, like several members of the PSD leadership, was a *umunyanduga* and the south erupted in anger. Unluckily for him, Martin Bucyana the CDR chairman was travelling there. Angry PSD supporters attacked his car in Butare and lynched him and his driver. This in turn called for CDR retaliation and on the 23rd and 24th the rioting in Kigali approached civil war intensity, leaving thirty-five dead and 150 wounded in the streets[26]. The RPF's answer to these events was remarkably muted. The Front simply declared that there were three groups of people with an interest

25. SWB, RTBF, 19 and 20 February 1994.
26. SWB, RTBF, 23 February 1994.

in putting off the institutional transfer of power by killing Gatabazi. These were Justin Mugenzi, whose fraction of the PL was resolute in its campaign to marginalise Landwald Ndasingwa and recover the totality of the Parti Libéral's share of seats; the President himself who was ready to use all and any means to postpone the swearing-in of the BBTG; and the CDR activists who had declared war on the whole concept of the democratic transition[27]. The Front did not accompany this analysis with any threat that it would start the war again, even after several members of its leadership fell into an ambush as they were driving down to Kigali from the north on the 23rd.

President Habyarimana had actually gone to the Conseil National du Développement (CND, the parliament building) on the 22nd and declared: 'The RPF and the PSD representatives are absent, so are the two Prime Ministers acting and designate as well as the president of the constitutional court.'[28] Without any allusion to the violence of the situation the President simply concluded that the absence of these participants from the transfer of power was a 'denial of democracy', and he 'called on the Rwandese population not to be discouraged'. (Whether or not the last remark should be taken as gallows humour was left for his listeners to decide.) Michel Moussali, UNHCR special delegate to Rwanda, warned of the danger of a 'bloodbath' if the political deadlock were not broken. The same day, President Habyarimana acted almost convincingly the role of the man of goodwill who has been forced into an unmanageable situation by unreasonable people when he declared at a press conference (23 February):

> 'We have two Prime Ministers, one for a government which does not work any more and the other for a government which has not yet managed to come together. [...] I do not know what to do any more after all these consultations and these discussions. If anybody has a better brain than I, he should offer suggestions.'

Apparently no suggestions were forthcoming and, as the last crisis slowly subsided, the President settled down again to his

27. SWB, Radio Muhabura, 22 February 1994.
28. SWB, Radio Rwanda, 23 February 1994.

usual round of postponements, manipulations, denials and jerry-built pseudo-solutions in the hope of surviving, Mobutu-like, through a state of stagnating turmoil. The Belgians had sent him their Minister of Defence, Léo Delcroix, who had told him: 'Belgium cannot wait indefinitely for the setting up of the transitional institutions'[29], a threat which did not seem to disturb him unduly. On 16 March the manager of a tea plantation, his wife and three employees were ambushed and killed as they drove down from Kinihira through the demilitarised zone. The MRND(D) and the RPF accused each other of responsibility for the attack, which was probably the work of neither. The most extremist of the *Interahamwe* were now operating on their own.

The CDR, which hitherto had scornfully refused to take any part in the new Arusha-engineered government, now found a new way to create an obstruction. It went back on its previous refusal to have a single seat in the TNA and asked to sign the future National Assembly Code of Ethics. This of course infuriated the opposition parties, who retorted that the CDR philosophy was incompatible with democratic institutions. This enabled President Habyrimana to fly to the rescue of the CDR and refuse any transfer of power without its participation. Everything was blocked again. Then the President recanted and announced that he would agree to a transfer of power on 25 March – but when that day came there was no transfer of power. It had been postponed to the next day, first, because the President wanted to include not only the CDR in the transitional government but a certain PDI representative then embroiled in a court action to claim his TNA seat against a fellow politician; and secondly, because one of the future MDR Members of Parliament was also embroiled in a court case against a fellow party member for control of his seat. By the next day nothing had been resolved and the transfer of power was again postponed to Monday 28 March.

The whole thing looked like a bad comedy of errors, but the general feeling in the country was that President Habyarimana

29. SWB, Radio Rwanda, 10 March 1994.

was down to his last few shots. He could conceivably pull off one or two more tricks, and his often greedy and quarrelsome adversaries might provide him with a few more opportunities for delaying, but the end was in sight. After yet another postponement on 28 March[30] foreign pressure became intense. UN special envoy Booh-Booh, the Papal nuncio, all the ambassadors who had attended the signing of the Arusha agreement and the Tanzanian facilitator met to make a solemn appeal to the parties. Even Russia, which had never been much involved in the situation, was called on to assist in the attempt at diplomatic pressure, and it issued a statement on 29 March 'regretting the failure of the transitional institutions to assume office' and promising 'to support all efforts towards that end'. On 2 April Booh-Booh warned that the UNAMIR budget would come up for examination soon in New York and that 'severe conditions' might be attached to any renewal of the Mission's mandate, while on 3 April, in the name of the European Union, the German ambassador called for a prompt inquiry into the deaths of Gatabazi and Bucyana, solemnly asked the President to implement the provisions of the Arusha agreement, and expressed his concern at the prolonged absence of government. More important, he hinted at a donors' boycott if the officially-sanctioned violence went any further:

> The European Union has to express its deep concern about the climate of insecurity which is increasing in the country and particularly in the capital and its surrounding areas. It is alarmed at the proliferation of weapons and wishes to point out the unacceptable role of some media which are blocking the indispensable climate of national reconciliation[31]. The European Union reiterates that its support for the peace process will only be effective if the parties speedily implement the provisions of the Arusha accord.[32]

30. The pretext was more difficulties with the PDI and MDR future members. Enoch Ruhigira, the director of the Office of the President, was naive enough to admit that 'even if the CDR question were solved . . . other problems would arise' (SWB, Radio Muhabura, 28 March 1994).
31. A clear allusion to the provocative broadcasts of *Radio Television Libre des Mille Collines* (RTLMC).
32. SWB, Radio Rwanda, 3 April 1994.

It was becoming obvious to President Habyarimana that he could not resist diplomatic pressure of this order for much longer. On 4 April the UN Secretary-General Butros Butros Ghali, in a report to the Security Council, threatened to 're-examine' the UN presence in Rwanda if the Arusha agreement were not quickly implemented. Even the regional 'dinosaur'[33], 'Marshal' Mobutu Sese Seko felt that he had to give some fatherly advice and called both Habyarimana and the Provisional President of Burundi Cyprien Ntaryamira to his Gbadolite residence in northern Zaïre. In the ensuing communiqué the main topic that had been discussed was described as 'ways and means to ensure public security . . . in the subregion'[34].

All this tension, this violence, these constant diplomatic pressures beg one question: was it possible at the time to know about the approaching Apocalypse? With the benefit of hindsight, this has been asked repeatedly, and France in particular has been accused in the strong words of François-Xavier Verschave of having been an 'accomplice' of the genocide[35]. As we see in the next chapter, some people had knowledge of 'death lists', and some public figures such as the former manager of the Central Bank, Jean Birara, tried to warn foreign governments. But the main colouration of the impending violence was deeply Rwandese, deeply embedded in the ambiguous folds of the national culture. The Rwandese rightly call the period between the Arusha agreements and the genocidal explosion *Igihirahiro* (the time of hesitation or uncertainty) – which it was.

What we would call 'Hutu popular culture' kept harping ceaselessly on the same themes, i.e. the intrinsically evil role of the Tutsi in Rwandese history, the errors of the deluded *ibyitso* and the need for 'vigilance'[36]. The RTLMC kept reminding its

---

33. This is the graphic title of a biography of Mobutu by the Belgian journalist Colette Braeckman, *Le Dinosaure*, Paris: Fayard, 1982.
34. SWB, Radio Rwanda, 5 April 1994.
35. François-Xavier Verschave, *Complicité de Génocide? La politique de la France au Rwanda*, Paris: La Découverte, 1994.
36. From this point of view the work of the popular singer Simon Bikindi is fascinating. In songs such as '*Akabyutso*' (the small awakening) or '*Bene sebahinzi*' (son of peasants) he kept propagating with talent a highly confrontational and slanted version of Rwandese history and culture.

listeners that soon 'one would have to reach for the top part of the house'[37] that the Tutsi were evil and that 'we have learnt about it at school'. Rumours were rife and a sense of foreboding was in the air. But even if this sounds like playing the devil's advocate, it was indeed difficult for Westerners – and especially for French Cartesian minds – to make a meaningful connection between such obscure cultural allusions and the magnitude of the horror then being planned.

African politicians might have been expected to have a greater awareness of the pressure building up. The final talking-to was supposed to be given to Habyarimana by his regional peers. On 6 April he flew to Dar-es-Salaam to meet President Ali Hassan Mwinyi of Tanzania, Kenyan Vice-President George Saitoti, Cyprien Ntaryamira of Burundi and President Yoweri Museveni of Uganda. The agenda was regional and the main topic was supposed to be the situation in Burundi. But the discussion soon turned to Rwanda and became an indictment of Habyarimana's refusal to implement the Arusha agreement. The attack was led by Museveni and Ali Mwinyi, but even Ntaryamira, Habyarimana's 'Hutu brother' and as such supposed to be sympathetic, eventually spoke up, reproaching the Rwandese President for endangering the security of Burundi by his strategy of tension. Habyarimana had to face a solid wall of verbal criticism laced with implicit threats in case he failed to comply. President Museveni accompanied the somewhat shaken Habyarimana back to the airport and solemnly asked him to honour his signature[38]. The presidential jet, a spotless four-year-old Falcon 50 flown by a three-man French crew, a gift of President Francois Mitterrand to the Rwandese state, was waiting. As President Ntaryamira was tired and as his own propeller-driven aircraft was much slower and less comfortable than the Falcon, he asked his Rwandese colleague for a lift. It was then decided that the two heads of state would fly to Kigali first. Then, after dropping Habyarimana there, the plane would go on down to Bujumbura, a short hop of twenty-five minutes, and deliver President

---

37. I.e. the place where traditionally weapons were hung.
38. Interview with President Museveni, Kampala, 6 July 1994.

Ntaryamira to his destination before flying back to Kigali. This was never to be. At about 8.30 p.m. local time, as the Falcon 50 was coming in low to Kigali airport for landing in the early evening dusk, two missiles were fired from just outside the airport perimeter. The aircraft received a direct hit, crashed in the garden of Habyarimana's house and immediately burst into flames, killing all aboard. Rwanda had fallen off the cliff.

7

GENOCIDE AND RENEWED WAR
(6 April–14 June 1994)

The enigma of President Habyarimana's death

At the time of going to press, there are still no certainties about who killed President Habyarimana, or even exactly why he was killed. To suggest a motive for his murder is, in a sense, to suggest also a likely culprit if we accept the legal maxim *Fecit qui prodest* (The culprit is the beneficiary). There are several conflicting theories and we will look at each in order of increasing probability. The most bizarre is probably that of the Belgian journalist Colette Braeckman who wrote that the President's plane had been shot down by two French soldiers of the Détachement d'Assistance Militaire et de l'Instruction (DAMI), the military structure the French had not completely dismantled when they left in December 1993[1]. She gave no reasons why the French would have wished to see Habyarimana dead but said that her sources tallied with the findings of the Belgian commission of inquiry which had been set up to find out the exact circumstances under which ten Belgian soldiers had been killed[2]. Since Ms Braeckman later gave as a motivation for the French Turquoise operation in Southern Rwanda 'an attempt at exfiltrating their men and at recovering sophisticated equipment they had left behind with the FAR' – a rather unrealistic view

---

1. Colette Braeckman, 'L'avion rwandais abattu par deux Français?', *Le Soir*, 17 June 1994. The author develops her point in her book *Rwanda. Histoire d'un génocide*, Paris: Fayard, 1994, pp. 188–97.
2. See the section entitled 'The second week of April 1994' below. The Belgian Prime Minister Jean-Luc Dehaene contradicted Ms Braeckman the next day, saying that none of the Commission's findings enabled it to say that French citizens had anything to do with the shooting down of the presidential plane.

of the whole problem[3]. There were no sectors of the French power structure that would have had any interest or desire to see their old ally dead, least of all the cloak-and-dagger boys who had been his most faithful supporters.

The next most unlikely theory is that first put forward by the Rwandese ambassador in Kinshasa, Etienne Sengegera, and later enthusiastically taken up by several other members of the Habyarimana power group: the President's plane had been shot down by UNAMIR Belgian soldiers[4]. To back up his theory, the ambassador said: 'Certain Belgian circles are involved in supporting the RPF for reasons unknown to us. We might make a geostrategic analysis and find that Rwanda is probably not the only country targeted.' He made the true observation that the airport perimeter, including Masaka Hill from which the missiles were fired, was patrolled by Belgian UNAMIR soldiers (he forgot to mention that it was also patrolled by Rwandese Presidential Guards). He added some obvious fabrications, e.g. that dead bodies of white soldiers fighting alongside the RPF had been found on the battlefield, and when asked what had happened to the three Belgian missile operators who he alleged had been captured by the FAR, he said that 'they had been immediately shot dead by the angry Rwandese soldiers', a convenient way of not having to account for an important part of the evidence.

Even the Belgian government had no more interest in the death of President Habyarimana than the French, there is nevertheless an important element in both these tall tales: the men thought to have fired the missiles were depicted by several eyewitnesses as having been white. They were seen driving off

---

3. Even if the theory is absurd, it contains at least one element of truth. Between forty and seventy French military advisers did stay discreetly behind after the December 1993 withdrawal of French forces to help the FAR in case of need (see interview of French Cooperation Minister Michel Roussin on Radio France Internationale, SWB, 30 May 1994). But there was absolutely no need for such a large and expensive operation as 'Turquoise' simply to pull out a few dozen men who could easily leave on their own. As for the sophisticated weapons, they would have been of no use in this poor man's war and existed only in Ms Braeckman's imagination.

4. SWB, *Voix du Zaire* (Kinshasa), 20 April 1994.

in a vehicle on Masaka Hill minutes after the plane crashed, and although nobody saw them actually fire the missiles, their extreme hurry makes it credible that they were fleeing from the site. Of course they did not show their passports to anybody and there was no attempt to stop them. Their identities are thus a complete mystery. So there is a definite presumption that the missile operators were indeed white and that Ms Braeckman and Ambassador Sengegera did not wholly invent their stories. But the problem is rather at the interpretative level. No European government had any reason at that time to want President Habyarimana dead[5].

The next and more interesting theory is that the presidential plane was shot down by the RPF. The first version of this theory was interestingly the work of a US-based Ugandan exile group, the Uganda Democratic Coalition, a motley collection of all the various strands of anti-Museveni opinion. Although mostly made up of northerners nostalgic for the days of Nilotic dominance in Uganda, it also contains some conservative ex-Democratic Party members. While close to the right wing of the US Republican Party during the administration of President George Bush, it has since developed an almost pathological hatred of the United States, which it accused after President Clinton's election of betrayal for supporting the 'Marxist' Yoweri Museveni. In a document distributed to foreign embassies and journalists soon after President Habyarimana's death[6], the Uganda Democratic Coalition accused the United States pell-mell of training RPF guerrillas, of 'seeking to destabilise Burundi, Uganda, Zaïre, Angola, Kenya, Ghana, Ethiopia and other African states' and of conniving at President Habyarimana's assassination. Prudence Bushnell, Deputy Assistant Secretary of State for Africa and Arlene Render, director of the Central African Bureau, both of the State Department; and Patricia Irvin, Deputy Assistant Secretary of

---

5. This does not invalidate the possibility that the men who pulled the trigger were whites. It simply makes it unlikely that they were acting on behalf of a European governmental authority.
6. Uganda Democratic Coalition, *Who are behind the Rwanda Crisis?*, Langley Park, MD, 12 April 1994.

Defense for Humanitarian and Refugee Affairs at the Pentagon, were specifically accused of being 'conspirators with dictator Museveni and RPF leaders in the assassination plot'.

This version of events was quickly seized upon by a number of *akazu* members or supporters[7], most vigorously by Mme Habyarimana and her controversial special adviser, former Captain Paul Barril. In the early 1980s this career *gendarme* had been the head of the crack French anti-terrorist unit GIGN which operated in close cooperation with the anti-terrorist unit in the President's Office led by his friend and mentor Major Christian Prouteau. These connections helped to develop in him a disturbing tendency to place himself above the law, an attitude which eventually resulted in his being drummed out of the army on the charge of tampering with evidence in a court case. The relationship between Barril and the Habyarimana family seems to have considerably pre-dated his signing of a contract with the President's widow on 6 May 1994 to 'undertake all the investigations necessary to shed light on the President's assassination'[8]. As we have seen already[9], a close friend and business associate of his worked for the Habyarimana family as early as January 1990, and it is reasonable to assume that since by then Barril and his friend Pierre-Yves Gilleron had together started their 'special services' company[10], they shared their business contacts. In late 1993 Paul Barril could be found in Burundi as security adviser to President Melchior Ndadaye. Barril's advice cannot have been foolproof since the Burundi President was murdered on 21 October 1993. As it happened, he had left the previous day for Kigali, where he was in close contact with the exiled

7. See for example the favourable presentation given to a translation of the Uganda Democratic Coalition document in the long cover story entitled 'Le complot' by Marie-Roger Biloa in *Africa International*, no. 272 (May 1994).

8. Hervé Gattegno and Corinne Lesne, 'Rwanda. L'énigme de la Boite Noire', *Le Monde*, 28 June 1994.

9. See Chapter 4, footnote 4.

10. See Hervé Gattegno, 'Les missions impossibles du capitaine', *Le Monde*, 23 August 1994. Barril's company was flamboyantly called 'Secrets Inc.' Gilleron was a former employee of the Direction de la Sécurité du Territoire (DST), the French counter-espionage agency.

Burundese Hutu ministers belonging to the extremist wing of Frodebu who were encouraging 'resistance to the attempted coup' (read 'massacre of the Tutsi minority in reprisal for the President's murder')[11]. These extremists, such as Minister Jean Minani, were broadcasting their appeals from RTLMC, the CDR extremist radio. Barril evidently was not working then for the Hutu extremists, but he was in contact with them. Within the framework of his contract with Mme Habyarimana he appeared on 28 June 1994 on the French TV channel Fr 2 during the 1 o'clock news and made a number of accusations. The first was that the presidential plane had been shot down by 'RPF terrorists', which he could prove because he had in his possession the plane's cockpit voice recorder which contained data to that effect. In support of his accusation Barril displayed a small black metallic box with a few electric wires dangling from it, which he said was manufactured by the British firm Litton. Secondly, he also possessed satellite photographs 'taken on the evening of the assassination' showing 'lorries massively rushing from Uganda to Rwanda in order to assault the government troops'. Thirdly, he claimed that the fatal missiles had been fired from Masaka Hill, 'an area under RPF control', and that he had retrieved the launchers used in the attack. Finally he claimed to have access to tapes held by the FAR recording conversations between RPF units where one could hear the voices of 'Europeans speaking English with a Belgian accent'.

It was a strange performance. The former captain seemed in a great state of excitement, and he insisted that the massacres being carried out in Rwanda at the time were 'only disinformation', an astonishing claim to make in late June 1994. His accusations were made with great aplomb. Nevertheless, two of his statements were inaccurate. The first one was easy to spot: Masaka Hill, from which the missiles had indeed been fired, was not then in RPF hands. It did not fall to RPF soldiers till several

11. See Eric Laurent, 'Barril accuse les "terroristes" du FPR', *Libération*, 29 June 1994.

weeks later, when full-fledged fighting had developed inside Kigali. At the time of the President's death, the hill was patrolled by the presidential guard (GP) while the RPF battalion was housed in the Couseil National pour le Développement (CND), the parliament building, several kilometers away; it did not come out of that building till the morning of 7 May, when it was attacked with mortar fire[12]. In terms of plausibility, it would have been extremely difficult for RPF troops to move in an area patrolled by both the UNAMIR and the presidential guard without being spotted. The RPF battalion would also have needed to smuggle in anti-aircraft missiles[13] and accept heavy losses in the subsequent fighting[14] since all its heavy weapons had been left behind before entering the capital.

The other inaccuracy was more difficult to spot for anyone without technical expertise. It had to do with the piece of metal equipment which the former captain showed as proof of his inside knowledge. In fact it looked suspiciously small for a cockpit voice recorder and furthermore this type of equipment is made by the Sundstrand company and not by Litton, which quickly issued a statement to that effect. What is most likely is that the object shown on TV by Barril was a piece of the automatic pilot, which certainly could not hold data on who shot whom, and indeed it later transpired from the aircraft maker Dassault Aviation that this particular plane had probably never been fitted at all with a cockpit voice recorder, which is an optional piece of equipment. In the following days none of the 'proofs' supposedly held by Barril materialised, neither the missile-lauchers, the satellite photographs nor the tapes with men speaking English with a Belgian accent. Mme Habyarimana,

---

12. Interview with Jacques Bihozagara, Paris, 22 June 1994, and with Faustin Kagame, Geneva, 15 June 1994.
13. The RPF had taken three SAM-7s with them from Uganda in October 1990. Two of them scored hits, bringing down a Cessna light transport aircraft and a Gazelle helicopter at the very beginning of the war. The third was lost. The new missiles would then have had to be bought on the free arms market; this was difficult though not impossible.
14. These losses were indeed incurred in the subsequent fighting when the battalion lost about 250 of its strength of 600 men.

who had announced that she would file a lawsuit against unknown parties over her husband's death, seemed to forget all about it.

So the question remains: why should Paul Barril have deliberately uttered inaccurate statements on TV, assuming that he did so? Barril seems to be one of those people who enjoy being in the public eye, and his public appearances are seldom without some ulterior objective[15]. Because it is doubtful that he would have performed his TV act out of either an ideological commitment to radical Hutu power or an abstract commitment to justice, we are left with a different hypothesis.

The former head of GIGN works in the shadowy business of 'security' where many of his contacts are former regular military men turned soldiers of fortune. If we remember the testimonies about white men on Masaka Hill being sighted on the evening of 6 April, and that firing anti-aircraft missiles is a relatively specialised trade, it is possible that Paul Barril could have known the men who had shot down the plane and on whose behalf they had acted. His unproven accusations against the RPF could have been made for the purpose of shifting attention away from other persons, known to him, capable of recruiting experienced white mercenaries for a hit contract on President Habyarimana. If such people existed at all, their only possible patrons, as we see later, were the *akazu* elements who by then had decided that President Habyarimana was more of a liability than an asset to the cause of Hutu power.

15. An excellent example is his role in the legal defence of the terrorist Illich Ramirez Sanchez, alias 'Carlos', alias 'the Jackal', who was sold by the Sudanese government to the French Interior Minister Charles Pasqua on 15 August 1994. The defence of such a notorious client was going to be difficult. Miraculously, a few days later on 21 August, ex-Captain Barril declared on French TV that years ago as a secret service man he had received orders to murder Ramirez Sanchez's advocate Maître Vergès, a famous and controversial lawyer well-known for his extreme left-wing sympathies. Vergès also 'happened' to be Barril's lawyer in his court case about planted evidence in 1982. This accusation, again unsupported by any proof, material or otherwise, cleverly created a cloud of uncertainty whereby murders committed by 'the Jackal' began to look commonplace, appearing as just some private violence which could be equated with the (alleged) government violence. It is not unreasonable to ask oneself whether the former secret service man had flown to the rescue of Me Vergès for purely selfless reasons.

The exact identity of the killers may never be known, and it cannot be proved whether Paul Barril knew them. They could have been mercenaries or even misguided elements in DAMI acting in support of their FAR comrades-in arms[16]. They could even not have been white at all, and the supposed eyewitness reports to the contrary could be deliberate falsehoods or the result of mistaken identity. But the Barril *akazu* RPF hypothesis still does not stand up to the test of probability for at least two reasons.

First, it was not in the political interest of the RPF to kill President Habyarimana. It had obtained a good political settlement from the Arusha agreement and could not hope for anything better. The President was already a political corpse anyway and the problem for the RPF was not going to be with him but rather with the 'Power' groups in the former opposition parties. Killing him meant renewed civil war, the possibility of direct French military intervention if the plot was uncovered, and a leap into the unknown. The result can be seen today, when the RPF victory is, to say the least, fraught with difficulties. Secondly, if the RPF had planned to kill President Habyarimana, it would have been prepared to leap forward militarily. This was not at all the case. The Falcon 50 was shot down in the evening of 6 April and there was no RPF reaction. The stories to the contrary are fabrications[17], using the beginning of the civilian massacres on the one hand and the fighting between the GP and the regular army on the other hand as a smokescreen. In any case, how could the RPF have planned to do anything in Kigali with 600 lightly armed men to contend with at least 15,000

16. If the French government ever knew of the involvement of any of its nationals in the Habyarimana death plot, its first reaction would probably have been to try to hide it for fear that it would be taken as an official action. But this is only due to the poor record of France in the whole Rwandese crisis and to an illogical sort of 'guilt by association'. The French government is highly unlikely to have killed President Habyarimana, not because it could never do such a thing but simply because it was not in its interest.

17. See for example Philippe Gaillard and Hamid Barrada, 'Rwanda. L'attentat contre l'avion présidentiel', *Jeune Afrique*, 28 April 1994, and Marie-Roger Biloa, 'Le complot', op. cit., mentioned above in footnote 7.

troops equipped with armoured vehicles and artillery? The RPF did not decide to fight till 8 April, when the massacres had become evident, and then it did not manage to reach its beleaguered battalion in Kigali from the north till the afternoon of the 11th. Far from it being able to 'attack the Presidential Guard' as has been alleged, the fact that this battalion and the civilians it had taken under its protection were able to survive at all for five days in such conditions was in itself a miracle[18].

This leaves us with the last and most probable hypothesis – President Habyarimana was killed by desperate members of his own *akazu* circle who had decided to gamble on their all-or-nothing 'final solution' scheme when they began to fear (or perhaps to know) that the President was finally going to comply with the provisions of the Arusha agreement.

Technically, the attack posed no problem once trained technicians could be found to fire the anti-aircraft missiles, which is why the eyewitness reports about white mercenaries make sense. The FAR were equipped with only one type of missile, the French anti-tank 'Milan'. This is highly efficient against vehicles but by no stretch of the imagination could it be used against an aircraft in flight. The missiles used in the 6 April attack were either US-built 'Stingers' – or as is more likely since they can more readily be obtained on the international arms market – Russian-made SAM-7s or the more advanced SAM-16s. Both, though relatively simple to fire, nevertheless require an operator trained in their use, and the only missile which FAR personnel knew how to fire was the 'Milan'. Hence the possible need for outside technicians.[19] As for the topography of the attack, the Presidential Guard (GP) would have had no problem in choosing a suitable firing site since the whole area was

---

18. Faustin Kagame, 'Je n'ai pas vu le même film d'horreur que vous', *L'Hebdo*, 19 May 1994. Interviews with Faustin Kagame, Geneva (15 June 1994); Jacques Bihozagara, Paris (22 June 1994); and Seth Sendashonga, Mulindi (5 July 1994).
19. Some observers believe that the Falcon 50 was shot down with RPG rockets, which is possible at low altitude. See J.F. Dupaquier, 'Révélations sur un accident d'avion qui a coûté la vie à un million de personnes', *L'Evènement de Jeudi* (1–7 December 1994).

patrolled by them and bordered directly on the big Kanombe military camp.

The possibility that President Habyarimana might be eliminated by some of his more extremist followers had existed ever since Defence Minister James Gasana, acting on his orders, got rid of some of them, such as Colonel Rwagafilita, Colonel Serubuga and a few others in 1992. This was Mme Habyarimana's side of the *akazu*, the 'real northwesterners', the representatives of the 'small Rwanda' which had conquered the big one. Their anger at the President went hand in hand with their growing dreams of a 'final solution' which would solve both the ethnic problem (killing *all* the Tutsi) and the threat of democratisation (killing *all* the moderate Hutu). Only in a small, tight, well-organised country like Rwanda could such a plan have any chance of success. And only a tight, mostly military leadership could possibly carry it off.

There are several facts that point to 'the two sides of the same plot'[20] i.e. a common origin to both the shooting down of the President's plane and the massacres that followed. First of all, the notion of a genocide had become common talk in Kigali during 1993-4. The fact that a magazine could coldbloodedly publish a headline saying 'By the way, the Tutsi race could be extinguished'[21] caused no shock or even surprise. Lists of names had been drawn up. They were small at first but they grew and several people eventually got to see them[22]. Twice in early 1994, the CDR extremist Hassan Ngeze wrote articles in *Kangura* predicting that President Habyarimana would die in March 1994,

---

20. Henri Faÿ, 'Rwanda. Deux volets d'un même complot', *Le Monde*, 28 May 1994.
21. *La Médaille Nyiramacibiri*, February 1994. *Kangura* was even more explicit in its no. 55 (January 1994), when it wrote: 'Who will survive the March War? [...] The masses will rise with the help of the army and the blood will flow freely.'
22. According to Jean Birara, former governer of the Central Bank (*La Libre Belgique*, 24 May 1994), there were only 500 names on the death lists in April 1993. He claimed that his relation, General Deogratias Nsabimana, the army commander-in-chief, had showed him a list of 1,500 names for Kigali alone on 20 February 1994 and that the lists were later expanded. He also said that he had mentioned the existence of an annihilation plan 'at a very high political level in Belgium' but had not been believed although the Belgian ambassador in Rwanda, Johan Swinnen, confirmed his declarations.

and even went so far as to say that his killer(s) would not be Tutsi but Hutu. And then there was the fact that during the last few days before the President's death, various clues were dropped about the imminence of 'something very big'. The clearest of those hints was an enigmatic broadcast by RTLMC late on Sunday 3 April: 'On the 3rd, 4th and 5th, heads will get heated up. On 6 April, there will be a respite, but 'a little thing' might happen. Then on the 7th and the 8th and the other days in April, you will see something.' Some people had even been warned in advance. In the interview already quoted in *La Libre Belgique*, Jean Birara said that an officer friend had told him on 4 April that 'very serious things were in the making' and that he did not know whether 'he would still be alive in a week's time'.

But apart from these advance warnings, the strongest support for the view that the President's assassination and the ensuing massacres were connected came from the speed with which the situation moved from one to the other. The plane was shot down at around 8.30 p.m., and by 9.15 there were already *Interahamwe* roadblocks everywhere in town and houses were being searched[23]. This was the cause of the shooting that began to be heard less than an hour after the President's death and not any imaginary fighting with the RPF. Fantastic tales have been written about those crucial hours on the evening of Wednesday 6 April 1994. According to the already quoted piece by Marie-Roger Biloa in *Africa International*, 'Groups of desperate Hutu were throwing themselves armed only with sticks and stones against RPF elements armed to the teeth. And they were shouting "They have come to kill us! They have come to kill

---

23. Interview with Carlos Rodriguez, UNHCR delegate in Kigali till April 1994 (Geneva, 15 May 1994). Rodriguez was having dinner with some friends at the house of the US ambassador when one of his employees called at about 8.45 p.m. on his portable phone to inform him of the President's death. After a short discussion, all those present decided to cancel their dinner and go home, fearing trouble. When Rodriguez came out of the ambassador's house at about 9.15 p.m., he found the first militia roadblock just around the corner.

us!"'[24] The reality is that on the evening of the 6th the lightly armed RPF battalion prudently stayed on the alert inside the thick CND cement walls, listening to the radio like everybody else. While Radio Rwanda remained neutral and confined itself to information bulletins, RTLMC started to broadcast direct incitements to deliberately murder 'to avenge the death of our President'. Within the next few hours the calls turned into hysterical appeals for ever greater quantities of blood. It was difficult to credit that normal people could broadcast such things as 'You have missed some of the enemies in this or that place. Some are still alive. You must go back there and finish them off.' or 'The graves are not yet quite full. Who is going to do the good work and help us fill them completely?'[25]

Obviously the *Interahamwe* and *Impuzamugambi* militia were on full alert. The GP was also on alert, since it immediately went out into the town and started killing[26]. The death-lists had been carefully distributed to the future killers, who acted in coordinated and systematic ways in order to catch their intended victims. There was little spontaneity in the whole process, apart from some street urchins joining in the bloody fun, and everything went ahead with the precision of a well-rehearsed drill. Would such quick efficiency have been possible if the

24. Ms Biloa can be excused for writing tendentious novellas. She was a close personal friend of the late President who had helped her financially in her journalistic endeavours.

25. The author would remind his readers, particularly Western ones, of some of the more outrageous pronouncements of the anti-semitic activists in Eastern Europe in the 1930s and 1940s. In France the Vichy government official René Bousquet, who was in charge of deporting Jews to Germany, complained to the Germans that he did not want any children left behind because 'he did not know what to do with them'. The Germans then also took the children (under twelve years old), whom they had previously neglected to carry off. See Pascale Froment, *René Bousquet*, Paris: Stock, 1994 (chapters 15–17). One should also keep in mind that, just as in Europe, the organisers of the genocide were not primitives. RTLMC's 'godfather' was Professor Ferdinand Nahimana, the talented historian.

26. Both the former commander of the GP, Colonel Léonard Nkundiye, and its present head Colonel Mpiranya were later among the coordinators of the countrywide massacres. See Human Rights Watch Africa, *Genocide in Rwanda (April–May 1994)*, London, May 1994, p. 6.

organisers of the 'final solution' had ignored what was going to happen to the President's plane? And finally there is the strange episode of what happened during the night of 6 to 7 April. The UN special envoy Jacques-Roger Booh-Booh received a call in the middle of the night from a somewhat tense Colonel Bagosora who told him: 'Don't worry, this is a coup but everything is under control. We will succeed and save the nation but Colonel Rwagafilita and Colonel Serubuga have to be called back into active army service to help me handle the situation.'[27] Booh-Booh replied that he had no mandate to approve or disapprove what seemed to be going on but that he thought the whole thing mad. Later that same night, Colonel Bagosora also visited the US ambassador with the same message.

Now, if we admit that the men who shot down the President's plane were probably some of his close associates, some questions remain: had President Habyarimana by then actually become a liability to the *akazu*? How did the conspirators actually see themselves and their action? Was it feasible for a group of men to kill the President, re-start the civil war, get away with mass-murder and still rule the country? The whole plan sounds fantastic, but in fact it was largely carried out. Some people actually thought they could carry it through, mad or not. It is of course risky to try imagining other people's thoughts, but keeping in mind the general political and cultural climate of Rwanda at the time, it is not impossible to guess the lines of reasoning along which the coup-cum-genocide planners were thinking. First of all, at the level of self-representation they would certainly not have called what they were undertaking a genocide, they probably regarded it as 'self-defence', as a national upsurge of the 'majority people' against their Tutsi persecutors[28]. They must have seen themselves as heroes and their Hutu democrat adversaries as traitors, which is why their ulterior lack of remorse

---

27. Interview with Faustin Twagiramungu, Paris, 24 May 1994.
28. In *Mein Kampf* Adolf Hitler depicts the German people as innocent victims of a Jewish conspiracy. Later decisions organising the genocide of the Jews were undoubtedly taken in a self-righteous spirit and seen as part of a justified defence mechanism.

was not so much the product of cynicism as of a complete absence of self-doubt.

This is where the notion of 'Hutu ideology' discussed in Chapter 2, comes in. As always in situations where a social group has to transgress generally accepted norms of behaviour in order to defend its interests, it is extremely difficult to do so without the justification of an ideology depicting the transgression as justified, not for the group of perpetrators, but for a wider social circle whose ultimate good justifies the transgression. It is of course better if the transgression can, by a moral sleight of hand, become justifiable in absolute terms. This was exactly the purpose that was fulfilled by the Hutu radical ideology inherited from the 1959 'social revolution'. This ideology, as is often the case for similar constructions, started from a verifiable social fact. The socially subordinate and economically deprived Hutu population of Rwanda had acquired, through the events of 1959 to 1961, a new dignity and an array of social and economic opportunities it never had before. But to achieve that benefit it had had to commit a certain number of violent acts which, as often in revolutionary situations, both enhanced and sullied the revolution's results. The ideologues boldly seized this mass of facts and feelings and solidified them into a sacred icon. The Hutu became the essential embodiment of democracy in Rwanda through the very fact of their demographic dominance, and their violence acquired an almost 'sacred' character. The Tutsi, in turn, became the evil opposite, essentially 'feudalistic' and anti-democratic because they were the minority, and any violence from their side was considered illegitimate. They had lost, they were the minority, they should shut up and accept the mercy of the 'majority democrats'.

So when the political situation looked as if these very Tutsi were going to come back to positions of power with the help of treacherous Hutu who questioned the essential validity of Hutu 'democracy', such a desperate threat called for desperate remedies. Killing had become an act of self-defence because evil incarnate was now threatening to destroy the peaceful agrarian democratic Hutu republic. And, in perfect logic, women and children had to go too. This was not war and there was no time for chivalrous attitudes. It was a matter of survival and the mistake of 1959 could not be repeated: if the evil race had been thoroughly eradicated then, their children would not have been threatening us now. Simple but true. This was Old Testament reasoning, closer to the world of the Deuteronomy than to post-modernist moral posturing.

Of course, saving the 'majority people' from their evil foes was not an entirely altruistic exercise. Democratisation, that is the irruption of both the RPF and of the Hutu opposition parties, meant first and foremost an élite upheaval. This was, among other things, largely a fight for good jobs, administrative control and economic advantage. The evil ones were those planning to take the money-making arrangements (legal or otherwise) away from the old boys. And all this talk of democracy was only a ploy to steal what we had rightfully acquired. Which means that when the President began to show signs of agreeing to go along with that 'peace and democratisation', he changed in status from protector to enemy, or at least an *ibyitso*, an accomplice of the enemy.

By late 1992, the CDR extremists had begun to fear a betrayal of their ideological commitment to Hutu power and some members of the *akazu* had become convinced that the President was ready to sacrifice their material interests to his future political manoeuvring. It was from that convergence of threatened privileges with ideological frustration that the genocide plans got their emotional fuel. As long as the President had seemed to go along with such plans[29], he had remained the leader, but when it began to look as if, with his back finally against the wall, he would eventually prefer carrying out the Arusha agreement provisions than go for Armageddon, his fate was sealed. Nevertheless, it was impossible for the plotters to proclaim openly what they had done. President Habyarimana had for so many

---

29. According to several testimonies, he knew very well of the planned massacre and kept that option open as long as possible, probably both because he actually considered it as a policy alternative and also to humour its promoters.

years been the very incarnation of Hutu power that it was impossible for a group following the same ideology to admit having killed him. This is why the complicated masquerade of the provisional government set-up was organised (see below), and why it was resolved not to have anyone look too closely at the circumstances surrounding the President's death – to the extent that the GP stood guard around the wreck of the Falcon 50 for several days, preventing the French experts from examining it. The Minister of Cooperation, Michel Roussin, had to intervene personally three times to recover the bodies of the French three-man crew. It is of course this 'eyes off' policy of the massacre organisers which makes the collaboration ex-Captain Barril was to get from them later in his retrieval of the magical 'black box' surprising.

One last point remains to be examined: did the plotters actually think they could carry it off ? Obviously they did, because they tried it. But the whole thing was less mad than it seemed. They had counted on foreign and, more precisely, UN passivity and got it. They had counted on domestic popular support for the genocide, and more or less got that too. They had counted on the unwavering support of the armed forces and got it with a few exceptions. They had counted on their capacity to keep a reasonable degree of administrative efficiency during the slaughter process; that was more difficult, but they could more or less manage it. And they had counted on their capacity to resist the RPF militarily and it was their miscalculation on that factor – and that factor alone – which defeated them.

Cynical as it may sound, if the RPF had not existed, or if they had been able to defeat it militarily, the plotters would probably have succeeded. After the genocide, there would have been a period of shocked reprobation; then possibly a UN-sanctioned (partial) economic boycott; then many violations of the boycott, some probably discreetly organised from Paris; then renewed relations with some non-respectable countries such as Serbia, China or Iran (building one or two mosques might have done the trick); and then, arguing on the basis of their 'traditional ties', the French, the Belgians and possibly the

Germans would have come back too. After all, Hutu power, genocidal or not, presents no threat to European interests. Who remembers the half-million Chinese killed on the orders of President Suharto of Indonesia in 1965? Or the hundreds of thousands of natives the same President has massacred in Timor over the years? Aung San Suu Ky is still under house arrest despite her Nobel Prize, and the Rangoon military dictatorship is still in power after slaughtering thousands of its own unarmed citizens who dared to ask for a free society. It is not necessary to be as powerful as China for the foreigners to forget about one's little Tien An Mens.

The second week of April 1994

As soon as the President's plane crashed, militia roadblocks appeared all over the streets of Kigali. Shooting was heard, coming from two sources. On the one hand, militiamen and Presidential Guards had started a house-to-house search for 'enemies' and were killing them; on the other, some FAR elements were trying to stop the slaughter. Fighting between 'loyalist' FAR elements and the GP lasted sporadically throughout Thursday 7 April and most of Friday, involving in some cases the use of artillery. The reason for this fighting was that the new army commander-in-chief, Colonel Marcel Gatsinzi, was not involved in the plot, while Colonel Mpiranya, head of the GP, was[30]. Colonel Gatsinzi tried to keep the army out of the 'final solution'. But many of his subordinates were already collaborating. And by 8 April, when news came that the RPF had decided to enter the fray, he had to bow to majority feelings and accept reconciliation with the GP and the *Interahamwe*.

---

30. The army commander-in-chief, Colonel Deogratias Nsabimana, had been killed in the plane with President Habyarimana. He was hated by the plotters but they were outmanoeuvred by the moderates during the night of 6–7 April and they had to accept Gatsinzi, whom they also thoroughly disliked, as the new supreme commander. It took them ten days to remove Gatsinzi and replace him with General Augustin Bizimungu, a well-known extremist and former Northern Front commander who had taken part in the January 1993 Bagogwe massacres.

The first victims of the massacres had been carefully selected. Among them was the Prime Minister, Agathe Uwilingiyimana, who was attacked in her house by an angry crowd. She was 'protected' by a detachment of ten Belgian UNAMIR soldiers, whom GP officers requested to lay down their weapons. Since the ten men were privates and did not even have an NCO with them, they tried to do what they thought was in keeping with their mandate and complied. They were taken away to a nearby military camp and killed. Meanwhile their charge was assassinated in her house and it was only through the courage of neighbours that her five children escaped death. The President of the Constitutional Court, Joseph Kavaruganda, was killed, both because of his liberal political opinions and because any sort of constitutional succession which he was supposed to organise was made impossible by his death. A number of priests were killed at the Christus Center because they were known to support the democratic transition. Their cook was killed simply because he happened to be there. Charles Shamukiga, the businessman and civil rights activist, was killed. Landwald Ndasingwa, leader of the democratic fraction of the Parti Libéral, was killed together with his Canadian wife and two children. The PSD leader and Minister of Agriculture Frédéric Nzamurambaho was killed, as was his assistant Théoneste Gafaranga and several of their party comrades, almost wiping out the PSD leadership. Their colleagues Marc Ruganera, Minister of Finance, Joseph Ngarambe and Sylvestre Rwibajige were among the very few who escaped death. The journalist André Kamweya, whose newspaper *Rwanda Rushya* was hated by the extremists, was slaughtered. Monique Mujawamaliya, the civil rights activist, survived by hiding in the ceiling of her house and later managed to leave the country after harrowing experiences[31]. The former Foreign Minister and negotiator of the Arusha agreement, Boniface Ngulinzira, was murdered, as was the Information Minister Faustin Rocogoza. The killers

31. On her case, see Laurence Weschler, 'Lost in Rwanda', *New Yorker*, 25 April 1994.

who had been detached to kill Prime Minister-designate Faustin Twagiramungu had the address slightly wrong, so while they were searching a house next to his, he had time to climb over the garden fence and take refuge with the UNAMIR forces[32]. But although the pogrom was clearly focused on liberal politicians and other democrats, the victims were not only well-known people. The lists were long, detailed and open to extension. Tutsi were killed simply because they were Tutsi, i.e. ontological *ibyitso*, 'accomplices' of the RPF, and this even in the case of people who had absolutely no sympathy with the guerrillas[33]. Hutu who were either members or simple sympathisers of democratic opposition parties were also killed[34] because their opposition to 'the democratic majority' had turned them into objective *ibyitso*, no better than Tutsi. Several journalists were killed because they had written too freely about corruption among senior officials. Many priests and nuns were killed because they tried to stop militiamen from killing others. Some well-dressed people, or people who spoke good French, or people who owned a car and were not known MRND(D) supporters were killed simply because these marks of social distinction made them natural suspects for holding liberal opinions. This social aspect of the killings has often been overlooked. In Kigali the *Interahamwe* and *Impuzamugambi* had tended to recruit mostly among the poor. As soon as they went into action, they drew around them a cloud of even poorer people, a *lumpenproletariat* of street boys, rag-pickers, car-washers and homeless unemployed. For these people the genocide was the best thing that could ever happen to them. They had the blessings of a form of authority to take revenge on socially

---

32. Interview with Faustin Twagiramungu, Paris, 24 May 1994.

33. Such a case is vividly described by Charles Rubagumya, a thirty-year-old Tutsi librarian from Kigali, in 'L'engrenage du génocide vécu par un jeune Tutsi', *Le Monde*, 5 August 1994.

34. It was relatively easy to know about people's political choices because, in their enthusiasm for the new democratic political culture, many Rwandese had taken to wearing badges or hats bearing the colours and symbols of the political organisation they supported. In every neighbourhood political affiliations were public knowledge.

powerful people as long as these were on the wrong side of the political fence. They could steal, they could kill with minimum justification, they could rape and they could get drunk for free. This was wonderful. The political aims pursued by the masters of this dark carnival were quite beyond their scope. They just went along, knowing it would not last.

In fact there was no contradiction between the ethnic and the social aspects of the killings since, in Kigali at least, the Tutsi tended to be better off than the Hutu. Political power had been in Hutu hands for thirty-five years but, thanks to the Belgian social and educational favouritism towards the Tutsi for the forty years before that, the Tutsi community was still able to do well for itself socially and economically. This did not only mean the big Tutsi businessmen; it also meant that most of the local personnel in foreign embassies and in NGOs and international agencies were Tutsi, that there were many Tutsi in the professions and even that the best and highest-priced bar girls, the ones to be encountered in the big hotels, were Tutsi. Social envy came together with political hatred to fire the *Interahamwe* bloodlust.

Politically, the situation was extremely confused. During the night of 7–8 April, Colonel Bagosora and Colonel Rwagafilita quickly assembled a Comité de Salut Public (Committee for Public Salvation) which was to pick a provisional government. They wanted a cabinet which would leave them and the other coup-makers in the shadows where they could go on pulling the strings, but which would be their creature and closely reflect their radical political option; and which would try to pass itself off as multiparty in the hope of satisfying the foreigners. On 9 April Radio Rwanda announced the composition of the new government through the voice of Théodore Sindikubwabo, Speaker of the Assembly, who was able to assume the vacant Presidency of the Republic by means of a somewhat free interpretation of article 42 of the June 1991 Constitution. Sindikubwabo was a mainstream MRND(D) person, old, in poor health and dumbly ambitious, manipulating him would not be difficult. His Prime Minister was Jean Kambanda, who had been the unsuccessful MDR extremist candidate for that position in July 1993. The communiqué declared that the new cabinet was made up of five political parties, the MRND (D), the MDR, the PSD, the PDC and the PL. This was technically true, but all the 'opposition' parties were represented by their 'Power' components which had rallied to the 'Final Solution' now tearing Rwandese society apart. Apart from Kambanda, the MDR was represented by Jérome Bicamumpaka (foreign affairs), Straton Nsambumukunzi (agriculture) and Eliezer Nitegeka (information). Nsambumukunzi was a little-known figure, but Bicamumpaka was one of the most extreme advocates of ethnic domination in the 'Power' group and his colleague Nitegeka had been an organiser of the Kibuye massacres in 1992. As for the PSD, it was represented only by Emmanuel Ndabahizi (finance), a somewhat lacklustre character who was one of the few 'Power' sympathisers in his party. The Parti Libéral was represented by the veteran Justin Mugenzi, who kept his Trade Ministry, and Agnes Ntamabyaliro (justice), both 'Power' members, and the PDC by its 'Power' leader Gaspard Ruhumuliza (environment and tourism, a grimly comic appointment considering the circumstances). The twelve other cabinet posts all went to the MRND(D) with the key Interior portfolio going to the CDR sympathiser Faustin Munyazesa. Not all the ministers were extremists. Some, like Prosper Mugiraneza (civil service) and the former University rector Daniel Mbangura (higher education and culture) were middle-of-the-roaders who had been in the previous cabinet and merely allowed themselves to be passively carried along by the movement. But none of them ever protested at the massacres or could be credited with a single independent political or even humane gesture to try to limit the slaughter.

In his inaugural speech, the new Prime Minister set forth three priorities for his government: to stop the violence and looting, reopen talks with the RPF, and help the displaced. The first priority was apparently neglected altogether and the third was impossible to achieve. As for the second, Major-General Kagame had answered it late on Friday 8 April when he decided to renew hostilities. RPF troops started to move down from the north the next day[35], but a new factor had come to complicate the situation. At the same time as the RPF troops went on the move, French Air Force planes were landing soldiers directly at Kigali airport and Belgium announced the dispatch of another expeditionary force.

Although there were at the time 2,519 UNAMIR troops in Rwanda[36], neither Paris nor Brussels – which had the largest expatriate communities living in Rwanda[37] – felt that the UN soldiers could guarantee their security. In fact, as we have seen, the UN soldiers were not even in a position to protect themselves, and the massacres were taking place right before their eyes while they had neither a mandate nor equipment enabling them to do anything.

The French landed 190 paratroopers on the morning of the 9th as part of the code-named 'Operation Amaryllis'. Their mission was to evacuate all foreign nationals who wanted to leave but no Rwandese. They were not to intervene in the local political or security situation. The 250 Belgian soldiers who arrived on the morning of Sunday 10 April had also come mainly to rescue their nationals from the growing anarchy in Kigali. But the political background was somewhat different. Willy Claes, the Belgian Foreign Minister, had asked the United Nations to modify the UNAMIR mandate to allow the international soldiers to intervene militarily and stop the slaughter. Belgium, still smarting after the killing of its ten Blue Helmets, wished to intervene, but only under a UN umbrella. There were plans to have the 250 arriving paratroopers join the Belgian UN contingent already on the spot, but Paris was adamantly opposed to such an idea. The RPF had already declared on the 9th that

35. Inside Kigali the RPF battalion which had been under mortar fire since the afternoon of the 7th came out and counter-attacked on the 8th. They clashed with the army around the Kimihurura barracks but were repulsed. Fighting was going on around the national stadium and the King Faysal hospital.
36. They came from twenty-three countries, but the majority contingents were from Bangladesh (937), Ghana (841) and Belgium (428). They were placed under the command of the French-Canadian General Roméo Dallaire.
37. The Belgians were about 1,500 and the French 650. There were perhaps another 800 foreigners of various nationalities, including 258 Americans.

it would fight the French if necessary and there was fear in Paris that, given France's past record in Rwanda, any form of 'humanitarian' intervention, even under a UN mandate, might be mistaken for an attempt at supporting the provisional government and lead to military clashes with the RPF[38].

The hurried evacuation was a disgrace. Some Tutsi who had managed to board lorries heading for the airport were taken off the vehicles at militia roadblocks and slaughtered under the eyes of the French or Belgian soldiers who, obeying their orders, did not react. In other cases, the African partners in mixed-race couples were refused access on board; a tearful Russian woman married to a Tutsi pharmacist was not only forced to abandon her husband but had to plead to be allowed to take her half-caste children on the plane. The French embassy was full of dignitaries of the Habyarimana regime who did not trust the situation and were trying to flee, while the embassy's Rwandese personnel, who were mostly Tutsi, was cold-bloodedly abandoned to certain death[39]. The *akazu* hard core including Mme Habyarimana, her children, her brother Séraphin Rwabukumba with his death-squad colleague Alphonse Ntirivamunda and a bevy of other extremists, were welcomed by the French authorities. Ordinary people clinging to the gates were pushed back by the French *gendarmes*. A French Africanist who was present, Professor Andre Guichaoua of Lille University, had to distract the attention of the French officers in order to sneak the five children of the murdered Prime Minister Agathe Uwilingiyimana on board a Paris-bound aircraft after they had

---

38. This problem was to resurface two months later when the French changed their minds and belatedly decided on a 'humanitarian' military expedition.

39. Joseph Ngarambe, 'Les responsables du massacre étaient là', *Le Nouvel Observateur*, 14–20 July 1994. Joseph Ngarambe, a PSD member, was one of very few opponents who managed to find asylum in the French embassy. Apart from him there was only Procuror-General Alphonse-Marie Nkubito. The feeling of the *akazu* members that this was *their* embassy was such that the former minister Casimir Bizimungu protested when he saw Nkubito, and asked 'What is *he* doing here?' As for the refusal to evacuate French embassy employees of Tutsi origin, see Vénuste Kayimahe's testimony in *La lettre de la FIDH*, nos 548–9 (28 July 1994).

been refused political asylum[40]. But the French evacuated a large number of 'employees' of the Sainte-Agathe orphanage (formerly a charity of Mme Habyarimana): these were exclusively male, they did not seem to know the children they were supposed to be taking care of, and they vanished as soon as the plane landed. The French authorities evacuated in that way about forty leading members of the MRND(D), who might be useful later in a different political context.

The disagreements between the French and the Belgians over what to do next developed into a highly tense situation right at the airport, with mutual threats of violence. Actually, when several shells fell close to the French aircraft, the 'Amaryllis' officers strongly suspected that they had been fired by their Belgian colleagues in an attempt to deter them from taking off[41]. On Tuesday 12 April Ambassador Jean-Philippe Marlaud locked up the French embassy and walked away. Apart from a handful of missionaries and devoted secular humanitarian workers such as Marc Vaiter, who managed to keep his orphanage open throughout the battle of Kigali[42], the whites were in full flight. Probably less than thirty of them were left in the whole country, a factor which was to make the massacres easier, far from prying Western eyes.

The slaughter spread to the interior of the country as early as the afternoon of 7 April[43]. Systematic massacres were started in several *préfectures* and word of the slaughter spread into the hills, both informally and through administrative and party channels. By the 12th, fully-fledged fighting had developed in Kigali between government troops and the RPF whose forces were pouring in from the north. The UNAMIR General Roméo

40. Interview with Professor Guichaoua, Lille, 8 June 1994.
41. Interview with a French Defence Ministry official, Paris, 17 May 1994.
42. See Michel Peyrard, 'Le SOS de Marc Vaiter', *Paris Match*, 9 June 1994. Vaiter remained with the orphans throughout the fighting, sheltering both Tutsi and Hutu and always managing to fend off the demands of the militiamen for ethnic lists. He later published a memoir of the experience – *Je n'ai pas pu les sauver tous*, Paris: Plon, 1995.
43. Telefax sent by Jeff Vleugels, a missionary of the White Fathers in Kigali, to his superiors on 7 April 1994 at 1.45 p.m.

Dallaire had tried to broker a cease-fire between the combatants, but the RPF did not seem interested in any kind of negotiation. The provisional government fled to Gitarama the same day to escape the intensification of the fighting, a move which increased administrative confusion. The only authority remaining in Kigali on the 'government' side consisted of General Augustin Bizimungu and his troops. General Dallaire tried again to bring about a cease-fire. The answer came indirectly from Théogène Rudasingwa, the Front's secretary-general, in an interview on Radio France Internationale: 'There will be no negotiations with these criminals.'[44] This was clear. The war was now on, but it was not the war which was killing most of the people. It was the enormous wave of civilian massacres now gathering momentum and sweeping right across the country. It was in fact a genocide.

The Genocide

Genocide is a value-laden word, it is a tragic word, and its use, infrequently applicable in the history of mankind, cannot be made without serious justifications. Such large-scale killings, even of very large size, as the the punitive expeditions of the Duke of Alba in the Low Countries in the sixteenth century or the bombing of Dresden in the twentieth, unpleasant as they are, are not genocides because the *purpose* of a 'final solution' is lacking and the slaughter stops when the killers are tired or feel that the enemy has learned his lesson. And thorough destructions of a limited population such as that of the population of Samarkand by Timur Leng in the fifteenth century, although quasi-genocidal, are not real genocides because the target is geographically limited. There are few genocides in history, especially in distant history where social action, including massacres, tended to be less systematised. Without any doubt, and contrary to the superficial 'explanations' that the 'primitiveness' of Rwanda was a cause of the genocide it suffered, genocides are a modern phenomenon – they require organisation – and

44. SWB, Radio France Internationale, 13 April 1994.

they are likely to become more frequent in the future. The conquering Romans, Arabs, Turks and even Mongols, contrary to their sombre legend, did not try to annihilate the populations they conquered. They reduced them to varying degrees of subjugation and often ended up more or less deeply mixing with them. The first modern genocide was that of the American Indians, and it was largely 'successful'. The genocides of the Armenians, the Jews and the Gypsies were also racial. The Communist system, with its notion of the 'New Man', created a new type of genocide of the political and social kind where the victims belonged to the same racial stock as their killers and were killed because their social behaviour was deemed contrary to the dominant ideology of the state. But the same criteria apply as in ethnic genocide, i.e. the systematic organisation of the killing and the attempt at completely erasing the targeted group – in this case socially or politically unorthodox people. Stalin's purges of the Kulaks followed by his massive administrative massacres of 'opponents' showed the way in that direction, later to be followed by the massive 'political' genocides in China and Cambodia. We have chosen to use the word genocide here not only because of the magnitude of the killings, but because of their organised and selective nature and because there was an attempt to carry them to the point where targeted populations would be completely annihilated. It is not because of its 'primitiveness' that Rwanda could suffer from a genocide; quite the contrary. If we take some of the largest African bloodlettings of recent times into consideration, neither the quasi-genocidal war between northerners and southerners in the Sudan nor the Somali clan wars of the late 1980s and early 1990s reached a truly genocidal stage simply because the killers were too disorganised and the killing field was too big and uncontrolled. In Rwanda, all the pre-conditions for a genocide were present: a well-organised civil service, a small tightly-controlled land area, a disciplined and orderly population, reasonably good communications and a coherent ideology containing the necessary lethal potential.

As we will see, the Rwandese genocide is of a mixed type –

partly classical genocide with the systematic massacre of an allegedly racially alien population, and partly political with the systematic killing of political opponents[45]. To avoid an understandable but somewhat sterile emotional treatment of the genocide, we will try to deal with it analytically and ask certain questions.

Who were the organisers? By 'organisers', we mean here the people who actually carried out the organisation of murder squads, distributed weapons and gave or relayed instructions at a high level. We do not mean the intellectual inspirators such as Ferdinand Nahimana or Casimir Bizimungu, great as their responsibility may be. We do not mean either the gun- and machete-toting actual killers.

As in any genocide, the question of who actually gave the orders is not an easy one to answer. Even in the the well-researched case of the German genocide of the Jews, although everyone knows by now relatively well how it was carried out, the precise decision-making mechanism which set the process in motion remains shrouded in uncertainties. But in the case of Rwanda, after a number of political actors have spoken of their roles, doubts are relatively limited and they concern more the 'how' than the 'who'. The same names crop up again and again, whether in the

---

45. For a discussion of the Rwandese genocide *qua* genocide, see Alain Destexhe, *Rwanda. Essai sur le génocide*, Brussels: Editions Complexe, 1994. Destexhe disagrees with the idea that the term 'genocide' can be applied to people killed for political and not ethnic reasons. This author takes a different view. The difference between simple – even if bloody – political repression and a political genocide has to do with three factors. In a political genocide the victims are killed wholesale, just as in an ethnic genocide, without always making sure that they do indeed support the opposition; the intention of the killers is not to frighten the opposition into submission, but to clean up the opposition by total physical annihilation; and there is no strategy or possible negotiation involved: members of the targeted group will be killed even if they 'repent', as if their 'guilt' is ontological and cannot be renounced even by abjuration, just as in an ethnic massacre. By any and all of these criteria, the Rwandese genocide was political as well as 'ethnic'.

reports of human rights groups[46] or in the testimony of independent observers of various political persuasions[47].

It seems that, inasmuch as there was a general organiser of the whole operation, this distinction has to go to Colonel Théoneste Bagosora, director of services in the Ministry of Defence and behind-the-scenes creator of the 'Provisional Government'. It seems to have been he who coordinated the 'final solution' activities as long as they retained enough coherence to be coordinated. Next in the line of responsibility is the Defence Minister, Major-General Augustin Bizimana, who oversaw the logistics and also influenced the reluctant elements in the FAR so that they would not stand in the way. His military aides were mostly Colonel Aloys Ntabakuze, commander of the paratroopers, and Lieut.-Colonel Protais Mpiranya, head of the Presidential Guard (GP). Other military men who seem to have played an essential role in articulating army resources and militia action are Lieut.-Colonel Leonard Nkundiye, the former GP commander, Captain Pascal Simbikangwa who supervised militia killings in Kigali, and his second-in-command Captain Gaspard Hategekimana. All these people acted at the national level. Locally one can mention *Gendarmerie* Colonel Nsengiyumva who directed the slaughter in Gisenyi and Colonel Muvunyi who did the same in Butare. Many civilians were also directly involved such as Joseph Nzirorera, the secretary-general of MRND(D), who coordinated the *Interahamwe* operations; Pascal Musabe, a bank director who was one of the militia

---

46. Such as the information found in the reports of Human Rights Watch Africa, *Genocide in Rwanda (April–May 1994)*, op. cit., and African Rights, *Rwanda: Who is killing? who is dying? what is to be done?*, London, May 1994. The most detailed list of the genocide organisers is provided in African Rights: *Rwanda: Death, despair, defiance* (henceforth quoted as *Rwanda: Death*), London: African Rights, 1994, pp. 97–100.

47. The informants interviewed on the question of the organisation of the massacres include Faustin Twagiramungu, Seth Sendashonga, Pasteur Bizimungu, James Gasana, Denis Polisi, Rakiya Omaar, Alphonse-Marie Nkubito, Joseph Ngarambe, Jean-Marie Vianney Ndagijimana, Faustin Kagame and several others who wished to remain anonymous. They also include several French army officers, as well as UNHCR officials, NGO staff members and ICRC officials who are all professionally obliged to remain anonymous.

organisers at the national level; the businessman Félicien Kabuga who financed the RTLMC and the *Interahamwe*; and Robert Kajuka, leader of the CDR militia, the *Impuzamugambi*, although he himself was a Tutsi. In the interior, the local organisers of the massacres were almost invariably the *préfets*, with particular distinction for viciousness going to Emmanuel Bagambiki, *préfet* of Cyangugu and Clement Kayishema, *préfet* of Kibuye. In some cases the main organiser could be a militant outsider, as with Rémy Gatete, formerly a simple *bourgmestre* of Murambi *commune* in Byumba, who had moved to Kibungo *préfecture* by the time of the genocide and who organised the massacres in the east before fleeing to Tanzania and becoming a 'refugee leader' at Benaco camp.

These people seemed to think according to a pattern familiar to those who have studied the work of various 'negationist' historians of the Nazi genocide. Verbally attack the victims, deny – even in the face of the clearest evidence – that any physical violence is taking place or has taken place[48] and fudge the responsibility issue so that, although there are victims, the killers' identities remain vague and undefined, almost merging into non-existence[49]. When talking to your supporters never claim any 'credit' for what you are actually doing but hint at the great benefits derived from the nameless thing which has been done, sharing complicity in the unspoken secret with your audience[50].

So we can see that the actual organisers of the genocide were a small tight group, belonging to the regime's political, military

---

48. See for example the quip by French negationist historian Henri Faurisson that 'in Auschwitz, the only things that were ever killed were lice'. This combines a blunt denial of fact with the dialectical advantage of the double meaning one can give to the word 'louse'.

49. On 15 May, Robert Kajuka, head of the *impuzamugambi*, could describe the killings in those terms: 'It is just the population which got angry after the death of the President. It is hard to tell who is responsible for these massacres' (*Le Monde*, 17 May 1994).

50. Thus 'Provisional President' Théodore Sindikubwabo in a speech in Kibuye in May, congratulated the audience on 'the return to a quiet situation . . . now that all the troublemakers have been dealt with'.

and economic élite who had decided through a mixture of ideological and material motivation radically to resist political change which they perceived as threatening. Many of them had collaborated with the 'Zero Network' killer squad in earlier smaller massacres, and shared a common ideology of radical Hutu domination over Rwanda. They did not belong exclusively to the inner circle of *akazu* if by this expression one means the people closest to President Habyarimana. Rather it seems that the leaders in the conspiracy were the people who had once been close to the President but who had somewhat parted company with him. On the whole, they seem to have been closer to the 'other side' of the *akazu*, that is Mme Habyarimana and *'le clan des beaux-frères'*. Their efficiency in carrying out the killings proves that these had been planned well in advance[51]. But the particularly chilling quality of that efficiency is that, as in other genocides, it would not have been enough had it not been for two other factors: the capacity to recruit fairly large numbers of people as actual killers and the moral support and approbation of a large segment – possibly a majority of the population.

Who were the killers? There are some differences between the situations in the capital and in the interior *préfectures*. In Kigali things developed rapidly. They were also highly centralised. The executions were begun by the Presidential Guards as early as the evening of the 6th. They started killing during the night and they managed to dispose of most of the 'priority targets' – the

51. There were many testimonies to that effect in the press. See for example Jean-Philippe Ceppi, 'Comment le massacre des Tutsi a été orchestré au Rwanda', *Le Nouveau Quotidien*, 13 April 1994; Jean Chatain, 'Des survivants de l'opposition accusent', *L'Humanité*, 9 May 1994; Jean-Philippe Ceppi, 'Témoignages de rescapés du Rwanda', *Libération*, 9 May 1994; Keith Richburg, 'A carefully organized massacre', *International Herald Tribune*, 9 May 1994; (anonymous), 'Le massacre organisé', *Jeune Afrique*, 12–18 May 1994; Jean Chatain, 'Rwanda. Rukara tente de revivre', *L'Humanité*, 18 May 1994; Marie-France Cros, 'Nous avons été entraînés pour éliminer tous les Tutsi', *La Libre Belgique*, 24 May 1994; and Alain Frilet, 'Kigali, l'enfer de l'église Sainte-Famille', *Libération*, 17 June 1994. The reason why so many sources are quoted is to dispel for good the still prevalent notion that the genocide was an act of 'spontaneous violence' carried out by 'angry peasants'.

politicians, journalists and civil rights activists – within less than thirty-six hours. The GP had a strength of about 1,500 – enough to terrorise the capital within a short time. But they immediately called for help from the *Interhamwe* and *Impuzamugambi* militias, which had been waiting for such a moment from the date of their conception.

These militias tended – usually though not always – to be recruited from low-class people. The camaraderie, the numerous material advantages and even a form of political ideal made them attractive to some middle-class young people. Country-wide, their numbers were estimated at about 50,000[52], that is approximately the strength of the regular armed forces. Their equipment was simple, some AK-47 assault rifles, a lot of grenades and the all-purpose slashing knives or machetes called '*panga*' in Swahili[53]. Many of them had received a military training, often thanks to the French army as we have seen. In Kigali they manned the roadblocks and took part in the house-to-house searches. They also acted as the executioners. It could be that in a given neighbourhood, some local people would work 'part-time' as *Interahamwe*, either for the sake of looting the victims' houses or, on the contrary, to be seen as 'one of the boys' and be able to protect their own house against looters[54]. On the whole, their discipline was poor, especially among new members recruited in the heat of the action. Since these new members tended to be street boys who were drunk most of the

52. See the already-mentioned interview with Jean Birara in *La Libre Belgique* dated 24 May 1994.

53. The panga, along with the hoe, is the commonest agricultural tool in East Africa, and there is nothing particularly sinister about peasants carrying machetes on their way between the *rugo* and their fields. But, according to the confidential letter *La Lettre du Continent* (16 June 1994), the local representative of the Chillington company, the largest producer of pangas and other agricultural hand-tools in East Africa, sold more machetes in February 1994 than in the whole of 1993. The militias had been armed – but crudely. It was clear that if their masters had succeeded in their scheme, there would have been a law-and-order problem after the successful conclusion of the genocide and then a disarmament period. Men with machetes are easier to disarm than men with firearms.

54. Florence Aubenas, 'L'éxil doré des profiteurs Rwandais au Zaïre', *Libération* (30 July 1994).

time, the militias crumbled into armed banditry in the later course of the war as the administrative structure which had recruited and supported them fell apart.

Till this late stage though, the killers were controlled and directed in their task by the civil servants in the central government, *préfets*, *bourgmestres* and local councillors, both in the capital and in the interior[55]. It was they who received the orders from Kigali, mobilised the local *Gendarmerie* and *Interahamwe*, ordered the peasants to join in the man-hunts and called for FAR support if the victims put up too much resistance. There was only one case of non-compliance with the killing orders. It came from Jean-Baptiste Habyarimana (no relation to the late President), the only Tutsi *préfet* in the country who was at the head of the Butare *préfecture*. Nothing happened in Butare for two weeks till, angered by his 'inaction', Interim Government President Sindikubwabo (one of the rare Butare men in the government) came down and gave an inflammatory speech, asking the people if they were 'sleeping' and urging them to violent deeds. On the 20th the *préfet* was replaced by the extremist Sylvain Ndikumana, GP elements were flown down from Kigali by helicopter, and the killing started immediately.

The efficiency of the massacres bore witness to the quality of Rwandese local administration and also to its responsibility. If the local administration had not carried out orders from the capital so blindly, many lives would have been saved. This fact will of course cause immense problems for any future government which has to run a country where almost the entire local civil

---

55. See for example the description by French journalist Alain Frilet of the situation inside the Sainte-Famille and Saint-Paul churches in Kigali where almost 5,000 potential victims had found refuge. Each time the militiamen came in to take away a contingent of refugees for slaughter, they carried with them authorisations duly signed by every administrative echelon, all the way from the lowly 'Madame Odette' (Odette Nyirabagwenzi) who was the local *mayumba kumi* person in charge up to Defence Minister Augustin Bizimana by way of the *préfet* and the *bourgmestre*. Of course, murders were not always carried out according to procedure, but constant efforts were made by the administration to keep the genocide from degenerating into all-out anarchy (Alain Frilet, 'Kigali. L'enfer de l'eglise Sainte-Famille', *Libération*, op. cit.).

service should be charged with crimes against humanity. In the horror at the behaviour of an administration cold-bloodedly prepared to massacre its own population, there is a mitigating circumstance the mention of which is hardly reassuring. All these administrators were not only civil servants, but also MRND(D) members and as such doubly responsible to the state. As we saw in Chapter 1, there had always been a strong tradition of unquestioning obedience to authority in the pre-colonial kingdom of Rwanda. This tradition was of course reinforced by both the German and the Belgian colonial administrations. And since independence the country had lived under a well-organised tightly-controlled state. When the highest authorities in that state told you to do something you did it, even if it included killing. There is some similarity here to the Prussian tradition of the German state and its ultimate perversion into the disciplined obedience to Nazi orders.

Political scientists tell us that the state can be defined by its monopoly of legitimate organised violence. Where· does the legality of the exercise of that monopoly stop? In time of war, people who refuse to carry out orders to commit violent acts can be shot. And we will see that violence and compulsion were used in the Rwandese case. This obviously constitutes no excuse, especially since, as we will also see, some people found in their religious faith or simply in their individual conscience the strength to resist the orders. But we have to realise that this is a society where two factors combine to make orders hard to resist. Thr first is a strong state authoritarian tradition going back to the roots of Rwandese culture. The Tutsi *abami* were definitely not constitutional monarchs, and killing was even an accepted sign of their political health – the difference being of course in the order of magnitude and social inscription of the killings. The second is an equally strong acceptance of group identification. In Rwanda, as elsewhere, a man is judged by his individual character, but in Rwandese culture he does not stand alone but is part of a family, a lineage and a clan, the dweller on a certain Hill. On top of this age-old feeling, the tight administrative practices (and regional discriminatory policies) of the regime had reinforced this 'collective grounding of identity'. When the authorities gave the orders to kill and most of the group around you complied, with greater or less enthusiasm, it took a brave man indeed to abandon solidarity with the crowd and refuse to go along. And such a heroic position would not be without personal danger. Sadistic killers such as the notorious Murambi *bourgmestre* Rémy Gatete seem to have been in a small minority and heroes such as *préfet* Jean-Baptiste Habyarimana were even rarer. The vast majority of civil servants carried out their murderous duties with attitudes varying from careerist eagerness to sullen obedience.

The Tutsi and opposition Hutu were duly listed, their houses were known, and few of those marked out to die had a chance to hide. To carry out their task the administrators relied first on the *Gendarmerie*, this rural police of whose training the French were so proud. The *bourgmestre* simply called on the next *Gendarmerie* unit and they fanned out among the *ingo*, shooting and flushing people out of their houses. But the *Gendarmes* could not perform such a herculean task as attempting to kill about 10% of the population all by themselves. Inter-service collaboration was needed, and so was the enrolment of 'volunteers'. The FAR did not at first take a leading role in the genocide. But after the failed attempt by Colonel Gatsinzi to keep them out of the unfolding tragedy[56], they were slowly drawn more and more deeply into the collective slaughter.

Other actors in the genocide were the Hutu Barundi refugees who had fled Burundi after the murder of President Melchior Ndadaye in October 1993 and the inter-communal massacres following that event. The MRND (D) had started recruiting them into the *Interahamwe* soon after their arrival in Rwanda and

---

56. After being deposed as commander-in-chief, Colonel Gatsinzi was sent to Butare as commanding officer and it was largely his presence which enabled the *préfet* Jean-Baptiste Habyarimana to keep things peaceful there. Gatsinzi was removed at the same time as J.-B. Habyarimana and replaced by Colonel Muvunyi who immediately changed the previous policy and launched the FAR into massacres (*Libération*, 29 August 1994, and African Rights, *Rwanda: Who is killing? Who is dying? What is to be done?*, op. cit.).

the UNHCR felt obliged to complain (without effect) to the Rwandese authorities[57]. After 6 April many of them took an active part in the killing.

Nevertheless, the main agents of the genocide were the ordinary peasants themselves. This is a terrible statement to make, but it is unfortunately borne out by the majority of the survivors' stories. The degree of compulsion exercised on them varied greatly from place to place but in some areas, the government version of a spontaneous movement of the population to 'kill the enemy Tutsi' is true[58]. This was the result of years of indoctrination in the 'democratic majority' ideology and of demonisation of the 'feudalists'. So even in the cases where people did not move spontaneously but were forced to take part in the killings, they were helped along into violence by the mental and emotional lubricant of ideology. We can see it for example in the testimony of this seventy-four year-old 'killer' captured by the RPF: 'I regret what I did. [...] I am ashamed, but what would you have done if you had been in my place ? Either you took part in the massacre or else you were massacred yourself. So I took weapons *and I defended the members of my tribe against the Tutsi.*'[59]

Even as the man pleads compulsion, in the same breath he switches his discourse to adjust it to the dominant ideology. He acknowledges that he killed (under duress) harmless people, and yet he agrees with the propaganda view (which he knows to be false) by mythifying them as aggressive enemies. If the notion of guilt presupposes a clear understanding of what one is doing at the time of the crime, then there were at that time in Rwanda, to use the vivid expression coined by the historian Jean-Pierre Chrétien, a lot of 'innocent murderers'. Such 'victim-killers' were often disgusted and horrified at what they were doing

---

57. See the Kigali UNHCR letter to the Minister of External Affairs (18 November 1993) quoted in African Rights, *Rwanda: Death*, op. cit., p. 59.
58. For chilling examples of this see Patrick de Saint-Exupéry, 'Rwanda. Les assassins racontent leurs massacres', *Le Figaro* (29 June 1994), and African Rights, *Rwanda: Death*, op. cit., p. 397, where a wounded schoolboy says he was hit while being escorted by *Interahamwe* 'even by women on their way to fetch food'.
59. *La Libre Belgique*, 24 May 1994.

which is partly why large groups of Hutu peasants started to flee their Hills even before the arrival of the RPF troops. In Tanzania, the objective of the first stage of this mass exodus, some of the refugees denounced their own *bourgmestres* who were walking along in the crowd. A Tanzanian police officer, Jumbe Suleiman, who saw them as they were crossing at Rusumo was struck by their reaction: 'When Gatete [Rémy Gatete, *bourgmestre* of Murambi] crossed the bridge over the river which marks the border between Rwanda and Tanzania, people started to shout: "This is Gatete! He is a murderer! Arrest him!" If we had not intervened, he would have been lynched.'[60] In the hysteria of Rwanda in April 1994, almost anybody might turn into a killer. But the responsibility lies with the educated people – with those in positions of authority, however small, who did not have the strength (or maybe even the wish) to question the poisonous effluents carried by their cultural stream.

There was of course also an element of material interest in the killings, even in the countryside. The killers looted household belongings and slaughtered the cattle. Meat became very cheap, and grand feasts were held, as if in celebration of the massacre. Villagers also probably had a vague hope that if things settled down after the massacres they could obtain pieces of land belonging to the victims, a strong lure in such a land-starved country as Rwanda. But greed was not the main motivation. It was belief and obedience – belief in a deeply-imbibed ideology which justified in advance what you were about to do, and obedience both to the political authority of the state and to the social authority of the group. Mass-killers tend to be men of the herd, and Rwanda was no exception.

Who were the victims? The vast majority of victims were people belonging to the Tutsi social group. All of them were slated to die. The killers did not spare women, old people, children or even babies. The 'bush clearing', to use the *interahamwe*

---

60. Jean-Philippe Ceppi, 'Des tueurs Hutu réfugiés en Tanzanie', *Libération*, 20 May 1994.

euphemism, was absolutely thorough. In the countryside, where people knew each other well, identifying the Tutsi was easy and they had absolutely no chance of escaping. Since Hutu and Tutsi are not tribes but social groups within the same culture, there was no separate dwelling pattern. They lived side by side in similar huts, and given the demographic ratio, each Tutsi household was usually surrounded by several Hutu families, making concealment almost impossible. In the countryside, in contrast to the city, there was no noticeable difference of economic level between Tutsi and Hutu. The 'small Tutsi' from the Hills were in no way different from their Hutu neighbours, except perhaps in their physical appearance. But it did not matter because the Tutsi or Hutu identities of the villagers were public knowledge.

It was not the same thing in the towns and even more in Kigali where people did not know each other. There the *Interahamwe* manning the roadblocks asked people for their identity cards. To be identified on one's card as a Tutsi or to pretend to have lost one's papers meant certain death. Yet to have a Hutu ethnic card was not automatically a ticket to safety. In Ruhengeri or Gisenyi and at times in Kigali, southern Hutu suspected of supporting the opposition parties were also killed. And people were often accused of having a false card, especially if they were tall and with a straight nose and thin lips. Frequent intermarriage had produced many Hutu-looking Tutsi and Tutsi-looking Hutu. In towns or along the highways, Hutu who looked like Tutsi were very often killed, their denials and proffered cards with the 'right' ethnic mention being seen as a typical Tutsi deception.

Of course, Hutu militants or sympathisers of the opposition parties were also killed, a fact which gives this genocide its peculiar mixed character both racially and politically. And as in many such situations, intellectuals were also a target: journalists, professionals and university people were highly suspect because they thought too much and as such were probably not good citizens, even when they were Hutu. In Butare, almost everybody who lived on campus, both students and teachers, the vast majority of them Hutu, were massacred after 21 April. So too were almost all the doctors at the hospital.

Although it seems that few people were killed purely for robbery, there was nevertheless a strong element of social envy in the killings, and in the rural areas this could work at a very simple level. In the vivid words of a survivor, 'The people whose children had to walk barefoot to school killed the people who could buy shoes for theirs.'[61]

Were there any bystanders? The bystanders were mostly the churches. Although, as we will see, there were admirable acts of courage among ordinary Christians, the church hierarchies were at best useless and at worst accomplices in the genocide. And the first to be appalled by this attitude were those priests who had supported human rights as a modern incarnation of Christian values and who found themselves betrayed. As two of them declared to a French journalist:

> 'Why did not the Bishops react? They made a few vague speeches but had no prophetic commitment. If they had spoken out, the massacres might have stopped. [...] Most of the priests who were killed were those who had defended human rights. [...] Only two bishops [out of nine] spoke out clearly, those of Kibungo and Kabgayi. The Bishop of Rwankeri even dared to ask the Christians to support the [interim] government.'[62]

Throughout the crisis, Fathers Vleugels and Theunis of the White Fathers sent frequent faxes to their head office to inform their Order of the developments in Rwanda. The general tone is most revealing: there are precise lists of priests killed but nothing about the massive killings of their parishioners. One

---

61. Interview with M.L., a Tutsi teacher (Paris, 12 July 1994), who was away from home when the killers reached his *rugo*, and lost his wife and four of his five children in the genocide. His fifth child, aged eighteen months, was saved by a Hutu neighbour who just grabbed it and ran off.

62. Jean Chatain, 'Deux prêtres témoignent sur les atrocités au Rwanda', *L'Humanité* (3 May 1994). Although most clergy who died were Tutsi, many Hutu priests who were known supporters of human rights and had denounced government atrocities in the past were also murdered.

almost has the impression of reading a trade union or diplomatic list where only the welfare of insiders is of concern. Violence is described as 'happening' but the perpetrators are never identified. One has the surrealistic impression of reading about murders being committed by armies of ghosts whose faces are forever blurred. The only moment when names are named is when the two Fathers can at long last pin a particular crime on the RPF. Then all the necessary details and particulars are given[63].

If some of the foreign priests could have such a distorted and ambiguous relationship with the reality surrounding them, little could be expected of the native Hutu clergy. As a baffled foreign observer remarked after visiting Kirambo parish near Cyangugu after the massacres had ended: 'There was not the slightest trace of collective guilt among the Christian clergy.'[64] Worse, the church placed itself in an advantageous moral position, simply because, like every other institution, social body or profession in Rwanda, it had paid heavily in the genocide. Even such an otherwise respectable publication as the monthly *Dialogue* used the list of the 192 members of the clergy killed in the general slaughter as a kind of badge of courage[65] claiming for the church the status of a martyr. There were few cases of priests being killed trying to defend their charges. Foreign priests were spared, but Tutsi and liberal Hutu priests were killed like their counterparts in the general population and, despite some courageous exceptions, most of the Hutu priests looked the other way. This situation was of course the result of the many years of close association between the Hutu republic and the Catholic church. This attitude had political consequences, even abroad, since the Christian Democratic International took an ambiguous attitude

---

63. See for example the telefax dated 19 May 1994. Even when the RPF so much as asks the Fathers to leave a certain area 'for their security', the demand is described in such a way as to hint that the Front wants to hide unspeakable things it is about to commit
64. African Rights, *Rwanda: Death*, op. cit., p. 516.
65. *Dialogue* no. 177 (Aug.-Sept. 1994), 'Liste des prêtres, religieux, religieuses et laïcs consacrés tués au Rwanda', pp. 123–35.

towards the RPF and never got around to an open condemnation of the Hutu extremists.[66]

As for the Protestant Churches, although their association with the regime did not have the historical depth of the Roman Catholics', their attitude was little better. But at least there was an admission of guilt at a higher hierarchical level. In the courageous words of the Revd Roger Bowen, 'Anglican Church leaders were too closely aligned with the Habyarimana government. The Archbishop spoke openly in support of the President and his party. [...] The ethnic issue also ran deep within the churches and all the Anglican diocesan bishops were Hutu.'[67]

The result of this violence is that there is now a 'church in exile' in Nairobi whose bishops staunchly refuse to denounce the genocide[68] and which is rejected by the Tutsi 'returnees' from Uganda and Burundi now flocking to Rwanda.

In the Catholic Church, the extreme point of bad faith was reached by the twenty-nine priests who on 2 August 1994 wrote a collective letter to the Pope in which they denied any Hutu responsibility for the genocide and attributed it to the RPF, denouncing the idea of an international tribunal to investigate crimes against humanity and defending the FAR.

Although written about the Protestant Churches, the Revd Jorg Zimmerman's words could apply to all the Christian denominations: 'What I witnessed was a sort of collective psychological repression phenomenon. Rwanda has to be re-evangelised and quite differently if we do not want such carnages to come back regularly. But unfortunately, the minds are not ripe yet.'[69]

---

66. See Marie-France Cros, 'L'échec de l'Internationale IDC', *La Libre Belgique* (11 July 1994).
67. Revd Roger Bowen, 'The role of the Churches in Rwanda: Anglican Perspectives', mimeographed document dated 8 December 1994. Protestants make up an estimated 15% of the population in Rwanda. See Tharcisse Gatwa and André Karamaga, *Les autres Chrétiens Rwandais. La présence protestante*, Kigali: Urwego, 1990.
68. See Mark Huband, 'Church of the Holy Slaughter', *Observer* (5 June 1994).
69. Revd Jorg Zimmerman of the United Evangelical Mission, quoted in African Rights, *Rwanda: Death*, op. cit., p. 517.

The only faith which provided a bulwark against barbarity for its adherents was Islam. There are many testimonies to the protection members of the Muslim community gave each other[70] and their refusal to divide themselves ethnically. This solidarity comes from the fact that 'being Muslim' in Rwanda, where Muslims are a very small (1.2%) proportion of the population, is not simply a choice dictated by religion; it is a global identity choice.[71] Muslims are often socially marginal people and this reinforces a strong sense of community identification which supersedes ethnic tags, something the majority Christians have not been able to achieve.

Patterns of killing. The overriding feature in the mechanics of the genocide was geographical. The dense population, the garden-like aspect of the Rwandese landscape, the virtual absence of wild country – these left few possibilities of escape for those being hunted. Since people were being attacked even by their neighbours, they tried to run and hide anywhere. Inside town houses, a favourite hiding-place was the false ceiling typical of European-type tropical housing, which leaves just enough room to crawl between ceiling and roof. Some people survived in these confined spaces for days or even weeks, depending on the kindness of strangers for providing food and removing excrement. Others tried to hide in banana groves, in abandoned car wrecks, in pit latrines, in swamps, in cupboards, almost anywhere that might not be noticed. Many were betrayed by their neighbours while neighbours protected and hid many others – it is impossible to say which attitude was the more prevalent.

There were several places where people regrouped in the hope of benefiting from collective protection. These were mainly churches. Apart from the three big ones in Kigali itself (Sainte-Famille, Saint-Paul and Saint-André) the other churches in the countryside, with the exception of the Great Seminary at

---

70. Such as the one given in African Rights, *Rwanda: Death*, op. cit., p. 419.
71. See on this José Hanim Kagabo, *L'Islam et les 'Swahili' au Rwanda*, Paris: EHESS, 1988, chapter 3.

Kabgayi, were very poor hiding places. In many places such as Nyamata or Shangi, the local church proved to be a death-trap for those who were going to be victims. Even if the priests pleaded for the life or their charges (for which in some cases they were killed), the *Interahamwe* tried to kill the mass of refugees. When their sheer numbers proved to be too much for them to handle (there could be up to 4,000 people huddled together in some of the larger churches) they went to call on the Army which fired mortar shells through the roof or threw hand-grenades through the windows in order to flush the people out. Sometimes the killing had to be spread over several days because the militiamen could only finish off a few hundred a day with the primitive means at their disposal.

In Kigali, several thousands of refugees managed to get inside Amahoro stadium where they survived because the UNAMIR troops firmly forbade the *Interahamwe* to get in. Still trying to get a few of the civilians inside, the FAR bombarded the stadium with artillery shells and scored a few murderously successful hits. The people who had taken refuge in hospitals or been carried there because they were wounded, fared even worse. In the words of an employee of Médecins Sans Frontières:

> Any wounded person (supposed to be Tutsi, since he had been wounded) was killed. Right in front of our eyes, the army men would come inside the hospital, take the wounded, line them up and machine-gun them down. . . . It was also the first time in any of our operations that we saw our local personnel being killed on a massive scale. All our Tutsi medical staff, doctors and nurses, were kidnapped and murdered in Kigali in April. Over two hundred people. We had never seen anything like it[72].

Schools could not be places of refuge either and Hutu teachers commonly denounced their Tutsi pupils to the militia or even directly killed them themselves. As one of them told a French

---

72. MSF employee in *Télérama* (27 July 1994). Quoted in François-Xavier Verschave, *Complicité de génocide? La politique de la France au Rwanda*, Paris: La Découverte, 1994, p. 103.

journalist: 'A lot of people got killed here. I myself killed some of the children. [. . .] We had eighty kids in the first year. There are twenty-five left. All the others, we killed them or they have run away.'[73] The relations of targeted people were often killed too, simply because of the family connection. So a relation's house was a trap rather than a place of safety and the presence of somebody who was being hunted would endanger any relation who might otherwise have been spared.

The horrors. For most people living in OECD countries and too young to have lived through the Second World War, the verb 'to kill' remains an abstraction. Some Third World readers will be painfully familiar with the material presented here. But for anyone wishing to understand the depths of the Rwandese genocide, some elements of raw experience have to be provided.

First of all, there was the matter of quantity – the many thousands of bodies appearing in a very short time. In Kigali, even in the midst of the fighting, teams had to be organised to pick them up for fear of infection. Given the magnitude of the task, they had to resort to using garbage trucks[74] and by mid-May some 60,000 bodies had been picked up and summarily buried. In the hills, the bodies of the victims often remained where they had fallen after finding a temporary refuge, and were often piled to a height of four or five feet, rotting for weeks and months since there was nobody to bury them[75]. Some rivers, such as the Kagera, were filled with bodies and this in the end seriously polluted Lake Victoria where 40,000 bodies were eventually picked up and buried on the Ugandan shore.

The killings were not in any way clean or surgical. The use of machetes often resulted in a long and painful agony and many

---

73. Patrick de Saint-Exupéry, 'Rwanda: les assassins racontent leurs massacres', op. cit.
74. Médecins Sans Frontières, *Bulletin* (April 1994).
75. Jean-Paul Mari, 'Rwanda. Voyage au bout de l'horreur', *Le Nouvel Observateur* (19–25 May 1994). The smell of the rotting bodies filled the air and it took a visitor several days to get rid of the feeling (at least psychologically) that it was sticking to his skin.

people, when they had some money, paid their killers to be finished off quickly with a bullet rather than being slowly hacked to death with a *panga*[76]. Sexual abuse of women was common and they were often brutally killed after being raped[77]. If some children joining the *Interahamwe* became killers, others were victims, and babies were often smashed against a rock or thrown alive into pit latrines[78]. Mutilations were common, with breasts and penises often being chopped off[79]. In some cases, they became part of macabre rituals which would have puzzled a psychiatrist: 'Brutality here does not end with murder. At massacre sites, corpses, many of them those of children, have been methodically dismembered and the body parts stacked neatly in separate piles.'[80]

Survivors emerging from piles of bodies were often tracked down, such as those from the massacre of 800 people at the headquarters of the Kibungo diocese who were sought out from among the corpses by the militiamen and systematically clubbed to death[81]. Sadism linked with racism could reach unbelievable extremes. On the campus of Butare University, a Hutu teacher whose Tutsi wife was in an advanced state of pregnancy saw her disembowelled under his eyes and had the foetus of his unborn child pushed in the face while the killers shouted 'Here! Eat your bastard!'[82] In some cases, militiamen tried to force women to kill their children in order to save their own lives[83]. Some people were burnt alive as their relations were forced to watch before being killed themselves. In other cases the *Interahamwe*

76. United Nations, Commission des Droits de l'Homme, *Rapport sur la situation des Droits de l'Homme au Rwanda soumis par Mr Degni-Ségui, Rapporteur Spécial de la Commission* (28 June 1994), p. 9.
77. Jean-Philippe Ceppi, 'Témoignages de rescapés du Rwanda', *Libération* (9 May 1994).
78. African Rights, *Rwanda: Death*, op. cit., pp. 342–44.
79. Stephen Smith, 'Kigali livré à la fureur des tueurs Hutu', *Libération* (11 April 1994).
80. 'Rwanda: no end in sight', *The Economist* (23 April 1994).
81. Véronique Kiesel, 'Massacres au Rwanda. Le fond de l'horreur', *Le Soir* (6 May 1994).
82. Private communication to the author.
83. African Rights, *Rwanda: Death*, op. cit., p. 337.

told families that if they would kill a certain relation the rest of the family would be spared[84].

This catalogue of horrors should definitely not be seen as an attempt at sensationalism. But the gruesome physical and psychological reality of the genocide has to be present to the mind when the political situation is being assessed. Whether one considers the possibilities of a coalition government in post-genocide Rwanda or the depth of foreign responsibilities, one should never forget how great were the horror's which the survivors experienced. Even close foreign observers (including this author) cannot avoid a feeling of shock in spite of their attempts at scientific detachment. This is why – and here again the comparison with the genocide of the Jews is rather strong – it will be difficult to treat the Rwandese case as just another piece of *realpolitisch* business as usual.

Complexities of the situation. The genocide phenomenon placed people in incredibly complex moral and social situations. While some could be denounced and sent to their death by neighbours whom they had known all their lives, others could – incredibly – be saved by a kind-hearted *Interahamwe!*[85] Some people were denounced by their colleagues who wanted their jobs or killed by people who wanted their property, while others were saved by unknown Hutu disgusted by the violence. The situation was particularly difficult for mixed couples. Thus a Hutu husband had to give all his money to be allowed not to kill his Tutsi wife and her relations when they were stopped at a militia roadblock[86]. A Tutsi wife who had managed to run away with her Hutu husband asked him to kill her after they had been hunted in the hills for several weeks. They both knelt

84. Ibid., pp. 341–7.
85. Ibid., pp. 321–2. There was the odd case of the local *Interahawame* leader Yosia Pimapima on Nyabitaru hill near Kigali, who managed to save almost all the people on his hill by telling the authorities that 'there was no need to send any men, I have already killed all the enemies'. He narrowly escaped arrest after the RPF victory. (Interview with Justice Minister Alphonse-Marie Nkubito, Kigali, 16 January 1995.)
86. African Rights, *Rwanda: Death*, op. cit., p. 576.

to pray for God's forgiveness, And then he killed her as she had asked. The man later confessed his 'crime' to a priest and asked him if God would forgive him[87].

Some of the so-called 'Hutsi' (those of mixed parentage) were saved by their Hutu relations while Tutsi members of their family were slaughtered[88]. Some people's attitudes were so complex that it was difficult to say whether they were heroes or villains. This was most remarkable in the case of Father Wenceslas Munyashyaka, the curate of Sainte-Famille church, who sheltered 8,000 refugees but who also agreed to let the militia come and pick off those they wanted. On the one hand he shepherded thousands of people to relative safety but on the other hand he freely agreed to select victims from his flock from the lists brought to him. Towards the end, he also tried to prevent people from finding refuge in the RPF zone, especially the Hutu whom he felt were 'betraying him' by 'going over to the *Inyenzi*'[89].

There were even many killings which appeared absurd. Thus a man who was an MRND(D) member and a Habyarimana sympathiser saw twenty-two members of his family wiped out by the *Interahamwe*. The reasons for the treatment were tenuous: he had been an opponent when he was a student, one of his brothers, a cashiered army officer, had approached the RPF (although he had finally decided not to join), and several of the men in the family had married Tutsi wives. But the operation was intended to be a final solution, and all possible human ambiguities had to be 'cleansed out'[90].

In another case, a medical doctor of mixed parentage, married to a Tutsi woman and who had already seen seven (Tutsi) members of his family slaughtered, was saved *six times in a row*

---

87. Private communication to the author.
88. African Rights, *Rwanda: Death*, op. cit., p. 463.
89. Ibid., pp. 381–5, and private communications to the author.
90. Interview with Innocent Butare, Nairobi, 3 January 1995. Mr Butare survived only because he was on a business trip to Kenya at the time of the slaughter. He stayed in Kenya for fear of returning to Rwanda, where his MRND(D) past might have caused him problems with the new government.

from execution because of his medical profession. Eventually saved in August by the French *Opération Turquoise*, he was evacuated to Kenya only to learn there that eighteen (Hutu) members of his family had been killed by the RPF during its advance in Kibungo[91]. Life and death reached proportions of almost cosmic absurdity.

Unknown heroes. It was also a time of undisputed heroism by people who expected no reward but the satisfaction of a clear conscience. Many of these unsung heroes were Christians who believed deeply in their religion and whose charity and courage made up for the compromises of their church hierarchies. Thus the last message of a lay church worker:

> As for me, my nose protects me[92] even if my speech condemns me. I keep preaching against the violence. . . . Before mass I give a thirty minute sermon always centred around Matthew 5, 38–48. The *Inkontanyi* praised me on their radio so that my ethnic brothers who already did not like me very much because of my anti-war opinions now have reason to hate me even more. . . . In any case, I doubt if I will come out of this alive since both sides have reasons for killing me. That is without counting the bandits who are now all over the hills. As for me, I walk in those hills to try to alleviate this misery with the limited means of *Caritas*. . . . I use all my energy for life and against death, for the Prince of Life against the princes of this world[93].

Others were motivated not by faith but simply by a solidly grounded sense of human decency which the organised madness around them could not destroy. Thus for weeks on end a Hutu houseboy sheltered and fed a Tutsi schoolteacher, not even his master, who had taken refuge in the false ceiling of one of the school houses. Though threatened several times by *Interahamwe* who were sure their prey was nearby, he never lost his head and

---

91. Interview with Dr Théoneste Semanyenzi, Nairobi, 2 January 1995.
92. People with thin noses were generally killed, being considered as Tutsi whether it was true or not.
93. *Dialogue*, no. 176 (June-July 1994), p. 17.

went on with business as usual as if the apocalypse was not going on around him. In the end both he and the teacher came out alive[94]. In the same simple stubborn vein is the case of a Hutu housemaid who willingly married a militiaman to save the lives of the children of the Tutsi family which had employed her and which had been massacred[95]. In such extreme cases, even the refusal to kill (with the attendant danger to one's own life) was a heroic act. Thus the testimony of a primary schoolteacher: 'These people [the killers], they are just poor Hutu peasants, completely manipulated by the regime and the army. They are innocent. When they tried to get me to kill the Tutsi children in my class, I had to run away.'[96]

Sometimes, even the simplest gesture of common decency could mean death, as with the Hutu family who could not bear the sight of the naked body of their Tutsi neighbour and went to cover it with some banana leaves, and were all killed by the *Interahamwe*[97]. Some went beyond simple courage to attain something like sainthood, like the Hutu Catholic lay worker Félicité Niyitegeka in Gisenyi who systematically helped hunted people cross the border. Her brother, an army colonel, wrote to tell her that the militia were aware of her activity, but she refused to stop. When they finally came to get her, she had thirty refugees in her house. The *Interahamwe* said that she would be spared but that her charges would have to be killed. She answered that they would all stay together, in life or in death. To make her recant, the militiamen then shot the refugees one by one before her eyes. When the slaughter was over, she asked to be killed. The militia leader then told her she would die and asked her to pray for his soul before shooting her.[98]

94. African Rights, *Rwanda: Death*, op. cit., p. 315.
95. Ibid., p. 603.
96. Jean-Philippe Ceppi, 'Nouvelles menaces d'exode après le départ de Turquoise', *Libération* (3 August 1994).
97. African Rights, *Rwanda: Death*, op. cit., p. 595.
98. Telefax no. 17 sent to the White Fathers in Brussels (9 June 1994).

How long did it last? The massacres started during the night of 6–7 April in most of the *préfectures* with the exception of Butare where things remained quiet till 20 April when the authorities were replaced by extremists. Since UNAMIR troops were completely useless because their mandate prevented them from intervening, all that could stop the killings was military occupation by the RPF. So the *préfectures* which were occupied early on, such as Byumba, the eastern part of Ruhengeri and the northern part of Kigali and Kibungo, suffered for a shorter period. In the western part of Ruhengeri *préfecture* and in Gisenyi, killings stopped by late April because almost every Tutsi in that heavily pro-government area had been killed. Massacres went on for longest in the south (Kibungo, southern Kigali, Gitarama, Butare, Gikongoro) and the south-west (Kibuye and Cyangugu). Even the arrival of the French *Opération Turquoise* in June did not, as we will see, completely stop the slaughter which went on unabated in Kibuye where they were not present and remained sporadic even in Cyangugu and Gikongoro where French troops were too scattered to cover the whole ground and could save only Tutsi who were concentrated in large refugee camps such as Nyarushishi or those they encountered on their way. But after late May, the killings had taken a more whimsical aspect. The hurricane of death had crushed 80 per cent of its victims in about six weeks between the second week of April and the third week of May. If we consider that probably around 800,000 people were slaughtered during that short period (see next section) the daily killing rate was at least five times that of the Nazi death camps.

How many were killed? It is absolutely impossible to produce now an accurate figure for those killed in the Rwandese genocide. Only an estimate is possible.

At an early stage, figures became ammunition in the complex and at times perverse game which several of the actors (the RPF, the NGOs, the UN and the interim government) played with each other and with the media. The first estimate was made by the American NGO Human Rights Watch on 24 April 1994 when it mentioned the possibility that 100,000 had been killed so far. Four days later, MSF-Belgium doubled it by saying that the figure was more likely to be 200,000. Already the question of *who* was killing these people was being discussed. By 30 April, there were already 300,000 refugees in the Benaco camp in Tanzania and they were reporting horrendous tales of mass slaughter of Hutu as the RPF advanced southwards and eastwards. These reports had to be taken with extreme caution because, as the UNHCR remarked, there were only four or five people with gunshot wounds among the 300,000 refugees and when there had been real and documented reports of RPF violence, it had always been carried out with guns[99].

On 5 May, Radio Muhabura, the RPF radio, advanced the figure of 500,000 dead, which was immediately repeated the next day by the Oxfam director David Bryer. But on 15 May, Radio Muhabura adjusted this down to 300,000 without saying why it was now lowering its estimate. However, there had been no attempt at systematic counting in any form since the beginning of the genocide, and these figures were opinions rather than facts.

One of the first bases for calculation was given by an RPF soldier at the Rusumo bridge on the Tanzanian border on 9 May when he remarked that since he and his comrades had arrived on 22 April, they had counted about one body per minute in the Akagera river floating down towards Lake Victoria and that 'it slowed down only yesterday when we could count no more than 500 bodies during the whole day'.[100] This means that in Kibungo *préfecture* a minimum of about 25,000 people had been killed during the last week of April and the first week of May. The only serious body counts were made in mid-May in Kigali where the garbage trucks picked up 60,000 bodies and in late May in Western Uganda where the authorities estimated that

---

99. *Le Monde* (4 May 1994). On the contrary, when Operation Turquoise troops entered the southern part of Rwanda, many of the Tutsi survivors they found were covered with large gashes made by *pangas*.

100. Jean Chatain, 'Rwanda. Le torrent des suppliciés', *L'Humanité* (10 May 1994).

about 40,000 corpses which had floated over from Rwanda had been buried locally. On 3 June Colonel Kanyarengwe, the RPF chairman, declared on Radio Muhabura that one million people had been killed since the beginning of the massacres. Then there was a sort of lull in the estimates till 24 August 1994 when Charles Petrie, vice-coordinator of the UN emergency unit on Rwanda, said 'I do not think the figure of one million dead is an exaggeration.'[101] It was the first time Kanyarengwe's high figure received something like an official confirmation, and the figure was later 'confirmed' again by Philippe Gaillard who had been the ICRC representative in Kigali during the genocide. These various 'confirmations' were not based on any new assessment or counting. Then a UN report which was made public in New York on 2 October said that there had been 'between 500,000 and one million dead'. The gap between the two figures mentioned was of course enormous but it merely reflected the prudence of the international bureaucrats who realised that nobody had any idea of the true facts. Then in late November a new UN report[102] prudently scaled the genocide figure back to 500,000, which then seemed to become a sort of accepted wisdom.

In fact, the only way to try to assess the losses due to the 1994 genocide is to start from the August 1991 Rwandese census[103]. This document has a good claim to reliability because, unlike most African countries, Rwanda is small, densely populated and with a good communication network, and had at the time an efficient civil service. In addition, as we will see, there is no incentive to fiddle with the results except on the exact Tutsi/Hutu ratio[104]. The total population of Rwanda in August 1991

101. *Le Monde* (26 August 1994).
102. United Nations Commission of Experts Established Pursuant to Security Council Resolution 935 (1994) on Rwanda, *Final Report*, Geneva (25 November 1994).
103. République Rwandaise, Ministère du Plan, Service National du Recensement, *Recensement Général de la Population et de l'Habitat au 15 Août 1991*, Kigali (December 1991).
104. The alarming growth of the Rwandese population had been well documented since the 1940s, and the Kigali government never tried to tamper with population figures either upwards or downwards in previous years.

was counted at 7,148,496 say 7,150,000 for the sake of easier computing. Taking into account a growth-rate of 3.2 % (one of the highest in the world) we arrive at the following:

1992	7,378,000
1993	7,614,000
1994 (April)	7,776,000

Next comes the question of the proportion of Tutsi in the population. The government said 9%, or approximately 700,000, in April 1994. But this can safely be reckoned a low figure, first because the government systematically tried to underestimate the Tutsi population in order to ke p its school and employment quotas low, and secondly because the Tutsi themselves often tried to pass themselves off as Hutu, going as far as acquiring ID cards mentioning the wrong ethnic grouping to avoid discrimination. So a reasonable and even conservative estimate would make the Tutsi population no less than one-third higher, i.e. about 12%, which would give about 930,000 Tutsi living in Rwanda on 6 April 1994.

On the other hand we do have more accurate estimates of the Tutsi population surviving in late July 1994 through counting in the refugee camps. The following estimate has been computed by an international civil servant who visited the camps and organised population estimates for food distribution purposes[105]:

INSIDE RWANDA

	Nyarushishi	10,000
	Kigali	20,000
	Byumba	15,000
	East	10,000
	Rilima	20,000
	Sub-total	75,000
IN BURUNDI		
		30,000
	Total	105,000

---

105. This informant wishes to remain anonymous. While such estimates in 'normal' refugee camps are often grossly overestimated for purposes of 'milking the

To this figure one should add an estimated 25,000 Tutsi who survived inside Rwanda by hiding on hilltops, in forested areas and in private houses, and who did not go to the camps. So a grand total of 130,000 Tutsi survivors would seem like a fair estimate. This gives a casualty figure of around 800,000 Tutsi killed in three months, to which an unknown number of opposition Hutu (between 10 and 30,000) must be added. Thus the approximate number of deaths in the genocide could be placed at between 800,000 and 850,000, a loss of about 11% of the population – probably one of the highest casualty rates of any population in history from non-natural causes. This figure should be taken not as a factual body-count but as the least bad possible in late 1994.

The refugees. At this juncture of the conflict, the number of refugees was large (about 300,000) but not yet colossal. They had mostly fled to Tanzania with a small number going to Burundi. With the exception of these, who were both Tutsi and Hutu, the vast majority who had fled to Tanzania from Kibungo *préfecture* (300,000) were Hutu, and they were not fleeing massacres, as their leaders tried to pretend, but on the contrary they were the people who had just killed between 25,000 and 50,000 Tutsi in eastern Rwanda and were fleeing to escape what they felt would be the vengeance of the advancing RPF forces. Nevertheless some UNHCR workers rather blindly accepted their tales of RPF violence. Even after the UNHCR coordinator Panos Moumtzis had said to journalists on 3 May that given the extremely few wounded people among the refugees it was highly unlikely that anybody had attacked them as a group[106], a field officer could write on 21 May: 'The refugees seem in relatively good condition. Only a few wounded persons cross. It seems as if the RPF is doing a clean job. Those who are attacked

humanitarian cow', the state of physical and psychological exhaustion of the surviving Tutsi in those camps, as well as the absence of any political organisation motivating them, points to a fair assessment of numbers. Nevertheless, a slight downward estimate has been applied to all figures.

106. African Rights, *Rwanda: Death*, op. cit., p. 646.

die.'[107] Some more scrupulous (or less prejudiced) field workers had their doubts:

> Although we cannot discount the eyewitness reports of Tanzanians and refugees in the [reported RPF killing] incidents . . . many questions have arisen: (1) the quality of translators when talking to refugees and Tanzanian villagers, (2) the fact that there have been to date no eyewitness accounts of RPF killings by UNHCR or NGO staff , (3) the 'fear factor' in reporting events in the presence of other refugees, (4) the possibility that some (though not all) of the refugees are in fact guilty of committing atrocities inside Rwanda.[108]

This marked the beginning of a very difficult situation for humanitarian personnel working in the refugee camps. Apart from those whose loyalties were with the former Rwandese government because they had worked in close contact with it in better days, the majority of the personnel realised that the people they were trying to care for were those who had committed the reported horrors. This had nothing to do with the fact that the RPF did indeed commit a number of war crimes on its way east (shooting prisoners suspected of being *Interahamwe*, killing civilians around battle sites etc).

It had in fact started killing on a small scale around Byumba as soon as the conflict had restarted, according to a pattern which was to become painfully familiar after its victory: soldiers' indiscipline[109], revenge killings based on denunciations, witch-hunts of real or imaginary *Interahamwe*[110]. In some areas where militiamen managed to use the civilian population as a shield, RPF reaction could be murderously brutal[111].

---

107. UNHCR field officer J.F. Jensen, Kagera region situation report (21 May 1994).
108. Refugee International field officer Mark Prutsalis, situation report no. 12, Kagera region (20 May 1994).
109. The previously well-disciplined Front was beginning to show the effects of vast and indiscriminate recruitment during the previous eighteen months.
110. For several examples see the report by Human Rights activist Monique Mujawamaliya, *Rapport de visite effectuée au Rwanda du 1er au 22 Septembre 1994*, Montreal (mimeo), 1994.
111. Such as the massacre on 15 April on Kanazi Hill (Sake *commune*) in Kibungo Prefecture. (Interview with a survivor, Nairobi, 1 February 1995.)

These crimes deserved to be condemned and their perpetrators put on trial – something which at the time of writing is unlikely, and which will pose serious problems for any future international tribunal. But they were in a way the unavoidable dirty by-product of civil war, and on the government side the FAR had done and was still doing exactly the same thing in the context of the fighting. But such killings represented 1–2% of the casualties in Rwanda – which is, as we see below, one reason why linking the end of the massacres with a cease-fire was absurd. A real cease-fire, if it had happened, would have led to more and not fewer deaths, since in government-controlled areas the *Interahamwe* would have had their hands free to finish their grisly task without any interference from the RPF.

The refugees moved to the camps in perfect order, with their *bourgmestres* and communal counsellors at their head. Inside the camps they remained grouped according to their *communes* of origin and under the control of the very political structure which had just been responsible for the genocide. Thus a Protestant missionary who visited Benako could write:

> At the time of my visit, the well-known human rights violator Gatete was in Benako and his militias were laying down the law. Every night people were assassinated, mainly Tutsi. In this huge camp, old scores could be settled easily and anonymously. . . . Benako was no more Tanzania, it was part of MRND's Rwanda.[112]

Knowing that they were dealing with murderers or their passive accomplices was not an easy psychological position for refugee camp personnel to be in, which could even have been a reason why some of them tried at first to attribute a form of symmetrical genocide to the RPF. This may seem a minor point, but it is essential because of a number of facts which later become apparent. First, the refugee camps which developed into enormous institutions at later stages of the conflict all became festering political sores where murder was commonplace and where intact militia structures served to keep the civilian population under the control of the former government. Secondly, the

112. African Rights, *Rwanda: Death*, op. cit., p. 646.

(very real) sufferings of the refugee population were equated with the genocide and ended up blurring the issues. The order of magnitude of the casualties (i.e. ten times more in the genocide than in the refugee exodus) was lost sight of. And lastly, a number of friends of the former authorities (the French government, some Christian NGOs, a number of foreign intellectuals) and up to a point the UN started to put about the notion of the 'double genocide' which we discuss further in Chapter 9.

The war

The RPF had re-started their military operations on 8 April, almost forty-eight hours after the death of President Habyarimana and the beginning of the genocide. The creation of interim government, which was announced on Radio Rwanda on 9 April, drew an immediate reply from Major Kagame who denounced Colonel Bagosora as the real master of the country and promised to fight on[113]. RPF troops reached Kigali on the 11th at 4.00 p.m. and a battle which was to last for almost three months started for the control of the capital. On the next day, the 12th, the interim government fled to Gitarama, leaving General Augustin Bizimungu as the only real power in the city. While the Front remained stationary in and around Kigali, the RPF took over Byumba with hardly any fighting and pushed on westwards towards Ruhengeri. It also moved east into the northern part of Kibungo *préfecture*, reaching the Tanzanian border on 22 April. From there it started to move to the southern part of the *préfecture* in a slow but regular advance. All these operations were realised with a minimum of fighting. There were very few government troops facing the guerrillas and they tended not to put up much of a fight. The only two points where FAR resistance was strong were the cities of Kigali and Ruhengeri which soon polarised most of the FPR efforts. While the Front slowly infiltrated small groups of

113. SWB/Radio Uganda, 9 April 1994 at 10.00 a.m.

lightly-armed combatants into the south-east, it concentrated its artillery and all its heavy equipment to fight the battle for the capital.

As we see in the next section, many foreign observers tended to confuse the war and the genocide, even making out that the first had caused the second. Thus the United Nations kept insisting that the belligerents must reach a cease-fire 'to stop the massacres'. Some observers tried to point out that these were two completely different issues [114] but they had great difficulty making themselves heard. On 12 May, the UN was still mechanically asking for a cease-fire and the former French Secretary of State for Humanitarian Affairs Bernard Kouchner could declare with a complete lack of understanding of the situation: 'Peace and a cease-fire are the most urgent needs.' [115]

But the RPF was steadily pushing its military advantage. On 5 May, intense shelling had forced the closing down of the airport and on the 16th RPF troops managed to cut the Kigali-Gitarama road, thus making contacts between General Bizimungu and the interim government more difficult. On 22 May, RPF forces took the airport and the Kanombe military camp in a single move. This victory considerably decreased the intensity of the fighting in the capital where almost random artillery fire had caused many casualties. A week later, the most moderate of the FAR superior officers, Colonel Marcel Gatsinzi, was brought back from semi-disgrace in the south to negotiate with the most diplomatically-inclined of the RPF military leaders, the chief-of-staff Colonel Frank Mugambage. Their discussions were aimed at letting some 240 civilians and prisoners be exchanged between the two sides [116]. But Mugambage also secretly hoped that a segment of the army could be persuaded to dissociate itself from

---

114. Holly Burkhalter (director of Human Rights Watch), 'Make the Rwandan killers' bosses halt this genocide', *International Herald Tribune* (2 May 1994).
115. *Le Monde* (20 May 1994).
116. On the 28th the UN had already managed to evacuate a batch of refugees from the Mille Collines hotel in the centre of Kigali. The hotel's owner, the Belgian airline SABENA, did not forget to ask all its 'guests' to sign IOUs for their hotel bills.

the extremists. This hope did not materialise and on 30 May, the RPF took Kabgayi.

As it spread over more and more territory, the RPF pressed on with recruitment. In its early years it had lived well with the steady influx of volunteers from the diaspora. By the time the country exploded on 6 April 1994, the Front probably could count on 20,000–25,000 men. But that was definitely not enough for the task it now had in hand. More than 15,000 were engaged in the battle of Kigali, at least 5,000 were used to occupy the east and two-thirds of the country still remained to be conquered. So the Front began to recruit massively and much less selectively than before, something which led directly to its later misfortunes. The young men being newly recruited were either Tutsi survivors of the genocide, with a bitter desire for revenge, or else Tutsi exiles from Burundi who now began to feel that the RPF was going to win, and that if they and their families wanted to be well-placed in the subsequent sharing of the spoils, they should hurry while there was still time. Several thousands were taken in and put under training in the last weeks of May. The presence of these new men fundamentally altered the internal balance of power within the RPF. It remained of course dominated by the initial 'Ugandan' nucleus, men such as General Paul Kagame, Frank Mugambage or Patrick Mazimpaka. But more shadowy figures began to appear in the background who felt that just as the initial nucleus had based its authority within the Front on the former NRA soldiers, they could do the same thing with the new boys now coming in. One of the first effects of is new trend seems to have been the murder (3 June 1994) of Mgrs Vincent Nsengiyumva, Thaddée Nsengiyumva and Joseph Ruzindana, together with ten other priests, at the historic Catholic centre of Kabgayi recently occupied by the guerrillas. The official explanation, quickly given by the Front, was that the clerics had been murdered by young Tutsi soldiers recently recruited into the RPF forces, who had lost all their family and wanted to take revenge on the bishops and their entourage. So the 'hurried recruitment' was put to good political use, but it did not work well. There had been more than 25,000 refugees around Kabgayi. Through patient negotiations the clergy had managed to sacrifice only about 1,500, an excellent survival rate (93%) compared with most displaced persons' concentrations where the *Interahamwe* usually ended up killing most of the people. In fact, the bishops felt so little guilt about their activities in Kabgayi that, although they were Hutu and had seen several of their colleagues hurriedly retreating with the FAR as they lost ground, they decided to stay put and wait for the RPF. So the young men who were supposed to have killed them out of revenge must have been poorly informed.[117]

For people impolite enough to question the official RPF line, a second version was whispered[118], namely that the target had been Mgr Vincent Nsengiyumva, who was hated for his cosy relationship with the Habyarimana regime, his membership of the MRND central committee till December 1989, his hostility to the Tutsi and his many successful business deals. He was to die but the killer or killers were clumsy and wiped out all the people in the room. It seems however, that a third version[119] may have been the true one. The RPF had just taken over Kabgayi a few days before and, according to this version, the three bishops during that short time had broached with the Front the possibility of launching a mediation by the church to stop both the war and the massacres. They were in a good position to do so. Mgr Vincent Nsengiyumva, who had been a crony of Habyarimana, had changed tack, partly from genuine

117. They were also very hard to find. The killers were said to have been one, two or three according to the different versions of the event. One was shot on the spot by the Bishops' bodyguards (although they 'had not been able to prevent the massacre' – they cannot have been very efficient bodyguards since machine-gunning fifteen people takes some time) and the others, if they ever existed, vanished into thin air, in spite of the Front saying that they were 'actively sought after and would be tried'. Nothing more was heard of it.

118. In that case by a Tutsi civilian close to the Front (Paris, late June 1994).

119. It was also whispered, by another Tutsi civilian, also close to the Front but deeply disturbed by what he had to report (Paris, late June 1994). The only printed hint of that version, to the author's knowledge, can be found in the late June 1994 *Africa Confidential*, in a brief piece called 'Rwanda: Killings in the Church'.

horror at what was going on and partly too so as to be in
the good graces of those he now saw as the probable victors.
As for Mgr Thaddée Nsengiyumva, his liberal positions were
well known, his December 1991 manifesto had made a great
political impact, and he had been one of the main forces pushing
the Church to distance itself from the regime. Nevertheless,
during 1993–4 he had shown a certain willingness to accommodate the hardliners. So the two namesakes had all the political
qualities required for such an attempt. But according to that
version, this is exactly what some circles in the RPF who were
bent on total military victory did not want. They felt that the
whole operation was an attempt to cheat them of their hard-won
successes and salvage what could still be salvaged of the old
regime. They feared that such a church initiative would immediately benefit from the general support of the UN and the
international community and escape completely from RPF
hands. Thus in that perspective the elimination of the bishops
would have been a cold-blooded political murder. It is extremely
doubtful, if this is true (and the circumstantial evidence in favour
is strong, including the ambiguous behaviour of the RPF guards
during the last moments before the shooting[120]), that the
orders to kill the clerics would have come from the old nucleus
of the 'Ugandan' RPF. The present author's interpretation is
(if the truth were finally found to be on that side) that these
still unexplained murders were among the first signs of a shift
in the political centre of gravity within the Front. The Tutsi
supremacists, who had never been very numerous or popular
within its ranks, seem to have felt strong enough to act on their
own on a major issue, due to the change in the internal climate
brought by the recuitment of new raw radical elements.

120. Interview with a Catholic priest who was in Kabgayi at the time, London,
14 December 1994. Former pro-government Catholic circles lost no time in
exploiting the killings politically, relating them in a rather artificial fashion to
the murder of Father Joaquim Vallmajo, a priest killed by the RPF at Kageyo,
near Byumba, on 25 April 1994, after a non-political quarrel. See telefaxes nos 17
(9 June 1994) and 19 (24 June 1994) sent from Rwanda to the Brussels office
of the White Fathers.

On 6 June the FAR tried to launch a small counter-offensive south of Kigali and around Gitarama as it felt an increase of RPF pressure on the 'capital' of the interim government. But the counter-offensive quickly ground to a halt and Gitarama was occupied on the 13th, causing the interim government to flee to Gisenyi. The end appeared to be in sight for the remnants of the old regime. So when two days later the French government announced that it would start a 'humanitarian operation' in Rwanda, the RPF screamed that Paris was simply coming to help its old allies and deprive it of its victory on the battlefield:

> After hundreds of thousands of innocent lives have been lost, the French government which is responsible for this loss of life now claims that it will send troops to stop the killings. The intention is clear: the French troops will come to protect the murderers.[121]

Since on the same day interim government President Théodore Sindikubwabo, who was in Kinshasa, gave his full support to the French operation and since President Eyadema of Togo, one of France's staunchest allies in Africa, also expressed his approval of the proposed intervention[122], RPF fears did not seem to be unfounded. Another chapter of the crisis was about to start.

From the outside looking in

What then had been the attitude of the outside world towards the horror unfolding in Rwanda since 6 April 1994? If one believes Cornelio Sommaruga, president of the International Committee of the Red Cross, it had been one of desertion: The international community has disappeared from the country with the exception of a very small UN contingent, of Médecins Sans Frontières and of ourselves. [. . .] Never in its history has the ICRC seen such a unleashing of hatred resulting in the extermination of a large part of the civilian population. . . . We feel very lonely.[123]

The press was at first stunned into incomprehension, but then

121. SWB/Radio Muhabura, 16 June 1994.
122. SWB/PANA-Dakar, 18 June 1994.
123. *Libération* (5 May 1994).

after a fortnight articles began to pour out, documenting the magnitude of the disaster[124]. But TV coverage of the genocide was not available, given the near technical impossiblity of catching killers in the act. This was later to prove an important factor since in contemporary Western society events not seen on a TV screen do not exist. And since the refugee exodus to Zaïre and a cholera epidemic later in July and August *were* covered by TV, the relative perception of the two events shifted in the international consciousness – a point to which we return later.

More important than the press attitude (but largely conditioned by it) international opinion reacted very differently according to the country concerned. Among the countries with strong links to Rwanda, Belgium hardly reacted at all since it seemed that the government and the public had both been paralysed by the torture and death of their ten Blue Helmets in early April. After the repatriation of the Belgian forces, the chief of staff had gone to see Foreign Minister Dehaene and told him point blank that the army would never again take part in any peace-keeping operations under a UN command. They might do so but only with their own orders and officers[125].

The United States, still smarting from the fiasco of its disastrous operation in Somalia during the summer of 1993, wanted above all to avoid any possible entanglement in Rwanda. Thus, after a long period of embarrassed silence, the State Department, through its spokeswoman, Christine Shelly, declared on 10 June: 'Although there have been acts of genocide in Rwanda, *all* the murders cannot be put into that category.'[126] The obvious point of this contorted declaration was that the United States wished to avoid having to act according to the December 1948 international convention on the repression of genocides which made it mandatory for any of its signatories to

---

124. For an evalutation of French press coverage on Rwanda during the crisis, see François-Xavier Verschave, op. cit., pp. 140–1. For the same evaluation concerning the English-speaking press, see African Rights, *Rwanda: Death*, op. cit., pp. 198–9.

125. Interview with a Belgian civil servant, Brussels, 2 June 1994.

126. *International Herald Tribune* (13 June 1994).

take immediate action once a genocide had been clearly identified. If one goes by the State Department surrealistic reasoning, no intervention should have been made against the Nazi death camps since the German authorities were at the time also killing large numbers of non-Jews. In the short run, it justified not only the inaction of the United States, but even its extraordinary niggardliness when it came to help the UN in the few desultory attempts at 'peace-keeping'. Thus, when Secretary-General Boutros Ghali asked for some armoured cars to help General Dallaire in Kigali, the United States reluctantly agreed to provide them – but the APCs were not going to be given, but only rented! And they were not to be active duty vehicles but taken from among army stocks of mothballed APCs. Taking them out of storage and getting the UN Department of Legal Affairs to agree with the US State Department took three weeks.[127]

The OAU and the UN were at least somewhat more honest in calling the genocide by its proper name, although Secretary-General Boutros Ghali showed a very inaccurate grasp of the situation when he said that in Rwanda, as he saw it, Hutu were killing Tutsi and Tutsi were killing Hutu.[128] The UN had allowed 'Foreign Minister' Jerome Bicamumpaka to fly to New York and address the General Assembly, where he made a passionate and inaccurate speech about the situation in the country. But worse, on 21 April the international organisation had voted to reduce the size of the UNAMIR military mission by almost 90 per cent to 270 men. Of course one could say that it did not matter anyway, because their restricted mandate had obliged the Blue Helmets to watch helplessly as people were being slaughtered right before their eyes. Militiamen quickly understood that they had nothing to fear from these toy soldiers and that the worst atrocities could be committed in their presence with total feedom from interference. But the symbolic impact of the UN withdrawal was nevertheless disastrous. The

127. Interview with a US State Department official, Washington, DC (4 September 1994). See also *International Herald Tribune* (24 June 1994).
128. Remark made on 29 April 1994, quoted in African Rights, *Rwanda: Death*, op. cit., p. 688.

message to the killers was that the international community did not care and that they could go on with their deadly business without fear of intervention or even disapproval. The arms embargo voted at the beginning of the crisis had been the only concrete measure, and with French help it could be circumvented. As for France, despite its later self-righteousness when it launched *Opération Turquoise*, it voted with the other OECD countries for the UNAMIR troop reduction on 21 April.

The RPF raged as thousands of people were massacred in spite of UNAMIR's 'presence'. Théogène Rudasingwa asked for the resignation of the UN representative in Rwanda, Jacques-Roger Booh-Booh, on the grounds of incompetence[129] a not altogether unfounded demand, and Jacques Bihozagara, the European representative of the RPF, declared that his movement wanted no more UN troops since 'they had given the population a false feeling of security'.[130]

On 29 April, Secretary-General Boutros Ghali launched the idea of a new UN armed intervention, a proposal which received US support on 5 May. On 6 May, after much haggling, the Security Council voted Resolution 918 which provided for a 5,500-man deployment operating under Chapter 7, i.e. one notch higher in terms of potential use of force than General Dallaire's forlorn UNAMIR. But satisfied with this unusual display of energy, the main contributor and the world body itself stopped and waited. The new international force was not to be finally deployed till three months later. Vice Secretary-General Kofi Annan bitterly deplored this passivity:

> 'Nobody should feel he has a clear conscience in this business. If the pictures of tens of thousands of human bodies rotting and gnawed on by the dogs . . . do not wake us up out of our apathy, I don't know what will.'[131]

As, in a similar vein, did the Secretary-General himself:

129. *Le Soir* (30 April 1994).
130. SWB/Radio France Internationale (30 April 1994).
131. *Le Monde* (25 May 1994).

'We are all to be held accountable for this failure, all of us, the great powers, African countries, the NGOs, the international community. It is a genocide. . . . I have failed. . . . It is a scandal!'[132]

In his justified bitterness, Secretary-General Boutros Ghali was unfair to target the NGOs for, in spite of all their political limitations, their policy short-sightedness and of their organisational egotism, they alone actually did something to alleviate the sufferings of the Rwandese civilian population.

But their presence indirectly caused a problem cruelly but accurately pinpointed by Rony Brauman who, as a President of Médecins sans Frontières for eight years, knew what he was talking about:

> The humanitarian intervention, far from representing a bulwark against evil, was in fact one of its appendages. . . . The social and political role of humanitarian aid was simply to stage-manage goodwill, to organise the spectacle of compassion[133].

Too often the presence of humanitarian NGOs on the ground was an excuse for governments and the UN to keep quietly procrastinating, waiting for the genocide to be over so that they could finally intervene without any political or military risk.

Which brings us to the case of France, since that is exactly what it did. In France, as long as the press remained more or less muted in its reaction to the ongoing genocide, there were no official declarations. Two of the men most compromised in the genocide – 'Foreign Minister' Jerome Bicamumpaka and the CDR leader, Jean-Bosco Barayagwiza – had quietly come to Paris where they were received officially by President Mitterrand, Prime Minister Edouard Balladur and Foreign Minister Alain Juppé (27 April 1994). This did not raise much of a fuss since

---

132. *Le Monde* (27 May 1994).
133. Rony Brauman, *Devant le Mal. Rwanda, un génocide en direct*, Paris: Arlea, 1994. The first part of the quotation is on page 27, the second part on page 39.

at that stage the press was still very unsure of what Rwandese politics was all about[134].

In spite of some stirrings in the press about its heavy past record in Rwanda[135], the French government was trying to maintain a facade of indifference. But behind the scenes some people were acting frantically to *'save our allies'*, without much thought about violating the international arms embargo voted by the United Nations[136]. This did not prevent Admiral Lanxade, chief of staff of the French armed forces, to declare with a perfectly straight face: 'We cannot be reproached for having armed the killers. In any case, all those massacres were committed with sticks and machetes.'[137] One can reasonably doubt that the French government was in any position to ensure that the ammunition it was secretly delivering to the Rwandese interim 'government' would be used exclusively for military purposes against the RPF. But this did not matter. For some armchair geopoliticians, Rwanda had become a major world battlefield. One of the first signs of this Parisian *kriegspiel* was a one-page article in a confidential newsletter reputed to originate close to some French government circles[138]. Dramatically subtitled 'Considerable political and geostrategic interests are hidden behind the Rwandese heap of corpses', it put forward the following argument: first, the RPF leaders had been trained

134. This was in sharp contrast with the attitude of the Belgian authorities, which refused visas to the two men. The Belgian Ministry of Foreign Affairs had decided not to allow any Rwandese interim government ministers into the country as long as their 'government' did not apologise for publicly accusing Brussels of having ordered the murder of President Habyarimana.

135. See for example 'La France perd la mémoire au Rwanda', *Le Canard Enchaîné* (5 May 1994); 'Rwanda. Les amitiés coupables de la France', *Libération* (18 May 1994); and 'Les responsabilités françaises dans le drame Rwandais', *L'Humanité* (20 May 1994).

136. Such as Philippe Jehanne, a former secret service man serving in the office of Cooperation Minister Michel Roussin, who declared to this author on 19 May 1994: 'we are busy delivering ammunition to the FAR through Goma. But of course I will deny it if you quote me to the press.' The deliveries apparently continued into June, a fact later documented in a report by Human Rights Arms Watch Project, *Rwanda/Zaïre: rearming with impunity: international support for the perpetrators of the Rwanda Genocide*, New York, May 1995.

137. On Radio Monte Carlo. Reported in *L'Humanité* (29 June 1994).

138. 'Les enjeux diplomatiques de la tragédie Rwandaise', *La Lettre du Sud*, no. 27 (23 May 1994).

in the United States; secondly, the Americans were 'soft' on Uganda and did not try to push Museveni towards multipartism, contrary to their practice elsewhere in East Africa; thirdly, Washington regarded Uganda as the last bastion against the expansion of Sudanese Islamic fundamentalism towards the Great Lakes area; and finally Museveni therefore had to be supported in all his endeavours, including his 'takeover of Rwanda'. The article concluded:

> The region cannot be left in the hands of an English-speaking strongman completely aligned to American views and interests. This is why since 1990 France has supported the late President Juvénal Habyarimana in order to fight the RPF. It did not work out, so now the only choice left is to put back in the saddle the Zaïrean President Mobutu Sese Seko, the one man capable of standing up to Museveni.

Out of this mixture of outright lies, half-truths and tendentious interpretations, the last paragraph, and even more the last sentence were probably the only ones worth serious consideration since they described the situation as perceived by the French government. Already in the third week of April the Zaïrean President had succeeded in discreetly torpedoing a regional summit meeting on Rwanda due to be held in Tanzania, and received French support for his position. By early May, the switch-over was complete and the Mobutu regime, which Paris along with Brussels and Washington, had considered for the previous three years to be beyond the pale, could again not only count on French support for its policies but on the active help of Paris for any initiatives having to do with the Rwanda crisis[139].

The Sudan and its evil fundamentalists seemed to be the key to everything, either for the former leftists who were always ready to suspect the Americans of undue interference, or for the

---

139. On 9 May 1994, Bruno Delaye, special counsellor for African affairs in the President's Office, told the author: 'We won't have any of these meetings in Tanzania. The next one has to be in Kinshasa. We cannot let anglophone countries decide on the future of a francophone one. In any case, we want Mobutu back in, he cannot be dispensed with [the word used in French was *'incontournable'*] and we are going to do it through this Rwanda business.' Less than two years earlier, President Mobutu had been denied a visa to come to France on a private visit.

paladins of *la francophonie* who were shocked after the August 1993 Arusha agreement at hearing too much English spoken at diplomatic cocktail parties in Kigali[140].

Whether the French government really believed its own fabrications, and whether its fantasies were convenient decoys or deeply-held beliefs, is hard to say. But what had become clear by mid-June 1994 was that it was getting more and more difficult for the French authorities, which were under heavy pressure both to talk more about the past and to do more about the present, simply to stonewall it in the same style as they had used so far. So when in the afternoon of 15 June Foreign Minister Alain Juppé announced on Radio France Internationale that Paris was seriously considering an intervention in Rwanda, there was little surprise. Later in the evening the minister repeated his declaration on France 1 TV Channel and the next morning one could read under his signature in the daily *Libération*:

> We have a real duty to intervene in Rwanda. The time to look on at the massacre passively is over, we must take the initiative. . . . France is ready, with its main European and African partners, to prepare an intervention on the ground to put an end to the massacres and protect the populations threatened with extermination. . . . France will live up to its responsibilities[141].

These were brave words, even if their motivation was somewhat less than glorious. But whether it was for *la gloire*, for *realpolitik* or to cover their backs, the French political leaders, of both Right and Left in coordinated confusion, had decided to move back into Rwanda.

---

140. See for example François-Xavier Verschave, op. cit., Chapter 13, or in a very different vein Claude Wauthier, 'Appétits americains et compromissions françaises', *Le Monde Dplomatique* (October 1994).
141. Alain Juppé, 'Intervenir au Rwanda', *Libération* (16 June 1994).

8

'OPÉRATION TURQUOISE' AND GÖTTERDÄMMERUNG IN CENTRAL AFRICA
(14 June – 21 August 1994)

Deciding and preparing for the intervention (14–23 June)

Media pressure and lobbying by some NGOs had put the possibility of a French return to Rwanda back on the political agenda in Paris. But what finally pushed President Mitterrand into making up his mind was President Nelson Mandela's statement on 13 June about Rwanda at the Tunis meeting of the OAU: 'The Rwandese situation is a rebuke to Africa. . . . We must change all that; we must in action assert our will to do so.'[1] In Paris his declaration acted as a clarion-call. Here was another representative of the 'Anglo-Saxon world' who was openly saying that he was about to intervene in French-speaking Rwanda. This was no Museveni, but someone against whom nothing could be done: Mandela's years of political struggle and symbolic place in the continent's politics had turned the old anti-apartheid fighter into an almost Christ-like figure. The exact reasons for his apparent willingness to intervene were not even analysed – the danger was felt to be too pressing[2].

But given the divided nature of French politics in that summer of 1994, the decision was bound to be taken in a climate of

---

1. *International Herald Tribune* (14 June 1994).
2. In fact President Mandela's resolve to act in Rwanda came largely as the result of proddings by South Africa's white military establishment, which thought that intervening to stop the genocide and help the survivors would provide the army with a perfect opportunity for image-building. Later, some of the President's ANC political advisers made him see both the internal reasons for the operation and its dangers while other crises such as Angola were closer to home. (Interview with Professor Peter Vale, Bergen, 24 September 1994.)

careful mutual watchfulness[3]. The President's special counsellor
on African affairs, Bruno Delaye, was in Tunis. He was flanked
by Prime Minister Balladur's diplomatic counsellor Bernard de
Montferrand and his Africa man Philippe Baudillon. They
watched each other as keenly as they watched their African
partners[4]. Soon after their return, at the 14 June cabinet
meeting, President Mitterrand announced that France would
intervene. He also asked them to keep the decision secret for a
few days to avoid a media blitz[5]. The next afternoon, as was
mentioned in the previous chapter, Foreign Minister Alain Juppé
was on the air to talk about it and by the 16th he was writing
about it in a mass-circulation morning newspaper. Why? Well,
the idea looked good in the context of internal French politics.
Once more the Socialists would appear to have 'le monopole du
coeur' (monopoly of the heart), something which always vastly
irritated Conservative politicians, who were keen not to be seen
as cold-blooded financiers and technocrats. In other words,
Rwanda and its chopped-up babies now looked as if they could
give good political mileage in terms of public opinion ratings.

   At this juncture, the author has temporarily to leave aside his
instinctive modesty and start writing in the first person. On
17 June the Ministry of Defence asked for my inclusion in the
crisis unit which was then preparing what later came to be
known as 'Opération Turquoise'. This was an unexpected request.
My association with the Rwandese crisis had at first been only
peripheral and mostly in a scholarly context. As I explained

   3. In March 1993 the Conservative parties (the neo-Gaullist RPR and the centrist
      UDF) had won the legislative elections against the Socialists. But although
      Parliament now had a Conservative majority, President Mitterrand had to remain
      in power till the end of his constitutional term in April 1995. Thus the country
      had a dual executive, split between its Socialist President and Conservative RPR
      Prime Minister Edouard Balladur. What complicated the situation even further
      was that within the RPR both the Prime Minister and his former political
      mentor, Party Secretary-General Jacques Chirac, were potential candidates for
      the Presidency. So within the power structure most politicians had to be defined
      as being backers of either the President, or Balladur or Chirac.
   4. François Soudan, 'Rwanda. Pourquoi la France s'en mêle', Jeune Afrique
      (30 June–6 July 1994).
   5. Interview with a Ministry of Cooperation civil servant, Paris, 17 June 1994.

in the foreword, it came from a total failure of judgement on my part about the 1 October 1990 invasion of Rwanda. Later the various small civilian massacres which had punctuated the war years had led me to a certain involvement with human rights NGOs concerned about the situation. My visits to Rwanda, whether with the RPF guerrillas (1992) or on the government side (1993), had not met with much approval from the French authorities. As a member of the International Secretariat of the Socialist Party, I had a fairly easy access to various offices, which allowed me to express some strong criticisms of France's role in Rwanda. This did not make me popular with the President's office, the secret service Direction-Générale des Services Extérieurs (DGSE) or the army. So being called to serve in the Ministry of Defence crisis unit on Rwanda came as something of a surprise.

But the reason soon became apparent. The Defence Minister, François Léotard, was a Balladur man and the Prime Minister felt that the whole Rwanda operation was directed against him. Edouard Balladur is a typical financial technocrat, a pure product of the French bourgeoisie, with very little feel for the raw rough-and-tumble of African politics. He dreamed of 'multilateralising' France's relations with Africa, which in normal language means weakening them and making them less of a family melodrama. His preferred tools were the European Union and the World Bank. To him and his men in the cabinet, the Rwanda thing was both dangerous (if it failed, he was bound to be blamed) and of very little profit (if it worked, the initiators, i.e. Mitterrand and Juppé who is a Chirac man, would get the credit). So François Léotard's cabinet felt that it was advancing through a political minefield and should be very prudent. This is why including an academic heretic in the Rwandese team could be a good idea. He might draw attention to some unforeseen difficulties, which is what I immediately did. The first draft of the intervention plan in Rwanda was entirely based on the supposition that the French troops would enter the country through Gisenyi. I considered the idea very inappropriate for a number of reasons. The first one was that Gisenyi was the heart of

CDR-land, the 'blessed region' of the late President Habyarimana. French troops would be welcomed with open arms by the perpetrators of the genocide, surely an embarrassing situation. Secondly, the troops' entry point would be uncomfortably close to the fighting. The RPF was besieging Ruhengeri, only a few kilometers to the east, and we could count on our interim government 'friends' to do everything in their power to push us eastwards in the hope of engineering clashes between the French expeditionary forces and the guerrillas. And thirdly, since the official purpose of the mission was humanitarian, there was precious little to do at that level in Gisenyi and Ruhengeri *préfectures*. As a local Hutu trader was later to remark to a French journalist, 'We never had many Tutsi here and we killed them all at the beginning without much of a fuss.'[6] The French forces would find absolutely no one left alive to be paraded in front of TV cameras as a justification for the intervention.

Now another question quickly occurred to me. Was this not just a giant deceit and were not the French troops in reality being sent to bolster the interim government's failing forces, just as the RPF suspected? If this was the case, I wanted no part of it. I had agreed to join the crisis unit only because some friends at the ministry had told me that the intervention was now a foregone conclusion and that I could help to make it smoother rather than rougher. But (from my distant memories of American friends *vis-à-vis* the Vietnam conflict) I knew that social scientists tend to be fascinated by power and love to get under the bonnet to see how the engine works. They can easily get trapped in there. So I decided that the question of the troops' entry-point would be my litmus test: if the army general staff accepted a change of plan, it would justify the purpose of the operation. If it did not, there had to be a hidden agenda. With the help of a number of the Defence Ministry permanent staff who kindly lent me their expertise as well as their political

---

6. Florence Aubenas, 'De Kigali à Gisenyi. Le grand exode des Hutu', *Libération* (11 July 1994).

support[7], I fought for one of two solutions: either to fly our men to Bujumbura and enter Rwanda from the south; or else to land in Goma with the heavy transports, transfer the loads to lighter twin-engine Transall planes, fly down to Bukavu and enter through Cyangugu. The first solution had my preference: I felt that going through Burundi might have a stabilising effect on that country and that we might be able to kill two birds with one stone. But I had seriously underestimated the capacity of the RPF to use the mostly Tutsi UPRONA opposition party as a relay for its positions. There were demonstrations in Bujumbura against French intervention and FRODEBU Foreign Minister Jean-Marie Ngendahayo, whatever might have been his personal views on the matter, had to refuse Paris the right of transit for the troops[8].

The alternative plan, i.e. going through Bukavu and Cyangugu, was opposed by the military on financial grounds: unloading in Goma[9], reloading, flying down to Bukavu and unloading again would be very costly. Now the question was to find out whether this opposition was genuine or whether it hid something else. After talking with General Mercier who was in charge of the overall planning for the operation, I felt that he, at least, had no hidden agenda. But I could not be sure about some other officers who were grumbling in the aisles about 'breaking the back of the RPF'. The question was finally solved on Monday 20 June when Minister François Léotard made the decision to adopt the Cyangugu plan. I had had a lot of support on that and was thankful for it, but my impression was that the part of my argument which finally won the day was that at Nyarushishi camp near Cyangugu we could find the large stock of surviving Tutsi whom we needed for displaying to the

7. One should realise that being an outside expert carries no political weight whatever. Experts are like a bouquet of flowers, pleasant and decorative to have around, but definitely not integrated in a politician or civil servant's view of how to make decisions.
8. SWB/PANA-Dakar, 22 June 1994.
9. Large transport planes such as the Boeing 747s and Antonov 124s which the Ministry was planning to charter could only land in Goma. The landing run at Bukavu airport was too short for these giants.

TV cameras. A humanitarian intervention in a place where there was no longer anybody left to save would indeed have been embarrassing. The intervention juggernaut had now gained its full momentum. Everyone wanted to climb on board, hoping for good political dividends. President Mitterrand, whose idea it had been from the start, was irritated to see it being hijacked. On Saturday 18 June, while opening a conference at UNESCO unconnected with Rwanda, he made a speech mostly about Rwanda in order to try to regain the initiative from the Conservative Foreign Minister Alain Juppé, saying that, given the gravity of the situation, the urgency was extreme and that 'it was a matter not of days but of hours'. This was unexpected coming from a man who had seemed so unperturbed during the brutal slaughter of the last two months in Rwanda[10].

Not everyone felt the urge to go and stop a genocide which had already largely run its course when ulterior motives could be surmised. The RPF had already vociferously condemned the intervention as a French ploy to save the Sindikubwabo regime from eventual defeat. And one has to admit that all the evidence in the Front's possession pointed to just that[11]. But there were other more unexpected rebuttals. Faustin Twagiramungu, Prime Minister-designate under the Arusha agreement, also condemned the intervention from Montreal where he was on a visit[12]. Secretary-General Salim Salim, who, as a Tanzanian had to be another participant in the world-wide Anglo-Saxon plot,

10. The President was very sensitive about the press campaign then revealing the extent of French compromises in Rwanda. On the morning of his speech, special couriers delivered by hand to all newspapers a communiqué from the Elysée where one could read: 'Every time it came to know about exactions and human rights violations, France immediately intervened, making all efforts to have the perpetrators sought out and arrested.' Considering the past record of France in Rwanda during the mini-massacres since 1990, the statement can only be seen as rather naive propaganda.
11. I understood the radical lack of perception of the situation among the French General Staff when a senior officer, talking about the RPF, asked me with genuine surprise: 'But why don't they trust us?'
12. SWB/Radio France Internationale, 20 June 1994.

conveyed the condemnation of the OAU[13]. In Kigali UNAMIR General Roméo Dallaire had spoken of 'the initiative launched by the French and which they describe as a humanitarian task' with a distinct lack of enthusiasm[14]. At the same time, all sorts of bad smells kept coming out of the past. On 21 June, the morning daily *Libération*, the same paper which had published Foreign Minister Alain Juppé's call to arms five days before, came out with an article called 'Rwanda – a Death Squad Veteran accuses', in which a former Zero Network member said that he had been trained by French instructors[15]. Two days later, Amnesty International released a communiqué asking the French government to clarify its past involvement with the Rwandese death squads. A few days earlier, Colonel Dominique Bon, military attaché at the French embassy in Kinshasa, had virtually admitted that weapons were still being delivered to the FAR through Goma, a most embarrassing fact if the airport was now to be used for a humanitarian intervention[16]. In this deleterious atmosphere, the enthusiasm of Prime Minister Balladur waned even further. In a parliamentary speech on 21 June he set five conditions which should be fulfilled before the French army would actually be set in motion. It should get a UN mandate; a clear time-limit to the intervention should be set and stuck to; there should be no in-depth penetration of Rwanda, the operation being carried from just outside its borders; the operation should be purely humanitarian and have no exclusively military component; and allied troops should be involved – France was not to operate alone. The condition on no in-depth penetration

---

13. Ibid., 21 June 1994.
14. AFP News Agency, 19 June 1994. In private General Dallaire was even more severe. He knew of the French secret arms deliveries to the FAR and when he learned of the French initiative he said: 'If they land here to deliver their damn weapons to the government, I'll have their planes shot down' (interview with a UN civil servant, Geneva, 29 July 1994).
15. Stephen Smith, 'Rwanda. Un ancien des escadrons de la mort accuse', *Libération* (21 June 1994). The fact that *Libération*'s Africa specialist is of 'Anglo-Saxon' origin had already fuelled many rumours, several coming directly from the President's office, which attempted to portray him as a CIA agent.
16. *La Lettre du Continent*, 16 June 1994.

of course made no practical sense and could not be adhered to. As for the last condition, Paris went ahead without being able to fulfill it. But the three others were respected.

Of course, there was a problem which had not been much discussed: the French intended to carry out a humanitarian operation in a country at war while avoiding any armed confrontation. And it (or rather the Foreign Affairs Ministry) had had no contact whatsoever with the party most likely to shoot at them, namely the RPF. There seemed to be a mental stumbling-block in French official thinking where the RPF was concerned, caused by the dreaded Anglo-Saxon enemy's proximity. When I learned on Monday 20 June that the choice to enter Rwanda through Cyangugu had prevailed, I took it on myself to phone Jacques Bihozagara, the RPF European representative, at his Brussels office and learned from him that he had not been contacted by Paris. Through the Defence Minister's office, I put pressure on the Foreign Ministry to rectify this omission. When I called Bihozagara again to learn the result of my efforts, I thought he would choke on the phone: he had received a fax asking him to come to Paris to meet Mme Boisvineau, sub-director for Eastern Africa of the Direction des Affaires Africaines et Malgaches (DAAM) at the Quai d'Orsay. We both knew that, although she was a nice lady of genuine goodwill, her capacity for political decision-making was equal to zero. Bihozagara was angry: 'This is ridiculous. It is an insult. I have been in Europe for three years and I must have seen her six times at least. What good can I expect from seeing her once more? I won't go.' So I got back on the phone and tried again to get some kind of reasonable response from the Ministry of Foreign Affairs. By the next day, I was pleasantly surprised to learn through the press that the Foreign Minister was 'in constant touch with the RPF'. I then called Jacques Bihozagara in Brussels and found him even more exasperated than the day before. He had received a second fax asking him to go to Paris to meet the Secretary of State for Humanitarian Affairs, Lucette Michaux-Chevry, and DAAM Director Rochereau de la Sablière. Bihozagara said: 'We are not asking for any bloody humanitarian aid, this is a political problem for God's sake! And as for M. de la Sablière, he can't decide anything. Either I see the Minister or else I won't waste my time.' I relayed this answer to the Defence Minister's office where a certain modicum of irritation was evident. A Defence Ministry official said to me: 'God dammit! It is *our boys* going in there. And if they get shot up because of those idiots at Foreign Affairs, there will be hell to pay.'

I do not know what kind of message was relayed between the Boulevard Saint-Germain and the Quai d'Orsay, but the next morning on Wednesday 22 June, the RPF representatives were in Paris and were received personally by Alain Juppé. Although the Minister had nothing much to say to them, the symbolic value was great.

Managing later in the day to get the two RPF envoys inside the Defence Ministry made me think of trying to smuggle ladies of ill-repute into the Vatican. Great precautions had to be taken to prevent them meeting the 'hawks' on their way to General Mercier's office[17]. There we had to reckon with two other problems. First, the intended firepower of the French forces seemed to be too important for a humanitarian mission. And then the complete operational plan of the future *Opération Turquoise* was written on two sheets of paper. The RPF envoys were furious: how could we pretend that we were going to send 2,500 men all the way to Central Africa with masses of heavy equipment if the plans for the operation covered only two sheets of paper? Where were the hidden documents? We had to persuade them that there were none and that, yes, this was a bit flimsy, but we would soon have more detailed versions of our future arrangements. As for the firepower, General Mercier said that it was contingency planning; he had just come back from Bosnia and would hate to be caught unprepared. But if fighting was not called for, the heavy artillery, armoured vehicles and the aircraft would stay put in Zaïre. In the mean time, would

---

17. They did meet one anyway. In the tense atmosphere, the presence of a superior officer was useful in avoiding any physical confrontation.

the RPF agree to host a French liaison officer at Mulindi to coordinate things and avoid unwanted clashes?

There was a noticeable difference of attitude between Jacques Bihozagara and the 'Ugandan' Théogène Rudasingwa. Because Bihozagara who had grown up in Burundi as a refugee and spoke perfect French, was the more accommodating of the two, the worst suspicions of some of the officers were confirmed: 'That one, the one who speaks English only, he is the sneaky one, he is Museveni's man, spying on the other.' I asked Rudasingwa, who is by nature reserved, to at least smile, but met only with a half-success. But I could see that the very earnest and open presentation of our positions by General Mercier had had an impact. They had refused the idea of a liaison officer or 'spy' as they put it. But Jacques Bihozagara and his 'sneaky' colleague were not so sure any more that the French were going to enter Rwanda to fight them, even if their interviews in Paris were still full of defiance. Reading into Prime Minister Balladur's mind, if it had been possible, would have immediately reassured them. Edouard Balladur had been pushed into doing something he did not particularly want to do, and he was going to do it as quickly and cheaply as possible.

On the same day, the UN Security Council voted Resolution 929 which gave to the French an intervention mandate under Chapter 7 of the UN Charter[18]. It was now a matter of hours. On the 23rd at dawn, the first elements of Opération Turquoise were put in place in Goma.

---

18. There were five abstentions out of fifteen Council members, a reflection of the malaise surrounding the whole concept of the French intervention. The only diplomatic support Paris received was from its faithful African retainers. Some were even a bit embarrassing in their obviously interested eagerness to see the French prop up whatever was left of the old Habyarimana regime, such as President Omar Bongo of Gabon who asked (Libération, 17 June 1994) for an interposition force. Which, given the military situation on the ground, meant a way to stop the RPF progress.

From the intervention to the fall of Kigali (23 June–4 July)

The surprise of the RPF delegates in Paris when they learned about the planned amount of firepower *Turquoise* was understandable. For a maximum strength of 2,500 men, there were more than 100 armoured vehicles, a battery of heavy 120mm. Marine mortars, two light Gazelle and eight heavy Super Puma helicopters and air cover provided by four Jaguar fighter-bombers, four Mirage F1CT ground-attack planes, and four Mirage F1CRs for reconnaissance. To deploy this armada, the Ministry chartered one Airbus, one Boeing 747 and two Antonov An-124s to supplement a squadron of six French Air Force Lockheed C-130s and nine Transalls. The whole force was placed under the overall command of General Jean-Claude Lafourcade in Goma and his subordinate General Raymond Germanos operating from Bukavu/Cyangugu.

The contacts in Paris had partly mollified the RPF, and Colonel Mugambage declared that 'he was not opposed to a humanitarian mission by French troops'[19]. This in turn somewhat softened the OAU attitude which passed a resolution in support of the French effort. With somewhat exaggerated optimism Foreign Minister Alain Juppé declared: 'Our initiative is already reaping very substantial diplomatic benefits.'[20]. In fact Italy, the only European country which briefly seemed prepared to join Paris in its endeavour, backed down on its promise when the inexperienced Prime Minister Silvio Berlusconi was briefed by more realistic Foreign Ministry officials. Apart from France's Black African clients, there were some vague supportive noises including a brief offer of Tunisian troops, rumours about forty Egyptian 'observers' and the announcement of a Mauritanian medical team. Most of these offers never went beyond rhetoric, and Senegal was the only country which actually sent troops.

On the ground, the welcome given to the French troops by

19. SWB/Radio Muhabura (25 June 1994).
20. SWB/France Inter (25 June 1994).

the *Interahamwe* and the local authorities óf the former regime was enthusiastic[21]. Enormous French Tricolors were displayed everywhere, even on FAR military vehicles. They proved to be an embarrassment, not only because of the press, but because, on seeing French flags, hidden Tutsi would come out of hiding only to be immediately killed by the soldiers or the militiamen. The French troops, who had been given a properly slanted view of events beforehand, were rudely awakened when they began to realise the relationship France had entertained with the Rwandese authorities. As a French soldier protested, 'I am fed up with being cheered along by murderers'[22].

Efforts were made to justify the operation by 'saving' as many Tutsi as possible. Nyarushishi camp near Cyangugu made a good start, with 8,000 refugees. Little groups were found here and there, but not many. On the 27th French forces went up to Kibuye and east as far as Gikongoro. Two days later, the Defence Minister François Léotard and Secretary of State for Humanitarian Affairs Lucette Michaux-Chevry went to Goma to inspect the situation[23]. Probably they were not told that there had not been much efficiency in saving lives. The only people *Opération Turquoise* could really help were those who were in the least danger, i.e. in large concentrations such as Nyarushishi or Bissosero. For the many lost in the bush, nothing much could be done as the situation around Kibuye quickly showed. There the authorities were still killing at a fairly fast rate and, apart from Kibuye town itself and its immediate surroundings, the French forces were powerless to do anything.

---

21. Around Gisenyi, where the French only made a quick incursion, the RTLMC had been broadcasting messages for several days before the arrival of the French troops calling for 'you Hutu girls to wash yourselves and put on a good dress to welcome our French allies. The Tutsi girls are all dead, so you have your chance.' It could well be that there is a relationship between cold-blooded acceptance of the genocide and an abysmal self-image here so gruesomely juxtaposed. In a way the Tutsi had been paying for the years of Belgian glorification of their excellence and vilification of the lowly Hutu.

22. Patrick de Saint-Exupéry, 'Rwanda. Les assassins racontent leurs massacres', *Le Figaro* (29 June 1994).

23. SWB/RTBF-Brussels, 29 June 1994.

With insufficient numbers and transport capacities[24], they often had to stand by in medium-sized towns while the killing went on unabated in the hills a few kilometers away. The interim government authorities, with which the French were obliged to deal, constantly tried to push the French to a clash with the RPF, as when the Cyangugu *préfet* Emmanuel Bagambiki kept repeating: 'The French Army must go into the RPF area and free our civilian population taken as hostages by the rebels.'[25] In effect he was asking for the reconquest of the guerrilla-held territories by French troops. For the war continued to rage on and nobody knew exactly what would happen if there was a clash between the *Turquoise* troops and the RPF. I was particularly concerned by such a possible development because I felt that despite General Mercier's careful preparatory weeding-out, there were still extremist officers in the French force who itched for a chance to get at the RPF and help their old friends. In the absence of any agreed mechanism to defuse an eventual crisis, I kept pushing for the creation of a telephone hotline enabling the RPF general staff to get in touch quickly with the Ministry of Defence in Paris and with General Lafourcade. The idea was popular neither with the diehard supporters of Hutu power in Paris nor with some RPF elements who were persuaded that we would use the satellite telephone to eavesdrop on them electronically. I had finally to get a technician to explain to them that it was easy for us to do this from Goma anyway, without having to bother about putting a piece of equipment directly into their hands. We finally got the green light on 2 July and flew to Entebbe to enter the RPF zone and meet the RPF leadership. The telephone was a useful idea; it was also a good pretext for a political contact, something which had been sorely lacking

---

24. When they found small pockets of hunted Tutsi, the French would often tell them that because of their present lack of lorries they would 'come back the next day'. There were too many useless armoured cars and not enough trucks because the whole operation had been conceived as a fighting one, whereas *Turquoise* was mostly faced with a gigantic humanitarian problem. By the next morning the Tutsi the French had met the day before were usually dead.

25. *Libération* (25–26 June 1994).

since the beginning of the operation[26]. Our delegation met part
of the political bureau of the Front at Mulindi and we then drove
down to Kigali to find that the city had just fallen at last to
the RPF. General Kagame was quite open to the telephone idea
(we were carrying an Immarsat with us, complete with its
regulation generator), and we agreed to pursue the discussion
the next day in Mulindi. But things remained very fragile. The
next day, as we were sitting down to talk, General Kagame
received a despatch telling him of the military preparations
carried out by 'Colonel Thibaut' in Gikongoro[27]. 'Colonel
Thibaut' had stated publicly that in the event of a battle with
RPF forces, the orders would be *'pas de quartier'* (no quarter
given). General Kagame, who understands French but does not
know it well, did not know the expression. It was translated
for him by a bilingual ADC, who told him in English: 'Sir, it
means they will kill the wounded.' Kagame furrowed his brow,
turned towards us and said calmly: 'This is a hostile statement,
isn't it?'. I did not feel particularly at ease. It took a great deal
of talking to persuade the RPF leader that at times French
colonels did talk foolishly off the top their heads without
properly checking with Paris if what they were saying was in
accordance with their instructions. Understanding was eventually achieved, and Kagame promised that there would be no
attacks on French troops. To reciprocate, President Mitterrand
and Admiral Lanxade declared in Paris: 'The RPF is not our
enemy.'[28] Capturing Kigali probably helped the Front to

26. These had been more than limited. After General Kagame had refused to see them,
    former ambassador to Kigali Jean-Philippe Marlaud and former ambassador to
    Kampala Yannick Gérard had been received at Mulindi by Colonel Kanyarengwe
    on June 23rd. Marlaud was considered as a diehard Habyarimana supporter
    and Gérard was not really known to the RPF. The choice of Kanyarengwe to
    meet them was in itself a sign that the Front did not want to deal seriously with
    them.
27. See SWB/Radio France Internationale (4 July 1994) and *Le Figaro* (6 July 1994).
    The real name of 'Colonel Thibaut' was Thauzin. He was a former DGSE man,
    which could explain his preference for operating under a false name, even with
    the press. He was also a former military adviser to General Habyarimana during
    the war and was itching to 'get at' the RPF. He was later recalled.
28. *Le Figaro* (6 July 1994).

achieve this belated semi-recognition. (Beyond this point the author ceased to play any active role in the unfolding tragedy.)

The fall of the northwest and the refugee explosion (14–19 July)

Meanwhile the so-called Rwandese interim government was fast disintegrating. A group of moderate FAR officers led by General Leonidas Rutasira and Colonel Marcel Gatsinzi had organised themselves in Gikongoro, using the French umbrella and calling for national reconciliation[29]. Their initiative did not work out because the French, who did not want to get embroiled in political affairs, did not help them and because their brother-officers in the FAR hardly responded to their call at all. Thousands of civilians were streaming out of Kigali *préfecture*, moving on foot either to the northwest, which was seen as the last government bunker, or to the south where the newly created French *Zone Humanitaire Sure* (Safe Humanitarian Zone or SHZ) seemed to promise physical security away from the dreaded RPF. Many of the people now on the move were multiple displaced persons who had fled Byumba *préfecture* in 1992 and then moved on towards Kigali at the time of the February 1993 RPF offensive and were now seeking a new refuge. The RPF still inspired the same irrational fear, with its supposedly devil-like fighters and tales of massive killings everywhere; the interim government viewed the RPF more as if they were the Four Horsemen of the Apocalypse than a human enemy. Apart from the impact of the propaganda, it seems that there was also a strong element of psychological projection: 'They can only do to us what we did to their kith and kin.' The fear was far from being unfounded, as we see in the next chapter, and even some Tutsi were running away from their 'saviours'. Within a few days of the fall of Kigali, about 1.5 million refugees had moved to the Ruhengeri and Gisenyi *préfectures* and about the same number to the French SHZ. RTLMC, which had stopped broadcasting

29. SWB/France 2 TV, 9 July 1994.

from the capital on the 3rd, restarted its poisonous propaganda from Gisenyi on 10 July.

On 11 July, General Lafourcade caused embarrassment when he declared that members of the interim government would be allowed to seek asylum in the SHZ if Gisenyi fell. This of course drew return fire from the RPF, which said that it would follow them whatever the consequences[30]. There seemed to be less than perfect coordination between the Ministries of Defence and Foreign Affairs because on the 15th the latter declared that if the interim government ministers entered the SHZ, they would be interned[31].

French politicians were floundering desperately in the Rwandese mire, trying to glorify the *Turquoise* intervention in the hope of washing off any genocidal bloodspots in the baptismal waters of 'humanitarian' action[32]. With perfect composure Prime Minister Balladur declared in a speech at the United Nations in New York: 'France has sent its soldiers out of a moral duty to act without delay in order to stop the genocide and provide immediate assistance to the threatened populations.'[33] When a journalist asked him a question about persons responsible for the genocide having been allowed to stay in France, he answered with a straight face: 'We have not allowed any of these people to stay in France.'[34] As for his declaration concerning Resolution 935 (Creation of a Commission of Inquiry into the genocide), it held great promise for the future: 'France was a co-author of this resolution and will put at the disposal of the commission all the information it is able to gather.'[35] Since the Prime Minister must have been telling the truth, this will undoubtedly constitute a fascinating collection of documents for future historians.

30. *Libération*, (13 July 1994).
31. *Le Figaro* (16–17 July 1994).
32. For particularly severe indictments of this moral sleight of hand, see Stephen Smith, 'Humanitaire, trop humanitaire', *Libération* (8 July 1994), and Rony Brauman, *Devant le mal. Un génocide en direct*, Paris: Arléa, 1994.
33. AFP Press Agency dispatch, 12 July 1994.
34. *Le Monde* (13 July 1994).
35. Idem.

For his part, the President showed the same masterly freedom in dealing with unpleasant facts. In an interview on French television,[36] he claimed, first, that *Opération Turquoise* had saved 'tens of thousands of lives'[37]; that in 1990 President Habyarimana had been in the process of democratising Rwanda 'following the La Baule principles'; that France had nothing to do with the genocide since it happened after it had left; France could not intervene in Rwanda during the genocide because this was the job of the United Nations; and if the present Rwandese crisis restored the power of President Mobutu Sese Seko, this was due to 'unforeseen circumstances'.

An informed observer witnessing this display of machiavellian statesmanship would have hesitated between involuntary admiration for the President's constructive capacity for lying and disgust at the degree of contempt it implied for the citizen-spectators. Nevertheless, as we see later, those laborious displays of truth rectification slowly began to have an impact on French public opinion. People began to forget that the French SHZ covered only 20% of the country and talked as if France had secured all of it and made it safe. The mechanics of *Turquoise* on the ground were overlooked. The genocide began to recede into the misty past for millions of fast-zapping TV viewers, and with it any responsibility France might ever have had. Rumours of summary executions by the RPF began to spread, starting to give credibility to a notion we would see more fully developed later, that of the 'double genocide', the 'Hutu killing the Tutsi and the Tutsi killing the Hutu' as the UN Secretary-General Boutros Ghali put it. Rwanda was too much, and compassion fatigue was beginning to set in.

---

36. SWB/France 2 TV (14 July 1994). This was a Bastille Day interview, and thus particularly hell-bent on *la gloire*.
37. This was of course a typical example of the creative use of statistics. If we try to evaluate the impact of *Turquoise* on the humanitarian situation in south-western Rwanda and admit that the Tutsi in the Nyarushishi camp, as well as those picked up at smaller locations, would *all* have been killed (improbable but not impossible), then *Turquoise* might have saved 13,000 or 14,000 lives.

All the more so because Rwandese reality refused to let up.
On the contrary, as the RPF's pressure on Ruhengeri increased,
the hordes of refugees who had moved north from around
Kigali picked up and started to move west towards Gisenyi. The
enormous crowd of at least 300,000 people was a mixture of all
sorts and conditions: dispirited *Interahamwe* who no longer even
bothered to kill the few Tutsi walking along with them, civil
servants and their families riding in a motley of commandeered
vehicles that had belonged to their ministries, ordinary peasants
fleeing in blind terror, exhausted FAR troops trying to keep a
minimum of discipline, abandoned children with swollen feet,
middle-class Kigali businessmen in their overloaded cars, whole
orphanages, priests, nuns and madmen. Even though many were
fleeing of their own choice, the administrative authorities tried
their best to get everybody to leave before the arrival of the RPF.
In Ruhengeri, the *préfet* had warned any who thought of
staying behind that 'the majority of the population will be
massacred.'[38] In Butare, the militiamen ordered everyone to flee
and those who refused were killed on the spot.[39] Right on the
heels of those leaving, small numbers of Tutsi refugees who had
spent more than thirty years in Uganda were beginning
to filter back in, driving before them thousands of head of
cattle.[40] When on 13 July Ruhengeri fell to the RPF, the
human torrent swelled to incredible proportions. More than a
million people were now walking along a stretch of road barely
60 kilometers long. Sick or wounded people were collapsing on
the roadside and receiving no help. The Gisenyi *préfet* had sent
cars equipped with loudspeakers to stampede the crowd further
towards the Zaïre border, and FAR soldiers fired their weapons
in the air to urge the people on[41]. The rumble of RPF artillery
could be heard in the distance, and when two shells did fall into
the crowd, such was the panic that more than fifty people were

38. SEB/Radio France Internationale, 12 July 1994.
39. Monique Mujawamaliya, *Rapport*, op. cit., p. 9.
40. 16,000 Tutsi had crossed over from Uganda in the first two weeks of July
    (SWB/Radio France Internationale, 13 July 1994).
41. *Le Monde* (17–18 July 1994).

crushed to death. On 18 July, the RPF took Gisenyi. More than a million people had crossed the border into Zaïre in less than a week. The same day, a new government was formed in Kigali and General Augustin Bizimungu, the FAR chief of staff now in Goma, commented: 'The RPF will rule over a desert.'[42]

The new government and the cholera apocalypse (*19 July–1 August*)

The swearing-in of a new government in Kigali (19 July 1994) was an attempt at some sort of normalisation for the first time since 6 April. The previous three months had seen a combination of genocide and civil war which had killed more than 10 per cent of the population and forced another 30 per cent into exile. Those people still 'in Rwanda' were in a complete state of disarray. Many were displaced and living some distance from their *ingo*. A large number (especially among the Tutsi survivors) had lost all they had possessed including their houses. Many were hiding in the hills. The French SHZ had stabilised in the south-west around 1.2 million people who could start moving again at any time if they feared that their temporary situation was about to change. Psychologically most people were in various states of shock, and many women who had been raped were now pregnant with unwanted children. Most of the infrastructure had been brutally looted, with door and window frames removed, and electric switches pried from walls. Almost no vehicles were left in running order except RPF military ones, in the towns running water and electricity did not work any more and although the crops on the hills were ripe, nobody was there to pick them. The few former Tutsi refugees who were moving from Uganda into the Mutara or from Burundi into Bugesera had plenty of room to pasture their cows.

It is this scene of disaster that the new government was supposed to manage. Although its concept was partly derived from the cabinet which had been planned at Arusha (the various opposition political parties kept their Arusha portfolio

42. *Le Monde* (19 July 1994).

allocation), there were two big changes. First, the RPF had decided to give itself all the ministries that should have gone to the MRND(D); and secondly, a new post of Vice-President had been created and given to General Paul Kagame in order to place him in a position of general oversight and control of the government without making him President.

The President was Pasteur Bizimungu, the oldest and most important of the 'RPF Hutu'. In ethnic terms, the cabinet had a majority of Hutu (sixteen out of twenty-two ministerial posts, including the President and the Prime Minister). But this was important in terms more of political intentions than of real power. Most of the ministers did not even have a proper office, a secretary, stationery or a typewriter, even less a car. So whether it connived at the situation or not, the RPF remained for the time being the only source of real power in the country simply because it had vehicles, fuel, weapons and portable telephones[43].

Apart from Finance Minister Marc Rugenera (PSD) and Prime Minister Faustin Twagiramungu (MDR), none of the ministers had ever held a cabinet portfolio before. The Minister of Justice, Alphonse-Marie Nkubito, the human rights activist, was the former prosecutor-general. But most ministers' credentials lay in their strong opposition to the 'Power' fractions within their respective parties during 1993, whether it was the Parti Libéral Minister for Higher Education Joseph Nsengimana, the PDC Minister for Environment and Tourism Jean-Népomucène Nayinzira, or the MDR Minister for Primary Education Pierre-Célestin Rwigyema. There were few straight 'RPF Tutsi' in the cabinet: General Kagame as Defence Minister and Vice-President, Women's Affairs Minister Aloysia Inyumba, Transport Minister Immaculée Kayumba, Minister of Youth and Sports Patrick Mazimpaka and Rehabilitation Minister Jacques Bihozagara. The problem of course continued to lie in the relationship between the cabinet and the RPF or more specifically the Rwandese Patriotic Army (RPA), as the Front Army now became known. Conditions of almost total material dependence of one on the other were not the basis for a healthy rapport.

---

43. See Denis Hautin-Guiraut, 'Pouvoirs parallèles à Kigali', *Le Monde* (8 August 1994).

In the short run, the government could do nothing to stop two phenomenons which were to have serious consequences. One was the real 'colonisation' of some parts of the country (mainly Nyanza, Nyamata, Kibungo and of course Kigali) by an increasingly massive influx of Tutsi returnees coming partly from Uganda and much more from Burundi. They grabbed whatever dwellings were 'available' and at times evicted owners at gunpoint when the property they wanted was occupied. As a direct consequence of this state of affairs, there was of course a sharp increase in criminality which the RPA alone could not suppress since there were no civilian police to work locally and since many of the offenders were its own soldiers. The RPA now felt the full impact of its hasty recruitment in the early summer. Raw recruits with guns acted as bushwhackers in the hills, grabbing properties for their relatives coming out of Burundi. There were to be several consequences of this. On the one hand, tales of RPF violence tended to paralyse any return to normal international relations with a regime still regarded by many – not only in Paris – with some reserve, and this at a time when normalisation was vital in order to re-start the economy. These tales also gave comfort to the militia and MRND cadres in the camps in Zaïre and Tanzania, who were trying to keep the enormous mass of refugees under their control and especially to prevent them from returning home. Tales of violence coming out of Rwanda were a boon to the killer *bourgmestres*.

What is not obvious is that the RPF Tutsi leadership really minded this situation. The men who kept harping on the necessity of returning the refugees were the Hutu politicians, whether within the Front like Seth Sendashonga or Pasteur Bizimungu or outside it like Faustin Twagiramungu. For them the Hutu refugees were potential voters and they wanted them back. For the Tutsi military cadres the prospect was much less certain. They had, as Jacques Bihozagara put it in a private conversation [44], 'lost almost a million voters in the genocide' – a true if somewhat cynical assessment. So if nearly 2 million Hutu had written themselves out of the country's future political process

44. With Filip Reyntjens during the Hague conference (June 1994).

by leaving why not let them stay out ? There would be time to see later.[45]

In the short run, 'outside' was quickly turning into another version of hell. The human mass which had crashed on the shores of Lake Kivu lacked everything: food, medicines, proper latrines (it was extremely hard to dig into the volcanic lava ground), shelter and even clean water. The last item, combined with the sanitation problem, caused an enormous cholera epidemic with the first cases breaking out on 20 July. The overcrowding, the lack of even the most elementary hygiene, the impossibility to obtain clean water – every condition that favoured the epidemic spreading like wildfire was present. After a week there were 600 deaths a day and after two weeks 3,000. The French *Turquoise* rear echelon in Goma was forced to turn almost overnight into diggers of mass grave. The Defence Minister was writing proudly in an article entitled 'France must hold its head high':

> We have stopped the violence, cared for the victims and prepared the way for those who deserve the beautiful name of humanitarians.[46]

Meanwhile the popular evening paper *France-Soir* reported more humbly:

> The French military feel completely impotent in the face of these uncontrollable events. They simply stand by, looking helplessly at the nightmare.[47]

Bodies lay everywhere, All available shelter was crammed with dying people and corpses kept falling into the lake, further polluting the water. Newspapers and TV reporters jumped with relish into the midst of this massive horror and documented it

---

45. This was the impression received by former anti-MRND activist Monique Mujawamaliya when she went back to Rwanda at the end of the war (see *Rapport*, op. cit., pp. 27–8) and the US Human Rights activist and Rwanda specialist, Alison Des Forges, felt somewhat the same way. (Interview – Ashburnham Place, 14 December 1994.)
46. *Libération* (22 July 1994).
47. *France-Soir* (22 July 1994).

in detail.[48] This peculiar twist of fate which now condemned many of the late killers to an atrocious death had an important media and public opinion consequence, well analysed by the Secretary-General of Médecins Sans Frontières, Alain Destexhe:

> Yesterday the genocide of the Tutsi by the Hutu militia, today the genocide of the Hutu refugees by the cholera? This comparison, which one can see widely used in the press, puts on the same plane things which have nothing to do with each other. Through this confusion the original, singular and exemplary nature of the genocide is denied and the guilt of the perpetrators becomes diluted in the general misery.[49]

This is an important point. The terrible sufferings of the Hutu refugees in Goma, with their 'divine retribution' aspect, diffused the intensity of feeling linked with the previous genocide. The genocide became weaker, more 'diluted in the general misery' (especially since one had had better media coverage than the other) and finally lost the exceptional nature which could have led to the quick empanelling of an international tribunal. The first UN report on the genocide by René Degni-Ségui came out on 28 June and gave a serious international legal basis to the very existence of the genocide which some circles close to the Interim government had tried to deny; but the pressure to create a tribunal was partly weakened by the shock of the refugee ordeal in Goma, according to an unspoken argument which could be roughly summed up as 'What these people need is food and medicines, not a tribunal'.

Although suffering certainly cannot be measured by numbers alone, one should nevertheless not forget that the victims of the Goma epidemic numbered around 30,000[50] while the genocide

---

48. The literature on the Goma cholera disaster was abundant and the titles particularly dramatic: 'Rwanda – le choléra fait 3,000 morts par jour', *Le Figaro* (26 July 1994); 'Land of the dead and the dying', *The Economist* (30 July 1994); 'Hell on Earth', *Newsweek* (1 August 1994); 'This is the Apocalypse', *Time* (1 August 1994).

49. *Libération* (27 July 1994).

50. By the time they left (22 August), the *Turquoise* boys had buried 20,500 bodies with the large mechanical earth-movers they had at their disposal. They can be considered to have buried at least two-thirds of the corpses.

figure came into the 800,000 range. The horror and the compassion directed at the refugees dying in Goma tended to obscure such facts.

On 21 July, President Clinton promised a vigorous US approach to the problem, with a $76m budget and a large number of transport planes from bases in Germany. The Americans rushed headlong into the fray with more goodwill than efficiency. They landed an advance party of troops at Entebbe with three C-130s, and started immediate airdropping of supplies (25 July). The inaccuracy of their operation was such that French soldiers and refugees alike had to dive for cover as pallets crashed all over the camps. Rumours immediately spread among the refugees that this had been a bombing raid by the RPF.

But life was slowly getting organised in the six main camps around Goma. The old administrative authorities kept most of their control over their former subjects. People lived in the camps in lots arranged according to their *préfecture* and their *commune* of origin, obeying the orders of the same *bourgmestre* who had led them before, even into the genocide. The deeply-ingrained Rwandese respect for authority which we have already mentioned several times still operated. Actually, when the UNHCR camp authorities tried to organise the first repatriations to Rwanda in early August, one of the main problems, besides the fear of the RPF, was the refusal of the communal authorities to go back with 'their' peasants. And even when those realised that they were being treated as political fodder, they still obeyed. As one of them said:

> 'Very clever people pushed us into fleeing two months ago. The FAR soldiers were opening the way with a lorry. We had to follow them and there were others with guns pushing us from behind. We had to walk like cattle. . . . But in any case, *we do not know what to think since our local authorities are now gone. We hope for a new bourgmestre who could tell us what to do.*'[51]

---

51. Florence Aubenas, 'La longue marche vers Kigali', *Libération* (2 August 1994). Emphasis added.

Of course, Prime Minister Twagiramungu's clumsiness did not help. On 2 August, he had declared to the press that it would be necessary 'to try 30,000 people' to punish the genocide adequately[52]. The figure was of course absurd since there was not enough jail space in all of Rwanda to hold so many prisoners and the idea of having to carry out the massive death sentences hinted at was simply unthinkable. Since the new government was at the same time trying to persuade Paris to agree to a demilitarisation of the French SHZ after the planned 21 August *Turquoise* withdrawal deadline, this did not make matters any simpler.

'Turquoise is going away, the problems remain'[53] (1–21 August)

The main problem for Rwanda in the short term was population control. The idea that the refugees should return right away was a well-intentioned mistake and Mrs Sadako Ogata, the very able UNHCR high commissioner, decided against it on 1 August. There were several obstacles to a rapid return: the refugees could easily carry cholera with them back inside Rwanda and spread it in the hills as they went; militiamen and ex-FAR elements could infiltrate with them and increase the insecurity; and there was still no structure for them to be administered except the old MRND. If the MRND *bourgmestres* went back in anonymously, lost in a mass of returnees, the population would become uncontrollable. In the short run, the refugees were going to stay put until a partial return to normality had taken place.

The second most important problem was that of security. The rumours of RPF exactions were beginning to increase, both because they had a basis in truth and because the survivors of the now defunct regime exaggerated them. The main bone of contention between those who sympathised with the RPF and those who disliked it was the degree of intentionality of what was going on. In a way, as we have seen, this quarrel had a

52. *Le Monde* (4 August 1994).
53. This was the banner headline of *L'Humanité* on 22 August 1994.

false premise. There was of course no 'second genocide' as some circles later tried to pretend. The killings occurring in Rwanda were scattered, irregular and limited in numbers. They had all the signs of a mixture of private revenge killings and ordinary banditry.

At times, some of the RPF 'slippage' reached momentous proportions, as when they massacred several hundred people on 9 July 1994 after taking Butare in a massive bout of revenge killings.[54] Nevertheless the perpetrators were often RPA soldiers, and the attitude of the government (or rather the RPF) towards them was ambiguous. There was much talk of their being arrested and tried for their misdeeds (a few even were, to satisfy public opinion), but the civilian government had neither the means nor the political clout to do so. And as for the RPF itself, it acted with a mixture of sincere leniency ('these are our boys, they are good boys') and calculated tolerance of crime designed to keep the Hutu refugee mass scared and out. It is doubtful whether General Paul Kagame really agreed with this policy, but either he was not sufficiently opposed to it to think it worth a major political fight, or he no longer had full control of the RPF any more – a hypothesis which was going to become more convincing as the months passed.

The third most important problem was the state of the economy – or rather its quasi-disappearance. When it left Kigali, the interim government took with it all the Central Bank foreign currency reserves as well as very large amounts of cash in Rwandese francs. This was part of a general policy of leaving only a waste land to the victorious RPF. All fixed installations which could be destroyed before leaving were destroyed. Almost *all* available vehicles were driven over the border to Zaïre. Not a penny was left in the public coffers. There was of course

54. See Monique Mujawamaliya, *Rapport*, op. cit., pp. 22–5. After the author started to talk about these events while in Rwanda, she was threatened by RPF officers who feared that 'she would be just as fierce in defending her Hutu brothers as she had been in defending the Tutsi under Habyarimana'. She had to leave the country – under the protection of other RPF officers who disapproved of their comrades' attitude.

absolutely no tax revenue any more[55], while customs revenue had fallen to a ridiculously low level. Ripe crops were rotting for want of people to gather them. Transport was non-existent. Banks were closed after being looted of all their cash. Countryside stores were empty and the few manufacturing industries had all ground to a halt. Worse, the extreme prudence now being shown by foreign aid donors did not augur well for a quick reopening of these channels. It is only because of the extraordinary fertility of Rwanda's countryside and the capacity for forbearance of its inhabitants that there was no famine. People tightened their belts and survived on very little.

Paris had finally agreed to talk to the '*de facto government of Rwanda*', and sent a delegation[56] to meet Premier Twagiramungu in Kigali on 22 July. The RPF finally accepted on 2 August the principle of turning the SHZ into a demilitarised zone after the French departed. Nobody in Paris had many illusions over how long the former SHZ would remain demilitarised after the departure of the *Turquoise* troops, but what mattered was face-saving and the ministries concerned still hoped to avoid a Goma-like panic when French soldiers withdrew. Because withdraw they would: in spite of a variety of foreign appeals, mostly from the UN and the Americans[57], Prime Minister Balladur was

55. What made the situation even worse was that 1993 taxes had only been finally collected by late March 1994. President Habyarimana was killed and the civil war restarted a week later. Thus when the interim government looted the public purse, it contained a full year's taxes.

56. This delegation had been carefully pegged at a medium level of diplomatic representation, with Mme Boisvineau, under-director for East Africa at the DAAM; General Germanos, second-in-command of *Turquoise*; and Bertrand Dufourq, Secretary-General of the Ministry of Foreign Affairs.

57. The first contingent of US troops (sixty men) arrived in Kigali on 31 July and the White House was extremely worried in case they and their comrades still to come should get stuck there. The whole 'Support Hope' operation was conceived (very much like *Turquoise* but within a much less complicated domestic political context) as a public relations exercise, and General John Shalikashvili, chief of staff of the US forces, made it clear both to Chief Security Adviser Anthony Lake and to USAID director Brian Atwood that the army 'had no intention of playing nurse for very long' (interview with a State Department official, Washington DC, 4 September 1994). The US army folded up and left by 30 September.

resolutely sticking to the deadline which the French forces had been given in the UN Resolution 929 two-months mandate voted on 21 June. Incredible procrastination by the United Nations left UNAMIR at the desultory level of 1,000 men, while endless discussions prevented the contingent from being deployed to its full strength of 5,500 men. And problems were obviously going to develop. Admiral Lanxade, chief of staff of the French armed forces, declared that 'France has no mandate to arrest the members of the former government'[58]. Several of them had slipped into the SHZ after the fall of Gisenyi and were negotiating with the French military authorities to obtain safe-conducts out of the country. This in turn caused RPF anger, General Kagame declaring that by letting them into the SHZ, 'France had become an accomplice of the militiamen'[59]. The French retaliated by accusing the RPF of kidnapping several people and looting property after entering the SHZ illegally[60].

Refugees started to trickle back into the RPF-controlled part of the country, albeit slowly. By early August their numbers were estimated at around 100,000[61]. But the movement slowed down as the rumours of RPF exactions became ever more insistent. General Kagame denied that these exactions were taking place[62], which of course scared everybody even more because this diplomatic lie was taken as an example of sinister duplicity confirming in the refugees' minds the existence of the 'Secret Tutsi Plan' the MRND had always been talking about. Everyone 'knew' that returning would mean annihilation[63]. Premier Twagiramungu's rueful admission that the government held only 200 people on suspicion of participating in the genocide after he had talked of putting 30,000 people on trial was

---

58. SWB/Radio France Internationale, 18 July 1994.
59. SWB/France 1 TV Channel, 5 August 1994.
60. SWB/Radio France Internationale, 6 August 1994.
61. SWB/RTBF-Brussels, 7 August 1994.
62. Le Monde (7–8 August 1994).
63. For a good analysis of these politico-psychological stumbling blocks, see Noël Copin, 'Un peuple malade de la peur' (a people sick with fear), La Croix (3 August 1994).

symptomatic of the paucity of means at his disposal[64] – not a reassuring factor. Many refugees would have preferred to see a strong government, RPF or not, which could at least have separated the perpetrators of the genocide from the rest. The lack of domestic means and the indifference and vacillation of the international community on the question of creating a UN-sponsored tribunal – everything pointed at a sort of confused, shadowy and unjust punishment for the genocide as the most probable pattern of 'judgement'. Since almost nobody, not even the real innocents, was sure of being able to prove his or her 'innocence' under such circumstances, there was no building of trust – in a situation where from the start such trust was unlikely to exist. This situation was of course ideal for the members of the former regime who were confident that at some point sooner or later things would swing back their way:

> Mr Nzirorera, former Secretary-General of the MRND, was telling us, as he received us in his splendid villa on the shores of Lake Kivu, about the refugees who a few kilometers away were dying of cholera in their overpopulated camps: 'They prefer to die of cholera rather than going home. They do not like the RPF.' The man saw in this suffering mass only one thing: his vademecum for the future, his passport to political life. Because they were there, he and a few dozen others could one day hope to get back in power.[65]

As the deadline for the French withdrawal in the southwest drew closer, a new exodus got under way, out of the SHZ towards Bukavu in Zaïre. The French were trying to reason with the displaced people in their area, but nobody would listen any more. The mixture of fear of the RPF and obedience to authority came into play again, and long columns of refugees started to stream on foot towards the border. In their desperation at seeing the flimsy SHZ structure collapse even before they were due to leave, the French authorities swallowed their pride and brought Seth

---

64. Despatch from AFP press agency, 8 August 1994.
65. Patrick de Saint-Exupéry, 'Rwanda. Une réconciliation impossible', *Le Figaro* (8 August 1994).

Sendashonga the (Hutu) RPF Minister of the Interior and his (Tutsi) Rehabilitation colleague Jacques Bihozagara by one of their military helicopters to Kibuye so that they would try to talk the population out of running away. But there were also increasingly objective factors in civilian Hutu fears. Although the RPF did not pursue a policy of systematic persecution, some Tutsi did so, especially the thousands of former refugees now streaming in from Burundi. In the southeast of Rwanda where they would arrive first as they came up from Ngozi and Kirundo provinces on the other side of the now traversed border, they evicted the Hutu from properties which they claimed had been theirs thirty years earlier. In the first two weeks of August, 13,000 new Hutu refugees had crossed the Burundi border southwards while probably three or four as times that many *former* Tutsi refugees were crossing it northwards. And the former government policy reinforced this. On 16 August, the UNHCR had been forced to cancel its first organised repatriation convoy from Goma after death threats to the returnee candidates from the ex-FAR[66] – threats that were far from being empty. Every day political murders were committed in the camps – of alleged RPF 'spies', of Hutu suspected of anti-MRND feelings, but mostly of people who had said they wanted to go home.

As the deadline drew nearer and the panic in the SHZ increased, defensive statements by French politicians multiplied. The Minister of Defence François Léotard, declared on 19 August:

> 'We did all that was possible to stabilise and reassure the population. [. . .] It is now up to the RPF to make the necessary gestures. . . . I don't think it is fair to say that our intervention has only saved people temporarily. . . . Let us not forget that the SHZ now contains a greater population than all the rest of Rwanda put together.'[67]

This strange defence and illustration of the intervention con-

---

66. *Le Figaro* (17 August 1994).
67. *Libération* (20–21 August 1994).

cept (about which, to be fair, the Defence Minister had never felt sanguine) rested on a factual error: the French SHZ sheltered about 1.5 million people, while there were some 3.2 million in the rest of the country. And then it was impossible not to feel slightly puzzled at such a statement being made forty-eight hours before total withdrawal, while thousands were streaming out of the area. The safety/stabilisation process definitely could not be seen as having been anything other than temporary. Foreign Minister Alain Juppé, one of the two godfathers of *Turquoise* the other being President Mitterrand, were keenly aware of this, claiming defensively in a radio interview that: 'We have taken all the necessary precautions. We did not merely leave during the night, putting the key under the doormat.'[68] Although the exodus had been less catastrophic than in the northwest, about half a million refugees had fled the SHZ for Bukavu by the time the French left on 21 August. As François Léotard had said, it was now – somehow – up to the RPF.

68. SWB/Radio France Internationale, 22 August 1994.

9

AFTERMATH OR NEW BEGINNING?
(22 August – 31 December 1994)

The new refugee problem

The mass exodus of July/August had led nearly 2 million Rwandese out of a total of some 7 million to cross the country's borders. Estimates of the refugee population were not always coherent: by mid-November 1994 the UNHCR gave a figure of 2.1 million, while the US Committee for Refugees thought it was only 1.7 million and the French medical organisation Médecins Sans Frontières (MSF) even less at 1.3 million. As for their geographical distribution, UNHCR figures, even if probably exaggerated, give a good idea of the general order of magnitude in each location[1]:

Points of concentration	Approximate figures
Northern Burundi	270,000
Western Tanzania	577,000
South-western Uganda	10,000
Zaïre (Goma)	850,000
Zaïre (Bukavu)	332,000
Zaïre (Uvira)	62,000

Even if we take the lower US or MSF figures, the proportions between the various refugee masses remain the same. In addition to these outside refugees, Rwanda contained by the fall of 1994 an enormous number of internally displaced persons, 1.8 million according to the new Kigali authorities, or 1.3 million according to the US Committee for Refugees. Thus one could say that in

---

1. UNHCR Special Unit for Rwanda and Burundi, *Rwanda and Burundi Information Meeting*, Geneva (16 November 1994).

a population of slightly over 7 million about half were displaced in one way or another, at a tremendous cost in human suffering. The various agencies trying to cope with this disaster were hoping that the refugees could rapidly come home. There was a certain hope that this might be happening when about 140,000 people returned, mostly from Goma, during August. But by early September, the return movement had completely dried up: we shall see why. The return movement from Tanzania occurred slightly later, during September–October, and was much smaller, bringing back only about 20,000 people. Then it too dried up, partly for other reasons than in the Zaïre case.

The main problem of the refugee camps was the question of their political control. UNHCR and other agencies had no real control over what went on in the camps, a situation which eventually led to strong protests from some of the biggest and most efficient NGOs[2]. Faced with the passivity of the UN and its incapacity to re-establish order in the camps, MSF eventually walked out, first from the Zaïre camps (mid-November) and then from those in Tanzania (mid-December). This was not a fit of pique but a political choice which other organisations might have followed, but for the funding and image problems which they feared.

The refugee camps were (and are at the time of writing) monstrous places. After the July–August cholera emergency, they were quickly brought under humanitarian control and the food/health/shelter emergency ceased to be a major problem. Death rates quickly declined to almost acceptable levels for a population living in refugee conditions. But this only compounded the political problem. The refugees had left under very special circumstances, as related in the last chapter. They were largely herded, willy-nilly, by the FAR and by their civilian authorities. Once they had crossed the border, they were almost militarily organised, by *préfecture*, by *commune* and by *section*,

---

2. Jean Hélène, 'Les organisations humanitaires menacent de quitter les camps de réfugiés du Zaïre', *Le Monde* (5 November 1994). There had been a common communiqué from fifteen organisations, including CARE, Oxfam and MSF.

with their former *bourgmestres* and communal personnel at their head. In a way, this simplified work for the UNHCR, the Red Cross and the other organisations. This was no Somali refugee camp with total and permanent confusion. Here food could be distributed in an orderly fashion. There were authorities and even a form of order. But this order was the order of death which had prevailed in April–July. The authorities were the old MRND ones and had no intention of giving up. Their ideology, their 'administrative practice' had remained the same. Already by late August, the UNHCR made no secret of the prevailing situation. One of its officials, Ray Wilkinson, said: 'We are in a state of virtual war in the camps.'[3] The reason was simple: the political logic of the genocidal state clashing with the humanitarian logic of the international organisations, and winning a clear victory.

The exodus had been masterminded by the ideologues of the genocide. As the former CDR leader Jean-Bosco Barayagwiza boasted in an interview, 'Even if the RPF has won a military victory, it will not have the power. It has only the bullets we have the population.'[4] The former leaders kept almost total control of their subjects. Whoever disagreed with them was quickly murdered, a quick way to stop returns to Rwanda after the first few weeks. They monopolised the distribution of humanitarian aid and inflated the numbers of people actually registered to get more than what was needed. In the distributions, they gave first priority to themselves, and then to the ex-FAR or *Interahamwe*; after that they sold the extra rations to obtain cash for the financing of further political or military operations. UNHCR, the Red Cross and the NGOs were powerless when confronted with the total ruthlessness of the political cadres and the passivity of the ordinary population[5].

3. Speaking to AFP (SWB/AFP, 27 August 1994).
4. African Rights, *Rwanda: Death, Despair and Defiance*, op. cit, p. 657.
5. See Raymond Bonner, 'Aid is taken hostage in Rwandan camps', *International Herald Tribune* (1 November 1994), and Laurent Bijard, 'Les tueurs Hutu se portent bien', *Le Nouvel Observateur* (3–9 November 1994).

Humour was a weak safety valve and the UNHCR workers soon learned the cruel but justified nickname of their organisation: *'Hauts Criminels Rassasiés'* (Well-fed Top Criminals). The Top Criminals were well-fed indeed and the paradoxical structure of the problem made any political adjustments extremely difficult. We will see in further sections that the demands of the international community – often set as a pre-condition for the re-starting of aid – that the Kigali government 'ensure the refugees' return' and 'broaden its political base' by, in fact, including some of the criminals in its ranks, has met so far with uncomprehending amazement from the new authorities. It seems that at times the international community lives in a world of transparent abstractions where concrete realities have no place. The refugees' return is a desirable goal, and it would be healthy indeed to broaden the political base of the present regime, but the question is how. The control of the genocidal authorities over the refugee population is almost total. Their lack of remorse is almost absolute. Where does one start from there? In fact there could be no start at all except a re-start of the hostilities. One of the complaints of the Kigali regime is that international aid is not really feeding refugees but refitting an army preparing for invasion[6], and there are many signs that such statements may be more than political propaganda.

The first signs came from the infiltrations which started as early as September. The UN admitted them[7] and late in the month they had developed into significant fighting between the Rwandese Patriotic Army (RPA) and the ex-Forces Armées Rwandaises (FAR) in Cyangugu *préfecture*. This was probably

6. See General Kagame's interview on Radio France Internationale in which he says that unless the international community is capable of regaining political and even military control of the camps, it will keep helping 'an army in exile preparing for war' (SWB, 6 December 1994).

7. See declaration by UN Special Representative Shahryar Khan about infiltrations in Cyangugu *préfecture* (SWB/Radio France Internationale, 8 September 1994). Major Plante, spokesman for UNAMIR, confirmed them and said that the infiltrees moved into Nyungwe forest. It is likely that if further operations take place, the mountainous forested area which stretches in the west of Rwanda all the way from Cyangugu to Gisenyi *préfectures* will be the chosen path of penetration.

a ground-testing process because after the stiff RPA reaction there was a lull in the clashes. But infiltrations took place later (December) in Gisenyi *préfecture* where the clashes caused more than sixty deaths. There were also attacks across Lake Kivu into Cyangugu *préfecture*. This was a reflection of the total loss of UN control over the camps. As a confidential UN report said at the time:

> Former soldiers and militiamen have total control of the camps. . . . They have decided to stop, by force if necessary, any return of the refugees to Rwanda. [. . .] It now looks as if these elements are preparing an armed invasion of Rwanda and that they are both stockpiling and selling food aid distributed by caritative organisations in order to prepare for this invasion.[8]

The former authorities did not try to hide what they were doing, and even boasted of it, as if they thought that nobody could or would want to stop them. On 7 October, Augustin Bizimungu, the former FAR chief of staff and 'Minister of Defence' in the interim government, and Mathieu Ngirumpatse, the MRND secretary-general, announced that they would attack Rwanda 'in case of the failure of a negotiated settlement'[9].

In late September some FAR forces began to move to the Ngara camp in Tanzania under the pretext of 'joining their families'. And in the following weeks, large elements of logistics and men began to slide southwards to Chimanga and Kanganiro military bases, not far from Bukavu, where the topography was more favourable for an attack than in the Goma area. They were under the leadership of Colonel Théoneste Bagosora who said that he would provoke internal disturbances in Rwanda to coordinate with his guerrilla attacks 'in the same way as the Palestinian intifada'[10]. The French seemed to regard the prospect with glee, with Bruno Delaye, African special adviser in the President's office declaring to a visiting journalist: 'We won't invite the new Rwandese authorities to the next Franco-African

---

8. *Africa News Report* (28 November 1994).
9. SWB/AFP in English, 7 October 1994.
10. Chris Mac Greal, 'Hutu exiles in training', *The Guardian* (19 December 1994).

summit. They are too controversial and besides they are going to collapse any minute.'[11] Nobody in Paris seemed greatly disturbed by the possible consequences, among them the fact that the RPA might decide to hit FAR rear bases in Zaïre in hot pursuit after open attacks, with all the attendant consequences in terms of regional violences[12]. Indeed General Kagame was considering that possibility, and his first visit abroad took him to Tripoli, one of his only possible sources of weapons[13]. And on the other side also, preparations were going ahead with training and the purchase of weaponry.

However, the former Rwandese government was not operating in a diplomatic vacuum – its actions seemed to have a very direct Zaïrean seal of approval[14]. The Zaïrean lobby on Rwanda had already met at Gbadolite in late April 1994, in the midst of the genocide, to decide what to do in the increasingly likely event of an RPF victory. The following were present at the meeting:

– *Herman Cohen*, former Under Secretary of State for African Affairs under President Bush, president of the Global Coalition for Africa, married to a French wife, and francophone himself. A strong lobbyist in Washington for President Mobutu. He had remained a vital player in the US/African field because of the low profile of the current Under Secretary of State, George Moose.

– *Michel Aurillac*, former French Minister for Cooperation under Prime Minister Chirac in the *cohabitation* cabinet of 1986–8. He

11. Private communication to the author (17 October 1994).
12. Colette Braeckman, 'Le Kivu craque sous les réfugiés', *Le Soir* (22 Nov. 1994).
13. SWB/Jana News Agency, 4 October 1994. The connection was Ugandan. Pressed by both the United States and the Sudanese Muslim fundamentalists, Colonel Gaddafi had an extremely small margin of manoeuvre. President Museveni was probably the last friend who could put in a good word for him in Washington. So General Kagame was very warmly received in Libya.
14. According to several sources (see *La Lettre du Continent* of 22 December 1994), President Mobutu made it possible for Mme Habyarimana and her brother Séraphin Rwabukumba to accompany him to Beijing when he went there on an official visit in late November. See also Human Rights Arms Project, *Rwanda/Zaïre: Rearming with Impunity . . .*, op. cit.

had remained one of the Africa experts for the Chirac fraction of the RPR neo-Gaullist party.

– *Robert Bourgi*, formerly a Shiite member of the Lebanese community in Dakar, now converted to Christianity. He had long been a trouble-shooter on both Middle Eastern and African affairs for the RPR. Formerly a Chirac man, he now appeared to have gone over to the Balladur-Pasqua camp in the pre-election political struggles in Paris.

– *Jacques Foccart*. A legendary figure, now in his eighties, he was a former secret service operative who became top adviser on Africa to General de Gaulle in 1958. President Pompidou wanted to get rid of him after his election in 1969 but had had to keep him on: he was bringing too much money in African contributions into the political coffers of the RPR to be dispensed with. However, he was fired by President Giscard d'Estaing in 1974. In spite of this he always remained a shadowy figure in the very peculiar Franco-African political underworld. During his brief tenure as Prime Minister in 1986–8, Jacques Chirac gave him back his old job as special adviser on Africa. A good friend of Herman Cohen with whom he remained in close touch, he was back in Gbadolite to reconcile President Mobutu and his Prime Minister Kengo wa Dongo on 8 August 1994.

– *Max-Olivier Cahen*, son of Alfred Cahen, the current Belgian ambassador in Paris. As a young man, his father helped Mobutu in his climb to power in the 1960s. The son was now one of the Belgian Socialist Party's advisers on Africa and a consultant in that field.

All these men constituted a sort of informal (but not entirely disinterested) Mobutu lobby. Their purpose in meeting was to plan the strategy which would enable the Zaïrian President, who had been radically marginalised for the last couple of years, to make a diplomatic comeback through the Rwandese crisis. The goodwill of Paris was secured, but Brussels and especially Washington were tougher nuts to crack. But former Under Secretary of State Herman Cohen, who at the time of writing probably has more power on African affairs than anybody else in Washington, took it upon himself to make sure that things went the right way, and to achieve US support for the French positions. Of course, there was a price to pay. President Mobutu had no sympathy for Yoweri Museveni whom he considered an insolent upstart and a dangerous revolutionary[15]. His fears were not totally unfounded. Eastern Zaïre feels culturally and economically part of East Africa, and people in that area could seriously consider secession if the disintegration of Zaïre went any further. And President Museveni had had contacts with the survivors of the old Mouvement National Congolais (MNC), Patrice Lumumba's party and Mobutu's mortal ennemies. As for the Zaïrian President, he considered the RPF to be a direct surrogate of the Ugandan regime and that given the large Banyarwanda population in the east, its victory posed a direct danger for Kivu. If one adds to these reasons Mobutu's old friendship with the dead President Habyarimana and his familiarity with many of the MRND barons, it is easy to see why he was strongly opposed to the new regime which had just arrived to power in Kigali. And as if this was not enough, the man in the leopard-skin hat also strongly disagreed with his Prime Minister on the Rwandese issue[16]. So any support of this lobby for a public relations facelift of Mobutu's regime would also have to assume the burden of fighting Museveni, fighting the new Rwandese regime and supporting the perpetrators of the genocide.

Due to the French support, the lobby did not do badly. *Opération Turquoise* had a powerful rejuvenating effect for President Mobutu who was rapidly reintegrated into the international diplomatic game as a guarantor of the 'stability' of Central

---

15. 'Zaïre/Ouganda: la guerre secrète', *La Lettre du Continent* (28 April 1994).
16. President Mobutu and his Prime Minister Kengo wa Dondo disagree on practically everything. But the President is resigned to Kengo's presence for several reasons: first, he is not a 'true' Zaïrean and therefore cannot aspire to the presidency; secondly, the foreigners like him; and thirdly, he has used his Jewish connection (his father was a Polish Jew who emigrated to Belgium and thence to the Congo) to good advantage to secure US and Israeli support. But Kengo's mother is a Rwandese Tutsi and he has no sympathy for the former MRND regime.

Africa, whatever that may have meant. On 15 September, a UN special representative, Mohamed Shahryar Khan, found it necessary to meet him to discuss the Rwandese refugee problems, and he was invited to the coming Franco-African summit conference in Biarritz (8 November) from which the RPF was banned. On 28 September, a World Bank meeting in Paris about debt rescheduling and aid to Burundi was the occasion for the US delegate to speak privately about Rwanda: the French could be happy, Washington was miraculously aligned on their position, and Kigali would not get the money it needed to start reconstruction if it did not show proper remorse (see next section)[17]. The international press soon picked up the news of Mobutu's comeback[18].

On the question of the refugee camps and the danger they represented, the new government in Kigali was trying to deal with Prime Minister Kengo wa Dondo rather than with the President. On 22 October, Prime Minister Faustin Twagiramungu and his Zaïrean counterpart signed a tripartite agreement with the UNHCR for the progressive repatriation of the refugees. Not that it made much practical difference in the short run, given the lack of UNHCR control over the camps and the reluctance of the Zaïrean armed forces to help enforce it. But at least it provided the UNHCR with a legal framework from which to operate.

President Mobutu kept his Rwandese friends on a tight leash.

---

17. Interview with a French Foreign Ministry civil servant, Paris, 29 September 1994. This development was in a way particularly ironical: Paris had always justified its opposition to the RPF with the argument that it was a stooge of Museveni and, through him, Washington and of the evil 'Anglo-Saxon world'. The turnaround of the US position on the question of providing the $4.5 million which could unblock the World Bank credits which the new Rwandese regime so badly needed, though perfectly understandable in the light of a rudderless US non-policy on the question which left the field open for the anti-Kigali Mobutu lobby in Washington, nevertheless amusingly negated of all the paranoid delusions the French authorities had entertained for years about 'US imperialism' over the small Central African nation.

18. As examples see 'Zaïre – la résurrection', *La Lettre du Continent* (13 October 1994); 'Mobutu redivivus', *The Economist* (15 October 1994); or 'Mobutu exploits the Rwanda crisis', *The New African* (November 1994).

They had brought 17 billions of Rwandese francs with them when they had fled the country, but most of it was stashed away in Zaïrean accounts, under the President's direct control. That way he could open or close the tap as he wished and so modulate the actions he wanted to undertake on Rwanda. The game was tight since Prime Minister Kengo did not want any action undertaken against the new regime in Kigali. In November he managed to block the formation of a Rwandese 'government in exile' planned by Stanislas Mbonampeka, Jerome Bicamumpaka, Jean Kambanda and a number of former MRND luminaries[19]. But despite the opposition of his Prime Minister, Mobutu remained in control because of the steady support he received from France. This was apparent in the open competition for the organisation of a regional summit on Rwanda towards the end of October. The Tanzanians had declared that they wanted to host it[20] almost at the same time as the Zaïreans[21]. Eventually nothing happened in Dar-es-Salaam, and there was a 'summit meeting' of the Communauté Economique des Pays des Grands Lacs (CEPGL) in Gbadolite. *La francophonie* had won.

Reconstruction and internal security

These two factors have continually been mutually contradictory alternatives ever since the beginning of September 1994. The UNHCR was saying 'We cannot send the refugees back to a country where private and possibly public revenge killings are the norm', while the government in Kigali said 'There can be no normalisation of the situation as long as large groups of refugees controlled by hostile forces remain on our doorstep.'

The fact is that both had a point – and that ultimately both were insincere. We have already seen that the repatriation process was something over which the UNHCR could have had no real control even if that had been what it wanted it because

---

19. SWB/La Voix du Zaïre, 11 November 1994.
20. SWB/Radio Dar-es-Salaam, 1 November 1994.
21. SWB/La Voix du Zaïre, 31 October 1994.

it did not control the camps. So in a way internal insecurity in Rwanda provided a nice excuse for procrastination. However, the UNHCR's accusations were far from baseless. The problem came from the situation mentioned earlier, namely the radical change in RPF recruitment after April 1994. Many young boys from inside Rwanda and even more from Burundi had been taken in and superficially trained. They found themselves with a uniform, a gun and none of the fighting tradition and discipline of the 'Ugandan' veterans. They also had relatives who were either dead or else aggressively alive. Boys from Rwanda had lost their families and understandably harboured strong feelings of revenge, unlike the 'Ugandans' whose families had remained safely behind in Uganda during the war years and the genocide. So they often killed Hutu just to get even with those they perceived as globally responsible for the death of their families. As for the Burundi refugees, they had often lost some of their relations in the Burundi massacres of October–November 1993 following the murder of President Melchior Ndadaye. But those who survived had often joined the Tutsi extremist militias which sprang up in early 1994 and dedicated themselves to killing Hutu in collaboration with the Burundi army. They were now coming to Rwanda with their experience of hatred and counter-hatred, of symmetrical massacres and minds poisoned by a political culture gone mad in ways perhaps more subtle than in Rwanda, but definitely just as lethal.

These new recruits with various axes to grind were faced with an absolutely chaotic situation. First of all, even if they were (more or less) fed, they were not paid. Six months after the end of the war, they still had not seen their first money. [22] So they tended to contract themselves out to private parties who needed a gunman, whether to scare off the owner of a coveted property or to murder somebody one wanted to get rid of. In addition to this, they were faced by sporadic *Interahamwe* attacks, especially in the former French SHZ zone which they had entered on 9 September. There, French presence had left behind many

22. They received their first pay in December 1994.

nests of militiamen who had believed either that the demilitarisation agreement would hold or that they could more easily hold their ground given the support they could receive from Bukavu and northern Burundi. They were periodically reinforced by FAR infiltrators from Zaïre, and firefights with the RPA were common. There were also bandits who, with no political commitment, were just out to loot and would even kill if they could do so without danger to themselves. Then there was also pressure, in the case of the sons of Burundi refugees, to 'help the family'. Relations tended to use a RPA son or nephew to grab whatever they could under the cloak of 'authority'. Denunciations of Hutu as former *Interahamwe* were common, just to get somebody out of the way and appropriate his house or land. The RPF authorities tried to denounce these practices but to no avail. Their control over the troops was wearing thin; at least, this is what they hinted at. The main question was obviously the degree of knowledge or control the Front had over its men. It was certainly far from perfect but it may not have been as bad as it seemed. That there were killings nobody could doubt[24]. But the two main bones of contention which fuelled the quarrel between UNHCR and UNAMIR were first, what was the extent of these killings? and were they the result of quasi anarchy or of a deliberate RPF policy? This is why the 'Gersony Report', produced by a UNHCR consultant in unclear circumstances tended to obscure rather than clarify the problem. This report apparently stated that the RPF murdered 30,000 Hutu in revenge killings between July and September 1994 and it was rumoured to present those killings as the RPF's deliberate policy[25].

23. The worst incident occurred on 7 January 1995 when an unauthorised RPF patrol was grenaded by unknown parties from Busanze refugee camp in Butare *préfecture*. The patrol went bersek and killed eleven refugees, probably not those responsible for the attack (SWB/Radio Rwanda, 8 January 1995, and author's field note).
24. See the interview of Alison des Forges, Human Rights Watch Africa officer, SWB/Radio France Internationale, 8 September 1994.
25. In *Libération* (2 October 1994) Stephen Smith wrote that Robert Gersony had interviewed people in '41 of the 143 communes of Rwanda', but on the same day in *Le Monde* (2–3 October 1994), Isabelle Vichniac was writing that the

Although the report cannot be discussed since it is not available, there must be strong doubts about its reliability, something which may explain the shroud of mystery surrounding it. The reason is simply than it is difficult to kill 250/300 people a day for more than two months without attracting a lot of attention and leaving a lot of traces in a country of 26,000 square km. The killings which have been documented beyond reasonable doubt always involve much smaller numbers, between 5–10 and in the worst cases 3–400. The total for the two months in question may be very roughly estimated at 5–6,000, itself an enormous number, and large enough to create conditions of extreme insecurity in the country.

The question of whether it was a deliberate policy of the government or not is not easy to answer. After some initial details by Colonel Frank Mugambage, General Kagame himself admitted that murders were taking place, and reprimanded the soldiers: 'Non-payment of salaries cannot be a pretext for people to commit the same offences which we have accused criminals of committing in this country.'[26] Prime Minister Faustin Twagiramungu was even blunter: 'We cannot deny that we have not provided satisfactory security. . . . People are still being killed like by the earlier ones. . . . I know we are all angry. But we cannot take spears and machetes and go on killing one another.'[27] It is extremely doubtful that people who would had organised a micro-genocide would incriminate themselves in

inquiries had been made 'in the refugee camps', something quite different. The most bizarre rumours began to circulate about the report, including one repeated to this author by a UNHCR official that the report did not exist, and was a mere verbal note. Then came news that it had been embargoed (if it existed) by the UN Secretary-General himself. To this day this author has never been able to speak to someone who actually saw the report, including journalists who 'quoted' from it. Undoubtedly this report came at a very opportune moment for the UNHCR. After it there was no further question of quick repatriation, and long-term planning for a large refugee programme could be assured. For a discussion of the 'methodology' of this mysterious document see Alain Frilet, 'Polémique sur les représailles Rwandaises', *Libération* (27 October 1994).

26. SWB/Radio Rwanda, 9 September 1994.
27. SWB/Radio Rwanda, 8 December 1994. This developed into a serious political crisis between the Tutsi and Hutu components of the government during December.

this way. However, the situation is not so straightforward. The growing wave of Tutsi extremism, which was especially strong in the 'Burundese' community, favours a kind of a 'let them die' attitude. The killings are not orchestrated deliberately but those that happen are seen by many Tutsi as something 'natural' given the preceding genocide. Very little effort is made to stop them even if they are unplanned. There seems to be a kind of winking and looking the other way on the part of the men on the ground, even if the leadership tries to restrain them[28]. Then there is the problem of private militias which the 'Burundese' have brought with them and are now operating between Kibungo and Butare, independently of any RPF authority.

The killings were also probably considered as useful by some members of the RPF hierarchy in discouraging Hutu refugees abroad from coming back, something which would cause considerable problems for the 'Burundese returnees' who had frequently grabbed their properties and might be forced by the RPF to return them in the name of 'national reconciliation'. Because, in a way, this was a struggle between groups in competition for access to a limited amount of land and very poor housing in an overpopulated country. Tutsi families and their children who had left since 1959 and had lived or even been born in exile, were coming back in massive numbers. The government's estimates tally roughly with those of the journalists: they were 100,000 in July, 200,000 in August and probably 400,000 by November[29]. They came from Uganda, Zaïre and Burundi, and each group had a different 'style', reflecting their different experiences in the countries of exile where they had lived for a whole generation. The 'Zaïreans' were the ones with the least money; but

---

28. This is the reason why the government has tried to set up separate military tribunals to deal more quickly and directly with RPA soldiers' offences which cannot be curbed by a non-existent civilian justice (SWB/Radio Rwanda, 10 October 1994). By January there were about 600 RPA soldiers detained for these officers. (Interview with a Rwandese security official, Kigali, 18 January 1995.)

29. *Le Monde*, 4–5 September 1994, and 'Evolution de la population Rwandaise depuis la guerre', a Rwandese government one-page document (no Ministry or Service mentioned) dated 21 November 1994.

they were also the most reluctant to come because in Kivu they usually had land and were not sure they would find similar opportunities in Rwanda. They were probably the only ones who at times were forced back into Rwanda by the RPF. The 'Ugandans' came in the most calculated and rational way. Although they had experienced persecution previously, this had begun to recede into the past and for the last seven or eight years their lives had been good. So they intended to go to Rwanda prudently, leaving relatives behind to look after Ugandan houses, and therefore a structure which would enable them to go back if things did not work out in Rwanda. It was they who were most easily accepted by the 'native' Rwandese, whether Tutsi or Hutu, because the political culture in which they had lived since Yoweri Museveni came to power was one that stressed the evils of tribalism, something of which they had had ample experience in Uganda between 1972 and 1984. And they had experienced discrimination not specifically as Tutsi but as Banyarwanda who saw Hutu being victimised right alongside them, a very different experience from the 'Burundese' one. As a result, their reactions to the Rwandese socio-ethnic situation were the most relaxed.

The ones everybody loved to hate were the 'Burundese'. They had the most money, the greatest aplomb and the most aggressive attitude towards the Hutu. They were even often aggressive towards the Rwandese Tutsi who had survived the genocide, accusing them of having 'collaborated' with the regime to survive. They tended to monopolise businesses, throw their weight about and support each other as a tightly-knit group. But behind their bravado lay deep fears; many had seen relatives die in the killings of October–November 1993 and they did feel, after the Rwandese genocide, that Tutsi moderates like General Kagame had not really understood the situation, that no quarter should be given or expected where the Hutu were concerned. They had usually left their life in Burundi behind without any hope of ever returning there, and they seemed to feel a desperate desire that things would work out well for them in Rwanda.

The land to which these exiles were 'coming back', which

many had never seen before, was a land deeply traumatised. The physical aspect of the country was tragic, with buildings destroyed, standing houses thoroughly looted and heaps of corpses still lying around. In some villages, children could be seen playing with skulls as if they were balls.

Psychologically, the place was full of walking wounded; traumatised Tutsi survivors who had lost everything – their friends, their relations, their houses – and were wandering around like ghosts, and traumatised Hutu survivors who could not believe what had been done to them, They were the 'natural' inhabitants, the *rubanda nyamwinshi*, yet had been hunted down like any Tutsi in spite of their being 'true citizens'. There were 114,000 children without parents trying to survive with nobody to care for them[30]. There were frightened Hutu who had done nothing or had perhaps mechanically obeyed orders, but who now lived in constant fear of being arrested or killed. There were also sullen Hutu who had killed or sympathised with the killers and whose souls seemed sick beyond redemption[31]. In this world of zombies, satisfied murderers and guilt-ridden killer-victims, it was not surprising that the returnees from Uganda or Burundi made good. They had a bit of money and, even more important, were more or less psychologically intact.

It was from this human material that the country had to be re-started. An amazing number of people seemed to buckle down to it, trauma or no trauma. There was an immense need for labour, with almost 40% of the population dead or in exile. But the economy was non-existent and the international community

---

30. UNICEF figure, January 1995.
31. While a Tutsi friend of the author was trying to find the body of a relative in a pile of corpses killed during the genocide, all that a passing Hutu woman could find to say was 'Why don't they bury all that stuff? It stinks.'
32. There was also another point made by the Youth and Sport Minister, Patrick Mazimpaka. The Tutsi survivors, even before the genocide, had lived for years as second-class citizens. They were psychologically damaged while the exiles were not. Part of the 'spite' felt by the returnees for their surviving brethen resembled the feelings of Israeli Sabras towards the old type of ghetto Jews. This 'superiority' was extremely painful for the survivors of the genocide. (Interview with Patrick Mazimpaka, Kigali, 17 January 1995.)

was strangely reluctant to give it any sort of serious help. About $1.4 billion had been spent between July and December in emergency humanitarian aid, but it was 'impossible' to find the $4.5 million needed to pay back World Bank debt repayment arrears so that the credit mechanism could be primed back into life[33]. As we will see, this chilly attitude of ultra-caution was a mixture of timidity and of French lobbying against the new Kigali regime in all the international institutions, strangely with the support of the United States.

So the name of the game remained humanitarianism, largely unconnected with the real economic needs of the country and with an efficiency at times highly questionable[34]. It would eventually lead to Premier Faustin Twagiramungu protesting at the lack of coordination, and the self-serving attitude of the 154 NGOs working in the country, which sometimes seemed to think that the country was a blank page on which they were the first to write. But when the European Union finally managed to find a $85 million credit, it was because the political criteria which we will now turn to had been (partly) satisfied.

What sort of political structure?

The terrible paradox of Rwanda's situation in the aftermath of the genocide was that, while it needed economic aid above all else in order to try and make a fresh start, the main preoccupation of the potential foreign aid donors was that the political conditions should be right. By this we do not mean that there were no political problems in Rwanda – far from it, as we will see. But the conceptual framework through which these were viewed by foreigners was fundamentally warped.

---

33. *Africa Analysis* (30 September 1994).
34. See 'New Rwandan battles: the NGOs versus the rest', *Africa Analysis* (9 December 1994). Rwanda was what was called 'sexy' in some NGO circles. Just like Afghanistan in 1982, Ethiopia in 1985 or Somalia in 1992, you had to be there if you wanted to get your funding. Many of the NGOs in Rwanda showed a marked haughtiness of manner, and questionable efficiency.

The central problem after the RPF military victory in the summer of 1994 was of course the kind of political system which would be chosen for governing what was left of the country. In some ways the new government sworn in on 19 July presented itself as a return to the Arusha agreement of 3 August 1993, which had been conceived not only as a 'Peace agreement' but as a constitutional law, providing a direct complement to the 10 June 1991 Constitution.

But there were several 'amendments' to the dispositions of Arusha. First of all, the ministerial seats which would have gone to the MRND had not been shared out between the various political forces of the new government, but had been taken *en bloc* by the RPF. Secondly, not only had the RPF taken the presidency with Pasteur Bizimungu, it had also created a vice-presidential post which had not existed in the Arusha agreement; this was given to General Paul Kagame, and made him the unofficial 'protector' of the Republic. And thirdly, by giving the Civil Service Ministry to Vice-Prime Minister and RPF Colonel Kanyarengwe, the Front made sure that it could control future appointments in the administration. This was a lot, especially since, as we saw in the last chapter, the extreme lack of resources condemned the 'government' to beg from the RPF for whatever limited means it could get. The former opposition political parties, now in government [35], protested so strongly against the RPF grabbing all the MRND ministerial posts that the Front dare not repeat the manoeuvre for the seats in the National Assembly. Here the MRND seats were shared out, with an additional two seats for the major forces (RPF, PSD, MDR, PL and PDC) and one additional seat each for the minor opposition parties (UDPR, PDI and PSR) which had managed to fall on the right side of the genocidal divide.

35. Although the situation was at times ambiguous. In order to protest against the monopolised MRND Arusha seats bring by the RPF and against the Front's manipulations in the nominations for the future National Assembly, Minister of Tourism and Environment Jean-Népomucène Nayinzira (PDC) claimed to be 'resolutely in the opposition' (SWB/Radio France Internationale, 15 September 1994).

The question of the relationship between the RPF and the former opposition was at the centre of the whole political process. Foreign Minister Jean-Marie Vianney Ndagijimana, in an interview he gave to a French magazine after defecting[36], listed as one of his complaints against the new regime the fact that as a 'party' minister he was constantly by-passed by more powerfully connected RPF colleagues. This was not a Tutsi/ Hutu divide, since he mentioned as his 'competitors' both Seth Sendashonga, the Hutu Minister of the Interior as well as Aloysia Inyumba the Tutsi Minister for Social and Women Affairs. But the impression was that a RPF minister was twice the minister his MDR or PSD colleague was. This state of affairs eventually led to the publication by the MDR on 25 November of an interesting working paper devoted to the constructive criticism of the political evolution in Rwanda since 19 July[37]. It is worth examining in detail because we find here a discussion of all the various problems faced by the new government.

The first MDR complaint concerned the fact that what the document called *La Loi Fondamentale* (Fundamental Law), that is the July 1991 constitution supplemented and amended by the August 1993 Arusha agreements[38], had been violated because the transitional period which was to have lasted twenty-two

36. *Jeune Afrique* (24–30 November 1994). Ndagijimana was a determinedly careerist diplomat. A mild MRND supporter who had been posted as ambassador to Paris, he switched sides soon after the death of President Habyarimana. He managed to impose himself on Prime Minister Twagiramungu as future Foreign Minister all the more easily since the only other logical candidate was Anastase Gasana (who replaced Ndagijimana on 24 November 1994), a political rival of the Premier. Ndagijimana then joined the Premier's party, but was soon disappointed by his experience as a born-again MDR minister, and defected while on his way to the UN Assembly in New York, having made sure he had enough government money to cushion his exile. But he is an intelligent man and his criticism of the new Kigali government is far from being unfounded.

37. Mouvement Démocratique Républicain, *Position du Parti MDR sur les grands problèmes actuels du Rwanda*, Kigali: MDR, November 1994.

38. Technically one should refer to them, as here, in the plural. As we saw in previous chapters, the Arusha negotiations were a long drawn-out process, lasting a year, and several different agreements (on army integration, on the status of refugees, on the duration of the transitional period) were signed along the way. It was only the formal crowning of the whole process which took place on 3 August 1993.

months had been pushed unilaterally by the RPF to five years. This was of course both true and disingenuous. Given the state of the country, twenty-two months were a very short time to organise any sort of election. But for the MDR, which was almost sure to win any election and dreamed of power acquired in this fashion, with all the necessary trappings of democracy opening a royal road to the World Bank vaults, five years was a very frustrating delay. Worse, it could be the prelude to a definitive confiscation of power by the RPF. For if there were a few Hutu in the Front, this was mainly due to the war, when men like Pasteur Bizimungu or Seth Sendashonga had made their choice, thinking (rightly) that armed struggle was the only way to remove the Habyarimana dictatorship. But now, after victory, ethnic politics were bound to reassert themselves, whether one wanted them to do so or not. Idealistic Tutsi moderates on the Kagame political line – who were mostly 'Ugandans' like Frank Mugambage or Patrick Mazimpaka – hoped for a Rwandese society where they could practise the Ugandan type 'no-party democracy'[39]. But this of course was an ambiguous recipe which on the one hand was sincerely trying to avoid the pitfalls of ethnicity and which on the other hand could also become a convenient disguise for Tutsi domination. The difference was that in Uganda there were thirty-two main tribes and not two, and that Museveni's balancing act was possible only because he played a masterly and complex game between all of them. The binary logic of Rwandese politics allowed no such refinements, and non-ethnic politics still belonged in the domain of pious wishes.

The RPF could not win elections as a political party because, even with some Hutu in its ranks and with moderate Tutsi at its head, it was going to be perceived as Tutsi Power. This was the experience President Buyoya of Burundi had painfully learned

39. See Nelson Kasfir, 'The Ugandan elections of 1989', pp. 247–78, and Apolo Nsibambi, 'Resistance councils and committees: the case of Makerere', pp. 279–96, both in H.B. Hansen and M. Twaddle (eds), *Changing Uganda*, London: James Currey, 1991. Also Gérard Prunier, 'La recherche de la normalisation', pp. 131–58, and Per Tidemand, 'Le système des Conseils de Résistance', pp. 193–208, both in G. Prunier and B. Calas (eds), *L'Ouganda Contemporain*, Paris: Karthala, 1994.

in April 1993 when all this goodwill and honesty failed to save him from defeat at the polls. So the MDR wanted elections for exactly the same reason as the RPF did not want them.

The next five points of the MDR document all also had to do with the problems posed by the duality of power between RPF and cabinet:

– There was a confusion of powers between the executive, the legislative and the judiciary (p. 3).

– The process of integrating the 1,000 or so former FAR officers and soldiers who had joined the RPA was too slow. And the document added on page 16: 'We must create a really national army, that is an army which will reflect all the components of Rwandese society.' For this read 'We want more Hutu in the RPA', something the Tutsi RPA officers were bound to view with extreme caution.

– It is necessary to clarify the juridical status of the RPF (p. 7) an obvious point, but which was akin to asking the protean RPF 'military-front-social-movement-political-party' to become a political party like any other. Or rather unlike any other. It would become *the* Tutsi political party. With the RPF turned into a party, how many Tutsi would there be in the MDR, the PSD or even the PL? And how many Hutu would the RPF retain?

– The document underlined the fact that there was no security, no due process of law and that there were many arbitrary detentions in military camps (p. 7), a point which came as a complement to the first above, adding on page 18: 'To restart agriculture, we must eliminate insecurity which prevents the peasants from cultivating their fields because they cannot be sure that they will still be alive a few days from now.'

– And finally there was a denunciation of the widespread property grabbing by the former refugees now coming back from Uganda and Burundi (pp. 7 and 22), the implicit criticism being that the RPF turned a blind eye on such acts or even connived with the voracious refugees.

Over the other points raised there was much greater consensus: establishment of some sort of a jurisdiction of exception to judge the perpetrators of the genocide and the creation of an international commission of inquiry in order to counter the fallacious idea of the 'double genocide' (p. 16).

This document should be read at two levels. First, it is documentary evidence of a number of the main political and social problems existing at this particular time in Rwanda. From that point of view it is extremely interesting. The document should also be analysed both as a political broadside aimed at the RPF as an over-powerful partner in a coalition government and as a political tract aimed at putting down other coalition rivals such as the PSD by demonstrating to Hutu opinion that even if Faustin Twagiramungu was Premier, he was no stooge of the RPF. But the document also had something of a 'holier-than-thou' quality. For example, on the question of arbitrary detentions, the MDR was very vocal about those of the judges Josephine Mukanyangezi and Claude Gatera[40], the journalist Dominique Makeri and the former vice-governor of the National Bank of Rwanda, Pierre Rwakayigamba. But it was less vocal about the detention of Sylvestre Kamali, a direct political adversary of Faustin Twagiramungu, who had probably been detained on the Prime Minister's orders[41].

But if there was one point on which the 'civilian' cabinet and

40. Although not charged with anything, the detained judges were usually arrested for being 'too soft' on Hutu detainees. Most of the time they simply did their job of releasing from custody prisoners whose file was empty. But the army does not see it that way, and for the soldiers a denunciation is often a presumption of guilt.

41. Kamali was a leader of the 'Power' fraction of MDR in 1993–4, but he distanced himself from his fellow 'Power' members and does not seem to have supported the genocide. This is why he came back to Kigali of his own free will instead of going to Goma. He was arrested soon afterwards. Of course, he could become another Gapyisi and, with a subtle form of moderate racist appeal which could be quite popular with the Hutu electorate, have stolen the MDR from under Twagiramungu. One should not forget that before the explosion Twagiramungu had lost control of his party and the 'Power' fraction held the majority. In any case, the problem of detentions was a nightmare because, as one minister said, 'given the intertwining of matrimonial and family relationships, many of us in the government, even the Tutsi, have relations who are guilty of having taken part in the genocide.' (Interview with Patrick Mazimpaka, Kigali 17 January 1995.) Shortly after this, two of the Hutu cabinet ministers were discovered concealing in their houses relations who had played a major part in the genocide.

its RPF colleagues were generally agreed, it was 'broadening the government's base' or the so-called 'Third Force'. This was a particularly sore point because it was directly linked to the resumption of international economic aid. Foreign countries persistently asked the new Kigali regime to open itself up and 'broaden' its political base. What did this mean?

With several countries such as the United States or Germany which were not very conversant with Rwandese politics, it was a simple misperception of reality. They thought that, as in a Western country, there were 'moderates' – 'middle of the roaders' who could be included in the cabinet. They did not realise that almost all the Hutu moderates who had not been killed were already in the government. The few who were not there, like the former Defence Minister James Gasana or the former Prime Minister Sylvestre Nsanzimana, had not come because they were waiting to make sure that the situation was indeed stable and because they still wanted to keep some lines open on the old MRND side.

But where some countries like Belgium and especially France (whose position we discuss more fully in the next section) were concerned, there was no innocent mistake. The pressure to force the new government to include some of the former MRND/CDR contaminated politicians, something it had absolutely decided not to do, was quite deliberate. As the Prime Minister said, 'Negotiations . . . sound like a mockery. They are mocking people when they say we must negotiate with the killers. This is tantamount to saying: well, Africans kill each other all the time. They can negotiate and we will see.'[42] The favourite candidate of the French was the former Prime Minister Dismas Nsengiyaremye, a former 'liberal' opponent who had turned to flirting with President Habyarimana and later with 'Hutu Power' once he had realised that the premiership was escaping him and that Twagiramungu was the one whom the Arusha agreement would put in the chair. Nsengiyaremye had floated down to Gitarama, seen that the interim government did not

42. SWB/Radio Rwanda, 15 September 1994.

have much chance of survival, and then gone straight to Kinshasa, avoiding the Goma trap. He now claimed a new political virginity in spite of showing strong signs of having remained on the 'Power' side of the political divide[43].

Some Belgians were also trying to put pressure on Kigali to 'negotiate', but in Brussels it did not come directly from the government of Premier Jean-Luc Dehaene. Rather it came from some personalities linked to the ultra-conservative wing of the Social Christian Party like former Minister Rita De Bakker and Senator Johan van Erps[44]. The same people were in close and friendly contact with the Goma exiled politicians. Because of French pressure, relayed by some of the Flemish Christian NGOs and the Christian Democratic International (CDI) lobby[45], most of the main aid donors kept insisting on the question of 'negotiation' as a prerequisite to any resumption of aid, while the country was choking under its debris. The problem was that there was really nothing to negotiate and nobody to negotiate it with, apart from a group of unrepentant mass murderers, trying to parley their strong-arm control over a primitive peasant mass into a number of cabinet seats and a share in the army.

43. On 5 November 1994, he created in Paris a new political party, the Union Démocratique Rwandaise (UDR) whose 11-page Manifesto still had a strong 'Hutu Power' odour. He nevertheless said to people he met in Paris that he still considered himself a member of the MDR.

44. See Colette Braeckman, 'La lutte politique se poursuit', *Le Soir* (19 September 1994) and 'Rwanda: European Pressure', *Africa Confidential* (November 1994).

45. The CDI, as a good relay of the Catholic church, had always been very close to the Habyarimana regime. But by the fall of 1994 the church was doing some soul-searching and could write: 'The Catholic church has been in the service of General Habyarimana's power. This is the accusation one constantly hears against the Rwandese church. And it is unfortunately true!' (*Lettre des Missionaires d'Afrique*, 12 September 1994). The CDI had no such qualms and kept discreetly backing the MRND remnants of the old regime. As for the flemish NGOs, theirs was a peculiar situation, because, in Belgian tribal terms, the Flemish had always tended to identify more with the Hutu and the Walloons with the Tutsi. This was reinforced by the atmosphere of 'Christian virtue' surrounding the Hutu Republic which we have described in Chapter 2. The Hague conference in mid-September 1994, which was supposed to be convened for the purpose of helping Rwanda, had been an educational experience in watching some viscerally anti-Tutsi Belgian Christians at work.

The attitude of the international community

Soon after the creation of the new government, some foreign countries started to reopen their embassies. By early August Germany, Belgium and the United States had all reopened theirs. France was sulking and only sent Jacques Courbin to man a 'diplomatic cell' in Kigali[46]. But these diplomatic missions had very little to manage. Aid, the main problem of the fledgeling new regime, was blocked – not only that, it was also allotted, prepared, wrapped up and then dangled in front of the eyes of the new government, but not handed over. The same political conditions of 'negotiations' and 'broadening the base' were ritually repeated, and of course 'technical reasons' were given, such as, in the case of the World Bank which had $140 million earmarked for Rwanda, the need to repay $4.5 million in arrears before the new credit could be unblocked. While the technical arguments were true – the World Bank's statutes do not allow it to open a new line of credit if reimbursements have not been made – it was odd that while governments could find vast sums for other much more mundane purposes – e.g over $1,400 million for 'humanitarian' aid going to the supporters of the former regime and the remnants of their army, nobody could find $4.5 million to prime the financial pump in Rwanda where 5 million people were trying to come out of their nightmare. In the same vein, the European Union had some special credits for nearly $200 million, but the French veto prevented any unblocking till 25 November when part of it could be released. And none of the 'regular' Lome IV funds set aside for the old Rwandese regime could be touched. As *The Economist* wrote 'European aid ministers . . . would be less than honest if they continue to make their aid conditional upon the resolution of problems that aid itself could help resolve.'[47] Or, as Interior

---

46. Courbin had a reputation as being a heavy-duty diplomat, having served in Senegal during the Mauritania crisis and then spent two years in Beirut. His appointment was in itself a sign of how Paris viewed the situation in Rwanda. He was accredited as full ambassador in January 1995.

47. 'Abandoned Rwanda', *The Economist* (26 November 1994).

Minister Seth Sendashonga said to a French journalist, 'We are refused both political confidence and material means, and at the time we are being asked to straighten out right away a situation of massive disaster.'[48] This situation could in fact be largely attributed to the French. Many people in Paris felt that they had been 'defeated by the Anglo-Saxons'[49]. The 'Fashoda syndrome' was operating with maximum force. At the September conference in The Hague the French ambassador stood up and left the room when Rwandese President Pasteur Bizimungu gave his speech[50]. And when Paris convened the eighteenth Franco-African summit in Biarritz on 8–9 November, Rwanda was deliberately not invited.

The problem is that thinking on the question in France was polluted by a number of things. First, it had always been completely unrepentant and remained so. The authorities accepted no responsibility in anything; what they had done was always faultless. From that point of view former Minister for Cooperation Michel Roussin, the 'Africa man' of the French cabinet, was remarkable. When asked on French radio[51] in late May what France was doing for Rwanda, where it had had such an involvement before the massacres, he answered without batting an eyelid that 'there is a huge camp which has been visited by my colleague Douste-Blazy.'[52] He then denied that France had abandoned any of the personnel at its embassy to the killer squads at the gates. When the interviewer asked him what he thought of the RPF, he started to shout:

---

48. Patrick de Saint-Exupery, 'Loin de Biarritz – le Rwanda', *Le Figaro* (8 November 1994).

49. In early July, after Kigali had 'fallen to the RPF', this author overheard a French senior officer moan, 'The worst is yet to come. Those bastards will go all the way to Kinshasa now. And how in God's name am I going to explain to our friends [the francophone African heads of state] that we have let down one of our own?'

50. *Billets d'Afrique* no. 15 (October 1994).

51. SWB/Radio France Internationale (30 May 1994).

52. The Secretary of State for Health, a decent but politically lightweight member of the cabinet.

'What are you interested in? What are you interested in, madame? Is it the fate of these people horrific pictures of whom we see every day, or is it a political analysis which is no longer topical?

Questions concerning French instructors in the FAR drove him to incoherence:

'No, first of all the figure is wrong, it is – the figure is totally wrong, and, and also [pauses] I do not . . . Even if it were seventy instructors, it is not these people who started [pauses] the slaughter we have been witnessing . . . [pauses] We have not, we have cooperation . . . [pauses] It was very limited because as soon as the *Noroit* operation was dismantled and UNAMIR took over from it we no longer had any role apart from traditional cooperation. Therefore I believe that again these are more groundless accusations.'

He was later to deny again any involvement of French military personnel in the training of militias in the same unconvincing way: 'Me! Accuse me of having got people to train death squads! Let's be serious! *In all these crises, some people always find an excuse to attack France.*'[53]

The second point about French thinking about Rwanda is that once it stops being both self-pitying and self-righteous and finally tries to go beyond the 'Anglo-Saxon plot to humiliate France', the result is often extremely mechanical. As a colonial power, France formerly had an excellent reserve of *officiers des affaires indigènes* and competent colonial civil servants, and a remarkable school to teach them about the realities of empire, the Ecole de la France d'Outre-Mer. Those men knew their jobs, and they knew Africa. They are now dead or in retirement. The result is analysis of the type represented by France's Foreign Affairs

53. *Le Monde* (16 July 1994). The last sentence of this rather disconnected self-defence is interesting because it is typical of a certain type of French thinking. First the Minister considers that he embodies 'France' because he is a minister, and secondly, he feels, probably honestly, that any criticism of his government's policies is an attack by 'some people' (probably not French, or not *really* French) on France itself. This is in a direct line of thought from Louis XIV to François Mitterrand, through Napoleon I and Charles de Gaulle. Of course, at lower administrative levels small policy choices are routinely tacked on to the justifying *grandeur* of such models.

Minister of the Rwandese obligation to 'negotiate' before any economic aid is unblocked:

> What is the Rwandese nation? It is made of two ethnic groups, Hutu and Tutsi. Peace cannot return to Rwanda if these two ethnic groups refuse to work and govern together. [. . .] This is the solution France, with a few others, is courageously trying to foster.[54]

One tends to pity the *'few others'* who have been welcomed on board this *Titanic* of a policy.

Prime Minister Twagiramungu has humbly asked France to 'forget the past'[55] and it has already done so completely. In the opening speech at the Franco-African summit conference in Biarritz[56], President Mitterrand could say without embarrassment when talking about Rwanda: 'One cannot ask the impossible from France, which is so alone, when local chiefs decide to . . . settle their quarrels with bayonets and machetes. After all, it is their own country.' One wonders why France should have become involved in the whole mess in the first place if 'after all, it is their country'. But worse was yet to come. When President Mitterrand was asked by a journalist about the genocide, he answered: 'The genocide or the genocides? I don't know what one should say!'

This public accolade for the so-called 'theory of the double genocide' was an absolute shame. The 'double genocide gambit' is a well-known piece of historical sophistry, that has been used before by revisionist historians of the genocide of the Jews during the Second World War, who explain that the genocide was 'a war between the Germans and the Jews and the Germans had to defend themselves'. Then, when the person who disagrees mentions the great number of Jewish casualties, the revisionist historian counters with the bombing of Dresden and the slaughter of the German army on the Eastern Front. In the Rwandese case, the arguments follow the same line. The Tutsi

54. SWB/France 2 TV channel (20 November 1994).
55. SWB/Radio France Internationale, 2 December 1994.
56. *Le Monde* (10 November 1994).

were killed by the Hutu in a defensive war, and anyway they themselves were killed in equal numbers. The last point tries to make the four years of civil war, the Goma cholera epidemic and the confused revenge killings since July 1994 cohere into an intellectual and emotional pattern meant to catch simple minds. To find President Mitterrand, an elder statesman, a man of taste, a literary author and formerly not without dignity, not embarrassed to be caught passing off such counterfeit intellectual and moral merchandise is another sad confirmation of the validity of de Gaulle's saying that 'getting old is a form of human shipwreck'.

But what was worse than President Mitterrand's personally dubious moral positions and the accompanying intellectual black holes of official French thinking on the Rwanda question was that political conclusions kept being drawn from them. After playing an important part in one of the worst genocides of the twentieth century, French authorities persisted, because they were angry at their 'defeat', in taking up murderous positions. Thus the new French Minister for Cooperation, Bernard Debré, could say at the end of the year:

> 'The Kigali government is an anglophone Tutsi government coming from Uganda. . . . I am only asking them to make one step towards democracy, to create a healthy judicial system and to set a date for the elections. As for the refugees, they must go home to their houses and their fields. This is what I told the Minister for Health.'[57]

Hey presto, the French magic wand had solved all the problems! It would have been funny if in the mean time half-starving orphans had not kept playing with leg bones for sticks and skulls for balls, if the refugee camps had not turned into social bombs whose fuses were likely to be lit by desperate men whom France

---

57. *Le Monde* (29 December 1994). Minister Debré had derived his nuanced and extensive knowledge of the situation in Rwanda (where he had never been) from half an hour's conversation with the Rwandese Health Minister Joseph Karamira who had come to Paris for a conference on AIDS. Unfortunately Karamira, who was raised in Uganda, is one of the three cabinet ministers (out of twenty-one) who cannot speak French.

kept helping, and if a new and very imperfect regime which was making a modest attempt at improvement had not been systematically starved, as if to see how soon it would break into another bout of homicidal madness. If this happened, one could after all feel justified – these people were all savages, and this new bunch were no better than the ones we had supported earlier.

Strangely, this mixture of *realpolitik*, humanitarian self-satisfaction, half-baked ideology, stale imperialism and economic blackmail which made up the attitude of the international community towards Rwanda, ended up by becoming focused on the question of an international tribunal to be set up for judging the organisers and the perpetrators of the genocide. The UN had published a series of reports[58] giving a seal of official authentication for whomever might still have had any doubts. For the Rwandese survivors of the genocide it was the beginning of vindication. The next step had to be some kind of a solemn ceremonial rendering of justice. Many Europeans do not seem to understand that this is an absolute emotional, social and even political necessity.

First there is a very basic and burning desire for vengeance which was well expressed by a woman who survived the Saint-Famille church hell:

'I don't want to lie. . . . I expect vengeance. I want revenge. I am hurting so much inside. And do you think it is going to stop because we are safe now? So much death, so much grief, so many families wiped out, and we are to forget about it. The fire is out, at least here in Kabuga; but not the fear. And what about the fire inside?'[59]

Then there is the question of the country's future social cohesion. All the various segments of the population need the ritual cleansing of a mass public trial. First of all, there are the

58. The two reports by René Dégni-Ségui, one on the genocide (June 1994) and the other on the situation in Rwanda since the new government took power (November 1994), were both well informed and objective. Then there was also the Resolution 935 Report by Atsu Koffi Amega, Mme Haby Dieng and Salifou Fomba which also dealt with the genocide (November 1994). Though somewhat plodding and uninspired, it was factually correct.

59. African Rights, *Rwanda: Death*, op. cit., p. 735.

survivors. Since it would be mad to add a second genocide to the first, it is out of the question to kill all the killers[60]. But the desire for vengeance can be assuaged if the real organisers, the 'big people', go to the gallows. Then there are the people who did nothing, who were passive accomplices but did not kill – that is, the vast majority of the Hutu peasants. They are now restless and afraid, because the rumours of judgement combined with no clarity about its nature make them afraid that they will not be capable of proving their innocence. The abuses of 'justice' in the present state of disarray, the arbitrary detentions, the arbitrary killings, all make them fear the worst, that is a revenge genocide directed this time at *them*. Then we have the 'innocent killers', those people who were led into killing because of their passivity, of their typically Rwandese respect for authority, but an authority which had gone mad. They now realise that they were duped, and that as the privates in the army of crime they are those most likely to pay. Some who were in jail in Kibungo told a French TV team: 'We are being treated as scapegoats. The people who gave the orders, the bigwigs, they have gone abroad. They will not face trial.'[61]

To understand their guilt and its limits, to understand the monstrous nature of what they were led to do, they need to see their once respected leaders in the dock. As for the 'returnees', the former refugees now coming back from Uganda or Burundi, they must see that justice is being done, through public authority, and not by the lynch law now being practised. For the army too, this is the only way to stop it taking the law into its own clumsy hands. And as for the refugees abroad, the news that the 'big people' are having to pay their debt to society is the only thing that will make them believe that they, the 'small people', will not be in danger if they go back. Finally there is the political dimension. As General Kagame said, 'There can be

---

60. It is of course impossible to know their number. But if we take the not altogether unreasonable average of 8–10 victims per killer, we are faced between 80,000 and 100,000 murderers.
61. SWB/France 2 TV channel, 18 August 1994.

no durable reconciliation as long as those who are responsible for the massacres in Rwanda are not properly tried.'[62] Forgiveness can come *after* retribution and justice and not before, unless one is dealing with angels and not human beings.

The attitude of the international community in the face of this problem has so far been absolutely disastrous. On 2 August 1994, José Ayala Lasso, UN Human Rights commissioner, asked for 147 observers to monitor past and present abuses of human rights in Rwanda. He intended to deploy them by late September, at the cost of about $2.1 million, and received pledges for $2.4 million.[63] By early September there was *one* observer, Karen Kelly, and she had no budget, no car and no local staff. The disbursements received by the commissioner amounted to a grand total of $420,000[64]. Ayalo Lasso, who had meanwhile realised the almost total disappearance of the judicial system in Rwanda[65], returned to the subject and asked this time for $10.5 million, in order to be able to supply ten prosecutors, nine doctors and twenty lawyers over and above the 147 observers, and provide all these people with minimum supplies and logistics. Still the money did not arrive. By mid-November, there were *four* observers, without any means and Karen Kelly resigned in disgust[66]. Slowly, more observers came, but they were mostly inexperienced young people who often spoke no French, and of course no Swahili or

---

62. In a speech made in New York during his visit there in December 1994 (*Africa News Report*, 19 December 1994).
63. Including $233,000 from France.
64. $380,000 from the United Kingdom and $40,000 from New Zealand. Human rights in Rwanda are indeed an Anglo-Saxon plot.
65. Minister of Justice Alphonse-Marie Nkubito had no car. There were no prison vehicles. There was hardly any food for the prisoners, and Kigali prison, built for 1,500 inmates, was holding over 5,000. There were five judges, all without vehicles or proper offices (the Goma ruffians had seven judges!), and the minister was struggling to try to free several others illegally detained by the army. There were almost no police, and those few had no guns. People were detained almost anywhere, and several prisoners died while locked up in a metallic shipping container which got overheated in the sun.
66. SWB/Radio France Internationale, 11 November 1994.

Kinyarwanda[67]. Since the French government's paranoia over a massive anglophone invasion was a fantasy, they were mostly unable to communicate with the population except through interpreters who told them what they felt like telling them. The whole thing was a disaster, especially since 'According to the 1948 convention on the repression of genocide, it is not enough for prosecutors to offer the evidence of mass killings to secure a conviction: they must also prove genocidal intent.'[68]

On 8 November 1994, UN Resolution no. 955 went ahead and created an international tribunal anyway. One can only wish good luck to the South African judge, Richard Goldstone, who accepted the gigantic task of trying to make something out of nothing. It is easy to imagine the most likely outcome of this disastrous exercise, if it ever takes place: poorly prepared and endless court sessions in Arusha, with former ministers of the Habyrimana regime turning the trial into a political tribune, allegations of 'double genocide'; inconclusive evidence, long speeches on the inherently democratic nature of 'Hutu Power' since the Hutu make up 85% of the population; Belgian NGO Rwanda 'experts', with warm support from the French, testifying to the fundamental good sense of this line of argument.

At this point, before we attempt any more global overview of the Rwanda crisis, a fitting conclusion to this section on justice and the role of the international community would seem to be the following extract from a text by Colette Braeckman, a Belgian journalist with whom this author has several differences of opinion on many points concerning the recent events in Rwanda, but which he finds perfectly fitting for the present:

---

67. In Kibuye, this author found a Human Rights Observer Station manned by five people, none of whom spoke any French. They said that a Togolese had been assigned to their team; but 'he had gone on leave'. In Kigali several UN volunteers had resigned in disgust at the ineptitude of the way the whole operation was run. For an unsparing assessment of this dismal performance, see African Rights, *Rwanda: A waste of hope*, London: UN Human Rights Field Operation (March 1995).

68. Andrew Jay Cohen, 'On the trail of the genocide', *New York Times* (7 September 1994).

The people who organised the crime and their allies . . . have worked hard to blur analysis and reflexion. Thus, the war launched by the RPF in 1990 has been described as the root cause of all the violence. After the destruction of the President's plane . . . the extermination of part of the population and the war which the RPF had restarted . . . were put on the same footing. Today revisionism is getting worse than ever . . . and humanitarian action is being asked to help confuse everything. [...] Such an enterprise of deliberate disinformation ends up by minimising the genocide, making it appear ordinary and . . . giving the leaders of the old regime a sort of monopoly of representation of the Hutu masses. [...] These gaps in information, this systematic twisting of interpretations are not the product of chance or incompetence, but a deliberate enterprise to undermine the new authorities because those who have helped the hangmen of yesterday know that any sort of fair trial would end up exposing them. [...] This sabotage is designed to pave the way back to power not for those who have been directly responsible for the genocide, but for those who, by claiming legitimacy in the direct path of the old 'Hutu Power' system, remain in the former logic of intolerance and exclusion.[69]

Towards a provisional conclusion

It is of course extremely difficult to conclude on a matter which is still evolving and changing. The writers who address the more distant historical past have the advantage that, while they may err in their appreciations, they should normally not be wrong about their facts. Yet the historian of the more recent past is not entirely without advantages. As the past slowly solidifies into history under his eyes, he can see the parts which are fairly settled, to be assessed rather than questioned; he can distinguish the soft uncertainties of some segments of the present and can also tell roughly at what point the two articulate. If he can be accused of being influenced by the emotions of the moment, he also enjoys a freshness of view which those who have not been fated to live through the events will not have in the future.

69. Colette Braeckman, 'Rwanda: le temps du révisionnisme', *Esprit* (December 1994).

With the Rwandese genocide, its causes and its probable consequences, one is struck by a feeling of predictability, a social equivalent of the psychological mechanisms of Greek tragedy. Of course, hindsight encourages such a perspective. Yet Rwanda had indeed been a time-bomb waiting for the right moment to be detonated. There are probably few instances, in Africa or elsewhere, of a country which became the subject of myth to the extent that Rwanda was in the late nineteenth and early twentieth centuries. To be fair, one must realise that this was the period of what Eric Hobsbawm has called 'the mass production of traditions'[70]. At that time Europe produced 'traditions' as massively as Renaissance Italy produced pictures – and as indiscriminately. The local causes varied, but they were all rooted in a sense of loss, of change, which left the inheritors of the industrial revolution and of the French political revolution with a longing for stability, for solidity. Adolf Hitler, in his craving for a new Thousand-Year Reich, was a perfect son of the period. To this mild form of cultural neurosis Rwanda gave an open field. It was small, its historical traditions were largely blank, its society was incredibly complex yet it could be read fairly easily though an ideological prism. And the nature of the ideological vision which could be projected on Rwanda was in perfect coherence with the generally accepted prejudices of the time. The tall Tutsi invaders, 'Europeans under a black skin', were a confirmation of everything the turn of the century liked to believe: the inequality of 'races', their quasi-Linnaean ranking and ordering, cultural diffusionism and the biological basis of social phenomena. At the same time, this was agreeably efficient in terms of colonial administration because the beneficiaries of the 'scientific theory' of the superior race were quite pleased with the white man's approach, which they could use to pursue their own aims: consolidation of the monarchy over previously loosely-controlled areas, centralisation and almost absolute social control over the Hutu. Through the re-invention

---

70. In the brilliant volume he and Terence Ranger edited: *The invention of tradition*, Cambridge University Press, 1983. For Africa see Chapter 6 by Terence Ranger.

of tradition, what was in fact taking place was a conservative revolution of which the Tutsi were the beneficiaries. In unequal parts of course since it was the high lineage Tutsi who were creaming off most of the advantages. But since the ideology was based on a racial construct, the beneficiaries were reputed to be *all* the Tutsi without distinction, from the *Mubega* chief with 2,000 cows to his small *umugaragu* who cultivated the land alongside his Hutu brethen.

The transformation of the various forms of social contracts linking economic and personal dependence played an important role. Their hardening from forms of complex social interaction to the simplifications of quasi-rural proletarian relations were a product of the need for a 'respect of the African tradition', as seen by the colonial eye. This does not mean that the Tutsi and Hutu categories were invented by the Belgians; these were integral to Banyarwanda society. What the Belgians did invent were forms under which they were supposed to relate to each other in order to fit in with the ideological fantasies and practical needs of the European.

The problem with myths is that once created, they have a tendency to live a life of their own, as Mary Shelley's *Frankenstein* poetically demonstrates. In Rwanda, by 1940, the myth had become reality. Tutsi and Hutu conformed to the images which had forcefully been projected upon them. They behaved according to their 'traditional' patterns, obeyed their 'ancestral customs' and probably felt the feelings appropriate to their positions in life. Tutsi even those who wore rags – had become haughty lords – and the Hutu mass felt – and was – oppressed. This is why, although the 1959 revolution was a fake, it was nevertheless a fake based on truth. The feelings, the revolutionary hope for a better life, the willingness of the masses to organise were all present. But there were two basic contradictions: on the one hand, this was a racist revolution where the aristocratic oppressors were seen as race rather than class. This had several very unrevolutionary consequences. First, social and economic relations were viewed in a static, mechanical way, once the tall, thin bad guys were eliminated, everything would be all right. This precluded any analysis of the post-revolutionary intra-Hutu social, economic or political dynamics. Secondly, all Tutsi were pictured as oppressors, something obviously false. Thirdly, all Hutu were pictured as 'liberators', a ludicrous view in the perspective of later developments and finally the racist ideology which had dominated the previous oppressive society was not destroyed, but merely turned on its head, so that it now became virtuous to oppress the former oppressors. The damage done to the souls of both was particularly disastrous in the long run.

Then the second set of contradictions in the 'revolution' of 1959 has to do with its sponsors. Usually revolutions, however violent and barbaric they may be, have a soul-cleansing effect, a psycho-therapeutic value. The old values are upset, society – at least during the enthusiastic initial stages – breathes an air of new-found freedom, and the very concept of authority, even of revolutionary authority, is questioned. If things are pushed too far, anarchy threatens. But nothing of the sort happened in this case. The White Fathers told the 'revolutionaries' what to do, they set the starting date and blew the whistle to get everybody back inside when the game was over. A revolution executed under the direction of a colonial army colonel, with the support of colonial troops and the blessing of an all-powerful Catholic church, which comes out of the 'revolution' even more powerful and Constantinian than before is a strange one indeed.

What we had here was not the violent but healthy atmosphere of revolutionary freedom, but the scapegoating of a minority by a social system which had decided hypocritically to eliminate its old accomplices who were no longer in tune with the times. Once the obsolete 'oppressors' were liquidated, new ones were immediately put in place, without leaving the oppressed much time to breathe. And the new boys were in fact of a much better model than the previous ones. First of all, they had been oppressed for a long time, and the white man, in his goodness and wisdom, had 'liberated' them. They were therefore more likely to remain polite and properly subservient than the old aristocratic bunch who were often insolent and thought them-

selves as good as, if not better than, the white man. Now the
church, the Europeans and the new native masters had no more
to fear. The 'revolution' had been carefully stage-managed, the
former victims had all been told that they were now free
by decree, and a perfect 'democracy' reigned, since the *rubanda
nyamwinshi* (the 'majority people') were now supposed to be
'in power'.

One is struck when reading about Rwanda in the 1960s and
1970s[71] about how dull and stunted the place seems to have
been. The amount of repression, including sexual repression
under church supervision, was enormous. This point played an
important and underestimated role later. The genocide was like
an explosion taking place in a very small, overcrowded room.
In a perverse and sick way it was, at least in part, the real revolution of which the people had been deprived in 1959, with all its
wild unleashing of energy and upsetting of social conventions[72].

The Habyarimana regime was better than the Kayibanda one;
it was a more refined version of the same basic design. General
Habyarimana was neat, he ran a tight ship, he killed very selectively and with almost total discretion, corruption was minimal
and it could be considered by the foreign aid donors as a form
of taxation. Rwanda was the darling of foreigners. The blacks
were polite and everything was clean. Unsurprisingly, Rwanda's
main foreign backers tended to be in northern Europe. Italian
aid was everywhere, from next door in corrupt, anarchic Uganda
to distant warn-torn Somalia and Mozambique, but Rome,
Christian Democrat or not, was never much interested in the
hard-working peasants who did not offer generous kickback
systems to the 'donor'. Switzerland, on the other hand, had
made Rwanda the main recipient of its governmental foreign aid.

71. The author has no direct knowledge of this period, never having been to Rwanda
    till the 1990s. But some 'old Rwanda hands' can recount vividly what it was
    like to live in the virtuous and well-ordered *rubanda nyamwinshi* frugal democracy.
72. But even there it remained very Rwandese, very 'Swiss' (Rwanda was nicknamed
    'the African Switzerland'). Anarchy, rape, arson and murder were all carried out
    according to plan and under the supervision of authority. People were throwing
    repression to the winds; yet at the same time even the Apocalypse had to be in
    accordance with official guidelines.

A little bit less airtight than under Kayibanda, Rwanda was still virtuous, Christian, respectable and boring[73].

The whole system went wrong for reasons which at first were economic and then turned politico-cultural. Rwanda's slide from relative heaven to absolute hell is a perfect textbook illustration of the theory of dependence. The Third World in general, and Africa in particular, might have been in the past victims of what Pierre Jalée and Samir Amin called 'looting'. But this is definitely no longer the case. In Africa today it is infinitely more profitable for Europeans to loot the UN or bilateral aid than an African peasantry that owns little that can be looted anyway. But far from making the situation any better, it makes it worse. Because there is nothing of interest left to loot in Africa except aid contracts, Europeans have lost interest in the intrinsic workings of the African economies[74]. They have been left to stagnate in a kind of post-colonial aftermath, producing increasingly useless products which compete savagely on the world markets with the same commodities turned out more efficiently in Asia. In the case of Rwanda, the free fall of world coffee prices in the late 1980s corresponded with the political disintegration of the regime. The murder of Colonel Mayuya can even be said to mark a sort of official beginning. The élite of the *rubanda nyamwinshi* had been kept reasonably satisfied with the proceeds of coffee, foreign aid, tin and tea, roughly in that order. By 1989 coffee and tin prices were both near to total collapse, and foreign aid was shrinking. The élite started tearing each other apart to get at the shrinking spoils, *Abakiga* against *Abanyanduga*, then among the victorious northerners *Abashiru* against *Abagoyi*, and within the top *Abashiru* people between the various affinity groups or families. Mme Habyarimana, nicknamed 'Kanjogera' in memory of the murderous nineteenth-century *Nyina Yuhi*, emerged at the

---

73. Which is the basic reason this author could not get interested in it and much preferred the Ugandan circus which, in spite of the violence, was alive and vibrant with efforts and potential.

74. Except of course in the case of World Bank experts. But then they are very well provided for financially in order to motivate their interest.

top of the heap as the best player; she was the true mistress of the country, not her big *umugabo* of a husband.

Of course, the atmosphere quickly became suffocating. Corruption had become an open sore in a country co-administered by the Catholic church and priding itself on its virtue. Political murders were taking place with abandon among an élite which had known only one bout of eliminations, after Kayibanda's downfall, and was used to a peaceful life. The small men of *rubanda nyamwinshi*, in whose name all this was being done, started to grumble. And this is where the growing crisis went from the economic to the cultural. The place of the Tutsi exiles in the national consciousness had retained all these years the status of the primeval parricide which Freud places at the root of every society. Everybody knew of it, although it was not much spoken of, but its presence was felt and the shared guilt and satisfaction made up the founding cohesion of the community. It was indeed both a totem and a taboo.

On top of that, the open crisis in the virtue of the state was happening at the worst possible time for an authoritarian system. The Berlin Wall had just been brought down, Ceauşescu had been unceremoniously shot and the best dictatorial system in the world had crumbled within a few months. Marxism-Leninism had been, at the organisational level, the great source of inspiration for conservative African regimes; it offered the language of 'revolution' with the absolute certainty of reactionary power. Now it was all over.

As a result, cracks began to appear in the *rubanda nyamwinshi*. True idealists, frustrated careerists, marginalised members of the élite, ambitious outsiders and plainly bored people who hoped for a more open future all banded together in the first political movements challenging the single party state. For the descendants of the 1960s *Inyenzi*, the occasion was too beautiful to resist. We have seen why and how they regrouped in Uganda for an armed assault on what they saw as a sinking ship, and how they also completely misjudged the mood, mental make-up and fears of their 'fellow countrymen'. Half-genuine 'Ugandans' who thought 'Musevenism' would go beyond ethnic struggles in the way that Marxism had been expected to transcend the class struggles, half-deluded Tutsi who wanted to get back in (and on top), the *inkotanyi* were the cutting tool which ripped the contented hypocritical Rwandese mediocrity to shreds. Even if the internal Hutu opposition was far from welcoming these 'liberators' with open arms, it ended up using them against an increasingly desperate dictatorship which was becoming addicted to ever higher doses of blood to ensure its survival.

We do not need to go into more detail about the role of the French. These hapless foreigners, for their own mythical reasons, contributed to poisoning further an already disastrous situation[75]. But they did not *cause* it, an admission by this author which should cause great satisfaction to Messrs Mitterrand, Roussin, Juppé and Balladur who have been saying nothing else since the beginning of the crisis. It is true that giving brandy bottles to an alcoholic is not the genuine cause of his death. The question is: why did he start drinking in the first place? However, what the French did was terrible mostly because it fitted like the last missing piece in the jigsaw puzzle of the Rwandese political madness. Military and political pressures had combined to bring the Habyarimana regime to repentance. Arusha was an admission of defeat for Mme Habyarimana and her family, but there was one last card to play: blow it all to smithereens. And since at least some of the French had also seen Arusha as a defeat, they would support the cleaning-up. This is of course where an African political élite showed its provincialism. Whether France wanted to support them or not, it could not afford to do so any more in the world political terms. The *akazu* judged the world according to the standards of their provincial dictatorship, but they probably would not have gone off the deep end if they had been sure that total international

---

75. If we count the Belgian infatuation with the Tutsi supermen and their further infatuation with the virtuous little Hutu, this was the *third* occasion when meddling foreigners came to tell the Rwandese how to behave with each other. It was third time unlucky, with even worse results than on the two previous occasions.

isolation would result. Thus France was the unwitting catalyst of ultimate Rwandese descent into the bloodbath.

As for the mechanics of the genocide, we have already described them: unquestioning obedience to authority, fear of the Tutsi devils and the hope of grabbing something for oneself in the general confusion. There is of course one further added cause: overpopulation. This is still a taboo, because human beings are not supposed to be rats in a laboratory cage and Christians, Marxists, Islamic fundamentalists and World Bank experts will all tell you that overpopulation is relative and that God (or modern technology or the *Shari'a*) will provide. But let whoever has not at least once felt murderous in a crowded subway at rush-hour throw the first stone. This author knows of only two cases where overpopulation has been mentioned in straight unabashed fashion as a direct cause of the Rwandese genocide. One came from a geographer Jean-Pierre Raison[76], and the other from Mary Gore, wife of the US Vice-President, who said at the Cairo World Population Conference in September 1994: 'Rwanda is a tragedy and a warning. It is a warning about the way in which extremists can manipulate the fears of a population threatened by it own numbers and by its massive poverty.'[77]

Whatever else they may know, geographers know about land and women know about wombs. Both are to do with nature, which they know cannot be pushed beyond a certain point without kicking back. This has nothing to do with laboratory rats and everything to do with social and psychological repression as an instrument of government. The Rwandese crisis is completely atypical if one compares it with other contemporary African crises. In Liberia and Somalia the state has collapsed; in the Sudan it totters on the brink. And on the reverse side its progressive restructuring in Uganda has been accompanied by a return to civil peace. Here we have the exact opposite. The

---

76. Jean-Pierre Raison, 'Le Rwanda et le Burundi sous pression' in A. Dubresson, J.Y. Marchal and J.-P. Raison (eds), *Les Afriques au Sud du Sahara*, Paris: Belin, 1994, pp. 320–9.
77. *Africa News Report* (12 September 1994).

genocide happened not because the state was weak, but on the contrary because it was so totalitarian and strong that it had the capacity to make its subjects obey absolutely any order, including one of mass slaughter. There remains the question of the psychological mechanism of such a state of affairs. We have already mentioned the weight of history, which is absolutely fundamental. Without the authoritarianism of the Tutsi *abami* of old, modern Kanjogera and her relatives could not have unleashed the tempest. But the traditional psycho-historical implant had been given new life by modern components: the racist ideology of the Europeans turned upside-down and the increasing population pressure. This has to be understood in context: on a certain *umusozi* (hill) in 1990 there were eight times as many people as there had been in 1900. And on top of that, instead of ecstatic possesion by *kubandwa* spirits, one had to make do, where one's religious life was concerned, with virtuous, gloomy Christianity. In such an atmosphere economic frustrations, neighbourhood quarrels, marital problems all became much more difficult than they had been a century before. People were under enormous pressure – pressure to be good, pressure to bear their poverty, pressure to tolerate their neighbours, pressure to witness the bloody political circus and yet keep quiet. Then one day the order was given. It must have been a great moment of psychological release for many of these wretched people. Private frustrations were going to emerge, and the unspoken taboo of the mysterious Tutsi threat would finally be dealt with once and for all. It was literally the Apocalypse, ushering in the relief of the Last Judgement. And this is how over-population, in a certain ideological context, could contribute to the genocide. It is not a dehumanising view but on the contrary a refusal to avert one's eyes from certain segments of human reality because they seem too desperate.

What now? As usual the Europeans have understood nothing. The great needs are justice and cash, *in that order*. As we have seen above, justice requires a minimum of cash and it is the ony way to soothe the survivors, to reassure the innocent and pardon the innocent killers. But justice also means blood. The Europeans are shocked when they hear the Rwandese, and especially the gentle and apolitical Minister of Justice Alphonse-Marie Nkubito, ask for the trials to be held in Rwanda and for the death penalty to be used. But the Rwandese are right. The immensity of the crime cannot be dealt with through moderate versions of European criminal law made for radically different societies. This after all is something Europeans already know: after the Nuremberg trial the condemned were hanged in the name of the millions who had died. This is a political and religious question. To reassure the 'small guys' who used the machete and to assuage the immense pain of their victims' relatives, only the death of the real perpetrators will have sufficient symbolic weight to counterbalance the legacy of suffering and hatred *which will lead to further killings if the abcess is not lanced.* And the abcess has well-known names such as Jerome Bicamumpaka, 'Premier' Jean Kambanda, Colonel Théoneste Bagosora, Frodwald Karamira, General Augustin Bizimungu, Colonel Mpiranya, *bourgmestre* Gatete, 'President' Théodore Sindikubwabo among others: maybe 100 men who have committed not only a crime against humanity but a sin against the Spirit by locking up a whole nation into the airless sadomasochistic inferno. They have to die. This is the only ritual through which the killers can be cleansed of their guilt and the survivors brought back to the community of the living. Then money, the universal lubricant, has to flow. A modicum of economic prosperity will go a long way towards assuaging the pain, especially if the money is used first and foremost with a view to diversifying an agricultural economy which is choking within its own structural limits.

Of course, this author has no serious hope that either justice or money will come, since Rwanda is a small landlocked African nation without any strategic or economic interest. It is also populated with blacks, not much of a saving grace in the white minds of the men of power. If justice and money do not come, then death will return – and will duly be covered by an eager media, for the benefit of a conventionally horrified public opinion which will finance another round of humanitarian aid.

BIBLIOGRAPHY

Note This does not pretend to be an exhaustive bibliography on Rwanda. The works listed here are those which seem to us the most relevant for an in-depth understanding of the problem of the 1994 Rwandese genocide. The best bibliographical guide on Rwanda is M. d'Hertefelt and D. Lame, *Société, culture et histoire du Rwanda. Encyclopédie bibliographique (1863–1980/7)*, Tervuren: MRAC, 2 vols, 1987. Books mentioned in the footnotes but not directly or mainly dealing with Rwanda are not listed here.

Periodicals

Although Rwanda was fairly well covered during the genocide period in the British and American daily press, the best general long-term coverage of Rwanda is to be found in Belgian and French newspapers. The main titles in this connection are *Le Soir* and *La Libre Belgique* in Brussels and *Le Monde*, *Libération*, *Le Figaro* and *L'Humanité* in Paris. Special mention should be made of the excellent journalistic coverage of the early days of the genocide by Jean Chatain of *L'Humanité* and, equally impressive, 'Opération Turquoise' by Patrick de Saint-Exupéry of *Le Figaro*.

Apart from general Africanist publications in which scholarly background articles on Rwanda can be found, the monthly *Dialogue* published in Kigali from 1967 onwards and now temporarily in Brussels is a good source of analysis and commentary on Rwandese social and political issues from a Catholic viewpoint. The Belgian non-government organisation Coopibo publishes *Rwanda aujourd'hui et demain* and *Traits d'Union Rwanda*, which are also good sources of information. The Economist Intelligence Unit in London publishes once a year a *Rwanda and Burundi Country Profile* and every three months a *Rwanda and Burundi Quarterly Report*. Specialised publications such as *Africa Confidential* and *Africa Analysis* have also provided good detailed coverage of the crisis.

Books, reports and articles

Africa Watch, *Rwanda: Talking peace and waging war: Human Rights since the October 1990 invasion*, London (February 1992).
——, *Beyond the rhetoric: Continuing Human Rights Abuses in Rwanda*, London (June 1993).

—, *Arming Rwanda: the Arms Trade and Human Rights Abuses in the Rwandan war*, New York (January 1994).

—, *Genocide in Rwanda (April–May 1994)*, New York (May 1994).

African Rights, *Rwanda: Who is killing? who is dying? what is to be done?* London (May 1994).

—, *Rwanda: Death, despair, defiance*, London 1994.

—, *Humanitarianism unbound? Current dilemmas facing multi-mandate relief operations in political emergencies*, London (November 1994).

—, *Rwanda: A waste of hope*, London: United Nations Human Rights Field Operation (March 1995).

Amnesty International, *The Republic of Rwanda: A spate of detentions and trials in 1990 to suppress fundamental rights*, London (October 1990).

—, *Rwanda: Government Supporters and Regular Troops have commmitted Massacres all over the Country*, London (May 1994).

—, *Rwanda: Reports of killings and abductions by the Rwandese Patriotic Army*, April.August 1994, London (October 1994).

—, *Rwanda: cases for appeals*, London (November 1994).

Anonymous, *Historique et chronologie du Rwanda*, Kabgayi, 1956.

Anonymous, *Le Ruanda-Urundi*, Brussels: Office de l'Information et des Relations Publiques pour le Congo Belge et le Ruanda-Urundi, 1959.

Arnoux, A., 'Le culte de la société secrète des *Imandwa* au Rwanda', *Anthropos*, vol. 7 (1912) and vol. 8 (1913).

Association Rwandaise pour la Défense des Droits de la Personne et des Libertés Publiques, *Rapport sur les Droits de l'Homme au Rwanda (Septembre 1991–Septembre 1992)*, Kigali: ADL (December 1992).

—, *Rapports sur les Droits de l'Homme au Rwanda (Octobre 1992–Octobre 1993)*, Kigali: ADL (December 1993).

Bangamwabo, F.-X. *et al.*, *Les relations interethniques au Rwanda à la lumière de l'agression d'octobre 1990*, Ruhengeri: Editions Universitaires du Rwanda, 1991.

Barahinyura, S.J., *Le Général-Major Habyarimana (1973–88). Quinze ans de tyrannie et tartufferie au Rwanda*, Frankfurt-am-Main: Izuba Verlag, 1988.

—, *Rwanda. Trente-deux ans après la révolution sociale de 1959*, Frankfurt-am-Main: Izuba Verlag, 1992.

Bart, F., *Montagnes d'Afrique, terres paysannes. Le cas du Rwanda*, Talence: Presses Universitaires de Bordeaux, 1993 (numerous maps, illustrations and tables).

Berger, I., *Religion and resistance: East African kingdoms in the pre-colonial period*, Butare: INRS, 1981.

Bezy, F., *Rwanda. Bilan socio-économique d'un régime (1962–89)*, Louvain-la-Neuve: Institut des Pays en Développement, 1990.

Bindseil, R., *Ruanda und Deutschland seit den Tagen Richard Kandts*, Berlin: Dietrich Reimer, 1987.

—, *Ruanda im Lebensbild des Offiziers, Afrikaforschers und kaiserlichen*

Gouverneurs Gustav Adolf Graf von Götzen (1866–1910), Berlin: Dietrich Reimer, 1992.

Bizimana, S., 'Le langage des *imaandwa* au Rwanda', *Cahiers d'Etudes Africaines* vol. 14, no. 1 (1974), pp. 88–103.

Bourgeois, R., *Témoignages*, vol. 1, Tervuren: MRAC, 1982.

Braeckman, C., *Rwanda, histoire d'un génocide*, Paris: Fayard, 1994.

——, 'Rwanda: le temps du révisionnisme', *Esprit* (December 1994), pp. 191–3.

Brandstetter, A.M., *Herrscher über tausend Hügel. Zentralisierungsprozesse in Rwanda im 19. Jahrhundert*, Mainz: Titus Grab Verlag, 1989.

Brauman, R., *Devant le mal. Rwanda un génocide en direct*, Paris: Arléa, 1994.

Briey, Comte Renaud de, *Le sphinx noir. Essai sur les problèmes de colonisation africaine*, Brussels: Albert DeWitt, 1926.

Chrétien, J.P., 'La révolte de Ndungutse (1912). Forces traditionnelles et pression coloniale au Rwanda allemand', *Revue Française d'Histoire d'Outre-Mer*, vol. 59, no. 4, (1972), pp. 645–80.

——, 'Echanges et hiérarchies dans les royaumes des Grands Lacs de l'Est Africain', *Annales ESC*, vol. 29, no. 6 (1974), pp. 1327–37.

——, 'Des légendes africaines face à des mythes européens', *Cultures et Développement*, vol. 3 (1974), pp. 579–87.

——, 'Les deux visages de Cham', pp. 171–99, in P. Guiral and E. Témime (eds), *L'idée de race dans la pensée politique française contemporaine*, Paris: Editions du CNRS, 1977.

——, 'Des sédentaires devenus migrants. Les motifs de départ des Barundi et des Banyarwanda vers l'Uganda (1920–60)', *Cultures et Développement* vol. 10, no. 1 (1978), pp. 71–101.

——, 'Vocabulaire et concepts tirés de la féodalité occidentale et administration indirecte en Afrique Orientale', pp. 47–63, in D. Nordman, and J.-P. Raison, (eds), *Sciences de l'homme et conquête coloniale. Constitution et usage des sciences humaines en Afrique*, Paris: Presses de l'Ecole Normale Supérieure, 1980.

——, 'Hutu et Tutsi au Rwanda et au Burundi' in J.L. Amselle and E. M'Bokolo (eds), *Au coeur de l'ethnie*, Paris: La Découverte, 1985, pp. 129–66.

——, 'Les Bantous, de la philologie allemande à l'authenticité africaine: un mythe racial contemporain', *XXème Siècle* (October–December 1985), pp. 43–66.

——, 'Presse libre et propaganda raciste au Rwanda. *Kangura* et les 10 commandements du Hutu', *Politique Africaine*, no. 42 (June 1991), pp. 109–20.

——, 'Le régime de Kigali et l'intervention française au Rwanda. Sortir du silence', *Bulletin du CRIDEV*, no. 105 (Feb.–March 1992).

——, 'Le Rwanda et la France. La démocratie et les ethnies', *Esprit* (March 1993).

Communauté Rwandaise de France, *Memorandum sur la crise politique actuelle au Rwanda*, Paris, mimeo (December 1990).

Del Perugia, P., *Les derniers Rois Mages*, Paris: Phébus, 1970, 2nd edn 1978.

Des Forges, A., 'Kings without crowns: The White Fathers' in D.F. McCall and N. Bennett, *Eastern Africa History*, New York: Praeger, 1969, pp. 176–207.

——, 'Defeat is the only bad news: Rwanda under Musiinga (1896–1931)' Ph.D. thesis, Yale University, Ann Arbor: Michigan University Microfilm International, 1972.

——, 'The drum is greater than the shout: the 1912 rebellion in Northern Rwanda' in D. Crummey, *Banditry, Rebellion and Social Protest in Africa*, London: James Currey, 1986, pp. 311–31.

Destexhe, A., *Rwanda. Essai sur le génocide*, Brussels: Complexe, 1994.

Erny, P., 'L'esprit de l'éducation au Rwanda ou le 'caractère national' décrit par un groupe d'étudiants', *Genève-Afrique*, vol. 21, no. 1 (1983), pp. 26–54.

——, *Rwanda 1994*, Paris: L'Harmattan, 1994.

Fédération Internationale des Droits de l'Homme *et al.*, *Rapport sur la Commission d'enquête sur les violations des droits de l'Homme au Rwanda depuis le 1er Octobre 1990*, Paris/New York: Africa Watch Montreal: CIDPDD, March 1993.

Feltz, G., 'Evolution des structures foncières et histoire politique du Rwanda (XIXème et XXème siècles), *Etudes d'Histoire Africaine*, no. 7 (1975), pp. 143–54.

Ferney, J.-C., 'La France au Rwanda. Raison du prince, dé-raison d'Etat?', *Politique Africaine*, no. 51 (October 1993), pp. 170–5.

Gakuba, L., *Rwanda 1931–1959*, Paris: La Pensée Universelle, 1991.

Gasarabwe, E., *Le geste Rwanda*, Paris: UGE, 1978.

Gasarasi, C., *A tripartite approach to the resettlement and integration of rural refugees in Tanzania*, Uppsala: Nordiska Afrikainstitutet, Research Report 71, 1984.

Gatwa, T., and Karamaga A., *Les autres Chrétiens Rwandais. La présence protestante*, Kigali: Urwego, 1990.

Gordon, N., *Murders in the mist*, London: Hodder and Stoughton, 1993.

Götzen, Graf von, *Durch Afrika, von Ost nach West*, Berlin: Dietrich Reimer, 1899.

Guichaoua, A., *Destins paysans et politiques agraires en Afrique Centrale*, Paris: ILO/L'Harmattan, 1989.

——, *Travail non-rémunéré et développment rural au Rwanda*, Geneva: ILO, 1990.

——, *Le problème des réfugiés rwandais et des populations Banyarwanda dans la région des Grands Lacs Africains*, Geneva: UNHCR, 1992.

——, *Les crises politiques au Rwanda et au Burundi (1993–94)*, Lille: Université des Sciences et Technologies, 1995.

Hanssen, A., *Le désenchantement de la coopération. Enquête au pays des mille coopérants*, Paris: L'Harmattan, 1989.

Harroy, J.-P., *Rwanda, du féodalisme à la démocratie (1955–1962)*, Brussels: Hayez, 1984.

Heremans, P.R., *Introduction à l'histoire du Rwanda*, Brussels: A. de Boeck, 1973.

d'Hertefelt, Marcel, 'Mythes et idéologies dans le Rwanda ancien et contemporain' in J. Vansina, R. Mauny and L.-V. Thomas (eds), *The historian in Tropical Africa*, Oxford University Press, 1961, pp. 219–34.

——, *Les clans du Rwanda ancien*, Tervuren: MRAC, 1971.

——, and A. Coupez, *La royauté sacrée de l'ancien Rwanda. Texte, traduction et commentaire de son rituel*, Tervuren: MRAC, 1964.

Heusch, Luc de, 'Mythe et société féodale: le culte *kubandwa* dans le Rwanda traditionnel', *Archives de sociologie des religions*, vol. 18 (July–December 1964), pp. 133–46.

——, *Le Rwanda et la civilisation interlacustre*, Brussels: Université Libre de Bruxelles, Institut de Sociologie, 1966.

——, *Rois nés d'un coeur de vache*, Paris: Gallimard, 1982.

Hiernaux, J., *Les caractères physiques des populations du Ruanda-Urundi*, Brussels: Institut Royal des Sciences Naturelles de Belgique, 1954.

Honke, G. (ed.), *Au plus profond de l'Afrique. Le Rwanda et la colonisation allemande (1885–1919)*, Wuppertal: Peter Hammer Verlag, 1990.

Hubert, J.R., *La Toussaint Rwandaise et sa répression*, Brussels: ARSOM, 1965.

Human Rights Watch/Africa, *Human Rights in Africa and US policy*, New York (June 1994).

——, *The aftermath of genocide in Rwanda: Absence of prosecution, continued killings*, New York (September 1994).

——, *Rwanda: A new catastrophe?*, New York (December 1994).

——, *Rwanda/Zaïre: Rearming with Impunity: International support for the perpetrators of the Rwandan genocide*, New York (May 1995).

Imbs, F., Bart, F. and Bart, A., 'Le Rwanda. Les données socio-géographiques', *Hérodote*, nos. 72–3 (September 1994), pp. 246–77.

Jefremovas, V., 'Loose women, virtuous wives and timid virgins: Gender and the control of resources in Rwanda', *Canadian Journal of African Studies*, vol. 25, no. 3 (1991), pp. 378–95.

Johnston, Sir Harry, *The Uganda Protectorate*, London: Hutchinson, 2 vols, 1902.

[Diocèse de] Kabgayi, *Convertissons-nous pour vivre ensemble dans la paix*, Gitarama, mimeo (December 1991).

Kagabo, J.H., *L'Islam et les 'Swahili' au Rwanda*, Paris: Editions de l'EHESS, 1988.

Kagame, Abbé A., *Le code des institutions politiques du Rwanda précolonial*, Brussels: IRCB, 1952.

—, *Inganji Kalinga*, 2 vols, Kabgayi, 1959.

—, *L'histoire des armées bovines dans l'ancien Rwanda*, Brussels: ARSOM, 1961.

—, *Les milices du Rwanda précolonial*, Brussels: ARSOM, 1963.

—, *Un abrégé de l'ethnohistoire du Rwanda précolonial*, vol. 1, Butare: Editions Universitaires du Rwanda, 1972.

Kalibwami, J., *Le catholicisme et la société rwandaise (1900–1962)*, Paris: Présence Africaine, 1991.

Kamukama, D., *Rwanda conflict: Its roots and regional implications*. Kampala: Fountain Publishers, 1993.

Kandt, R., *Caput Nili. Ein empfindsame Reise zu den Quellen des Nils*, 2 vols, Berlin: Dietrich Reimer, 1905, 2nd edn, 1919.

Keiner, H., 'Allmählich schwand die Bewunderung für "Habis" Regime', *Frankfurter Rundschau* (5 November 1992).

Krop, P., *Le génocide franco-africain*, Paris: J.C. Lattès, 1994.

Lacger, Louis de, *Le Ruanda*, Kabgayi, 1939, 2nd edn 1959.

Lemarchand, R., 'L'influence des systèmes traditionnels sur l'évolution du Rwanda et du Burundi', *Revue de l'Institut de Sociologie de l'Université Libre de Bruxelles* (1962), pp. 2–24.

—, *Rwanda and Burundi*, New York: Praeger, 1970.

Linden, I., *Church and revolution in Rwanda*, Manchester University Press, 1977.

Logiest, G., *Mission au Rwanda. Un Blanc dans la bagarre Tutsi-Hutu*, Brussels: Didier Hatier, 1988.

Louis, W.R., *Ruanda-Urundi (1884–1919)*, Oxford: Clarendon Press, 1963.

Lugan, B. (ed.), *Sources écrites pouvant servir à l'histoire du Rwanda*, Butare: Editions Universitaires du Rwanda, *Etudes Rwandaises* (special no., vol. 14).

—, 'Entre les servitudes de la houe et les sortilèges de la vache. Le monde rural dans l'ancien Rwanda', unpubl. Ph.D. thesis, University of Aix-en-Provence, 1983.

Maquet, J.J., *Le système des relations sociales dans le Rwanda ancien*, Tervuren: MRCB, 1954.

—, *Le Rwanda. Essai photographique sur une société africaine en transition*, Brussels: Elsevier, 1957.

—, *The premises of inequality in Rwanda*, Oxford University Press, 1961.

— and M. d'Hertefelt, *Les élections en société féodale*, Brussels: ARSOM, vol. 21 (1959).

Mbonimana, G., 'L'instauration d'un royaume chrétien au Rwanda

(1900–1931)', unpubl. Ph.D. thesis, Université Catholique de Louvain, 1981.

Mboniyumutwa, S., *Rwanda, gouverner autrement*, Kigali: Imprimerie Nationale du Rwanda, 1990.

Meschi, L., 'Evolution des structures foncières au Rwanda. Le cas d'un lignage Hutu', *Cahiers d'Etudes Africaines*, vol. 14, no. 1 (1974), pp. 39–51.

Mouvement Démocratique Républicain, *Analyse de la situation actuelle au Rwanda et perspectives d'avenir*, Kigali: MDR, 1992.

——, *Position du MDR sur les grands problèmes actuels du Rwanda*, Kigali: MDR (November 1994).

Mujawamariya, M., *Rapport de visite effectuée au Rwanda du 1er au 22 Septembre 1994*, Montréal, mimeo (October 1994).

Munyakazi, J.C., 'Le pouvoir Nyiginya sur le Gisaka. Le cas du Gihunya (1850–1916)', Master's thesis, Université Nationale du Rwanda, Butare (director Professeur Nsanzimana), 1981.

Murego, D., *La révolution rwandaise (1959–62)*, Louvain: Institut des Sciences Politiques et Sociales, 1975.

Musabyimana, G., *Les années fatidiques pour le Rwanda. Coup d'œil sur les préparatifsi intensifs de la 'Guerre d'octobre' (1986–1990)*, Kigali: Kiroha, 1993.

Mvuyekure, A., 'Idéologie missionnaire et classification ethnique en Afrique Centrale' in Chretien, J.-P. and Prunier, G. (eds), *Les ethnies ont une histoire*, Paris: Karthala. 1989, pp. 314–24.

Mworoha, E, *Peuples et rois l'Afrique des Lacs*, Dakar: Nouvelles Editions Africaines, 1977.

Nahimana, F., 'Les Bami ou roitelets Hutu du corridor Nyabarongo-Mukungwa avec ses régions limitrophes', *Etudes Rwandaises*, no. 12 (1978), pp. 1–25.

——, 'Les principautés Hutu du Rwanda septentrional' in Centre de Civilisation Burundaise (ed.), *La civilisation ancienne des peuples des Grands Lacs*, Paris: Karthala, 1981, pp. 115–37.

——, *Le Blanc est arrivé, le Roi est parti. Une facette de l'histoire du Rwanda contemporain (1894–1931)*, Kigali: Printer Set, 1987.

——, *Le Rwanda, émergence d'un Etat*, Paris: L'Harmattan, 1993.

Ndagijimana, F., *L'Afrique face à ses défis. Le problème des réfugiés rwandais*, Geneva: Arunga, 1990.

Nduwayezu, J.-D., *Les fondements physiques, humains et économiques du développement au Rwanda*, Ruhengeri: Editions Universitaires du Rwanda, 1990.

Newbury, C., 'Ubureetwa and Thangata: Catalysts to peasant political consciousness in Rwanda and Malawi' in Centre de Civilisation Burundaise (ed.), *La civilisation ancienne des peuples des Grands Lacs*, Paris: Karthala, 1981, pp. 138–47.

——, *The cohesion of oppression: Clientship and ethnicity in Rwanda (1860–1960)*, New York: Columbia University Press, 1988.

Newbury, D., 'The clans of Rwanda: A historical hypothesis in Centre de Civilisation Burundaise (ed.), *La civilisation ancienne des peuples des Grands Lacs*, Paris: Karthala, 1981, pp. 186–97.

Nkundabagenzi, F., *Le Rwanda politique (1958–1960)*, Brussels: CRISP, 1961.

Nkurikiyimfura, J.-N., *Le gros bétail et la société rwandaise. Evolution historique des XIIème-XIVème siècles à 1958*, Paris: L'Harmattan, 1994.

Nsabimana, A., *La guerre et la paix au Rwanda*, Kigali: privately printed, 1992.

Nsanzuwera, F.X., *La magistrature rwandaise dans l'étau du pouvoir éxécutif. La peur et le silence, complice de l'arbitraire*, Kigali: CLADHO, 1993.

Pages, A., *Un royaume Hamite au centre de l'Afrique*, Brussels: IRCB, 1933.

Paternostre de la Mairieu, B., *Le Rwanda, son effort de développement*, Brussels: A. de Boeck, 1972.

Poincarré, N., *Rwanda. Gabriel Maindron, un prêtre dans la tragédie*, Paris: Les Editions de l'Atelier, 1995.

Pottier, J., 'Taking stock: Food marketing reform in Rwanda (1982–89), *African Affairs*, vol. 92 (1993), pp. 5–30.

— and Wilding, J., *Food security and agricultural rehabilitation in post-war Rwanda*, London: Save the Children Fund (September 1994).

Prunier, G., 'L'Ouganda et le Front Patriotique Rwandais in A. Guichaoua (ed.), *Enjeux nationaux et dynamiques régionales dans l'Afrique des Grands Lacs*, Lille: Faculté de Sciences Economiques et Sociales, 1992, pp. 43–9.

—, 'Elements pour une histoire du Front Patriotique Rwandais', *Politique Africaine*, no. 51 (October 1993), pp. 121–38.

—, 'La crise rwandaise. Structures et déroulement', *Refugee Survey Quarterly*, vol. 13, nos. 2–3 (Summer/Autumn 1994), pp. 13–46.

—, 'La dimension politique du génocide au Rwanda', *Hérodote*, nos. 72–3 (September 1994), pp. 270–77.

Raison, J.-P., 'Le Rwanda et le Burundi sous pression', in Dubresson A. *et al.* (eds), *Les Afriques au Sud du Sahara*, Paris: Belin, 1994, pp. 320–9.

Reporters sans Frontières, *Rwanda. Médias de la haine ou presse démocratique*, Paris: ASF, November, 1994.

Republique Rwandaise, *Le terrorisme Inyenzi au Rwanda*, Kigali: 1964.

—, *Le Rwanda et le problème de ses réfugiés. Contexte historique, analyse et voies de solution*, Kigali: Présidence de la République, Commission Spéciale sur les problèmes des émigrés Rwandais, 1990.

—, *Mémoire présenté à la Deuxième Conférence des Nations Unies sur les Pays les Moins Avancés*, Paris (3–14 September 1990).

—, *Livre blanc sur l'agression armée dont le Rwanda a été victime à partir du 1er Octobre 1990*, Kigali: Ministère des Affaires Etrangères et de la Coopération, 1991.

—, *Rapport préliminaire de la Commission Nationale d'Agriculture*, Kigali: Ministère de l'Agriculture (June 1991).

—, *Recensement Général de la Population et de l'Habitat au 15 Août 1991*,

Kigali: Service national du Recensement, Ministère du Plan. (December 1991).

Reyntjens, F., *Pouvoir et Droit au Rwanda*, Tervuren: MRAC, 1995.

—, 'Cooptation politique à l'envers. Les législatives de 1988 au Rwanda', *Politique Africaine*, no. 34 (June 1989), pp. 121–6.

—, 'Le *gacaca* ou la justice du gazon au Rwanda', *Politique Africaine*, no. 40 (December 1990), pp. 31–41.

—, *L'Afrique des Grands Lacs en crise. Rwanda et Burundi (1988–1994)*, Paris: Karthala, 1994.

Richards, A., *Economic development and tribal change: A study of immigrant labour in Buganda*, Cambridge: Heffer, 1956.

Rumiya, J., *Le Rwanda sous le régime du mandat belge (1916–1931)*, Paris: L'Harmattan, 1992.

Rwabukumba, J., and V. Mundangazi, 'Les formes historiques de la dépendance dans l'Etat rwandais', *Cahiers d'Etudes Africaines*, vol. 14, no. 1 (1974), pp. 6–25.

(Collective) *Rwanda. Depuis le 7 avril 1994, la France choisit le camp du génocide*, Paris: Agir Ici, mimeo (December 1994).

Sanders, E.R., 'The Hamitic hypothesis: Its origin and function in time perspective', *Journal of African History*, vol. 10, no. 4 (1969), pp. 521–32.

Schürings, H. (ed.), *Ein volk verlässt sein Land. Krieg und Völkermord in Ruanda*, Cologne: I.S.P., 1994.

Sirven, P., J.-F. Gotanegre and C. Prioul, *Géographie du Rwanda*, Brussels: De Boeck, 1974.

Speke, J.H., *Journal of the discovery of the source of the Nile*, London: J.M. Dent, 1969 (1st edn 1863).

Stoecker, H. (ed.), *German Imperialism in Africa*, London: Hurst, 1986.

Tabara, P. *Afrique. La face cachée*, Paris: La Pensée Universelle, 1992.

Taylor, C., *Milk, Honey and Money: Changing Concepts in Rwandan Healings*, Washington DC: Smithsonian Institute Press, 1992.

United Nations, Trusteeship Council, various *Reports* published in New York, 1948–61.

—, Conseil Economique et Social, *Rapport sur la situation des Droits de l'Homme au Rwanda soumis par Mr R. Degni-Ségui, Rapporteur Spécial*, New York (28 June 1994).

—, Conseil Economique et Social, *Rapport sur la situation des Droits de l'Homme au Rwanda soumis par Mr R. Degni-Ségui, Rapporteur Spécial*, New York (11 November 1994).

—, Commission of Experts Established Pursuant to Security Council Resolution 935 (1994) on Rwanda, *Final Report*, Geneva (25 November 1994).

Vaiter, M., *Je n'ai pas pu les sauver tous*, Paris: Plon, 1995.

Vansina, J., *L'évolution du royaume du Rwanda des origines à 1900*, Brussels: ARSOM, 1962.

Vassal-Adams, G., *Rwanda: An agenda for international action*, London: Oxfam, 1994.

Verschave, X., *Complicité de génocide? La politique de la France au Rwanda*, Paris: La Découverte, 1994.

Vicchi, S., G. Laghi and W. Schonecke, 'Rwanda. Le ombre lunghe del passato', *Nigrizia* (December 1994).

Vidal, C., 'Anthropologie et histoire. Le cas du Ruanda', *Cahiers Internationaux de Sociologie*, vol. 43 (July–December 1967), pp. 143–57.

——, 'Le Rwanda des anthropologues et le fétichisme de la vache', *Cahiers d'Etudes Africaines*, vol. 9, no. 3 (1969), pp. 384–400.

——, 'Colonisation et décolonisation du Rwanda. La question Tutsi-Hutu', *Revue Française de Sciences Politiques et Africaines*, no. 91 (1973) pp. 32–47.

——, 'Economie de la société féodale rwandaise', *Cahiers d'Etudes Africaines*, vol. 14, no. 1 (1974), pp. 350–84.

——, 'Situations ethniques au Rwanda' in J.-L. Amselle and E. M'Bokolo (eds), *Au coeur de l'ethnie*, Paris: La Découverte, 1985, pp. 167–84.

——, *Sociologie des passions*, Paris: Karthala, 1991.

—— and M. Le Pape (eds), 'Rwanda, Burundi 1994–1995 . Les politiques de la haine', special issue of *Les Temps Modernes*, no. 583 (July–August 1995).

Waller, D., *Rwanda: Which way now?* London: Oxfam, 1993.

Watson, C., *Exile from Rwanda: Background to an invasion*, Washington DC: US Committee for Refugees (February 1991).

——, 'Rwanda: War and Waiting', *Africa Report* (November–December 1992), pp. 51–5.

Willame, J.-C., 'La panne rwandaise', *La Revue Nouvelle*, no. 12 (December 1990), pp. 59–66.

——, and Peeters, A. 'Rwanda, miroir brisé', *La Revue Nouvelle*, no. 12 (December 1990), pp. 53–8.

——, 'Le *muyaga* ou la "révolution" rwandaise revisitée', *Revue Française d'Histoire d'Outre-Mer*, vol. 81, no. 304 (1994), pp. 305–20.

——, *Aux sources de l'hécatombe rwandaise*, Paris: L'Harmattan (Les Cahiers Africains no. 14), 1995.

GLOSSARY

Introductory note

The general system of word classification in Bantu languages is based on the use of variable prefixes. The prefix puts the nouns into certain 'categories'. Then the other elements of the sentence are all put in agreement with the prefix. Thus in Swahili, the only Bantu language with which this author is personally more or less conversant, we would have:

Mtu mrefu anakimbia	The tall thin man runs
Watu warefu wanakimbia	The tall thin men run

because the prefix (*m*) or (*wa*) announces the class reserved for living beings. Thus, less pleasantly –

Wadudu warefu wanakimbia	The long thin insects are running

or if we talk about a certain class of object –

Kijiko kidogo kinatosha	The small spoon is enough
Vijiko vidogo vinatosha	The small spoons are enough

This is only to explain that, in this text as in others, Bantu names at times appear with different prefixes, but this makes them no more different than 'mouse' and 'mice'. In this glossary, the nouns will be given in their singular form with the plural prefix between brackets when relevant. In the course of the book we talk of Tutsi and Hutu where we should properly have written 'Mtutsi' and 'Muhutu' in the singular and 'Abatutsi' and 'Abahutu' in the plural. The problem is compounded when one reads the old travellers who, in the nineteenth century, tended to use the Swahili prefix everywhere, thus writing about Watutsi[1] rather than the proper Kinyarwanda form 'Abatutsi'. Other words are at times found without their prefix such as '*biru*' for the court ritualists instead of the proper '*abiru*'. Our choice of the common spelling 'Tutsi' is a simple effort at clarity. But we must confess to several cases of 'Banyarwanda' ('the people of Rwandese extraction') when wanting to talk of people belonging to that ethnic origin, whether they are Rwandese citizens or not. This is important since there must have been at least 2 million 'Banyarwanda' outside Rwanda before the war started, without even taking into account the true 'refugee' population. We see why in the book.

---

1. Even 'Watussi' or 'Ouatoussi' in the case of German or French authors.

One last point concerns the rendering of pronounciation. Bantu languages do not make a distinction between the sounds L and R. Thus one can write indifferently *uburetwa* or *ubuletwa*, *abatwaale* or *abatwaare*. The letters G and K are also not pronounced very differently. There is also a certain uncertainty on the pronounciation (and writing) of the long vowels. Thus one can find *abatwale* or *abatwaale*, *Musinga* or *Musiinga*.

Akazu	'The little house'. In pre-colonial Rwanda this was the name given to the inner circle of the Royal Court. After 1985 it was the nickname given to the inner core of the Habyarimana regime, with a strongly critical connotation of power abuses and illicit enrichment.
Gufaha	To pay rent on an agricultural piece of land, without involving clientship relations.
Guhakwa	To pay court. The noun *ubuhake* (*q.v.*) is derived from that verb.
Ibyitso	'Accomplice'. Name given by the regime's extremist supporters to the Tutsi living in Rwanda after the 1 October 1990 invasion. After the democratisation movement got under way, the Hutu who supported the opposition parties also became *ibyitso* i.e. 'traitors' to the ideology of Hutu 'racial' superiority. The genocide of April–July 1994 was the killing of the *ibyitso*.
Igihirahiro	'The time of uncertainty'. The name the Rwandese gave to the period between the signing of the Arusha agreement and the explosion of the genocide.
Igihugu (ibihugu)	Country, land, region. Not a political term but rather a cultural and geographical one. Rwanda is made up of all its *ibihugu*.
Igikingi (Ibikingi)	Land concession given by royal order, later evolving towards a form of private property.
Ikigabiro (ibi-)	A royal burial site marked by a sacred grove. The varieties of trees planted there are carefully chosen.
Imana	The Supreme Being, God.
Imandwa	Initiates of the Kubandwa (*q.v.*) cult.
Inkotanyi	'The tough fighters'. Name given by the Rwandese Patriotic Front (RPF) to its soldiers. An old royal regimental name, with a monarchical connotation.
Interahamwe	'Those who work together'. This was described by the governement as the 'MRND youth movement'. It was the first civilian militia, officially created for tasks of social interest having to do with *umuganda*

(*q.v.*). They started to take part in killings as early as 1992 and were later the main perpetrators of the genocide. In one of these coded verbal allusions so frequent in Kinyarwanda, their name is a reminder *both* of the virtuous vocabulary of cooperative *umuganda* and in a more nasty way of the slogan of the 1959 massacres, '*Tugire gukora akazi*', 'Let us go and do the work'.

Inyenzi Cockroaches. Name given to the Tutsi guerrillas of the 1960–3 period, partly out of spite and partly because, like the cockroaches, they tended to move at night. After 1992 the CDR extremists and their allies started using the name again for the RPF fighters.

Inyangarwanda 'Those who hate Rwanda'. An expression with an interesting semantic evolution. Originally it was the name given to the rebels under the monarchy, but after 1959 it was used of the Tutsi exiles. After the beginnings of democratisation in 1990 it was used for anybody disagreeing with the regime.

Inzu 'Hut'. The smallest and most basic kinship unit. A loose grouping of people with a common agnatic ancestor going back up to six generations, beyond which point it tended to break up. The *inzu* was the basic unit for social solidarity: members of your *inzu* helped you pay for your son's brideprice if you could not afford it, pitched in to give you cattle if yours had died and avenged you if you were killed by members of another *inzu*. With its *inzu* council it was also the basic unit of political life.

Isasu (amasasu) 'Bullet'. Name of a secret extremist organisation in the Rwandese army which collaborated with the civilian militias and gave them arms.

Itonde Poise, self-assurance, stoicism, reserve. It is the quality on which high-lineage Tutsi pride themselves, and the basis for their feeling of superiority.

Itsembabmbaga Lit. 'Extermination of the Nation' (the genocide of 1994).

Kazi A Swahili word meaning 'work'. In colonial Rwanda it was used for the forced labour the Belgians demanded from the natives.

Kinyarwanda The language spoken by the Banyarwanda tribe, and *exactly* the same whether spoken by Hutu or Tutsi.

Even similar personal names are given indifferently to Tutsi or Hutu.

Kubandwa   From the verb *kubanda*, to put pressure on something, to seize, to grab, plus the *wa* suffix of the passive form, 'to be taken'. This was a very important initiatic cult of possession where the *imandwa* communed in the devotion to Ryangombe, the lord of the spirits. This cult, which was destroyed by Chistian evangelisation, played an important integrative social role since its initiates were indifferently Tutsi, Hutu and even Twa.

Kunywana   Lit. 'to drink each other'. A blood-brotherhood institution entailing the drinking of each other's blood from incisions on the belly. The '*Abanyawani*' (blood-brothers) had strong mutual obligations. They could belong to any strata of society.

Mshenzi (wa-)   Swahili word of Persian origin meaning a savage, a barbarian. Originally used by the coastal Swahili traders to refer to the populations of the interior, in Rwanda it means a pagan as opposed to a Christian. It has kept the same spiteful connotation.

Mshiru (Aba-)   The people from Bushiru, the *Akazu* élite.

Muyaga (wa-)   Low-altitude region, drier and hotter than *rukiga* (*q.v.*).

Mutagetsi (Aba-)   'The bosses', 'those who give orders'. The name given by ordinary Rwanda to their 'élite'.

Muzungu (wa-)   Swahili word used all over the interlacustrine area of the White Man. Also found in the Kinyarwanda form *umuzungu*, *abazungu*.

Ntore   From the verb *gutore*, to choose. Applied to several selected groups, mainly (a) the élite warriors of the King's regiments; (b) the troop of royal dancers; (c) after the advent of Christianity, the catechumens.

Nyina   Mother. Followed by the reign name of a king, it means the queen mother of that particular king, i.e. the second most important person in the kingdom. For example, Kanjogera, the terrible mother of King Yuhi V Musiinga, was called *Nyina Yuhi*.

Panga   Machete. This agricultural tool was the great weapon of the genocide.

Rubanda nyamwinshi   'The majority people'. A coded political expression used of the Hutu population with the connotation that one must be Hutu to be allowed to rule and that whoever rules in the name of the 'majority people' is ontologically democratic.

Rugo (ingo)   Enclosure around the home. The basic living unit of the Banyarwanda peasants.

Rukiga   High altitude region, cool and humid, as opposed to *Muyaga* (*q.v.*). By extension the northernmost part of Rwanda, on the border with Uganda, between Murera and Bufumbira (see *umukiga*).

Shebuja   Patron in the *ubuhake* contract, or by extension in any other form of contractual social subordination.

Ubuhake   The main form of personal contractual subordination in traditional Rwandese society. Contrary to much of the ideological writing about Rwanda, it was neither a happy element of social cohesion nor a form of slavery. Its real social and economic roles changed considerably over time and nineteenth century *ubuhake* in Nduga had little to do with something called by the same name in Cyangugu in 1930.

Ubureetwa   A form of corvée work developed by Tutsi chiefs in the nineteenth century and later incorporated in the Belgian system of tax and compulsory labour.

Ubwoko   Usually tranlated as 'clan', a highly ambiguous term in Kinyarwanda. In fact a better translation would be 'group' because there is no notion in it of a common ancestor. It comprises Tutsi, Hutu and Twa together, while both the *inzu* (*q.v.*) and the *umulyango* (*q.v.*) are made up of only one of the three catagories of the Banyarwanda population. *Ubwoko* seems to have been a rather synthetic classificatory element in traditional society. For example (an amazing thing if it been a real 'clan'), it was not exogamous. It is all the more surprising that this term was chosen to figure on the compulsory identity card to pinpoint the 'ethnic' element so dear to journalists. It is almost as if, in a prefect example of a Freudian slip, the leaders of the Hutu republic after 1961 had acknowledged that the colonial classification they had decided to retain was a modern social construct rather than an 'eternal' category going back to the dawn of history.

Umugaba (aba-)   The recruiters of the royal army in pre-colonial times. They were always Hutu.

Umugabo (aba-)	A 'real man', someone embodying the *ubugabo* virile quality (strength of body and character, sexual potency). President Habyarimana was often described as 'a true *umugabo*', not without a subtle note of irony because in modern times the *umugabo* image has taken on, in educated circles at least, a slightly ridiculous *macho* element.
Umuganda	Free labour demanded from the peasants by the Rwandese regime since 1974. It was supposed to be half a day per week or two days a month, but 'the touching enthusiasm of the laborious peasant masses tended to make them increase this time. *Umuganda* became one of the key elements in the regime', ideology, eliciting great admiration from foreign aid donors, the churches and the NGOs – as long as they did not look too closely into the actual workings of the 'voluntary' system.
Umugaragu (aba-)	Client in the *ubuhake* system. By extension, any person in a relation of subordination to another.
Umugererwa (aba-)	Client in the *ubukonde* type of land contract.
Umuhinza (aba-)	Title of the small Hutu princes in northern Rwanda who remained independent from the Rwandese *Abami* till the nineteenth century. Initially denoting a spiritual power of kingship, it evolved into meaning a rebel, somebody not submitting to the court's authority.
Umuja (aba-)	Female servants or concubines.
Umukiga (aba-)	Technically a member of the Bakiga tribe, a group closely related to the Banyarwanda but mostly living in the Ugandan district of Kigezi just over the Rwandese border. But because of the *rukiga* (*q.v.*) country, the name has been applied to the northern Hutu, somewhat interchangeably with *abakonde*. But contrary to *abakonde* which denotes economic prosperity and a lineage which has lived in the area for a long time, the connotation of *abakiga* is rather that of rough and uncouth people.
Umukonde (aba-)	Title of a rich northern Hutu landowner who rents out his land. The *ubukonde* were pieces of land traditionally belonging to certain northern Hutu lineages. If they were rented out, the tenant became known as *umugererwa* (*q.v.*), in a fashion rather similar to the *shabuja/umugaragu* relationship in the *ubuhake*

contract which mainly concerned cattle. Later, the name *abakonde* was often used of northern Hutu in general.

Umuka (aba-)   'The ones who shine' (with the glory of the Holy Spirit). Name given to the Christian charismatic revivalists.

Umunyabukenke (aba-)   'The chief of the pastures', royal functionaries who organised grazing and collected the relevant fees for the King up to the 1929 reform. They were always Tutsi. Also called *umutwale (q.v) wa inka* or *unutwale wa igikingi (q.v)*.

Umunyabutaka (aba-)   'The Chief of the Land', a royal functionary who organised agricultural matters and collected land taxes for the King up to the 1929 reform. They could be either Tutsi or Hutu. Also called *unutwale (q.v) wa butaka*.

Umunyanduga (aba-)   Somebody coming from Nduga country, i.e. the south-central part of Rwanda. During the colonial period this referred to the (mostly Tutsi) newcomers arriving from the South, often to act as agents of the court. The term quickly took on a derogatory connotation. After the 1973 coup and the assumption of power by a new *abakiga (q.v.)* élite, all southerners, whether Tutsi or Hutu, became known to the northerners as *abanyanduga*. Since Nduga was at the heart of the old kingdom, there is an element of envy and irony towards the supposed sophistication of the *abanyanduga*.

Umurenge   Sub-section of an *umusozi (q.v.)* that is part of a hill considered not geographically but as the basic administrative and tax unit. *Umurenge* was the sub-unit.

Umuryango   Lineage. This is an intermediate social unit, larger than the *inzu (q.v)* but smaller than the *ubwoko*.

Umusozi (imi-)   'Hill'. The next level in the living environment of a Rwandese peasant after his *rugo (q.v.)*.

Umutwaare (aba-)   Chief in general. Story with the *abanyabutaka (q.v.)* and the *abanyabukenke (q.v.)* the third type was the *umutwale wa ingabo* the 'chief of the men'. The *Umutwaare wa ingabo* was essentially a tax collector and like his colleagues looked at the population rather than at the crops or the cows. They were all abolished by the 1929 administrative reform.

Umwami (abami)	King.
Umwami w'imandwa	'King of the initiated'. The principal spirit medium of the *kubandwa* (*q.v.*) cult at the royal court.
Umwiru (Abiru)	Court ritualists. Their role was partly religious and partly to do with protocol. They surrounded the King and at times tried to manipulate him. Their rituals were essential in the succession process.

ABBREVIATIONS

BBTG	Broad Based Transitional Government	The government which was supposed to be put in place after the Arusha agreement of 3 August 1993.
CDR	Coalition pour la Défense de la République	Extremist party which supported President Habyarimana, then went into opposition when it found him too moderate. Later one of the main organisers of the genocide.
CND	Conseil National du Développement	National Assembly under the Habyarimana Second Republic.
DAMI	Détachement d'Assistance Militaire et d'Instruction	The French military mission, later accused of having trained not only FAR recruits but also the CDR and militiamen.
FAR	Forces Armées Rwandaises	Rwandese armed forces of the Habyarimana and Interim governments. Heavily involved in the genocide.
FRODEBU	Front pour la Démocratie au Burundi	The party of President Melchior Ndadaye.
GOMN	Groupement des Observateurs Militaires Neutres	OAU UN-sponsored monitoring body set up in 1993, before Arusha.

GP	Garde Présidentielle	Presidential Guard. They started the genocide.
ICRC	International Committee of the Red Cross	
MDR	Mouvement Démocratique Républicain	The main opposition party, later to become the main coalition partner in the July 1994 government.
MFBP	Mouvement des Femmes et du Bas Peuple	'Movement of the Women and of the low-born people', one of the 'political pygmies' and an MRND plant. Its leader was a very 'high born' bourgeois lady.
MRND(D)	Mouvement Révolutionnaire National pour le Développement (et la Démocratie)	Habyarimana's single party later revamped by the addition of a second 'democratic' D. Many of its leaders were among the main organisers of the genocide.
MSF	Médicins Sans Frontières	French medical emergency NGO.
NGO	Non Governmental Organisation	
OAU	Organisation of African Unity	
PADE	Parti Démocratique	Another political pygmy and MRND plant.
PAPERWA	Parti Révolutionnaire Rwandais	Same as PADE.
PDC	Parti Démocrate Chrétien	This Christian Democratic party was in opposition to

Habyarimana and thus not recognised by the Christian Democratic International which strongly supported the Rwandese regime. The smallest of the four 'serious' opposition parties.

PDI	Parti Démocratique Islamique	One of the 'pygmies', it nevertheless had a political reality in that it represented the small Rwandese Muslim community. Flirted with Habyarimana, then went into opposition and became a junior partner in the July 1994 government.
PECO	Parti Ecologiste	Under its mild name, one of the worst of the 'pygmies', closely allied with the MRND and later with the genocidal Interim government.
PL	Parti Libéral	An opposition party with many Tutsi members and a rather bourgeois well-to-do image. Ranked third among the opposition parties.
PPJR	Parti Progressiste de la Jeunesse Rwandaise	Another pro-MRND 'pygmy'.
PSD	Parti Social Démocrate	The second largest of the main opposition parties, later a coalition partner in the July 1994 government.
PSR	Parti Socialiste Rwandais	A 'pygmy' which flirted for a while with the MRND then went into opposition. A junior partner in the July 1994 government.

RPA	Rwandese Patriotic Army	The RPF army.
RPF	Rwandese Patriotic Front	The political arm of the anti-Habyarimana guerrilla force and dominant coalition partner in the July 1994 government.
RTD	Rassemblement Travailliste pour la Démocratie	Another pro-MRND 'pygmy'.
RTLMC	Radio Télévision Libre des Mille Collines	The 'free' radio station set up by Hutu extremists after the state relinquished its monopoly on broadcasting. A main orchestrator of the genocide.
UDPR	Union Démocratique du Peuple Rwandais	A 'pygmy' which went over to the opposition and became a junior partner in the July 1994 government.
UNAMIR	United Nations Assistance Mission to Rwanda	The powerless UN 'military' force which watched the genocide without being allowed to lift a finger.
UNHCR	United Nations High Commission for Refugees	
UNUROM	United Nations Uganda/ Rwanda Observer Mission	A short-lived UN group which preceded UNAMIR and was supposed to monitor the Uganda-Rwanda border.

INDEX

Ababega 24 and n., 68, 85
abagaragu 13, 20, 31, 39, 43, 47, 86;
    see also *umugaragu*
Abagoyi 350
Abahinza lineage 86
Abakiga 350
abakonde 57, 61, 371
abami 38, 57, 61n., 85, 245, 354: see
    also *mwami*
Abanyandugu 196, 350
Abashiru 350
abayinginya (see also clans) 85
abazungu (Europeans), see Europeans
abiru 9, 31, 54, 366, 373
Africa Unit, see *Cellule Africaine*
akazu 85, 87, 123, 129, 130n., 145,
    154, 166, 167, 168, 169, 182, 203,
    216, 219, 220, 221, 222, 225, 227,
    235, 242, 352, 367, 369; see also '*le
    Clan de Madame*'
Amasasu 200
Amin Dada, Idi 67 and n., 74, 81,
    113
Amin, Samir 350
Amnesty International 287
Annan, Kofi 276 cit.
Anglican church 252
'Anglo-Saxon', French conception
    of 99, 104, 106, 114, 116n., 148,
    178, 281, 286, 288, 320n., 337,
    338, 343n.
APROSOMA (Association pour la
    Promotion Sociale de la Masse) 47,
    48, 49, 51, 58
ARD (Alliance pour le Reinforcement
    de la Démocratie) 171n., 182
Arusha agreements 1993 150, 151,
    159–64, 166, 167n., 170, 171, 173,
    174, 177, 179, 180, 185, 187n.,
    189, 190, 191, 192, 193n., 194, 196
    and n., 197, 200–5, 208, 210, 211,
    227, 230, 280, 286, 299, 329 and
    n., 330, 334, 367, 374

Astrida préfecture 33, 48, 51, 53; see
    also Butare
Astridiens 46, 57
Aurillac, Michel 317

Bagambiki, Emmanuel 240, 293 cit.
Bagaragaza, Thaddée 129
Bagogwe 29, 136 and n., 139, 175,
    197
Bagosora, Colonel Théoneste 85, 163,
    167 and n., 168, 225, 232, 240,
    268, 316, 355
Bahutu, see Hutu
'Bahutu Manifesto' 45–6 cit.
Baker, Sir Samuel 7
Bakker, Rita De 335
Balladur, Edouard 277, 282 and n.,
    283, 287, 290, 296 cit., 307, 318,
    352
Bantu people 6, 7, 71, 155
Bantu language 5, 366
Banyarwanda 13, 15 and n., 17n., 39,
    56, 63, 64 and n., 68 and n., 69,
    70, 71, 72, 73, 74, 93, 95, 98,
    116, 117, 139, 153n., 319, 326,
    347, 366, 370
Banyingana, Major (Dr) Peter 91, 93,
    94, 95, 96, 114
Banyinginya dynasty 18, 24, 47
Barahinyura, Jean Shyirambere 128 and
    n.
Barayagwiza, Jean-Bosco 129, 165n.,
    277, 314 cit.
Barril, Captain Paul 128n., 216 and
    n., 217–19 and n., 220, 228
Batutsi, see Tutsi
Batwa 22, 26, 34n.; see also Twa
Baudillon, Philippe 282
BBTG (Broad-Based Transitional
    Government) 173, 189, 190, 191,
    192, 193, 196, 206, 207, 374
Belgian Congo, see Congo

378

Belgium and Belgians 11, 12, 13, 25
and n., 26, 27, 29–34, 35 and n.,
42, 43, 46, 47, 48, 49, 50, 51, 52,
53, 54, 58, 66, 68n., 80, 81, 89n.,
101, 107, 108, 116, 125, 131n.,
141, 151n., 153n., 157, 162n.,
204n., 205, 208, 213 and n., 214,
222n., 228, 230, 232, 234 and n.,
236, 245, 274, 278, 292n., 334, 335
and n., 336, 344, 347, 352n., 368,
370
Benaco camp 241, 262, 267
Berger, Iris 34 cit.
Berlusconi, Silvio 291
Bertello, Giuseppe, papal nuncio 132
Bicamumpaka, Jérôme 233, 275, 277,
321, 355
Bihozagara, Jacques 116, 197n., 204,
218n., 221n., 276 cit., 288–9 cit.,
290, 300, 301 cit., 310
Bikindi, Simon 210n.
Biloa, Marie-Roger 223 cit., 224n.
Birara, Jean 210, 222n., 223 cit.
Bizimana, General Augustin 197n.,
237, 240, 244n., 268, 269, 299 cit.,
316, 355
Bizimungu, Casimir 86, 101, 235, 239
Bizimungu, President Pasteur 90, 153,
160, 163, 195 and n., 197n., 204,
205, 240n., 300, 301, 329, 331, 337
Boisvineau, Mme 288, 307n.
Bon, Colonel Dominique 287
Bongo, Omar, President of
Gabon 290n.
Booh-Booh, Jacques-Roger 204, 206,
209, 225, 276
Bourgi, Robert 318
bourgmestres 52, 53, 75, 76, 136 and
n., 138 and n., 173 and n., 196,
241, 244, 246, 267, 301, 304, 305,
314, 355
Boutros-Ghali, Boutros 210, 275, 276,
277 cit., 324n.
Bowen, Revd Roger 252 cit.
Braeckman, Colette 213 and n., 215,
344, 345 cit.
Brauman, Rony 277 cit.
Briey, Count Renaud de 8

Brosse, Fr Etienne 8
Bryer, David 262
Bucyana, Martin 129, 206, 209
Buganda 64, 67
Buganza 18, 21
Bugesera 18, 21, 51, 56, 137, 139 and
n., 145, 147, 168 and n., 299
Bujumbura 54, 64, 66, 171, 179, 195,
198, 202n., 211, 285
Bunyenyezi, Major Christopher 71,
93, 94, 96, 114
Buregeya, Colonel Bonaventure 167
Burgt, Fr van den 7 cit. and n.
Burundi 2, 5, 7, 10, 51, 55, 56, 59,
60, 62, 78 (table), 81, 116, 153,
191, 195, 198, 201, 202, 211, 215,
252, 264 (table), 265, 270, 285,
290, 299, 300, 310, 312 (table),
322, 323, 325, 326, 327, 331, 342
Bush, President George 215, 317
Bushnell, Prudence 215
Butare *préfecture* 53, 57, 89, 90, 75n.,
125, 135, 203n., 206, 240, 244,
246n., 249, 256, 261, 298, 306,
323, 325; see also Astrida
Butare, Innocent 258n.
'Butare Mafia' 57
Buyoya, President Pierre 198, 202, 331
Bwanakweri, Chief Prosper 46, 48, 56
Byumba *préfecture* 135, 136, 171, 174,
177, 196n., 241, 261, 264 (table),
268, 272n., 295

Cahen, Max-Olivier 318
Casati, Gaetano 7
Catholic Church and Catholics 30–4
and n., 38, 43, 44, 59, 69, 75, 81,
82, 83n., 89, 125 and n., 132–3,
174, 270–2 and n., 335n., 348, 351
CDR (Coalition pour la Défense de la
République) 128–9, 131, 154, 162,
164, 165, 166, 169, 170, 171 and
n., 173, 179, 182, 185, 186, 188,
189, 197, 199, 200, 201 and n.,
203, 204, 206, 207, 208, 209n.,
217, 222, 227, 233, 241, 277, 284,
314, 334, 368

Cellule Africaine 100, 101, 103, 128n., 165n., 177n.
CEPGL (Communauté Economique des Grands Lacs) 79, 321
Chirac, Jacques 282n., 283, 317, 318
Chollet, Lieut.-Colonel 149
Chrétien, Jean-Pierre 36 cit., 247 cit.
Christian Democrats and CDI 59, 107–8, 125, 251, 335, 349
(Le) Clan de Madame 85, 87, 167; see also Mme Habyarimana
Claes, Willy, 205, 234
clan (see also *ababega, abayinginya, ubwoko*) 14n., 15, 16 and n., 20, 23, 24, 45, 85, 245, 370
Classe, Mgr Leon 26 cit., 32, 41 cit., 50
Clinton, Bill, US President 215, 304
Cohen, Herman 317, 318
Cold War 47, 52
Comité de Concertation de l'Opposition 133, 135
Comité du Salut Public 232
Commission Spéciale sur les Problèmes des Emigres Rwandais 90–1
Congo, Belgian 49, 55, 63
Conseil National du Développement (CND) 77, 207, 218, 224
Courbin, Jacques 336 and n.
(Le) Courier du Peuple newspaper 129
Crédit Lyonnais 148 and n.
Cyangugu préfecture144n., 284, 288, 291, 292, 293, 315 and n., 316

Dallaire, General Roméo 234, 236–7, 275, 276, 287 and n.
DAM (Direction des Affaires Africaines et Malgaches) 288, 307n.
DAMI (Détachement d'Assistance Militaire et de l'Instruction) 213, 220
Dar es Salaam 25n., 55, 66, 79, 182, 184n., 191, 194, 211, 321
Debarge, Marcel 149, 177 cit., 178, 183
Debré, Bernard 340 cit. and n.
Decraene, Philippe 154n.
Degni-Segui, René 303, 341n.

Dehaene, Jean-Luc 213n., 274, 335
Delaye, Bruno 165n., 177n., 279n., 282, 316–17 cit.
Delcroix, Léo 208 cit.
Destexhe, Alain 303 cit.
DGSE (Direction Générale des Services Extérieurs) 176, 178, 283
Dialogue periodical 81n., 132n., 251, 259n.
Dufourcq, Bertrand 307n.
Dumas, Roland 100

(The) Economist 336 cit.
Entwicklungsdiktatur, 77; see also Keiner
Erps, Senator Johan van 335
Ethiopia 7, 10, 16, 172, 215
Europeans 5, 6, 19, 25, 26, 31, 39, 44, 140, 157, 217, 341, 346, 349, 350, 354
European Union 209, 283, 328, 336
Eyskens, Mark 108

FAR (Forces Armées Rwandaises) 94, 96, 110–14 passim, 119, 135, 144, 149, 150, 165, 166, 167, 169, 174, 176, 182, 184, 187, 193, 196 and n., 213, 214 and n., 217, 220, 221, 229, 240, 244, 246 and n., 252, 254, 267, 268, 269, 271, 273, 278n., 287 and n., 292, 295, 298, 304, 305, 310, 313–17 passim, 323, 332, 338, 374
Foccart, Jacques 318
Force Publique (Congo) 49
Forum, 185; see Gapyisi
FPR (Front Patriotique Rwandais), see RPF
France and French 89n., 91, 94, 96, 99 and n., 101 and n., 102, 103 and n., 104–7, 110, 111, 113, 114, 118, 127, 135, 145, 147, 148 and n., 149, 163–5, 169, 176–9, 184 and n., 191, 194, 204, 210, 211, 213, 214n., 220n., 228, 234 and n., 235, 236, 243, 268, 273, 276–8, 280, 281–20 passim, 328, 334, 336 and n., 337, 338 and n., 339–41,

344, 352, 353; see also *Opération Turquoise*
Frodebu Party (Burundi) 125n., 198, 217, 285
FRONASA (Front for National Salvation) 68

Gabiro 94, 96, 109
Gafaranga, Théoneste 130, 181, 230
Gahengayire, Anne 115
Gaillard, Philippe 263
Galla 7 and n., 17n.; see also Oromo
Gapyisi, Emmanuel 147, 154, 180, 182, 185, 186 cit., 188, 383n.
Gasana, Anastase 330n.
Gasana, James 145, 149n., 163, 167 and n., 197n., 222, 240n., 334
Gasana, Thadée 136, 175
Gatabazi, Félicien 130, 144 cit., 181, 197n., 206, 207, 209
Gatera, Claude 333 and n.
Gatete, Rémy 138, 241, 246, 248, 267, 355
Gatsinzi, Colonel Marcel 167, 229, 246 and n., 269, 295
Gaulle, Charles de 103, 106, 318, 338n., 340 cit.
Gebeka Project 88
Gendarmerie 240, 244, 246
Genocide 96, 137, 169–70, 213, 224n., 225, 229–36, 237–80
Germanos, General Raymond 291, 307
Germany and Germans 23–6, 32, 35 and n., 59 and n., 68n., 81, 108, 141, 162n., 209, 229, 245, 335, 337
'Gersony Report' 323–4
Gilleron, Pierre-Yves 128n., 216
Gisaka 18, 21, 29, 35
Gisenyi *préfecture* 14n., 19, 51, 86, 123, 136, 150, 161, 171, 240, 249, 260, 261, 273, 283, 284, 292n., 295, 296, 298, 299, 308, 315n., 316
Gitarama 48, 53, 57, 85, 123, 135, 237, 261, 268, 269, 273, 334
Gitera, Joseph 47, 49
Goldstone, Richard 344
Goma 303 and n., 304, 307, 310,

312, 313, 316, 333, 335, 343
GOMN (Groupe des observateurs Militaires Neutre) 194
Gore, Mary 353
Gorju, Fr 7
Götzen, Graf von 3n., 9 and n., 80
GP (Garde Presidentielle) 214, 218, 220, 221, 224 and n., 225n., 228, 229, 230, 240, 242–3, 244
Guichaoua, Professor Andre 65 cit., 88, 235

Habanabakize, Thomas 129
Habyarimana, Jean-Baptiste 244, 246 and n.
Habyarimana, Juvenal, Major-General, later President, and regime 58, 61, 74, 75, 76 cit., 77, 82n., 83–7n. passim, 89–91, 94, 96, 98–101, 107 and n., 108, 109, 110 cit., 112, 115, 120, 121–5 passim, 127, 128 and n., 129, 130, 133, 134, 133, 134, 141, 145–8 and n. passim, 150, 151, 154 and n., 155, 156, 157, 160, 161 cit., 162–4, 166, 168, 170 cit. and n., 171 and n., 172, 178–83 passim, 185–190 and n. passim, 191, 195, 196 and n., 198, 202, 203, 205, 207 cit., 208, 210, 211, 221, 222, 224, 225–9, 235, 241n., 242, 252, 258, 268, 271, 278n., 279, 284, 290n., 294n., 297, 306n., 307n., 319, 330n., 331, 334, 335n., 344, 345, 349, 352, 371, 374, 376; theories about assassination of 212–29
Habyarimana, Mme Agathe (née Kanzinga) 86, 87n., 123, 166, 167, 168, 187, 203n., 216, 217, 218, 222, 235, 236, 242, 317n., 350, 352; see also 'Clan de Madame'
Hakizamana, Colonel Pontien 167
Hammarskjöld, Dag 52
Harroy, Jean-Paul 47–8 cit., 58n.
Hategekemana, Captain Gaspard 240
Hirth, Mgr 44
Hobsbawm, Eric 37n., 346 cit.
Huchon, General 148

Hutu 5, 6, 11, 16 and n., 22, 25n.,
    26, 35, 40, 41, 42, 43, 45, 46, 47,
    49, 50, 51, 57, 75, 76, 86, 109,
    111n., 112, 122, 124, 128, 129,
    145, 150, 154, 161, 165, 170, 183,
    185, 189, 195, 198, 199, 200,
    201n., 205, 210, 217, 219, 223,
    232, 236, 246, 248–52, 254,
    256–60, 262–5, 271, 275, 284,
    292n., 293, 297, 300, 301, 303, 306
    and n., 310, 322, 323, 325, 326,
    327 and n., 330–333 and n., 334,
    335n., 339, 340, 342, 345–8, 352,
    369, 370, 371, 372, 377;
    principalities of 19, 20, 21, 25;
    exclusion from élite 22–7, 39, 44,
    45; republic of 41–92; growth of
    counter-élite 43–7; ideology during
    republic 58–60, 66, 112–113, 226;
    and massacres 135–50 passim,
    192–206 passim, 213–65 passim;
    281–95 passim; refugees 136,
    246–327 passim
'Hutu Power' group later referred to
    as 'Powers' 188, 197n., 199, 200,
    220, 233, 333n., 335n., 344, 345

ibihugu 18, 367
ibyitso 121, 128, 138, 142, 143, 162,
    172, 210, 227, 231, 367
igikingi (ibikingi) 20, 21, 29, 46n., 367
Igihirahiro 210
ILO 79
Impuzamugambi militia 165, 184, 224,
    231, 241 and n., 243
Initiative Paix et Démocratie 147
inkotanyi (see also RPF) 179, 201, 259,
    352, 367
Interahamwe militia 165, 169, 171,
    182, 184, 203, 208, 223, 224, 229,
    231, 232, 240, 241, 243, 244, 246,
    247n., 249, 254, 256, 257 and n.,
    258, 259, 260, 266, 267, 271, 292,
    298, 314, 322, 323; newspaper 131
International Commission on Human
    Rights 173, 176, 183
International Committee of the Red
    Cross (ICRC) 70, 97, 240n., 263,

273, 314, 375
Inyenzi (Tutsi commandos) 26n., 54,
    55 and n., 56, 57, 60, 73n., 83,
    143n., 151, 171 and n., 258, 351
Inyumba, Aloysia 115, 300, 330
inzu 3, 15, 368, 370, 372
Irvin, Patricia 215
Isibo newspaper 131, 144n.

Jalée, Pierre 350
Janssens, General 49
Jehanne, Philippe 278n.
Johnston, Sir Harry 10
Joxe, Louis 100
Juppé, Alain 277, 280 cit., 283, 286,
    287, 289, 291, 311, 352

Kabera 24 and n., 25
Kabuga, Félicien 241
Kagame, Abbé Alexis 36–37, 58, 59
Kagame, Faustin 189n., 221n., 240n.
Kagame, Major (later Major-General)
    Paul 68, 70, 91, 92 and n., 93 and
    n., 94, 96, 114n115, 119, 120, 152,
    155n., 156, 195, 204, 205 and n.,
    233, 268, 270, 294 and n., 300,
    306, 308 cit., 315n., 317 and n.,
    324 cit., 326, 329, 331, 342n3 cit.
Kagera River Basin Organisation
    (KBO) 79
Kajeguhakwa, Valens 90, 117
Kajuka, Robert 241 and n.
Kalinga sacred drum 10, 47
Kamali, Sylvestre 333 and n.
Kamarampaka newspaper 131
Kamarampaka referendum 1961 131,
    151 and n.
Kambanda, Jean 190, 232, 233, 321,
    355
Kampala 70, 72, 73n., 94, 98, 115,
    117, 149, 163, 202 and n., 294n.
Kamweya, Andre 132, 230
Kandt, Richard 3n., 12
Kangura newspaper 129, 131, 165–166
    and n., 188 and n.,222 and n.
Kanjogera 23, 24, 25, 86, 350, 354;
    see also Habyarimana, Mme
Kanyarengwe, Colonel Alexis 115,

128, 177, 195, 196n., 205 and n.,
   263, 294n., 329
Kanyarushoki, Ambassador
   Pierre-Claver 163
Kanyemera (alias Kaka), Major
   Samuel 91, 93
Karamira, Frodwald 183, 188, 190 and
   n., 201n., 355
Karamira, Dr and Colonel
   Joseph 197n., 340
Kavaruganda, Joseph 196n., 230
Kayibanda, President Grégoire 45 and
   n., 47, 48, 53, 57, 59, 60, 61n.,
   75, 76, 82 and n., 85, 120, 123,
   124, 134, 198, 349, 350, 351
Kayishema, Clément 241
Kayitare, Captain 114
Kayumba, Immaculée 197n., 300
Keiner, Pfarrer Herbert 77 cit., 81n2
   cit., 83 and n.
Kelly, Karen 343
Kengo wa Dongo 318, 319n., 320,
   321
Khan, Mohamed Shahryar 315n., 320
Kenya 50, 98, 130, 215, 258n., 259
Kibungo préfecture 256, 261, 262, 265,
   266n., 268, 301, 325, 342
Kigali (capital and seat of
   government) 56, 58n., 66, 73n., 74,
   77, 79n., 82n., 83 and n., 85, 88,
   90, 94, 96, 97, 99n., 101, 102,
   103, 107, 108, 109, 118, 120, 121,
   124, 129, 135, 137, 138, 143, 148
   and n., 149, 162n., 163, 165n.,
   176n, passim, 184, 187n., 190n.,
   194n., 195, 202, 203n., 205, 206,
   207, 211, 212, 216, 218, 220, 222
   and n., 229, 231, 232, 234 and n.,
   236, 237, 240, 242, 243, 244 and
   n., 249, 253, 254, 255, 257n., 261,
   262, 263, 264 (table), 268, 269 and
   n., 270, 273, 275, 280, 294, 295,
   298, 299, 301, 306, 307, 312, 315,,
   319, 320, 321, 328, 333n., 334,
   336, 337n., 343, 344n.
Kigeli V 54, 55
Kigwa 47
Kinyamateka newspaper 45 and n.,

81n., 132n., 174 cit.
Kinyarwanda language 5n., 18, 32,
   41n., 81n., 129, 131, 166, 170n.,
   344, 366, 370
Kiswahili language 12n., 66, 343, 366
Kouchner, Bernard 269 cit.
Kubandwa cult 15, 33–34 and n., 354,
   369, 373
kunyawana 34n., 369
Kuypers, Senator Willy 168

La Baule Franco-African summit,
   1990 89, 106, 297
Lacger, Louis de 7, 10 cit., 15 cit.,
   17 cit. and n., 18, 30 cit.
Lafourcade, General Jean-Claude 291,
   293, 296
Lakwena, Alice 71 and n., 98, 119
Lanxade, Admiral 294, 308
Lasso, Jose Ayala 343
League of Nations Mandate 25–26
Lehmann, Orla 44–45 cit.
Léotard, François 283, 285, 292, 310,
   311
[Le] Liberal newspaper 132
Linden, Dr Ian 41 cit.
Lizinde, Colonel Théoneste 82 and n.,
   84, 115n., 119, 120, 128
Logiest, Colonel Guy 49 cit., 51, 53,
   54 cit., 58n.
[La] Loi Fondamentale 330

Maasai 8
Majyambere, Silas 118, 121 cit. and n.
Makeri, Dominique 333
Mandela, President Nelson 281 and n.
Maquet, Jean-Jacques 14 and n., 20n.,
   57 cit.
Marlaud, Jean-Philippe 154, 236, 294n.
Martens, Willy 108
Martre, Georges 102, 147, 148n.,
   154n., 176
Mau Mau movement 50
Maurin, Lieut.-Colonel 149
Mayuya, Colonel Stanislas 84, 87, 350
Mazimpaka, Patrick 115, 149, 152,
   163, 270, 300, 327n., 331, 333n.
Mbangura, Daniel 233
Mbonabaryi, Noël 85

Mbonampeka, Stanislas 145, 172, 181, 183, 188, 321
Mbonyumutwa, Sub-Chief Dominique 48
MDR (Mouvement Démocratique Républicain) 122, 124, 129, 131, 133 and n., 134, 135, 145, 150, 151, 164, 170, 173, 179, 180, 181, 183, 185, 188, 189 and n., 190, 192, 197 and n., 201n., 204, 206, 208, 209n., 233, 300, 329, 330, 331, 332, 333 and n., 335n.
Médecins Sans Frontières (MSF) 254, 273, 277, 303, 312
Mercier, General 285, 289, 290, 293
Michaux-Chevry, Lucette 288, 293
Minani, Jean 217
Mitterrand, President François 89 and n., 100, 148n., 154n., 163, 164, 165n., 211, 277, 281, 282 and n., 283, 286 and n., 294, 297, 311, 339 cit., 340, 352
Mitterrand, Jean-Christophe 100, 101 cit.
MNC (Mouvement National Congolais) 55
Mobutu Sese Seko (President of Zaïre) 55, 82, 101, 109, 186, 208, 210 and n., 279 and n., 297, 317 and n., 318, 319, 320 and n., 321
Moi, Daniel Arap (President of Kenya) 98, 108
Montferrand, Bernard de 282
Morandini, papal nuncio 132
Moose, George 317
Moumtiz, Panos 265
Moussali, Michel 207
Mouvement des Femmes et du Bas-Peuple (MFBP) 127, 179n., 375
Mpiranya, Lieut.-Colonel Protais 224n., 229, 240, 355
MRND (Mouvement Révolutionnaire National pour le Développement) 76–8, 83 and n., 85, 90, 91, 109, 112, 113, 121, 123, 125, 128, 129, 271, 301, 305, 308, 309, 310, 314, 316, 319 and n., 321, 329 and n., 334

MRND(D) (Mouvement Révolutionnaire National pour le Développement et la Démocratie) 126, 127, 128, 129, 134, 145, 146, 147, 149n., 151, 155, 156, 161, 167, 168, 169, 170, 171 and n., 172, 173, 179, 182, 185, 189n., 190n., 192, 195, 196n., 201, 203, 205, 208, 231, 232, 233, 236, 240, 245, 246, 258 and n., 300
Mouvement Social Muhutu (MSM) 47, 48
Mubega 347
Mugambage, Colonel Frank 115, 152, 269, 270, 291, 324, 331
Mugenzi, Justin 130, 181 and n., 188, 197n., 207, 233
Mugesera, Lon 171–172 cit.
Mugiraneza, Prosper 145, 197n., 233
Muhutu see Hutu
Mujawamaliya, Monique 230, 266n., 302n., 306n.
Mujyanama, Théodore 109 cit., 134
Mukamugema, Immaculée 128; see also Barahinyua
Mukanyangezi, Joséphine 333 and n.
Munyazesa, Faustin 145, 233
Murego, Donat 181, 183, 188, 190 and n.
Musabe, Pascal 240
Musamgamfura, Sixbert 131, 144n., 178n.
Museveni, Yoweri (President of Uganda) 67–8, 70, 71, 72, 73 and n., 93, 95n., 97, 98, 100, 104, 108, 115, 118, 119, 152, 155n., 171, 191, 195, 202n., 211 and n., 215, 216, 279, 281, 290, 317n, 319, 326, 331, 351
Musitu, Commandant 91
Muslims in Rwanda (see also PDI) 127n., 253, 376
Mutara 18, 109, 136, 139, 299
Mutara III Rudahigwa 30, 31, 34, 36, 38, 54 and n.
Mutesa III, King of Uganda 56 and n.
Mututsi see also Tutsi)
mutwale 11, 12

Muvunyyi, Colonel 240, 246n.
muyaga 41
Muyaneza, Augustin 82 cit.
mwami (king) 9 and n., 10, 11, 18,
    25, 31, 49, 57, 58, 86
Mwinyi, Ali Hassan (President of
    Tanzania) 191, 211

Nahimana, Professor Ferdinand 19n.,
    25n., 37 cit., 86n., 137n., 146,
    152n., 197n., 224n., 239
[*La*] *Nation* newspaper 131
National Reconciliation Conference
    1961 53
National Transition Assembly (NTA,
    TNA) 191, 193, 208
Nayinzira, Jean-Népomucène 181 and
    n., 197n., 300, 329n.
Ndabahizi, Emmanuel 233
Ndadaye, President Melchior 191, 195,
    197, 198, 199, 200, 201, 202, 203,
    216, 246, 322, 374
Ndagijimana, Jean-Marie
    Vianney 240n., 230 and n.
Ndahindurwa, Jean-Baptiste see Kigeli
    V
Ndasingwa, Landwald 125 cit., 146n.,
    188, 197, 207, 230
Ndikumana, Sylvain 244
Ndindiliyimana, Colonel 167
Ndorwa 18, 21
Nduga 18, 21, 30
Nduguta, Major Stephen 71, 93, 114
Nduwayezi, Augustin 87-8 cit.
Newbury, Catharine 42 cit.
Newbury, David 16 and n.
Ngarembe, Joseph 230, 235n., 240n.
Ngango, Félicien 130
Ngendahayo, Jean-Marie 285
Ngeze, Hassan 129, 165, 222
Ngirumpatse, Mathieu 173, 316
NGO (Non-Governmental
    Organisation) 83, 131, 232, 240,
    261, 268, 277, 281, 283, 313, 314,
    328 and n., 335 and n., 344
Ngulinzira, Boniface 145, 149, 161,
    163, 170-1 cit., 197n., 230
Nitigeka, Eliezer 233

Niyitegeka, Félicité 260
Nkubito, General Alphonse-Marie 109
    cit., 235n., 240n., 257n., 300,
    343n., 355
Nkundiye, Lieut.-Colonel Léonard
    224n., 240
Nkurikiyimfura, Jean-Népomucène
    13n., 21n., 22n., 28n., 29 cit.
    and n. '*Noroit*' 110, 111, 112,
    149n., 338; see also France and
    French
*Notes on the Social Aspects of the Racial
    Native Problem in Rwanda* 45-6 cit.
NRA (National Resistance Army, see
    also Uganda) 70, 71, 72, 74, 90,
    92-95 passim, 98, 118, 119, 152,
    153n., 155, 270
NRM (National Resistance Movement)
    68n., 95n.; see also Uganda
Nsabimana, Colonel Deogratias 16,
    222n., 229n.
Nsambumukunzi, Straton 233
Nsanzimana, Sylvestre 134-7 passim,
    145, 334
Nsekalije, Colonel Alexis 87n.
Nsengimana, Joseph 300
Nsengimana, Nkiko 147
Nsengiyaremye, Dismas 145, 161, 163,
    167, 180, 182, 183n., 186, 187n.,
    189n., 197n., 334, 335n.
Nsengiyumva, Colonel 240
Nsengiyumva, Mgr Thadée 132,
    142n., 270, 272
Nsengiyumva, Ngr Vincent 83n., 132,
    270, 271
Ntabakuze, Colonel Aloys 24
Ntagerura, André 145, 197n.
Ntambyauro, Agnès 145, 197, 233
Ntaryamira, President Cyprien 210,
    211-2
Ntirivamunda, Alphonse 168, 235
Nyakibanda 33, 45n., 57
Nyina Yuhi 350, 369; see also
    Kanjogera
Nyirabawenzi, Odette 244n.
Nyiramashuhuko, Pauline 197n.
Nyiramutarambirwa, Félécula 89
Nyirinkindi, Gaspard 116

Nzabahimana, François 125, 146
Nzamburambaho, Frédéric 130, 181,
    197n., 230
Nzirorera, Joseph 86, 240, 309

OAU (Organisation of African
    Unity) 194, 275, 287
Obote, Milton (President of
    Uganda) 56 and n., 67n., 69, 71,
    72, 73, 119, 153n., 155; see also
    Uganda
OECD 179, 118, 148, 159n., 162n.,
    255, 276
Office Rwandais d'Information
    (ORINFOR) 146 and n., 147
Ogata, Sadako 305
Omaar, Rakiya 240n.
Omutone, Christine 116
Opération Amaryllis 234, 236; see also
    France and French
Opération Turquoise 184, 213, 259,
    261, 276, 281–311 passim, 319; see
    also France and French
Oromo 7 and n., 17n.; see also Galla
OXFAM 262

Pagès, Fr 7, 20n., 32
Paix et Démocratie newspaper 132
Palipehutu Party, Burundi 125n., 198
panga 243 and n., 256, 262n., 369
PARERWA (Parti Révolutionnaire du
    Rwanda) 127, 171n., 375
PARMEHUTU (Parti du Mouvement
    et de l'Emancipation Hutu, formerly
    MDR/PARMEHUTU) 48, 51–53,
    85, 86, 122–4, 134, 145, 151n.,
    182, 188; see also MDR
PDC (Parti Démocratique
    Chrétein) 125, 145, 173, 179, 181,
    183, 188, 189n., 233, 300, 329
PDI (Parti Démocratique
    Islamique) 127, 164, 179n., 208,
    209n., 329
Pauwels, Fr 32
PECO (Parti Ecologiste) 127, 164,
    171n., 179n., 376
Pelletier, Jacques 101
Perraudin, Mgr 45n., 47

Petrie, Charles 263 cit.
Pimapima, Yosia 257n.
PL (Parti Libéral) 124, 125, 130,
    131n., 134, 137 and n., 145, 150,
    164, 173, 179, 181, 183, 188,
    189n., 197 and n., 204, 207, 230,
    233, 300, 329, 332
Polisi, Denis 116, 240n.
PPJR (Parti Progressiste de la Jeunesse
    Rwándaise) 179
Presidential Guard, see GP
Protestant churches, Protestants 69,
    252
Prouteau, Christian 128n., 216
PSD (Parti Social Démocrate) 124,
    130, 131, 134, 144, 145, 150, 162,
    164, 170, 173, 179, 181, 188,
    189n., 206, 207, 230, 233, 235n.,
    300, 329, 330, 332, 333
PSR (Parti Socialiste Rwandais) 127,
    164

Racial theories 5, 6–9, 16n., 17, 28n.,
    45, 50, 80, 346
RADER (Rassemblement
    Démocratique Rwandais) 48, 51, 56
Radio Muhaburu 162, 189, 262, 263
Radio Rwanda 163, 164, 189, 224,
    232, 268
RTLMC (Radio Télévision Libre des
    Mille Collines) 129, 133, 188, 189
    and n., 200, 210, 217, 223, 224
    and n., 241, 292n., 295
Raison, Jean-Pierre 353
Rambuka, Fidele 196
RANU (Rwandese Alliance of
    National Unity) 67, 72, 73
Red Cross, see International
    Committee of the Red Cross
Render, Arlene 215
Reyntjens, Filip 156 cit., 168, 193,
    301n.
Rocard, Michel 110 cit.
Rogoza, Faustin 230
Roscoe, John 7
RPA (Rwanda Patriotic Army, see
    RPF)
Rodriguez, Carlos 223

Roussin, Michel 228, 278n., 337 cit., 338 cit. and n., 352

RPA (Rwanda Patriotic Army, see RPF)

RPF (Rwandese Patriotic Front) 17n., 64n., 73 and n., 74, 83n., 90–101 passim, 108–111 passim, 113, 114, 115, 117, 118, 120 and n., 121, 122, 125n., 128, 131n., 132, 135, 137, 138, 139 and n., 142, 143 and n., 144, 145, 147, 149 and n., 150, 151 and n., 152n7 passim, 161, 162, 163, 166, 167n., 168, 169, 172, 173, 174, 176–83 passim, 184 and n., 186, 187 and n., 188, 189 and n., 190–4 and n. passim, 195 and n., 196, 197n., 201–205 and n. passim, 206, 214–218 and n. passim, 220, 221, 223, 224, 227, 228, 229, 231, 233, 234, 237, 247, 248, 251 and n., 252–9 passim, 261, 262, 265–72 and n. passim, 273, 276, 277, 278, 283–6 and n., 288, 289, 290 and n., 291, 293–301 passim, 304, 305, 306, 308, 309, 310, 311, 314, 315, 316 and n., 317, 322, 323, 324, 329 and n., 330–4 passim, 345, 368

Rubagumya, Charles 231

rubanda nyamwinshi 75, 183, 185, 203, 327, 349 and n., 350, 351, 369–70

Rucunshu *coup d'état* 24, 25

Rudasingwa, Théogène 115, 152, 163, 237, 276, 290

Rugenera, Marc 145, 197n., 230, 300

rugo 3, 12, 184, 243n., 370

Ruhengiri *préfecture*48, 57, 86, 90n., 119, 120, 123, 124, 135, 136, 150, 156, 161, 170, 175 and n., 196n., 205, 249, 261, 268, 284, 295, 298

Ruhigira, Enoch 209n cit.

Ruhumuliza, Gaspard 181, 183, 188, 197n.

Rukeba, François 55

Rumiya, Professor Jean 28n., 172 cit.

ruriganiza 87

Rutalindwa 23, 24

Rutaremara, Tito 116, 195

Rutasira, General Léonidas 295

Rutaysire, Wilson 115

Ruzindana, Joseph 270

Rwabugiri, King (Kigeri IV Rwabugiri) 13, 15, 21n., 23, 24, 38

Rwabukumba, Séraphin 85, 235, 317n.

Rwagafilita, Colonel Pierre-Célestin 85, 167, 187, 222, 225, 232

Rwagasore, Prince Louis of Burundi 55

Rwakayigamba, Pierre 333

Rwamasirabo, Dr Emile 116

Rwambuka, Fidèle 138, 196

Rwanda Rushya newspaper 132, 230

Rwandese Patriotic Army, see RPF

Rwibajige, Sylvestre 230

Rwigyema, Major-General Fred 68, 70, 73, 91–6, 114, 152

Rwigyema, Pierre-Célestin 300

RWWF (Rwandese Refugee Welfare Foundation) 67

Ryangombe 15, 18; see also *Kubandwa*

Ryckmans, Pierre 11 cit. and n.

Sablière, Rochereau de la 288

Sagatwa, Colonel Elie 85, 87n., 168

Saitoti, George (Vice-President of Kenya) 211

Salim, Salim 286

Sebyeza, Sub-Chief Gabriel 55

Secyugu, Paul 181

Sendashonga, Seth 153, 197n., 240n., 301, 309–10, 330, 331, 337 cit.

Semanyenzi, Dr Théoneste 259n.

Sengegera, Etienne 214 cit., 215

Serubuga, Colonel Laurent 85, 87, 167, 187, 222, 225

Service Central de Renseignements (SCR) 146

Shamukiga, Charles 185, 230

shebuja 13, 39, 43, 86, 370; see also *ubuhake*

Shelley, Christine 274 cit.

SHZ (*Zone Humanitaire Sûre*) 295, 296,

299, 305, 307, 308, 309, 310–11, 322; see also France and French
Simbikangwa, Captain Pascal 240
Sindambiwe, Fr Silvio 89
Sindikubwabo, President Théodore 232, 244, 273, 286, 355
Société des Transports Internationaux Rwandais (STIR) 129–30
[*Le*] *Soleil* newspaper 131 Sommaruga, Cornelio 273 cit.
Soubielle, Fr 31 cit.
Speke, John Hanning 7, 10, 11
Ssezi-Cheeye, Teddy 95 and n.
Structural Adjustment Programme (SAP) 160
Swinnen, Johan 222n.
Switzerland and Swiss 56, 57, 64, 81 and n., 163, 349 and n.

Tanganyika 5, 35, 51, 55, 59
Tanzania 59, 62, 68, 70, 78 (table), 81, 87, 116, 135n., 150, 184, 191, 241, 248, 262, 265, 279 and n., 286, 301, 312 (table), 313, 316, 321
Tega, Frank 116
[*Le*] *Terrorisme Inyenzi au Rwanda* report 57
Theunis, Fr 250
Toparchies 18; see also *ibihugu*
TRAFIPRO Cooperative 45 and n.
Tutsi (see also Batutsi, Mututsi, Burundi, RPF, Uganda) 5, 6, 7, 20, 22, 26, 31, 33, 36, 38, 40, 43, 45, 46, 47, 49–52, 75, 76, 86, 97, 111n., 117,122, 124, 129, 139, 142, 145, 150, 152, 165, 180, 185, 188, 198, 199, 201, 205, 210, 211, 212, 225, 226, 231, 232, 235, 236, 244, 246–249, 251, 252, 254, 256, 265n. passim 270, 271, 272, 275, 284, 285, 292 and n., 293n., 295, 297–301 passim, 306n., 308, 310, 322–7n. passim, 330, 331, 332, 335n., 339, 340, 346, 347, 348, 351–4, 368, 369, 370, 371, 372, 376; theories about origins of 5–8; kingship and social organisation under 11–23; and colonial rule

25–80 passim; and Catholic church 31, 33, 34, 41n., 43, 75; '*petits Tutsis*' 43, 49, 65, 80, 249; refugees and diaspora 51–94, 98, 102, 116, 180, 184, 195, 196; genocide decided 169; massacres analysed 137–44 and n., 184
Twa 5, 6, 14–15, 34n., 50, 369, 370; see also Batwa
Twagiramungu, Faustin 129, 130, 131, 132, 180, 181 and n., 185, 189, 190 and n., 197n., 204 cit., 205n., 206, 225n., 231 and n., 240n., 286, 300, 301, 305, 307, 308, 320, 324 cit., 328, 330n., 333 and n., 334 cit., 339

ubuhake 13–14, 18, 21, 29–30, 31, 42, 46n.
ubukonde 14n., 20, 28 and n.
ubuletwa 12 and n., 13, 21, 27
ubwoko 15, 16, 76n., 122 and n; see also clan
Uganda 5, 10, 35, 51, 53–6 passim, 59, 62 and n., 63, 64 and n., 67, 69, 70, 71, 74, 78 (table), 81, 86, 91, 9n. passim, 100, 106, 107n., 113, 115, 116, 118, 130, 135, 152, 153 and n., 155, 157, 176, 178, 179, 191, 194, 195, 202n, 205, 215, 217, 252, 255, 262, 270, 272, 279, 290, 298, 299, 301, 312 (table), 319, 322, 325, 326, 327, 331, 332, 340 and n., 342, 349, 351, 353
Uganda Democratic Coalition 215 and n.
umuganda 79, 87, 138
umugaragu 347; see also *abagaragu*
umunyanduga 206
Umurangi newspaper 132
umuryango 15
umusanzu 87
UNAR (*Union Nationale Rwandaise*) 47, 48, 49, 51, 53, 65
Union Democatique du Peuple Rwandais (UDPR) 121, 164, 329, 377
United Nations (UN) and agencies 35n., 45, 47, 52, 53 and

n., 106, 149n., 184, 194, 204, 205, 206, 209, 210, 225, 228, 234, 235, 261, 263, 268, 269 and n., 272–8 passim, 287, 290, 297, 303, 307, 308, 313, 315 and n., 316, 320, 341, 343, 344 and n., 350

UNAMIR (UN Assistance Mission to Rwanda) 194, 203, 204, 205, 206, 209, 214, 218, 230, 231, 234, 236, 254, 261, 275, 276, 308, 309, 315n., 323, 338

UNESCO (UN Educational, Scientific and Cultural Organisation) 286

UNHCR (UN High Commission for Refugees) 62n., 63, 97, 207, 223n., 240, 246, 247n., 262, 265, 266 and n., 304, 305, 310, 312, 314, 320, 321, 323, 324n.

UNICEF (UN Children's Fund) 100, 327n.

UNUROM (UN Uganda/Rwanda Observer Mission) 194 and n.

United States 81, 162n., 215–16, 274–5, 304, 307n., 328, 334, 336

UPRONA Party (Burundi) 55, 285

Usumbura see Bujumbura

Uwihoreye, Colonel Charles 120 and n.

Uwilingiyimana, Agathe 145–6 and n., 189, 190, 197n., 230, 235

Vaiter, Marc 236 and n.

Vallmajo, Fr Joaquim 272n.

Verschave, François-Xavier 210 cit.

Vidal, Claudine 23 cit., 37 cit., 59–60 cit.

Vleugels, Fr Jeff 125n cit., 250

Voisin, Governor Charles 26, 27

Wasswa, Lieut.-Colonel Adam 93

White Fathers (Pères Blancs) 32, 125n., 250, 348

Wilkinson, Ray 314 cit.

World Bank 79, 88, 119 and n., 160, 283, 320 and n., 327, 331, 336, 350n., 353

World Food Program, see United Nations and agencies

World Food Programme 184

Gérard, Yannick 294n.

Yuhi V Musinga 21n., 24, 30, 31, 66n., 86, 369

Zaïre 1, 62, 63, 64, 78 (table), 82, 86, 101, 109, 113, 116, 135, 186, 191, 202n., 210, 215, 274, 279, 289, 298, 299, 301, 306, 309, 312 (table), 313, 317, 318, 319 and n., 320, 323, 325

'Zero Network' 168, 169, 182, 200, 242, 287

Zigiranyirazo, Protais 85, 203n.

Zimmerman, Revd Jorg 252 cit.